By Stanley Kauffmann

Novels

The Hidden Hero
The Tightrope
A Change of Climate
Man of the World

Criticism

A World on Film
Figures of Light
Living Images

Editor

(with Bruce Henstell)
American Film Criticism: From the Beginnings to *Citizen Kane*

Stanley Kauffmann

LIVING IMAGES

film comment and criticism

HARPER & ROW, PUBLISHERS

NEW YORK, EVANSTON, SAN FRANCISCO, LONDON

1817

to my friends at Yale 1967–1973

The poem by Roy Campbell on page 81 is "On Some South African Novelists" in *Adamastor* (Dial, 1931).

The verse by Wallace Stevens on page 136 is from "Le Monocle de Mon Oncle" in *Poems* by Wallace Stevens (Vintage, 1959).

This work originally appeared in *The New Republic, Performance,* and *Horizon.*

LIVING IMAGES: FILM COMMENT AND CRITICISM. Copyright © 1970, 1971, 1972, 1973, 1974, 1975 by Stanley Kauffmann. All rights reserved. Printed in the United States of America. No part of this book may be used or reproduced in any manner whatsoever without written permission except in the case of brief quotations embodied in critical articles and reviews. For information address Harper & Row, Publishers, Inc., 10 East 53rd Street, New York, N.Y. 10022. Published simultaneously in Canada by Fitzhenry & Whiteside Limited, Toronto. Kauffmann, Stanley, 1916

FIRST EDITION

Designed by Sidney Feinberg

Library of Congress Cataloging in Publication Data

Kauffmann, Stanley, 1916
  Living images.
    1. Moving-pictures—Reviews. I. Title.
PN1994.K32   791.43′7   74-1822
ISBN 0-06-012269-2
ISBN 0-06-012268-4 (pbk.)

contents

preface

SOME people have paid me the compliment of reading my first two collections of film criticism. For them—and possibly for others!—I offer this third collection. Its purpose, as with the first two books, is to put in permanent, accessible form some material that appeared in journals through several years, further evidence of a continuing relation with an art.

All the reviews were published in *The New Republic* between 1970 and 1974. Many of them have been slightly revised. The eight articles in the Reviewings section appeared in *Horizon* between 1972 and 1974 and are here somewhat altered and expanded. The last essay in the book has not been published before, except for a brief portion that comes from an article of mine in *Film Comment*. (Thanks here to Roger Copeland for a reference he suggested.)

I offer this last essay in place of the introduction that often precedes collections of reviews or separate articles. Such an introduction often runs the risk of imposing explicit principles on a collection, principles that may better be found inductively. I put my "introduction" at the close; it does not enunciate principles, it attempts a historical comment, particularly on the period covered by this and my first two collections.

In the back of the book I have also included a combined alphabetical listing of all the films reviewed in those first two books, for readers who may want to refer to those reviews. The index to this third book comes right after that list.

My chief professional debt is, as before, to *The New Republic,* its editor Gilbert A. Harrison, and its readers. My chief debt of all is, as always, to L.C.K.

S.K.

May 1974

REVIEWS

reviews

Borsalino

(August 15, 1970)

CURIOUS, the relation between Hollywood and the film making of other countries nowadays. It's interesting to see which country fixes on which Hollywood element. Japan makes monster pictures, Italy makes Westerns, France makes gangster movies.

Godard's *Breathless*—the most prominent example of the last—is really about the effect of the Bogart persona, rather than a straight gangster movie. But a new French film, *Borsalino,* is the thing itself—an attempt to re-create a Cagney-Bogart crime epic, and with a nice double view: the past thirty years never happened; on the other hand, the past thirty years give the film an ambience of affection.

This story of the rise of two young hoods in Marseilles in the early

3

1930s is like a gorgeous ballet danced to the memory of *Angels with Dirty Faces* and *The Roaring Twenties*. Jean-Paul Belmondo is himself, quizzical, sexy, strong; Alain Delon does a fine reproduction of George Raft, lacquered hair and all (the Cagney-Bogart reference is one of temper, not specifics). The whole feeling is as if this were a lost film that had suddenly been discovered in the Warner Brothers vaults—for some mysterious reason made in French thirty years ago, with English subtitles.

Remember these scenes (or their equivalents)? The first shot is Delon walking out the prison door in ill-fitting clothes, meeting two waiting pals. Then, in slick clothes, Delon and his pals go to the bar of the guy who squealed on him, and they set fire to it. Then he finds the guy (Belmondo) who took his girl while he was in stir, and they slug it out; and we know, as they punch each other against walls and over pool tables, that this is simply ritual, no one is being hurt, they are testing each other's mettle, and will end up friends.

As they do. The plot need not be detailed, but here are a few more recognition-points. Each of the major characters is given a character-tag: one gang chief is fat and wears a white hat, another is thin and carries a lap dog whom he feeds at table. There is plenty of shooting—including the obligatory bizarre setting, a wholesale meat market, with death among the beeves—and there is lots of veneration of that venerable sacred object, the Tommy gun. Hardly two consecutive minutes without blood, or explosions ripping the backs of jackets, or spinning and clutching of guts, but none of it painful, really, just part of violence-as-ritual. The fabulous quality is underscored at the close by the arbitrary way the story ends. It simply stops, and there is a note on the screen to tie it off—followed by a series of black-and-white stills from the color picture we have just seen. An album of snapshots from a film that was itself an album.

The screenplay is by Jacques Deray, who directed, Jean-Claude Carrière, who has collaborated with Buñuel, Claude Sautet, also a director, and Jean Cau. They all had fun. The picture owes considerable to a catchy tune by Claude Bolling which we first hear on a honky-tonk piano as part of the score, but is later used "inside" the picture on a phonograph and by a dance band. The clothes by Jacques Fonterey are magnificent—especially the suits for Belmondo and Delon, which epitomize a vulgarity that is by now endearing. The title refers, of course, to the famous Italian make of hat, which I suppose is being worn in the film, but this is never specified.

Two of the most tired words in film discourse are "camp" and "*hommage*." I wish, at the moment, that the terms were less tired. *Borsalino* takes off its hat to a popular art form that was once done non-camp, and so becomes a formal tribute, amidst the gore, to what the gat begat.

Diary of a Mad Housewife

(*September 12, 1970*)

THIS film is a prototypical contemporary American cultural artifact. It is well finished, well acted, brightly written, but all its assorted talents and technological smartness are turned to the varnishing of mediocrity. And it is not about what it thinks it's about.

Eleanor Perry, whose last script was *Last Summer,* wrote the screenplay from a novel by Sue Kaufman. The story is of a young Manhattan woman, wife of a young successful lawyer, mother of two small girls, chatelaine of an expensive, very *consciously* furnished apartment: her tribulations, her humiliations, her fineness, her first extramarital affair, her ultimate reliability. (The word "mad" may apply to the novel which I haven't read, but not to the film—in either sense. She is rarely angry, and no one thinks she's insane. She goes to group therapy at the end, but, one may almost say, who doesn't?)

The ostensible theme is the New Materialism of Affluence. The husband is a connoisseur—of wine, of clothes, of social status, of business investment. His anxieties about all these things are intended as a picture of the sterilities and false values that lead him to under-prize, for instance, his wife. At one point he remembers how different they used to be when they were "young" (he's now in his early thirties!), and he says that all the idealism went out of them when JFK was assassinated. If that passage were meant satirically, it would be the best moment in the film, a statement of the kind of bankruptcy that is relieved to have found an occasion to declare itself. But I think the lines are offered as a deep social perception. Anyway, the husband's present empty busyness has turned him into an urbane nag.

From the very first moment, he is nagging. He nags his wife awake, nags her while she dresses, nags at breakfast, and so on. His nagging is sometimes supposed to be witty, sometimes flattering, sometimes kittenish (when he wants a "roll in de hay"). But underneath his vaudeville, he is nothing but a conceited, nagging boor. And that's not all the wife has to endure. Her children are nasty smart alecks. Her household work is endless (and unappreciated). Her party-going is dismal—until she virtually solicits attention from a prowling young novelist. She is driven to his bed by her husband's egotism. Subsequently she is literally thrown out by her lover because she wants humanity as well as sex. Then her husband, who has been busted by a snobbish investment in a French vineyard and whose job in his law firm is now threatened, comes to her for comfort, which she gives, aware that new success will once again make him what he was. At the last she goes to a therapy group and tells her problem, whereupon she is promptly attacked, by men and women, as spoiled and self-pitying. *Nobody* understands her.

In short, what is presented to us as a devastating picture of modern urban mores is in fact a modernized version of a dozen Joan Crawford–Ruth Chatterton films, yet another spayed version of *A Doll's House*. Ibsen gave us the awakening of a woman who has been spiritually brutalized by her marriage and who resolves to break out of it. *Housewife* gives us a woman who is essentially unchanged from beginning to end: she is noble all the way; and she stays with her husband at the end in order to go on being unappreciatedly noble. No other person in the film has anything like her vision or decency—not a shred of it. She is solitary in nobility. And so the film's depiction of male conceit shrinks beside its profounder, unintended depiction of female vanity. I hazard, further, that the Lib ladies will dislike the film because it shows this oppressed woman resolving to persist in her proper place as egotist's helpmeet and brats' ma.

There is something else operating here, too, a larger cultural current of which this picture becomes a tiny part. Here we have an attractive intelligent young woman, a Phi Beta Kappa out of Smith, who allows herself to be treated like an amiable dimwit; whose husband is well-off but who, even with a part-time servant, lets herself be used as a drudge. True, love begets forbearance; true, too, some women like housework and even prospering husbands cannot afford, or get, the household staffs of yore. But from start to finish her husband is abusing or blatantly utilizing her, and she almost always accepts it meekly. She takes a great deal of bullying from her lover, as if it were part of her lot. Why does she accept all this? A sense of inferiority? Her family and intellectual background are at least the equal of her husband's. Masochism? Not proved. No, there is, finally, only one credible reason for her acceptance of continual abuse. *Because she knows the camera is there.* She has witnesses (us), who know what she is suffering and how fine she is, who are sitting in judgment of her harassers and will reward her—at least with our sympathy and high opinion—for the reticent courage with which she undergoes her trials.

Put literally, this means of course that the film makers know the camera is there, but the film is told so intensely from the viewpoint of a heroine among besiegers, it is so inexplicable and unbalanced without the other half of the equation, that it has the effect of her conscious autobiography for those who are watching. This effect—a sense that the protagonist of a fiction knows that he (or she) is being watched or read or listened to—has been a familiar one now for two hundred years. With the decline of belief in God, the omnipresent witness, the secret sharer and rewarder, various art forms have moved to fill the gap left by his departure. These art forms, subjective and inevitably self-aggrandizing, finally substantiate Hulme's definition of romanticism as "spilt religion." Mountains of fiction and poetry attest to this phenomenon; now this film is carrying it on. Religion is not mentioned, yet what could be sustaining this woman except some kind of faith that her disregarded virtues are not lost? (The kind of job God used to do.) Imagine her as unwitnessed, and the only thing that would then be credible is her quick flight or quick breakdown.

Much of this confidence in our presence comes from the performance of the role by a newcomer named Carrie Snodgress. She has attractive taciturnity and an unusual voice, reminiscent of Jean Arthur, and, like Miss Arthur, Miss Snodgress is always saying to us privately and winningly, "See?" Even in her bed scenes. Another film newcomer, Frank Langella, known in the New York theater, plays the lover with feline insolence. The husband is Richard Benjamin who again displays his limited, sure gifts of comic inflection and calmly arrogant italicization. The bright rich boy, grown partially up. Any differences between this performance and, say, Danby in *Catch-22* are simply differences in dialogue.

Frank Perry has done his best direction so far. As usual, he is good with his actors, and here he has "staged" things adroitly. For instance, the final quarrel between lover and wife: the man angrily shoves her flat on her back on the sofa and she has to argue upward at him. But in the past Perry has often seemed strained in pure cinema technique, and now he is as smooth and creamy as the best TV commercials—which, technically speaking, is a compliment. The best thing that can be said about his direction is that it is free of those incessant zooms and intercuts which many younger directors think essential to hipness. On the other hand, like so many currently developing directors, Perry's work is devoid of personal style.

This lack of style matches the general chic anonymity of the whole film. Its infinite accurate details do not make for specific truth, only for general recognition. Like *Bob and Carol and Ted and Alice,* it is a product of the very culture it means to examine critically. Its interest is not in any way that it takes us but in the way it can be looked at objectively.

The Rise of Louis XIV

(September 19, 1970)

THE photography for this film by Roberto Rossellini was done by Georges LeClerc, the costumes were designed by Christiane Coste, and I can describe the result only with the antique phrase "a feast for the eyes": because I had the figurative sensation of devouring scene after scene. This is no case of imposed prettiness, like *Elvira Madigan,* no sentimentally spurious selection of décor to support a romantic concept. Here the exquisite fabrics, the richness of texture, the modeling of space by light, all are used to validate a complex reality. Artists have arranged matters, but there is no straining for arty effects. So they get the best possible result for a historical film: this is how the mid-seventeenth century must have looked when it was new.

Louis XIV was made for French television (which may give us a hint about the high quality of the TV sets in French homes). When you consider that it was finished in 1965 (it was shown in the 1967 New York Film Festival), you recognize once again that critical pronouncements, in any country, about the state of film art don't reflect that state as accurately as they reflect the profit hopes of distributors. Getting a picture made is only Money Problem Number One for a film maker; Number Two is getting it distributed, in the country of origin and elsewhere. At any moment—at *this* moment—

there are films in existence in many countries that, one way or another, would seriously affect anyone's estimate of the current film situation, if he could see them. For the general public in the U.S., Rossellini's film has not existed for the first five years of its existence.

Rossellini, born in 1906, has had a long and influential career. He was one of the preeminent postwar Italian neo-realists (*Open City* and *Paisan*), and he helped launch both Fellini and Antonioni, among others. His work in the fifties, insofar as it was available here, interested me less than it did other people. His last previous picture that I saw—not the last one he made—was *General della Rovere* (1959), which started slowly but became a strong idealistic thriller.

The French title of the new film is more precise than the English: it translates as "The Seizure of Power by Louis XIV." Rossellini begins with the deathbed of Cardinal Mazarin in 1661. The royal ministers then ask the young king to whom they should report, and Louis makes his famous surprising reply, "To me." The film ends with the arrest of Fouquet, the establishment of Colbert as chief adviser, and the relish of kingship realized, as Louis embarks on what turned out to be fifty-four years of rule.

The picture has been called a psychological study and a re-creation of historical forces. In the usual senses, these terms seem to me misleading. In comparison with the way that Eisenstein's *Ivan the Terrible* is a psychological study, or the way that Jancsó's *The Red and the White* exposes the nerves of political kinetics, *Louis XIV* only glides on the surface. Rossellini creates his picture with pictures—not quaint tableaux but the realization of daily life in the great houses by following details; the doctors bleeding Mazarin, the maid sleeping on the floor outside the curtained fourposter where the king and queen repose, the dumpy progress of the little king plodding down the corridors, sentenced to immense journeys just in getting from one chamber to another. It's a species of naturalism, a reliance on surface fact to evoke inner truths, and is thus related to neo-realism. In *Open City* the facts were those that Rossellini's contemporaries knew: which was the whole point of Italian neo-realism—to show Italians recognizable Italy for a change. Here the factualism is in the past, but the artistic rationale is much the same. There is a scene in which Louis dines alone, with nobles (not servants) to serve him, with his brother on hand to provide the napkin, with dozens of courtiers standing below the dais to watch the king eat. The pace is natural, thus slow. The meal is a ceremony that reveals more about the evolution and power and responsibility of the institution of monarchy than most overt commentary or dramatization could provide. "Save the Surface and You Save All" is the slogan of a paint manufacturer; it is Rossellini's artistic credo here, and it works.

Music is also a strong element, in a unique way. At the start, we hear music of the period, and after it ceases, the picture seems to continue in the same stately tempo and sonority. From time to time, music rejoins the film, but always as if we had been hearing it all along.

The slow movement of the picture itself and of the characters within it has no relation to Eisenstein's tempo, where he often selects elements for Byzantine emphasis, nor to Antonioni's middle films, where he distends time for philosophic reasons. Rossellini is simply re-creating life—no, not simply, of course, but with the main intent of verisimilitude. And the rhythm and shape of that life are caught so well that the verism eventually takes on aspects of abstraction.

We get very few explanations of Louis's radical decisions. We never go "into" his head, and we see only a little of the exercise of shrewdness—in a scene with his mother. But all of his acts are credible, largely because of the performance of the role. Jean-Marie Patte, short and plump and plain, clumps his way to genuine regality with the full assurance of gracelessness. His very lack of stature and his disregard of that fact convince us that there must really be something in a man who has such assurance despite those physical odds. As Mazarin, an Italian actor called Silvagni and, as Colbert, Raymond Jourdan fill solidly the spaces assigned to them in the composition. Rossellini casts a pretty actress (Joelle Laugeois) as the neglected queen and a merely handsome actress (Françoise Ponty) as the king's adored mistress. Neat.

The script by Philippe Erlanger and Jean Gruault has its mechanical moments. The opening sequence creaks with old fashions: peasants discuss their troubles—for our edification—outside the chateau at Vincennes, then two doctors ride by en route to the sick cardinal, then we follow the doctors into the sickroom. The authors put a stranger in the court to whom another courtier can explain some things that need explaining to us. Rossellini, too, has a few awkward moments: more than once, a character gets up from a chair, takes a few steps, and returns to the chair. This trope, which is supposed to add movement to a static scene, is only staginess.

But the picture is a serene, savory delight. To the French, this

account of the Sun King's self-realization must be rich with reverbera-
tions. To other viewers, lots of other historical parallels are available.
More important than such parallels is the beauty with which a certain
portion of past time is made to flow through the glass once again.
This is the work of a film maker calm and sure enough to relax
without being lax: enjoying the fruit of long experience in the ease
and clarity with which he is now able to work.

Five Easy Pieces

(September 26, 1970)

Two months ago I was driving down through the Grand Tetons and
gave a lift to a young man. He turned out to be a Ph.D. candidate
from an eastern university who had just finished his course work and
couldn't get up enough interest to write his dissertation. The whole
process had turned futile on him. He had come out to Wyoming to
get a job with his hands; he didn't know how long it would be before
he went back. Perhaps never.

I thought of him when I saw *Five Easy Pieces*. This film is about
an oil-field worker named Bobby—a chain-slinging, beer-drinking
manual worker—who turns out to have been a concert pianist and a
member of a distinguished musical family, who chose to drop out of
his former life. Now he lives with an affectionate ninny named
Rayette whom he abuses but who forgives him when he pauses to see
that he *is* abusing her. Bobby reluctantly goes back to visit his family,
who live on an island in Puget Sound, because he learns that his
father has had a couple of strokes. And reluctantly he takes Rayette
along (though he stows her in a motel near the family home).

The scene shifts: from cheap little bungalow to spacious culture-
crammed country home: to bearded paralyzed patriarch and male
nurse, Bobby's adoring sister, stuffy brother and his fiancée. After a
brief fling with the brother's fiancée, Bobby explodes out of the house
with Rayette. Very soon after, he cuts loose from her and heads
off—somewhere.

I'm going to say some adverse things about *Five Easy Pieces*, so
I'd like to emphasize first that it ought to be seen by anyone who
cares about American film. To begin with, the photography by Laszlo

Kovacs is extraordinary in a time when extraordinary camerawork is becoming common. Kovacs, who shot *Easy Rider* with joy in the rolling landscape, has a particular gift for photographing air. The sunbaked air lies heavy on the oil fields; the air in the Northwest is soft and damp. His use of planes is sharp and telling. The very last scene is a long shot of a filling station, with a giant logging truck pulling away from us up a hill and in it Bobby fleeing from the waiting Rayette. In the middle ground, she gets out of their car at the gas pump and walks toward us, toward the men's room where she thinks Bobby is. This is using the very stuff of cinema to make drama, through the look of the whole shot and the different lines of motion.

Of course the director had something more than a hand in this. He is a thirty-five-year-old named Bob Rafelson, who wrote a lot of TV adaptations and then made a film with the Monkees called *Head* (which was fairly enjoyable). Rafelson has authentic gifts. He knows how to work with actors: individually to bring out everything each one has for the role, and in ensemble balance and synthesis. He has a feeling for veristic detail: the harsh metallic look of the oil rigs nearly bruises you in your seat. He has a sense of detail: when Bobby goes into an almost empty coffee shop, a baby in the background is squalling on his parent's lap (standard equipment for small-town coffee shops) and the waitress has a beehive hairdo like a seventeenth century Venetian wig. And Rafelson can understate nicely: a frenetic sexual scene, just enough of it to tell us something about Bobby; a parting from some hitch-hikers, whom we have met at some length, dismissed in one silent long shot—because there is nothing more to say.

The performances are very good, with their own intrinsic truth even where the film wanders a bit. Jack Nicholson, who pierced millions as the boozy small-town lawyer in *Easy Rider,* plays the hero, Bobby, and proves that he is probably on the screen to stay a while—a long while. He has tenderness, fire of several kinds, spontaneous charm and—which he especially needs here—conviction of some depth. Two moments are particularly fine. He tells Rayette that he is going up home without her and stalks out leaving her sulking in bed; he gets in his car, bursts into frustrated obscene rage, then quietly goes back inside and invites her to come along. And in the filling station at the end, there is a moment in the men's room when he looks in the mirror. Nothing changes in his face, but we know something is happening in him. (He comes out and hitches a ride on the logging truck to leave Rayette, looking for something else, whatever it is.)

On evidence so far, Nicholson has limitations. His peak moments are filled, but there is a sense in them that he is flat out, with no reserves (unlike Brando and Newman, for instance). His own rural accent doesn't jibe with everything—the speech of his family here, for instance. But within his limitations he has variety and strong appeal. He is starting a screen life somewhat later than James Stewart or Henry Fonda or Gary Cooper did, but he may become something of an anti-urban myth-figure like them.

Karen Black has an easy part in Rayette, the conventional good-hearted vulnerable bunny, but she handles it nicely. Lois Smith, as the sister, is excellent. What a wonderful emotional face for the screen. Susan Anspach radiates refaynment as the fiancée. Helena Kallianiotes carves an effective cameo as a nutty, probably lesbian hitch-hiker. William Challee, whom I used to see with the Group Theater and who has not acted in films, has a good mask for the mute father. (I have a photo of Challee and Bette Davis in a 1929 Provincetown Playhouse production—both looking so *new*.)

The theme of the film is—well, we have a choice. Either it's the aridity of American society and of traditional culture, or it's the "congenital" spiritual torment of a born Outsider. I vote for the latter because, unlike my Wyoming friend, there is very little hint of dissatisfaction in Bobby with the U.S. as is. He dropped out of his piano career because he didn't think he was much good; he still loves music as such. He moves on from one menial job to another, from one "world" to another, not because there is any subliminal hint that he is searching for something (as was the case in *Easy Rider*) but because he is fleeing. He tells his father—in an effective monologue—that he always moves on before things go bad on him. That is not a critique of U.S. 1970, it is a description of a spiritually disenfranchised playboy of the Western world.

This indecisiveness of theme is a chief flaw in the story—by Rafelson and Adrien Joyce. (Miss Joyce also wrote the screenplay, with pungent vernacular.) There is much material—bowling-alley and trailer-home ugliness—to suggest that the modern U.S. is Bobby's cross; but he never endorses this. On the contrary, he relishes it all, including the bowling and a fistfight, with sensual delight. The script harries him further: it excludes any opportunity of satisfaction for him. Rayette is vapid; his brother is stuffy; his father, with whom he has never been close, can't even speak; the brother's fiancée insists—quite rightly, I should think—on staying with the brother and not going off with Bobby, but she is supposed to be cowardly and square because of her decision. There is, in fact, no person of any class—excepting his sister—who is really fit to be on the same earth with Bobby.

And the contrasts between the prole life and the *very* highbrow life exclude alternatives. This arbitrary juxtaposition of extreme strata, as if they represented the entire world, has the flavor of melodramatic fiction: the jungle and Mayfair of Tarzan.

Also the script has too much of a fondness for "colorful" vignettes, a rather facile way both of jabbing up interest and seeming to tell encyclopedic truth. The lady hitch-hiker's diatribe about filth, a party girl's story about her chin dimple, are vaudeville acts of realism, facile ways to score. There is a scene with "intellectuals" near the end which is even worse because the vignette given that fine actress, Irene Dailey, is quite incredible.

Rafelson has evidently been ardent (and tasteful) in his filmgoing. The pair of hitch-hikers are handled in a way reminiscent of the way Bergman handled his different pair in *Wild Strawberries*. Bobby pushes his father's wheelchair across the horizon in what seems a clip from Fellini's *Juliet of the Spirits*. Rafelson has presumably remembered Truffaut's *Shoot the Piano Player* in this story of a former concert pianist (although Truffaut provided more connection between his hero's two worlds) and, as director, he has learned from Truffaut and Godard about the use of peripheral characters—a straw boss, a figure in a doorway in a recording studio—as contributors to both reality and mystery.

But Rafelson is very clearly trying to use what he has learned as his own, not merely in imitation. And *Five Easy Pieces* is particularly welcome because it is something still rare in American films—a personal picture, made primarily because it says something that its makers wanted to say. It can be criticized, not dismissed. Its overall effect can be questioned because of some sentimental mod assumptions, but many sequences crackle with intelligence and talent. Rafelson and Nicholson are members of a new producing group, which has so far made *Head* and *Easy Rider* and this film. I'm glad they exist, I wish them long life, and I hope they improve, all three.

As for the meaning of the title, several guesses are possible, including a sexual one and a reference to a piano album for beginners. But those are only guesses: I don't really know what it means.

P.S. Now I know. I've met Bob Rafelson and he tells me that my second guess was right.

The Wild Child

(October 3, 1970)

AT a press conference after the showing of his new film at the New York Festival, François Truffaut was asked why he had made it in black and white. He said that when he saw the zoom lens used in Pasolini's *Gospel According to Saint Matthew,* he found himself thinking that there was no zoom lens in the time of Christ; and similarly he felt that there was no color film in 1798, the period of *The Wild Child.* Asked why he himself played the doctor, he said that he wanted no mediator between him and the child; by playing the role he could direct the picture while he was in it. Asked why he used so many iris shots to begin and end scenes, he said that fade-outs have to be done in a lab and are always unsatisfactory; he could do the iris shots right in the camera.

Directors should not be burdened too heavily with the things they say in interviews: there seem to be two concurrent but separate professions—film making and interview giving. But Truffaut's replies are cute. (Besides the obvious cuteness of the first answer, it is also cute to pretend that he couldn't have directed the boy from behind the cameras as well as he did the boys in *Les Mistons* and *The 400 Blows;* and cute, further, to pretend that lab shortcomings forced him here to use the archaic iris device that he has often used before.) The cuteness is part of his film-making psyche these days (all those cozy "inside" references in *The Bride Wore Black* and *Mississippi Mermaid*), and it is one of the reasons why *The Wild Child,* which is generally interesting, is not as good as it might have been. The visual aim of the film is not to look like 1798, but to look like an old film, a cute objective rather than an artistic one: the many uses of the iris, the tone of the black and white which is almost like 1920s sepia, the management of the crowd scenes like those in old operettas, all these are consciously quaint devices.

The best element is the straightforward narrative, which is truly simple, not quaintly so. Truffaut follows the documents left by a Dr. Jean Itard who in 1798 acquired custody of a boy of twelve or so. This boy had apparently been living alone in a forest since he was old enough to feed himself; the guess was that he had been abandoned for dead when he was three or four. He now loped on all fours most of the time, was naked, and had no kind of speech. The chief psychiatrist of the day thought the boy was mentally defective, but Itard, a counselor of deaf and dumb children, thought otherwise, took the boy to his home near Paris, and, after various tribulations, brought him to utter his first high-pitched word and to show some sign of moral discrimination.

The film's viewpoints are mixed—sometimes objective, sometimes the boy's or the doctor's—and this mixture doesn't help a cumulative sense of the unhusking of a human soul. Sections of Dr. Itard's notes are read on the sound track—in English, necessarily (although the dialogue is French, with subtitles), but why did Truffaut himself do it so badly? Jean-Pierre Cargol, a gypsy boy, is only adequate as the wild child; it's hard to see how he could have done less and still have registered. Truffaut as the doctor is a nullity, with a tight constricted voice and no warmth. Another example of a director who thinks that, since he can be at ease in front of a camera, he belongs there.

Yet the picture has a certain deep-seated effect. I was bored through some of the middle because I knew, as anyone would, that we were going through a *gradus ad Parnassum,* that the original notion of idiocy was going to be disproved, that the savage boy was going to be transformed—to some degree, anyway—by civilized kindness and knowledge. Or else why would the picture have been made? Still there is a power in this old idea, partly because it flatters us. What a wonderful bunch we are, we civilized fellows, and how touching it is to see a forest creature being elevated to our midst. The figure of the boy is only occasionally pathetic, yet there is a tribal, almost smug pleasure in watching the doctor's gradual success with him.

But compare *The Wild Child* with the use that was made of a similar theme in *Kaspar,* a play by Peter Handke, the young Austrian playwright and novelist. Handke took the idea of Kaspar Hauser, the

Nuremberg boy who spent his first fifteen years alone in a dark hole somewhere, and used it for a complex, ambiguous inquiry into the very stuff of communication, cognition, and teleology. Truffaut merely builds on a series of flat assumptions in all these matters. Handke's work has a shadowy and disturbing texture; Truffaut's work asks very little and assumes pat responses.

The Wild Child has had an ecstatic critical reception. No surprise. When a sophisticated artist chooses an unadorned parabolic story and treats it in a consciously unadorned manner, it's a safe bet that the result will be hailed as profound simplicity, no matter how banal it may be. This film is neither a banal disaster nor a symbolic triumph. But it couldn't miss. *The Wild Child* by François Truffaut!—that theme chosen by a man who himself had a troubled childhood more or less chronicled in *The 400 Blows,* the new film dedicated to Jean-Pierre Léaud who played that earlier boy—why, this film hardly had to be made at all. The title credits and the dedication would have evoked practically the same reviews.

Tristana

(October 10, 1970)

LUIS Buñuel is back in Buñuel country, alas. His last two films, *Simon of the Desert* and *The Milky Way,* were wonderful recrudescent works by an old artist who was concentrating on Catholicism in his unique Iberian atheist surrealist way. In *Tristana* he has relapsed into sensationalism—underpinned by the matters mentioned above but not clearly focused; and the result, like his earlier *Viridiana,* is an essentially vapid series of briefly stunning images.

Once again Buñuel puts on that hairshirt in which he feels so comfortable: the hell of the flesh. Once again he defies ideas of divine order with blasts against priests and parades of deformities and fetishism. (The shoe, an item he favors, is now on the end of a detached artificial leg.) Once again his native land, Spain, is the cross of his consciousness, and the only thing he can do about the fate of having been born Spanish and Catholic is to rail like a defiant adolescent who also happens to have prodigious film-making gifts.

Julio Alejandro, who collaborated with Buñuel on the script of *Viridiana,* helped him write the script of this film from a novel by

Pérez Galdós. (Alejandro also collaborated with Buñuel on another Pérez Galdós adaptation, *Nazarin*.) Like Viridiana, this heroine is an innocent put in the care of an older man who is sexually attracted to her. (The same actor, Fernando Rey, is the older man again.) This time the old man sleeps with her, instead of hanging himself. She is her guardian's mistress for a while, then she runs away with a young painter and returns in two years when she gets a tumor of the leg. After an amputation, one-legged Tristana marries her still-devoted guardian. In a scene reminiscent of *The Little Foxes,* she does not call a doctor when he has a heart attack. The barely well-to-do old man had lately inherited much money; Tristana is left a rich widow.

Again we are in a world where sex is a curse—the heaviest burden of human existence. Again the theme is corruption. But of whom by whom? When we meet Tristana, she is fresh and fair; when we leave her, she is a vicious and vindictive utilizer of her maimed body. (Special sex thrills there for special connoisseurs.) When her guardian first proposes that they go to bed, she makes no slightest protest; she walks into the bedroom and takes off her clothes—if not with joy, certainly with neither horror nor boredom. She reviles him some time later for what he did to her. Why? Here was a man who loved her, who behaved very decently toward her as benefactor, and who also slept with her but not against her will. Where was the villainy?

Understandably, she runs off with a younger man, but when she is in trouble and comes back, the older man takes her in at once and after her operation, marries her. In return for his never-failing devotion, she figuratively murders him.

Superficially this is a story of purity tainted by lust, with the lust in time paying for its sin. But this view will not stand scrutiny. I see it (viewing it through middle-aged male eyes, of course!) as the story of an intelligent, free-thinking, though hardly selfless man who both worships his ward and wants to sleep with her—not a new high in human complexity. Belatedly the girl is corrupted, not by her guardian but by a society which demands that she feel corrupted. She ends up a vindictive bitch who likes to tease a deaf-mute servant into masturbation and who kills her jealous but sincere and pathetic lover-husband.

Now this reversal, this truth worked out under a trite formula, would make a good film; but if Buñuel had it in mind, he has not put it on the screen, except obliquely and in fragments. The focus is lost in a parade of sadistic and diabolic effects, often graphically done but not knit toward a central vision, as they were in his last two films. The result is a picture that ends with a fuzzy, incomplete feeling, a sense that all this grave apparatus must have been intended for *something,* but only retrospection shows what that something might have been and how it was missed. *Tristana* is more of Buñuel's peculiar self-indulgence, in his own peculiar manner.

The story has been updated to the 1920s, and the exteriors, shot in Toledo, are caught in exquisite muted tones by Jose F. Aguaio. Catherine Deneuve is the heroine and does some of her best miming as she moves from virgin to vixen, but it *is* miming; her role has been dubbed in Spanish by someone else, and part of the unusual effect of her acting is that this time she has an interesting voice. Franco Neri plays her young lover, also dubbed in Spanish, and once more is an ambulatory phallus, the same function he fulfilled in the recent *Virgin and the Gypsy*. Fernando Rey, the guardian, is subtly quirky and dignified.

No Buñuel film lacks good touches. Some of them here: the way Tristana eats throughout the film as an index of sensuality, the glimpses of Spanish small-city life and the position of an atheist in such a city. But *Tristana* wobbles because again Buñuel overestimates the specific gravity of his grotesque and sexual effects.

Well, he's only seventy. Still time to regain the stride of his last two films. I look forward to his next.

Buster Keaton Festival

(October 24, 1970)

COMPREHENSIVE exhibits of neglected artists can have contrary effects. Sometimes a big exhibition only makes clear that a man's few well-known works are all that ought to be well-known. But sometimes a retrospective exhibit can do exactly what it was intended to do: reinforce our high opinions of a man's known work, let us see how much of his good work is insufficiently known, and in general lift him to a higher stature than ever.

That's exactly what the current Buster Keaton Festival in New York is accomplishing. The festival, which is at the Elgin Theater and will soon be seen around the country, includes every one of the ten features that Keaton himself produced, between 1923 and 1928, and each feature is shown with at least two shorts to make a bill of two hours. It's all wonderful.

There is often a tendency to get nostalgically lush when talking about old films, particularly old comics whom one loved as a child. Looking at these Keaton films as judiciously as I can, I'd like to repeat what I just said of this festival: it's *wonderful*.

Keaton has never been forgotten, but he has been comparatively neglected. That comparison is, obviously, with Chaplin. Now some points seem clear. As performer, Keaton is certainly Chaplin's equal. As director, he is Chaplin's superior, more flexible in his camera movement, more sensitive to pictorial quality as such. As producer of whole, organic works, he is not quite as good as Chaplin. As manager of his career, he is not remotely in Chaplin's league. Chaplin had great business and promotive sense; Keaton had practically none. (Sam Goldwyn once said, "Charlie has no business ability—he only knows the figure he won't take a penny less than." If only Keaton had shared this conviction of the Divine Right of Comedy Kings.) Chaplin had intellectual and political concerns that made him attractive to many kinds of writers. It's impossible to imagine Keaton hobnobbing with Shaw or Wells or Einstein or Churchill. I'm not sorry that Chaplin got his reputation; I'm sorry that Keaton did not get an equal one.

There are signs already, in discussion of the Keaton Festival, of the "heavyweight champ" complex that operates in film criticism. There must be a "best." In order to give Keaton his due, Chaplin will have to be "reevaluated." This is nonsense. But let me continue comparisons with Chaplin as a way of treating this festival, instead of trying to discuss each Keaton film individually. Both men were born of theatrical families, Chaplin in 1889, Keaton in 1895. Both came out of the popular theater, Chaplin from the English music hall, Keaton from American vaudeville. Both began young, but Keaton began almost as an infant. When he was about three, his father and mother tossed him about the stage in their act, and he soon became known as "The Human Mop." (At one New Haven performance in 1903, his father *threw him into the audience*—at some rowdy college boys!) Both Chaplin and Keaton got on well in the theater, Keaton even more successfully. Chaplin entered films in 1913, aged twenty-four, Keaton, four years later, aged twenty-two; and both saw very quickly that their theater knowledge could prosper only if they understood the idea of the camera. Chaplin's career, because of his gift for self-guidance, went up like a rocket and never came down. Keaton started well and, after an eleven-month interruption for service in World War I, continued well, largely due to the management of his brother-in-law, Joe Schenck. When Schenck and he parted, his career went wobbly and his private life hit some miserable low spots. Toward the end, his luck began to pick up. He was in *Limelight* (1952) with Chaplin, as well as in some other pictures, and in 1965 he appeared, with almost cosmic fatalism, in the virtually solo role of Samuel Beckett's film, *Film*. He died in February 1966. Chaplin not only managed career and money better, but also longevity. I'm delighted for him but wish Keaton had managed all three as well.

Artistically, there are close similarities and wide differences between them. Both understood the body as the source of comic life, both had incredible control of their bodies—an identification of physicality with comic performance that may never be seen on stage or film again. (Where is any young performer going to learn it?) Both understood that mere physical miracle was eventually sterile, that it had to be used in support of a character, a basically fixed character, as in the ancient tradition of clowning. In Chaplin's earliest shorts, one can see him moving toward the Tramp. In *Coney Island,* where Keaton supports Fatty Arbuckle, one can see him moving toward *his* character. (And, incidentally, disproving the myth that he never smiled.) Both pantomime artists dreaded the coming of sound, and neither was at his best in speaking roles. (*Film* is silent, except for just one sound: a minor character says, "Ssshhh!")

The differences between them are also interesting. In a primary but not exclusive sense, Chaplin is balletic, Keaton acrobatic. It would not be Chaplin's best style to do the skip across a table, over a man's shoulders, and the dive headfirst out a transom that Keaton does in *The Goat*. Keaton would not have done the globe dance in *The Great Dictator*. Intrinsic to Chaplin's silent films is an unheard music, to Keaton's the unheard sound of daily life. Chaplin's recurrent images are the theater and the road, Keaton's are boats (*Balloonatics, The Navigator, Steamboat Bill Jr.*) and trains (*Our Hospitality, Go West, The General*). Many of Chaplin's long films have better structures than Keaton's: Chaplin would never have let a film run ten minutes or more, as does *Our Hospitality,* before we get the first hint that it's a comedy. Most of Keaton's pictures are more obviously carpentered together than most of Chaplin's; they build toward a big climax, but they also deliberately delay it, filling in with comic figurations. Most Chaplin films are works of genius. Most Keaton films are vehicles for a genius.

There is also a sharp basic difference between the "characters" of the two men. Chaplin is the outsider, whose natural enemy is the police, almost always unemployable, let alone unemployed. (The factory job in *Modern Times* drives him nuts.) He gets rich at the end of *The Gold Rush,* but it feels wrong; he should not be an accepted member of society. Keaton wants nothing so much as to be one of the bunch, to be accepted, to disappear in conformity; it is out of his failure to do this that most of his comedy arises. Sometimes he is born rich and conventional (*The Navigator, Battling Butler*). He is often employed, and when he is, he wants to make good. Compare the attitudes toward war in *Shoulder Arms* and *The General:* the former is a tragicomedy, the latter is a comedy. Chaplin is a visitor from another planet, whose formal, though ill-fitting clothes are never mussed, in a gutter or a Klondike cabin. Keaton is very much of this planet and tries earnestly to make us believe that he is one of us. Perhaps what all this means is that Chaplin is European, Keaton is American.

It is now trite, but nonetheless true, to note that Keaton's face is beautiful. Chaplin's face gets the same beauty in motion (the scene with the girl at the end of *City Lights*) that Keaton's face has in repose. The only other film comedian comparable to these two, the endearing Harold Lloyd, falls a bit short in this respect: his face never suggests the angel in the pratfall.

Raymond Rohauer, who put this festival together, was running a film theater in Los Angeles in 1954 when Buster Keaton, whom he had never met, turned up one day, Keaton said he had heard that Rohauer was interested in old films. "Yes, I certainly am," said Rohauer. Keaton said he had a lot of "junk" in his garage that he was going to throw out unless someone took it away. Rohauer went there next day and found, among other Keaton treasures, the *only surviving prints* of three features: *The Three Ages, College,* and *Steamboat Bill, Jr.* He then went to work scouring the world for Keaton material and has now found everything except two two-reel shorts, *Hard Luck* and *The Love Nest.*

Keaton had a lot of rotten luck in his last thirty years, and he couldn't believe (says Rohauer) that his pictures mattered anymore. If only he could hear the audiences at the Elgin.

Trash

(October 31, 1970)

Trash, faithful to a new esthetic, tries to conquer us with ugliness—close-ups of pimply behinds and dangling penises and buck teeth and East Village squalor. The film was directed, photographed, and written by Paul Morrissey, a member of the Andy Warhol stable. (Warhol produced the film.) "Written" is not quite the word: the dialogue was evidently improvised on a sketchy story line.

The title is meant to reverberate. A few of the characters live by collecting and selling trash, but any adolescent (*preferably* an adolescent) can see the ironic larger meaning. Besides, the title has a parodic echo of *M*A*S*H*.

Trash deals with a young junkie and his adventures with various girls. He is looking for money for junk, they are looking for sex; but he is impotent. The girl he lives with is played by a transvestite homosexual called Holly Woodlawn. (The actors' names in Warhol-land are its most amusing feature.) Woodlawn has some ability to vent bitchiness—more exhibitionism than acting, still occasionally it's lively.

There is a lot of the usual Warhol stuff: hand-held camera and hand-held organs, frank language and franker formlessness, lots of simulated sex, an attempted put-down of Hollywood slickness by using poor lighting and poor recording and clumsy editing and a cast of either non-actors or freaks. A cheery go-go girl has nice breasts; the junkie's junkie behavior is credible, but possibly he is actually on junk in the picture. (The real star is the needle.) In short, another Warhol-type film. But there is one difference. Warhol at least has the courage of his lack of convictions; he persists in his formlessness and tedium. His films don't end, they stop. Morrissey concludes Trash with a neat welfare-worker sketch right out of Second City.

What is particularly revolting about this film is not the language or the life style or the poor-to-nil technique. Naturalism, now widely rumored to be dead, was (is?) an honorable mode in art, another attempt to reach universality by a different method of selectivity. Trash—and the Warhol school, generally—depends on our conditioning by naturalism, so that we will accept mere data as result: buttocks and profanity and dirt as prima facie evidence of ruthless honesty and art. I don't believe that Warhol and Morrissey believe in or care about the point of naturalism. I think they get a kick out of the suckers who drool in best Pavlovian style when the naturalistic bell is rung: the ones who believe that we are automatically being told something about our society and its spiritual turmoil by candor and grubbiness.

Added to the opportunistic brew is what Morrissey has learned from Warhol about the mystique of film itself: by photographing something—anything—you give it at least momentary grandeur. This is true, just as the affects of naturalism are true; and the Warhol-Morrissey school uses both truths equally cynically.

Trash is disgusting, not for what is on the screen but for what is in the minds of the people who made it.

This Man Must Die

(*November 14, 1970*)

How pleasant to go to a film one liked seven years ago and find that it's now even a bit better. Claude Chabrol's *Landru*, which I reviewed in 1963 and saw again recently, is one of the truly fine pictures of its decade, disgracefully neglected. Chabrol's version of the Bluebeard story (script by Françoise Sagan) was attacked for its mixture of tones and its stylized settings. But the tonal mixture is carefully selected to represent the range from slapstick to tragedy inherent in this story, and the stylization is an abstraction to help the mythopoeic process—Landru as legend. Above all, Charles Denner's performance of the killer-sage presses us against the backs of our chairs with a hand of iron.

How pleasant to like a new Chabrol film. And what a change! *Les Biches* and *La Femme Infidèle* and *Le Boucher* (the last seen at the New York Film Festival) all were silken exercises in aggrandizement, failed attempts to make much of little by doing it dexterously. But, in *This Man Must Die,* the material justifies the skills—heightens them, in fact. The film has real force and feeling.

As usual, Chabrol is working with murder, which is his *madeleine* (of stimulus, not memory). As usual, the cinematographer is Jean

Rabier, whose subtlety, especially in color, has increased since *Landru*. Again the screenplay is by Paul Gegauff—from a novel by Nicholas Blake (pseudonym of C. Day Lewis, the British Poet Laureate). And again Chabrol relies on plot contrivances to break open shells and reveal character. This time it works.

A small boy is killed by a hit-and-run driver in a Breton village. We see that there is also a blonde in the car beside the male driver. The father of the boy is a widower, a well-to-do author of children's books. In a freezingly quiet way, he swears—to himself—to find the murderer and kill him. He learns the identity of the blonde and makes her his mistress; then she leads him, unwittingly, to the man he is seeking, her brother-in-law. The avenger finds out that the intended victim is a wretch whom several other people would also like to kill. The drama is played out in cool tensions and psychological strokes.

The two tricky points in the plot are the coincidence through which the avenger gets his first real clue and the patness of the killer's rotten character. The way Gegauff and Chabrol have handled these delicate spots is to confront them and italicize them. Coincidences and "caricatures of evil" occur in life, they say, so why not here? And their nerviness succeeds.

As the stricken father, Michel Duchaussoy is immediately credible, genuinely threatening. What might have been a lurid tale of vengeance is taut because of this furiously reticent performance. Caroline Cellier, the blonde, is quietly fine. She has two especially telling moments: when she confesses to her lover that she once slept with her brother-in-law and is disgusted by the memory; and when her lover reveals that he is the father of the dead child. Cellier has imagined these moments as freshly and has treated them as affectingly as, say, Bibi Andersson might have done.

The essence of Chabrol's camerawork and editing here is austerity, matching what he does precisely to what is needed. The cutting is parsimonious and exactly right, as in the sequence on the sailboat with Duchaussoy and his victim. The scene at the restaurant table when the camera pans slowly from Duchaussoy to Cellier's face as he discloses his true identity is a perfect fusion of good script, truthful acting, and crystallizing camerawork.

Chabrol drops a neat hint of how the hero became a widower—just a suggestion of his wife's illness in some home movies he reruns. There are some display effects—the intercutting of the headwaiter serving the duck in the restaurant scene mentioned above, the burning of a cigarette in an ashtray while Duchaussoy talks to the victim's abused son—but they serve as functional and symbolic stitching.

The New Wave, throughout its twelve-year existence, has made a lot of films from thriller novels. Most of the time this is an empty anti-literary, pro-cinema device that ends in various bankruptcies. But sometimes, when all the components are right, as they are here, the film really takes us back to the primordial sources of which the thriller novel is only a saran-wrapped convention. In its small-scale way *This Man Must Die* is about modern possibilities of total evil and total love and total despair. We believe that the death of his son has drained this father's life of meaning, as it might have done to an ancient king. Essentially this is a film of classic gestures performed in trousers and minis and Mustangs, and it is gripping.

The Owl and the Pussycat

(December 5, 1970)

SHE really ought to be called Barbra Strident. She comes on harsh and grating, seeking to win us by being unabashed about seeking to win us. One reason she does it, I think, is panic. *Funny Girl* fit her like a second skin, but then, bereft of Fanny Brice in the two musicals that followed, she grabbed at a lot of other imitations to support her out there in the Brice-less cold. In her latest comedy, increasingly desperate, she leans on all the crassness she considers sure-fire, like a comic running out of material who can at least drop his pants.

The Owl and the Pussycat, by Buck Henry from a play by Bill Manhoff, is about a Manhattan bookshop clerk who kids himself that he's a writer and a hooker who kids herself that she's a model. Their encounters strip away their delusions and their clothes, and they end up facing truth together. They "meet cute," and their story gets mechanically cuter all the way.

Henry has opened the play out of its original one room into a number of settings and has expanded the dialogue in the Manhoff patterns of punch-line rhythm. Rhythm is the important element in this standard brand of Broadway laugh manufacture, not words. For instance, just before a character exits (Character B in the following exchange), the rhythm usually runs something like this:

A: Dum-dum-da-dum-da-*dum?*

B: Dum-dum-da-dum—(*pause*)—dum-dum-da-dum—(*pause*) —dum-dum-dum-dum-dum-dum-da-DUM! (*Fast exit.*)

Yok. Boff. Sure-fire. The words themselves don't really matter, though of course a nice salty final expletive helps.

Herbert Ross, the director, has a choreographer's sense of these rhythms, but visually he is plagued by the Panavision, which he doesn't know how to use. Also he stages the final fight-and-reconciliation scene in Central Park, with the lovers throwing each other to the ground and walloping each other in front of dozens of people in the background who never even turn their heads to look at the battling pair. The color throughout is what used to be known in magazine art departments as borax. (Example: If Ed Sullivan were a piece of artwork, he'd be borax.)

George Segal plays the clerk, and there's a sharp contrast between him and his co-star. Segal has changed, from the flashy make-out actor of his first films, to an actor trying to probe for some truth. His range isn't wide and he lacks basic excitement—there's no kind of surprise in him—but he does try to validate his work. And here he plays opposite a vaudevillian who is looking only for effects: glitz or heart-tug or boffola, all the while underscoring her vulgarity so hard that she hopes to embarrass you into laughing at it. (Which you do, sometimes.) She's skillful, but she's a performer, not an actress; and Segal is trying to act.

If computers can ever turn out romantic comedies, the results will be a lot like *The Owl and the Pussycat.*

The Confession

(December 19, 1970)

In Poland, they did not execute their Gomulka, in Bulgaria and Hungary they executed one minister each, but the crop of Czechoslovak Stalinism was the richest of all.

Thus writes Ivan Svitak, the exiled Czech philosopher, and that crop is what concerns Costa-Gavras in his new film. The director of *Z* has turned from a melodrama with a political setting to a true political drama. With the same scriptwriter, Jorge Semprun, he has made a harrowing film from Artur London's autobiography, *The Confession*. London, a former Czech deputy foreign minister, previously a hero of the anti-Nazi underground, a staunch Communist then and now, tells the story of his arrest on charges of espionage in January 1951 and the consequences. Like the thirteen others arrested around that time, he eventually made a public and false confession of guilt in the infamous Slansky trial of November 1952. Eleven of the defendants were executed; London and two others were sentenced to life imprisonment, but in the post-Stalinist days he was freed and rehabilitated. He and his wife now live in France.

Cinematically, the challenge of this story was huge because the bulk of it is visually repetitious—a long series of walks down corridors, interrogations, denials, harassments in the cell. Costa-Gavras solves this basic cinematic problem very ingeniously. Even more than in *Z,* he deals in short shots, and almost every shot contains something in motion—a character or the camera itself. Almost no shot is held more than, say, ten seconds, and almost none is fixed. This syntactical method creates a sense of dynamics even when the material, by its very nature, struggles to remain in stasis: that is, London does not want to change.

Costa-Gavras is greatly helped by three factors. The physical reality of the film is superb: the dampness, the dark, the differing types of blindfold as London is led back and forth from his different cells, the freshly carpentered cubicles in which the defendants wait outside the courtroom, and so on. All of these touches are heightened by the photography of Raoul Coutard who did *Z* and who handles color as revelation, not as surface. (You feel that the walls are the same color all the way *through.*) Third, the performance of Yves Montand as London. I've never been a great admirer of Montand's acting, but there's very little high "emoting" to be done here, so the part lies well within his range. What's needed is facial evidence of worms eating slowly at the guts, and Montand makes this utterly genuine. His look, in the very first shot, when he comes down the ministry steps and spots the police agents waiting, contains the whole film in little. Later, during the months-long questionings, his weary, whiskered face seems a political map of twentieth-century Europe.

Simone Signoret, grown gross, is adequate as his wife. Gabriele Ferzetti, who was the architect in *L'Avventura,* plays Kohoutek, the chief interrogator. (Dubbed into French?) London writes that Kohoutek "had something of the professional salesman," and Ferzetti gets this quality quite well. The subtitles by Noelle Gilmor are, predictably, good.

But there is something missing. It may seem ridiculous to criticize a true story in terms of what it lacks artistically, but if art weren't different from life, we wouldn't need it. The obivous comparison for *The Confession* is *Darkness at Noon,* and Koestler is better. I'm not being flip about London's sufferings; I'm talking only about what is shown on the screen, and there we see a considerable gap between Koestler's novel and London–Semprun–Costa-Gavras. The chief difference is that Koestler's point is to show an intellectual transformation, a rationalization of harsh unjust fate into the fulfillment of one's purpose. No such transformation, or any other, goes on in *The Confession;* it simply presents a process of attrition and chicanery that wears its victim down.

Essentially, the film does little more than restate, with force, what we have known ever since the Moscow trials in 1938: Communist ethics are ahistorical. They have nothing to do with traditional concepts of truth and justice for the individual, they have only to do with programmatic success. They even implicitly (sometimes explicitly) acknowledge individual injustice but hold it irrelevant to the long view. The great question for the world is whether a philosophy that crushes individual justice as it chooses can ever realize the international justice for which it does the crushing. This is a more chilling question than the old one about whether the end (Communist triumph) justifies the means.

And this leads to the question: why did London hold out? Why didn't he confess at once, or soon, to the false espionage charges? He knew, better than any of us possibly could, what the examinations were for, what the trial would be for, where it would all end. He writes in his book:

In such conditions, it is not only impossible for a Communist to prove his innocence but it presents him with a grotesque conscience problem: if you agree to "confess," in the Party's eyes you enter the path of your redemption. But if you refuse to sign because you are innocent you are a hardened culprit who must be mercilessly liquidated.

Weren't his personal standards, which made him courageously refuse to "confess" for many months, essentially irrelevant? Inapplicable? Weren't they really standards of bourgeois individualism?

Harold Rosenberg criticized Koestler because

He did not attack the jailors of Rubashov for specific violations of socialist values but placed the responsibility on Rubashov himself as representing with them a metaphysical absolute—"the logic of history"—opposed to the individual by the nature of things.

Here there is no "author." A "Rubashov" wrote *The Confession,* a Rubashov who was formerly a powerful official in a Stalinist regime. This shifts the focus very considerably and makes idealistic sympathy, as distinct from human compassion, more shadowy.

The film is not meant to be anti-Communist. There are flashes forward, during the prison months, in which London talks with friends in France *post hoc* and declines to let his book be used as a weapon against his unchanged political philosophy. One must admire his refusal to revel in the embrace of eager red-baiters. But there is something inescapably mutton-headed in his insistence on personal ethics, his refusal to accept the facelessness that his Party—as it has proved thousands of times—relies on in him whenever it chooses to summon it. He has even seen that the Party thinks nothing of discarding its advertised credo for tactical purposes. All during the interrogations and the trial there was a stream of vile anti-Semitism. (London is a Jew, as were many of the other defendants.)

For whom, then, is he being individualistically virtuous? And what is the root purpose of this film? (Of the book, too.) Presumably to help humanize Communism. I should think it would be easier, though not much more likely, to humanize capitalism.

The film has one telling antistatist gesture, during the carefully rehearsed trial. One defendant is in the middle of his memorized testimony when his trousers drop, ostensibly because he has grown so thin. The crowd laughs, and he joins in; but Costa-Gavras holds it so long and so brutally that we see that the prisoner is making the only comment he could make, with his trousers, on the words he is forced to speak.

There are three final bitter moments. One day the rehabilitated London meets Kohoutek in the street. The ex-interrogator has himself been in jail. Now he shrugs off his past harassment of London and invites him to have a beer. Dazed, London drifts away.

Second, London returns to the "new" Prague in 1968 to have his book published, just in time to see the Soviet tanks roll in. (In his book he hails the post-Stalin Soviet Union after his release and says that his "confidence in the Party and the USSR" has returned. This heightening of the bitterness is omitted from the film.)

Third, and possibly unintentional, the last shot shows Prague students, during that Soviet invasion, painting a slogan on a wall: "Lenin, wake! They're going mad!" But if Lenin *had* awakened, then what? It was Lenin who ordered the Red Army to take Warsaw in 1920.

Costa-Gavras has made a gripping, tough, intelligent film about an agony toward which the Western world has been moving for centuries. It's a tragic story; but, like some other modern instances, the real tragedy is that the hero is his own antagonist, and the ground of the struggle is not virtue but irony.

Little Big Man

(*December 26, 1970*)

JUST six years ago I reviewed Thomas Berger's novel *Little Big Man* and said:

A chief function of the tall tale is as a free-flowing conduit of history, a catch-all vehicle that, by disregarding most probabilities and some possibilities, contains a lot of historical truth.

Like Vincent McHugh's *Caleb Catlum's America* (a neglected nugget), Berger's book performed the American tall-tale magic: it summarized a chunk of basically grim history in a breezy, darn-your-eyes manner, its very style implying the one virtue that possibly counterbalances the heavy deeds done—lively, humorous grit.

Calder Willingham's adroit screenplay condenses Berger's big book and, often sensibly, rearranges matters, as it tells the story of Jack Crabb, who survives a Pawnee attack on a wagon train when he is ten, is carried off by the Cheyenne and raised by them, and whose life then fluctuates between the Cheyenne and white civilizations until the two life styles collide at the Little Bighorn in 1876. Jack is the sole white survivor, and he survives until "now" when he tells his story into a tape recorder. In the novel (1964) he was 111 when he was talking; for 1970, he had to be made 121. (The film was done just in time; even tall tales are limited in height.) The most significant change is that, in the original, Jack's Cheyenne "grandfather" goes up on a mountain at the end to die, and dies; in the film the old man can't quite make it, and has to come down again with Jack, to live. I rather liked this change, as it leads nicely into the note of Jack's own astonishing survival.

Arthur Penn directs with all his customary skill and very little of his customary artiness. This time, happily, he leaves Beauty to the eye of the beholder, and doesn't label it for us. He tells his story in a clean, vigorous manner, with a generally fine sense of where the audience should be placed to get the most out of every moment, with his humanist concerns revealed in his handling of character relationships. His weak spots are his large-scale physical conflicts; he doesn't love action enough to handle it as well as a Ford or Peckinpah or Hawks would. Ralph Nelson is a far inferior director to Penn, but the slaughter of Indians by cavalry in *Soldier Blue* was more gruesome than in *Little Big Man*.

Penn's invention falters in his battle scenes, and he also fumbles some opportunities. When Custer's cavalry rides up out of the snowy mist along the Washita to murder the Cheyenne, instead of letting them materialize out of the whiteness (as he starts to do), Penn suddenly cuts to a long shot from a hilltop to show the troops proceeding down the valley. And at the Little Bighorn, the angles and the editing don't give us a clear idea of the closing of a trap; terrain and disposition are unclear.

But there is life in the film, and the core of it is Dustin Hoffman's performance of Jack Crabb. We hear his 121-year-old voice out of the silence under the titles—there's no music until we're well along, and very little then—when we see him in his (rubber-mask) antiquity. Later, after a boy actor and an early adolescent actor have marked his growing time, Hoffman himself takes up Crabb at about the age of fifteen and carries him through his "periods" of frontier schoolboy, young Cheyenne brave, carnival man, gunfighter, boozer, storekeeper, older Cheyenne brave, hermit, and cavalry mule skinner.

Bernard Shaw said that fine art is either easy or impossible, and as Shaw meant it, Hoffman proves it yet again. He's short, he has a Feiffer profile, his voice is no great shakes, and, although he has charm, he has no great force of personality. What he has is instant credibility. It never seems to cross his mind that he is anything other than what he claims to be at the moment, so it never crosses our minds, either. His secret is not only imagination, not only the requisite vitality, but a lack of objectivity, so great as almost to be simple-minded. It's as if Hoffman were saying, "What do you mean, I'm not a Cheyenne brave? I've been one all my life." This ability to shut out objectivity—to shut out any view of one's self *playing* the part—is an essential particularly for "chameleon" actors, and it's Hoffman's ace.

In Robert Hughes's documentary film about Penn, there is a sequence showing Penn and Hoffman working on a scene from *Little Big Man*. It's a small lesson in the interweaving of two kinds of talent, and the results are in this picture.

The other noteworthy performance is by Chief Dan George as Crabb's Cheyenne "grandfather." I was prejudiced in the chief's favor because he looks a lot like my Uncle Al, dead these many years, and he fed my prejudice with his dignity and humor. Penn's one failure with a performer is Faye Dunaway, a parson's prurient wife who later turns up as a whore. She misses no possible acting cliché. Besides, as a frontier parson's wife, she wears false eyelashes only a trifle smaller than ostrich fans.

Under the energy of the film, the ominous theme is the invincible brutality of the white man, the end of "natural" life in America. At the beginning, when Crabb's young interviewer uses the word "genocide," it irritates the old man, but the film—his story—only substantiates the term. Penn makes contradictorily sure we know his own sympathies. When Indians attack a stagecoach, the murders are supposed to be funny; when cavalrymen attack an Indian village, the murders are tragic.

The color is unobtrusive—certifying without being garish. The Panavision feels comfortable. Penn has made a tangy and, I think, unique film with American verve, about some of the grisly things that American verve has done.

Flap

(*January 23, 1971*)

IN *Custer Died for Your Sins* Vine Deloria, Jr., says:

America has yet to keep one Indian treaty or agreement despite the fact that the United States government signed over four hundred such treaties and agreements with Indian tribes.

This is the underlying theme of *Flap,* written by Clair Huffaker from his novel *Nobody Loves a Drunken Indian.* Which gives us our second pro-Indian, anti-white film in a month. (The other, *Little Big Man,* is based on one of the few books about Indians that Deloria recommends.)

Flap is a corny, ill-made picture full of tedious movie brawls. It takes considerable time to get started, and it misses no chance for familiar cinematic pattern—in fights or bordello hijinks or stuff with a bucking horse. Further, the color, at least in the print being shown in New York, is deplorable. Yet the picture has a root effect, and makes its slow, cinematically sentimental way along a hard, unsentimental base.

In brief, it tells the present-day story of a small symbolic uprising led by Flapping Eagle, a drunken, loafing ex-World War II sergeant—the doomed effort he makes to help his harassed and cheated friends on the reservation to get their rights. All the gestures of plot and camera are stale, but a core of residual truth comes through because of the quality of some of the performances.

By rights Anthony Quinn ought to be just a big bore by now—he's been so hearty and male and ethnic for so long. But, damn it, he's *good,* at least from time to time. He's been good as an Eskimo, a Greek, an Italian, and several Mexicans, and as this Indian, he's good again. He not only has the technique and power to sustain the big moments, he has the intensity of imagination to root the character in quiet reality. Once in a while I found myself asking, "Does Quinn really know where he is, or has he just been off-camera, between takes, phoning his agent in Madrid about the picture after next?"; but then I watched him *listening* to another actor in a two-shot, and he listened like Flapping Eagle. He makes no smallest move except as Flapping Eagle—or rather as Flap dramatized.

There are pleasant performances by Tony Bill and Claude Akins as other Indians, but there is an absolutely knockout performance by, of all people, Victor Jory. He used to be my idea of a stock-company leading man, not improved by such Broadway work as his John Gabriel Borkman some twenty years ago. Here he is Wounded Bear, a toothless, leathery, snappy old correspondence-school lawyer, who spends most of his time burrowing in old treaties for Indian rights, and he is excellent. Unlike most actors, Jory is growing, late in his career, and I hope we're going to see much more of him.

Carol Reed is the unlikely director, fresh from his grossly overrated *Oliver!* There is little grace or fluency in the making of this film, little to reflect Reed's long experience; he is particularly clumsy in getting the story started. But he does work well with actors. Quinn and Jory give this picture a truth too good for it.

Little Murders

(February 6, 1971)

FOUR years after its Broadway premiere, I'm now resigned to a future with *Little Murders* as a thorn in my side. Jules Feiffer's play will always fascinate me and will always dissatisfy me. Besides the first Broadway production, I've seen it off Broadway, have read it twice, and have now seen the film version. There are elements in this play that would do credit to the best surrealist playwrights, like Aragon and Vitrac, but it falters. And the film, I think, falters in its own way.

The Newquists, who live in hazardous Manhattan, have a college-student son and a twenty-seven-year-old bachelor-girl daughter, Patsy. She brings home her latest boy friend, Alfred, to meet her family. Alfred is a big, gentle, "apathist" photographer. Soon he and Patsy marry, and the violence of the city, which has been peripheral, reaches in when a sniper shoots Patsy. (Her other brother had been killed by a sniper a few years before.) This murder shoves the periphery into the center, and the play—the film, too—ends in a bacchanal of murder.

This last scene is one of the best in postwar American drama. Exalted in frenzy, it soars past black humor, past any snug or smug social satire, to a burning-clean comic distillation of horror and thwarted love. It frightened and moved me both times I saw it on stage and, almost again, on film. There are a few other moments in the play that approach this scene; there are many moments that are funny. But, in general, it's a bumpy trip from beginning to end, even though the least of *Little Murders* is above run-of-the-mill satire.

By now it's a commonplace (I'm one of those who have said it) that this play reflects a cartoonist's occupational predisposition—it's a collection of strips and panels. The film underscores this and other discrepancies. The play starts as a realistic comedy: with jokes about power failure, about a tiny TV set being taken out of a huge cabinet, and—the script's low point—the father's objection to being called by his detested first name, Carol. (As if he had just been given the name, as if he had not been married thirty years.) In spite of the realistic air, the family is incredibly cool about the son mindlessly murdered a few years before. The play begins as realistic satire and ends in surrealism. It keeps shunting back and forth throughout, neither consistent in texture nor consistently changing—with an accelerating spin from the real to the surreal.

But the main trouble is the main action, the drama between Patsy and Alfred. She keeps trying to convert the "apathist" to feeling and response. There are some arbitrary flip-flops in this tussle just before she is killed, but all this hassle is about a quite different subject from the ostensible theme of the play. That theme is the increasingly evident violence in our world, irrupting because of social and political forces that are pressing it out like pus from a boil. This is a very different subject from the matter of the placid affable calm in Alfred that Patsy is trying to heat up. He tells us, in a hilarious scene, that he has withdrawn from competitive involvement because of the absence of real values in the world. What has that to do with violence? He tells us, in a beautiful speech (regrettably condensed in the film), that the first chill he got was in college because of a government agent who was reading his mail. But how is this incident—a Kafka-like anecdote about insecurity and guilt—related to the pathology of the New York jungle? Alfred's apathy does not connect with the play, and the scenes between him and Patsy don't advance or dramatize the theme. When Patsy finally converts Alfred and at that moment is killed by a sniper, the shooting seems to change the subject, instead of capping the scene. (So the shooting never "works.")

In his film script, Feiffer has naturally opened up the play, making narrative of the original exposition. We see the young couple meet, and Alfred's first appearance is nicely prepared by the sounds of an off-screen fight. A resort hotel, famous for its mating games, comes in for a good workout. When the couple return from the hotel to Patsy's apartment, they find it wrecked and cleaned out by burglars, with anti-white-folks slogans on the wall, and they take it in calm stride—*c'est la vie New-York*. In the hippie church where they are married is a sign: "Support the Newark 85."

But some of the alterations don't help. Feiffer has inserted a visit by Alfred to his long-forsaken parents in Chicago, which gives us nothing but familiar cartoons on psychiatry and culture-vulturism and which muddles the abstract quality of Alfred by providing a dossier that isn't even a dossier. In the play, the first time we see Alfred after Patsy's murder, he is in high gear, cheerful and busy in his new mania of violence. This abrupt change is one of the best moments, in both its impact and its implications. In the film, after Patsy's death, Alfred goes through a period of catatonia, which injects a hurtful senti-mental note. Worse, his shift from catatonia into mania is made to depend on a walk in Central Park, which for no apparent reason is a catalyst. Worse still, the park scene looks so normal that it contra-dicts the atmosphere in the Newquist apartment, which is supposed to indicate a changed world outside.

There are some very good performances. Marcia Rodd is at last the right Patsy, both metallic and pathetic. Elliott Gould, who was Alfred on Broadway (he was unknown then!), is even better here, with bearlike gentleness and puzzlement. From the off-Broadway cast came Elizabeth Wilson and Vincent Gardenia, the parents, and Jon Korkes, the younger brother; the first two are first-rate, Korkes is all right in an easy part. Donald Sutherland floats through, as a hippie minister. Alan Arkin, who also directed, is good as Detective Prac-tice. A revue-skit bit like this, as opposed to acting, is the kind of thing he does best.

But Arkin's direction doesn't help the discomforts of the script. I had hoped that the film version might unify the work, by providing a consistent visual texture to blend the inconsistent modes: a surrealist *look*, even when the work is at its most naturalist. This isn't done. On the contrary, Arkin emphasizes the naturalism. A particularly bad moment is when the camera pulls back from Patsy's death to show us the actual sniper at an opposite window, thus raising questions of identity and motive in what had been simply some more blind stupid killing. And the moments where Arkin does attempt surrealism are bungled, partly because there is no preparation. The long speech of the old judge is one of the sharp moments in the play, a quintessential record of immigrant idealism, valid in itself, falling on deaf ears, which in fact is valid, too—a scene of really deep noncommunication. Arkin allows Lou Jacobi to shout the judge's speech from beginning to end, has him suddenly walk out of his chambers away from the couple as he talks, then continue the speech in a courtroom empty except for a stenographer taking it down, and finish it in a suddenly crowded courtroom. The whole sequence, instead of serving as visual comment on what it is presenting, simply seems irrational, failed cleverness.

So, too, is a sequence at the wedding. We see a number of quick shots of the father confiding to people that he gave the young couple $2500. The last of these shots is the father alone on a toilet, repeating the line to himself. Again, the unprepared touch, which had been intended presumably as a Freudian anal joke, collapses. The best we can think of it is that the father is momentarily demented.

Agile though he is, Arkin so far lacks the fundamental for a good director: a central concept, primarily visual, that controls all the film's elements: as, for instance, we are conscious from the first moments of *The Knack* and *How I Won the War* that, whatever their defects, every moment is tissue of a body. (*There* is the director—Richard Lester—who might have helped *Little Murders*!) Arkin seems only to have felt along the script for moments to be artful, and in between has been content to be inferior Billy Wilder.

So the film has not redeemed the play as, partially, it might have done. It's just a somewhat different set of pluses and minuses. But the pluses are so good, and the minuses so far above the ruck, that the picture confirms *Little Murders* as an unforgettable, imperfect work.

Bed and Board

(*February 13, 1971*)

AT the press screening of *Bed and Board* they gave us copies of a recent interview with François Truffaut in which he spoke at length of his admiration for the high Hollywood days and for the directors who could do three films a year. His new film makes clear that he is really speaking out of envy. In one sense Truffaut can be called a Hollywood director without a Hollywood.

Truffaut was one of the first *auteur* critics, in the early 1950s, one of those who proclaimed the greatness of those Hollywood directors who, far from being shackled by the assembly-line studios, the taboos, the vulgar script distortions, were stimulated by the difficulties of their work conditions. The triumph, said the *auteur* argument, was that these directors put their personal imprint on their assigned material through their shooting and editing style, and the fundamental virtue in their work is the tension between their talent and the limitations of show biz. It's a bit like Tevye, the impoverished milkman, rationalizing himself into feeling rich, still this view prevails among many (even though some of them, without changing their views, now boast that they no longer use the word *auteur*).

In daily Hollywood practice, what it came down to was that directors under contract to a studio were supplied with scripts by the studio. The director was simply one step, though a major one, in the manufacturing process from studio executive to consumer. If the director was big enough, he had the right to decline scripts—a limited number, anyway; and the ones he accepted soon provided a graph of his temperament and talent. But he didn't have to find his subjects himself—certainly not *in* himself—as artists, film or otherwise, have usually done.

This, I would guess, is the aspect of Hollywood that Truffaut misses most. He has seemingly run out of sources, novels or other materials that genuinely spark him, and even his latest autobiographical films have been thinned out into entertainments. Heaven, for Truffaut, would presumably be the chance to work in an old-time studio with no responsibility to originate material, with a front office that bombarded him with scripts, some of which he was obligated to direct. What a happy misery. Nothing to do but direct, just as if directing—in that merely executant sense—were film making.

His last previous work, *The Wild Child* was mildly interesting. In the threadbare film world, some are now calling it a masterpiece that failed at the box office because its spirit was meliorist in a nihilist age. Possibly. For myself, I couldn't see why people should flock to a picture that was only moderately rewarding, whose factual material was untransformed and unenriched, and whose tone was sentimentally simplistic. Still, it was a small recovery in Truffaut's career. With *Bed and Board* he retrogresses.

This film completes (?) his life story disguised as Antoine Doinel. The first installment was *The 400 Blows,* then there was an episode in the anthology picture, *Love at Twenty,* then the pleasant *Stolen Kisses.* But there was a great discrepancy between the first Antoine and the hero of that last film, and it's no easier to believe in the wholeness of the character now that the story is concluded.

Here we have Antoine newly married to Christine, scraping up a living briskly and merrily (ah, Paree!) frisking with his wife, having his first extramarital affair. That jolly Latin Quarter courtyard (out of René Clair), those happy-happy tradesmen, the downstairs bistro owner with a taste for culture, the bar-girl who lusts tastefully after Antoine, the colorful neighbors, including an opera singer (Clair again?)—they are all there, *mes amis,* as they have been there for forty years. Antoine has an affair with a Japanese girl; a job with an American company; a reconciliation; a baby.

Besides the scent of Clair, there are other "in" references (often called *hommages*), including a bit by Jacques Tati. Truffaut also gives his bistro owner one of the oldest Hollywood jokes. *Viz.,* MGM had a man on its staff to think up titles. A desperate producer asked him to title a picture in a hurry, no time to see the film. The titler asked: "Any trumpets in it?" "No," said the bewildered producer. The titler said grandly, "Call it *Without Trumpets*!" Truffaut includes the ancient wheeze here as if it were new. *Hommage*? Gall?

Style is what is being hailed in *Bed and Board,* but charm is what is being merchandised, as calculatedly as in any France-for-export film of the 1930s. Jean-Pierre Léaud is again Antoine, again exploiting his best asset—a private, introspective quality on which the camera seems to be intruding. Claude Jade is again the girl, to no special effect. Some other old Truffaut hands are on deck, like Pierre Fabre and Daniel Boulanger.

But for all the incessantly pumped *bonhomie,* the picture sags, with no such nice touches as the shoe-shop encounter or the lovelorn stranger in *Stolen Kisses.* If a fiction artist uses autobiography and it doesn't nourish his work, he *is* in trouble. Truffaut badly needs something in his life to fertilize his art, or he will indeed become—as I was worrying some time ago—a mere talented filmer of concocted scripts. Which is what he seems to want.

Jules and Jim and Catherine, you arrived less than ten years ago? Incredible.

The Hour of the Furnaces

(February 27, 1971)

A film phenomenon and a phenomenal film. This Argentine documentary runs four hours and twenty minutes, plus two intermissions, and is a clear, unambiguous call for revolutionary violence. It was directed by Fernando Solanas, thirty-five, who wrote the script with Octavio Getino, thirty-six. (Solanas also photographed, Getino did the sound.) Both of them have been making short films in the past decade. Their work here is sometimes crude, sometimes suspect, and is certainly not unfailingly gripping, but they have made an impressive, vehement film of immense energy.

It has three main sections, "Neocolonialism and Violence," "Act for Liberation," "Violence and Liberation," and there are numerous subsections. To criticize the argument of the film calls for a knowledge of Argentina—and a copy of the script!—to which I won't pretend. The thesis, varied and repeated, supported with news clips, commentaries, quotations, statistics, and interviews, can be stated fairly simply: Argentina began as a Spanish colony and, after independence (1816), continued as an economic and cultural colony of Great Britain. The U.S. developed great interests there and through this century U.S. power has supplanted British power, though the British still have a strong cultural hold. (See the dress and amusements of the upper class.)

The first really Argentine politics in Argentina was Perónism. Perón was maligned abroad, principally by the U.S., because his economic developments and social welfare programs, his payment of the foreign debt, all interfered with foreign investments and control. The U.S. conspired in the overthrow of Perón, nominally as a pro-democratic move, actually to install a regime more friendly to its influence. Post-Perón governments, like earlier ones, have been oligarchic, plutocratic, militaristic, and brutally repressive, and have depended heavily on outside cultural and economic resources. The largest political party in Argentina is still the Perónist one; it can be the spearhead of a people's revolution which is what is needed in all Latin America. "Two, three, more Vietnams," as Che said.

All the above is subject to some question, even on the basis of superficial knowledge like mine. But the size of the Perónist bloc (30 to 40 percent of the population) and the possible alliance between Perónism and the far left were reported in *The New York Times,* by Malcolm W. Browne, on October 3, 1970. Anti-Americanism is a great unifying force among political factions in Latin America. If it be argued that there are Latin-American countries much worse off than Argentina, there is also a country—Uruguay—that has always been much better off; and see the recent history of their Tupamaros.

Besides the questions that may nevertheless be asked of the film's facts, there are also questions about their presentation. What's the point of the gory slaughterhouse scenes? Argentina lives by beef production, and will do so presumably under the most popular government. We are told ominously—twice—that four people die a minute in Latin America. By my figures, this is also the rate in the U.S. We are told that true culture depends on the complete liberation of man—in which case we will never have true culture. (I would have thought that one reason for art is that man is *not* completely liberated, and will not be.) We are shown a man being beaten by a group of men in mufti, then being dragged face down through the mud. How do we know that he wasn't a CIA agent who tried to get into a Perónist meeting? There are many instances of beating and gassing where political sympathy is asked immediately for the victims, with no fixing of facts.

But, keeping one's guard up as well as possible, one still is overcome by a sense of selfish, cruel, exploitative power in the hands of a few. As usual in all tyrannical situations, East or West, black or white or brown, there is no slightest reason to believe that the oppressed are the moral superiors of their oppressors and will behave better if and when they triumph; but that's hardly a reason for the oppressed to accept things as they are, particularly if they are the majority.

So we come to the nub of the matter: the advocacy of violence. In politics, I don't see how a view on violence can be held as a universal absolute, which is why many of us who object to the Vietnam war still do not call ourselves pacifists. The Argentine peasant, who has inherited generations of wretchedness, who has seen women and children machine-gunned by police, is in a very different emotional and, I think, moral position, in regard to violence, from the American university student who is (rightly) protesting the campus presence of Dow Chemical. Although it is chilling to see this film come *three times* to a climactic call for violent revolution, I think that to deplore it in terms of the nonviolent campaigns which one advocates in the U.S. is almost to verge on the smug. It's a bit like people on a diet telling the underfed that they're better off thin. If violence is immoral, as it objectively is, we still have to recognize that there are situations where objectivity is impossible; that there are situations where violence may have to be used to drive out even greater immoralities.

In terms of cinema technique and imagination, Solanas has done everything he could to make his work a *film*—to break out of the old booby-trap of propaganda: which is that propaganda films rarely change anyone's mind, they only heat up the previously convinced or the susceptible. True, he says halfway through Part Two that his film is not for mere spectators, but I think that by then he hopes to have hooked those people—Latin-Americans, anyway—who started as mere spectators. He has worked to make his picture visually interesting. He used to work on advertising films, and one can see it in his use of varying optical techniques for the many words on screen. The editing is sharp, often with staccato intercutting of action and verbal message. The sounds and songs are effective. (I should probably specify that it's all in Spanish with subtitles.)

And sometimes the film is genuinely beautiful. There's a well-composed, deep-focus scene in which an old Patagonian peasant sits before his shack, speaking with simple stateliness of the horrible past and his undimmed socialist enthusiasm. There's a scene in which the camera travels past an odd assortment of silent men waiting in a cellar, then passes a curtain on the other side of which a young whore is seated on the edge of her bed, taking her lunch-break. There's a slow 360-degree pan over the Buenos Aires rooftops, while a voice speaks of its condition and history and the photography itself underscores what is being said.

In a further effort to break the film forward *off* the screen, to keep it from being something to watch, Solanas has arranged moments where the film can be stopped and discussed. And he has left it all open-ended, so that further testimonies and interviews can be added.

The Hour of the Furnaces has been shown only clandestinely in Argentina, but openly in some other Latin-American countries and in Europe. The gifted Italian director, Marco Bellocchio, has said, "It's not a film, it's a gun." But (as he knows) it would not be a gun unless it were a film. I hope the reality of that gun will be seen in this country, and I hope against hope that it may influence our policy abroad. Time runs out.

Solanas has made a message picture with more than one message. In its force and commitment and stature, it's the best film—of any kind—that I've seen from Latin America.

Ramparts of Clay

(February 27, 1971)

QUOTATIONS from Frantz Fanon are featured by Fernando Solanas in *The Hour of the Furnaces,* and a Fanon epigraph also introduces *Ramparts of Clay,* which is about a village in southern Tunisia. (Actually shot in nearby Algeria.) It's based on a book called *Change at Shebika* by Jean Duvignaud who spent five years in such a village, and it has been made something in the style of Visconti's *La Terra Trema:* inhabitants of the place enact sequences fashioned on events of their lives. There are only a few professional actors, one of them a girl, Leila Schenna, who looks like a young Irene Papas.

The purpose is, basically, to show us a life style of rock and poverty, sandstorm and desert, religion and folkway. Andreas Winding's chromatically subtle camera puts it all before us deftly, and Jean Louis Bertucelli, a director out of French television, has worked miracles of empathy with the villagers.

Bertucelli's film moves slowly, rhythmically, interestingly. The central incident is a strike by the men of the village, who work in a quarry, but the real theme is the abrasion between the hard life and the girl, who discovers that she wants to get out.

There is no travelogue feel (though the dialogue is sparse), there is a sense of entry into the dawn-to-dusk survival pattern, complete with a couple of harsh sequences about the use of animal blood—seen as the villagers see it. The only questionable moment is the last shot of a helicopter. Whose, for heaven's sake? But the sound of its motor at the end closes the circle begun by the very first sound of the squeaky well-bucket pulley. And in between is a film of dignity and grace.

Claire's Knee

(March 20, 1971)

AMONG my sins last year was my failure to review *My Night at Maud's* by Eric Rohmer. This French screenwriter and director, now forty-seven but virtually unknown in this country before *Maud*, has been working for years on a sextet of feature films which he calls *Six Moral Tales*. "In each tale," Rohmer said in a recent interview, "a man looks for one woman and finds another." *Maud*, which is immersed in Catholic ambience, is the third in the series. It's set in a small French city and concerns a serious man who does not make love to a beautiful woman in whose flat he spends the night; instead he has a thoughtful conversation with her. He marries a younger woman and, in a postlude a few years later, some psychological elements of the story at last fall into place.

Now we have *Claire's Knee*, which is the fifth of Rohmer's tales. (Numbers One, Two, and Four have not yet been shown here.) I liked it even more than *Maud*—for one reason, because it shows Rohmer to be a film maker with more than a style. To put it differently, it confirms that his style, courageously calm, derives from a large philosophical overview.

His work authenticates his claim to be the scion of seventeenth-century French classicism. Rohmer has seen classical form, classical *impulse*, as the source of his cinema. I emphasize this point: he is a man of film, one of the former editors of *Cahiers du Cinéma*, yet he has relied on a literary tradition. There is a great deal of conversation in his pictures and not much overt action, but the result is *film:* He has translated the techniques of French classical literature, its spirit, into film terms: of serial time, spatial deployment, sequences of images, and the very sound of words—even for one who has to rely on the subtitles, like me.

After admitting his debt to classicism, Rohmer says in the interview (*Le Monde Weekly,* January 20, 1971):

But one should not overemphasize the influence of classical culture on my film-making. You would probably be surprised to know that I learnt the rudiments of dialogue writing from a close study of detective stories!

Acknowledging that he is neither prig nor pedant, I still think the single most significant aspect of Rohmer's work is his success in transmuting a set of artistic concepts that were fashioned before film existed into a modern medium.

In *Claire's Knee* the serious games of love and desire and temptation and restraint are played principally by a man and a woman in their thirties and two stepsisters of sixteen and seventeen. Jerome is a diplomat who has come to Lac d'Annecy to sell his villa there. He encounters Aurora, a Rumanian novelist whom he knows and has not seen for some time, who is staying with a family on the lake and who is the means of his meeting the two sisters. Jerome is to be married in a month, to a woman we see only in a photograph; Aurora, we learn, is "resting" from sex-love life. He and she are very fond of each other and often touch as they talk, but I don't think we are to infer from this that they were once lovers, simply that they live in a culture where friends touch one another, almost as index of friendship *instead* of sex.

After he meets Laura, the younger daughter, Aurora tells him that the girl has fallen in love with him. From then on, Aurora suggests actions or nonactions to him, and he reports to her on what he has done or not done. He is, quite consciously, acting out the rough draft of a novel that she may one day write.

The brief flirtation with Laura ends, the older sister Claire arrives —cool and fair, where Laura had been dark and confiding. Claire is completely uninterested in Jerome; she has a boy friend of her own age, and is indeed the only one who is seemingly having an active sex life during the film. Possibly it's her indifference to him and his knowledge of her amour that fascinate Jerome. His desire is focused precisely on her right knee—not because he suddenly sees it—it's always visible, she wears brief skirts and swimsuits throughout. But one day Jerome sees her boy friend's hand on her knee and it suddenly becomes a sexual grail to him. In time he fulfills his quest, in a way that puts him and his disordered desires in order again, without Claire's ever being aware of what has happened.

Much of the fabric consists of Jerome's secrets, which he confides to Aurora, so we see his actions from an inner vantage point. We become a bit jealous of his having an Aurora to whom he can report and from whom he can get advice. ("Men are driven by love and self-love," says Rohmer, "but they also feel the need to confide in someone." He is not a Catholic for nothing.)

Every detail of the film is painlessly planned and finely articulated.

Jerome lives across the lake and travels by motorboat; every visit to Aurora and the girls, therefore, takes on the image of voyage and departure. The color photography by Nestor Almendros almost *speaks* in its clarity: the camera even makes upholstery patterns of the furniture part of the story. All the clothes have been carefully and, I'd say, wittily selected. There is not a note of music except when music is in the scene, and the silences and sounds also contribute.

Obviously a film like this depends very decidedly on its actors. They have to fill the screen, since the action is within them, not done by them. Rohmer has a canny gift for choosing the right people. Jean-Claude Brialy, familiar from *Les Cousins* and *King of Hearts* and many other pictures, is suitably complicated and gentle as Jerome. Aurora is Aurora Cornu, herself a novelist, who is appealing in a heavy, slightly hairy way. (Rohmer has left in several of her nonprofessional glances at the camera, as if to prove that she is a "real" person, not an actress.) But the best performances, the crucial ones, come from Beatrice Romand and Laurence de Monaghan as Laura and Claire. Their sensitivity and charm testify very strongly to the core of Rohmer's talent, which is to gain the confidence of his actors and to *present* them.

In this he resembles the older—and greater—French Catholic director, Robert Bresson. Also, as in Bresson's *Diary of a Country Priest,* Rohmer's film has a diaristic effect. Each sequence is introduced by a handwritten title, bearing the day and date; the story runs precisely from June 29 to July 29. (The rhythm of these sequences is neatly controlled, each one cut off astringently, their duration nicely varied.) And, although the atmosphere of *Claire's Knee* is much more voluptuous than anything I've seen in Bresson, there is almost the same feeling of ascetic selection of everything.

Two things are different from Bresson, which make Rohmer lesser. There is no passion; there is only intrigue, even though it is intrigue that involves the spirit and self. And, in *Claire's Knee* there is little feeling of accomplishment, of arrival at some revelation when it's over. (Not true of *Maud.*) When this film is finished, we feel only that we've spent 100 minutes in the company of some attractive and intelligent people. Drama, true drama, is concerned with the most important events that will ever happen to its characters. We can't feel that the events of *Claire's Knee* are the peaks of its characters' lives. All we have seen is some of their experience, experience which indicates what they are, more than it affects them for any change. But as they are all interesting and are in the hands of a fine talent, the 100 minutes are lovely.

Wanda

(March 27, 1971)

PROBABLY the most difficult subject to make interesting in art these days is the prole. For at least twenty years, our esthetic attention has centered on such matters as alienation, communication, and identity crisis, problems that are the prerogatives of those who don't have to worry about tomorrow's grub. When a film or play or novel deals with blue-collar folk, we get an anticipatory feeling of *déjà vu,* as if the subject has already been well dealt with in art and there is little to add. In certain senses this is true: snobbish as it sounds, the range of interest in the truckdriver tends to be smaller than in the advertising executive (even). Most proletarian art deals chiefly with injustice, and most of what changes from one proletarian work to another is the data.

Just because I believe this, *Wanda* is all the more welcome. It's about a working-class girl, and it goes past mere authenticity to some depth, to aspects of universality. At least equally impressive, it marks the writing and directing debut of Barbara Loden, who also plays Wanda and who distinguishes herself in all three fields. Loden is well known as a theater actress. Her performance of the Marilyn Monroe role is about all I remember favorably from the first production of Miller's *After the Fall.* Still I—and most others, I think—would not have expected her to be able to write and direct a film as good as this. Her performance, too, has surprising qualities.

Wanda, I guess, is meant as a homonym for wander. She's a Polish-American girl, from the Pennsylvania coal fields, who drifts away from her husband and two small children simply because she lacks the power to feel for them; drifts with no more luggage than her pocketbook into a motel with a traveling salesman; then drifts into a liaison with a nearly psychopathic criminal. Somehow his fits of fury bind her to him; she is unable to leave the comfort of that fury even when she knows she is coasting with him into crime. We sense that his outbursts are the strongest show of true feeling that anyone has ever offered her, and since she has no great depths of feeling to offer anyone else, she clings to the strongest feeling that has come her way.

The man's bank-robbing plan fails, and he is killed; through her persistent stupidity (she gets to the bank too late to play her part), she escapes. Then, after resisting a sexual assault from still another pickup and after bursting into tears for the first time, she seems launched on a career as a barroom hustler.

This is most distinctly not a crime story, not a low-budget *Bonnie and Clyde*. It concentrates on Wanda, on the accidents of her strictured life, which happen to include an encounter with a criminal. It's a modest account of a pilgrimage, even if unknowing and squalid, from beginnings that had numbed her powers of response or protest through various kinds of disregard and abuse, with almost complete acceptance. The film succeeds in large measure because it's quietly made, taciturn in its fierce concentration on this nearly dumb creature, and because it almost never asks for pathos. Every effort is at succinct chronicle, so gradually Wanda acquires, in her vulnerability and her humiliations, some aspects of an agonist. I know nothing of Loden's religious beliefs, but this strikes me as essentially a Catholic film.

Michael Higgins plays the robber with excellent egocentric madness, yet he tells us that this man is the product of his life, living it out as defensively as he can. Loden is very careful not to play Wanda as a victim; she makes her a victim by playing her as a girl who is struggling every moment of her life. The struggle is weak and handicapped, the results are misfortunes and defeats, but she never pities herself, until the very end. The last shot is a freeze-frame—one of the few really apt recent uses of that device—in which Wanda sees that the rest of her life is going to be a steep slide, and not a long one. Wanda looks like an easy part, but it would be easy only for an inferior actress. Loden succeeds beautifully because, inside the cage of inadequacy, we sense the bafflement and fruitless fight. Her performance is sure to be widely underrated because it's not the least bit showy; but it's a work of understanding, imagination, and talent.

Her direction and writing are not much less talented. The film was shot in 16mm, now blown up to 35mm, so the texture is grainy and the color mediocre, but—ex post facto rationale, perhaps—the look of it fits the subject. Some shots, like Wanda in white walking through the coal fields, are a little arty. But note, for instance, a sequence near the end: Wanda stands in front of a tavern window; a girl comes out of the bar, passes her, goes up an outside stairway, appears at a window on the other side, comes down again and comes around to Wanda—all shot from one position with a panning camera, the action designed so that one position could accommodate it and so that we get the feel of a web being woven around Wanda.

The virtues (considerable) and faults (few) of the writing can be shown in one passage. During her first night in bed with the robber, Wanda says to his back, "Mr. Dennis, don't you want to know *my* name?" A life is in that line. Without turning, he replies, "No." A touch too heavy. If he had just grunted or said nothing, but just let her line hang there, the point would have been unhammered.

In the last three or four years, a number of attempts have been made, of varying worth, to deal with American life as it is. Almost all of them have dealt with the young or near young, exemplifying aspects of complicated social or political crisis, with at least some attributes of intellection. But, as Robert Coles and others keep reminding us, most of the country, like most of the people on earth, do not live at that level; Hobbes's state of nature—with life nasty, brutish, and short—hasn't changed much for them in three centuries. Wanda came out of a society that had ravaged her afferent powers and her adaptive intelligence long before she was on her own. Loden's triumph is that she has realized this truth without stopping at case history; her writing, direction, and acting make *Wanda* a small, good work of art, and make Loden a very welcome addition to the film scene.

The Conformist

(*April 10, 1971*)

ANOTHER Italian leftist director has gone the way of Technicolor flesh. Like Luchino Visconti and Pier Paolo Pasolini and Elio Petri before him, here is Bernardo Bertolucci gone overripe. The first Bertolucci to be seen here, *Before the Revolution* (1965), was a quiet, direct film about radical dilemmas, with some youthful lift. It was in black and white. Then came color and, like drink in the wrong hands, it unsettled Bertolucci as it has so many.

In Shaw's play *The Doctor's Dilemma,* an old doctor says, "Chloroform has done a lot of mischief. It's enabled every fool to be a surgeon." Color has done a lot of mischief in the film world. It's enabled a lot of directors, fools or otherwise, to become esthetes.

Bertolucci's next pictures, both in color, were *Partner* and *The Spider's Stratagem,* which up to now have been seen here only at festivals. The first, garnished with Godarderie, was a *Doppelgänger* story of some interest. The latter was a rancidly arty allegory about fascism. Now, it's fascism and color again in *The Conformist,* based on Moravia's celebrated novel, but the film is a precious and perverse travesty of Moravia.

The dominant tone of the book—actually its real point—is its calm, as it tells the story of Clerici, a young Fascist official in the late 1930s. He is haunted by the (supposed) murder he committed at thirteen—he thinks he killed a chauffeur who tried to seduce him—and now he wants only to blend obscurely into the landscape, whatever the landscape is. On his honeymoon trip to Paris, he agrees to guide Fascist assassins to an ex-professor of his who is doing anti-Fascist work there. Clerici and wife see the professor and wife in Paris, with some personal complications, and the asssassins are alerted. Back in Rome, Clerici reads of the murder of the anti-Fascist pair. He is now even more part of the surrounding landscape. Some years later, on the day that Mussolini is deposed, Clerici discovers that the chauffeur is still alive. The trauma that caused his lifelong drive for conformism had never really existed. Next day Clerici and his wife and child are killed in an air raid—*really* flattened into the landscape. All in the same unruffled tone.

Bertolucci's pressure-cooking begins with his screenplay. He has chopped up the chronology of the book in a display of the "film mind" that makes hash of the story's progress and makes the hash difficult to digest. He has changed the hero to a strong silent sex-figure, and has given the dialogue lots of sudden leaps and ellipses, meant to indicate big boilings underneath. In the guise of dramatizing, he blatantly heats things up. For instance, in the novel the hero is ordered simply to identify the professor for the gunmen. Here he is given a gun and ordered to kill him. The delicacy of Moravia's point—perfectly filmable—is ground into cliché.

For Moravia's ending, Bertolucci substitutes distortion and illogic. After Clerici sees the chauffeur, he then lingers near and presumably beds with a young male whore. Moravia's psychopolitical point is debased into a sexual fillip—as if what had been bothering Clerici all his life was repressed homosexuality, inculcated by the chauffeur and now liberated by discovery that the "dead" man is alive. This for a story that was designed to show the psychic bases of political action.

But the screenplay is only where Bertolucci *begins* whooping things up. In the filming itself, he makes very sure we understand that the Age of Cinema has arrived and that he is a leading citizen. No millimeter of the screen is left unpregnant at any moment, no shot is spared ponderous meaning. Men carry sculptured eagles out of the dark, lights swing to cast moving shadows, the composition always transforms a recognizable place into an abstraction of itself, nothing ever happens in the foreground without some busy contrapuntal movement behind. The lighting is born out of sophomoric adulation of Fellini.

Bertolucci has cast two beautiful women—Stefania Sandrelli and Dominique Sanda—as the two wives, and he pores over them like a fussy, attitudinizing fashion photographer, never with feeling, always with a sense of utilization. With them, with everyone, the screen is crammed full of shots that were seemingly designed for reproduction in glossy film journals.

One's figurative solar plexus gets sore from so many esthetic punches. What is fundamentally wrong with the look of the film is that it completely controverts the intent of the work (as, in another way, the fragmented script does). The idea of the murderer's security among mass murderers, his happiness in conformism, is swamped and destroyed by the bordello style—even that of a high-class house. The visual aspects of fascism were inflated-heroic, never voluptuous.

Through all the stultifying pyrotechnics Jean-Louis Trintignant manages to give some coherence to the hero. Which makes one all the more angry that he wasn't allowed to play the part in a sane script, under a director who had interests in something other than himself. This film, supposedly about politics, seems to provide a refuge for its author's political frustration in a species of gluttony. Last year Visconti produced his chromatically intoxicated, sexually perverse version of Nazism in *The Damned*. Now, from Bertolucci, on a smaller scale, we get the Fascist equivalent. Call it *The Darned*.

Derby

(*May 22, 1971*)

ROLL on, Roman games. The crowd always wants blood, and some members of the crowd are always willing to draw that blood as a way of getting *out* of the crowd. True in the Circus Maximus, true in Dayton, Ohio. *Derby* is *cinéma-vérité* about roller derbies, shot mostly in Dayton, and gives us the thump of body contact on the floor, the mob's pleasure, and the story of a young factory worker who wants out of his job via a roller-derby team.

I've never seen a derby. Fans will know that there are male teams and female teams, and that besides speed, each contestant, male or female, needs the ability to whack others out of the way, to vault over shoulders, to punch and to take punches. It's much less a race than a running fight on wheels, whichever sex is racing. When I saw women slugging one another while the crowd cheered and applauded, I remembered that the very first show I ever saw on U.S. television was a wrestling match in mud between two women. The same principle is operating here.

The footage of the races and some of the locker-room stuff is pure documentary, a record of events that would have happened anyway, when and where they happened, even if no camera had been present. And there are some straight interviews. But the story of Mike Snell, the young worker, which is presumably true, has obviously been reenacted: the talks with his wife, the team manager, a loan company executive, and so on. The most surprising material is the sequence about Snell's dalliance with other women, in which he and a man friend are frank and in which his wife participates.

Robert Kaylor, the photographer-director, has done the essential thing for this kind of work, he has got the confidence of his subjects so that they will be easy in front of cameras and will reveal themselves. Helped by good editing, he has made a sharp film, just the right length, that slashes laterally across a stratum of society. This is not Middle America but prole America, and *Derby* is one more index (*Wanda* was a more subtle one) that the classic working class is still very much part of our world, no matter how much we talk about the middle class enveloping everything. That last is true in the cultural sense, not the economic one.

Derby cannot shake the veil of contrivance that, however gauzy, shades the verity in this kind of cinema. The basis of this film making is the pretense that no film is being made, so the truth is in fact a bit further removed than in good fiction films, like *Wanda*. But Kaylor delivers a short, hard jab to our assumptions of change. Besides his eye for ugliness, he has an eye for beauty in unlikely places: the silent wife of the team manager, Snell's wife, and even Snell himself—a slimmer Elvis Presley with a cockerel touch of Warren Beatty. One reason this film has some quality is that Kaylor's vision is open, not prejudiced.

Bananas

(May 22, 1971)

THE trouble with Woody Allen's films—which he writes, directs, and stars in—is quite simple. He is a very funny writer and (on TV) a fairly funny stand-up comic. As a director and actor, his talent is, so far, absolutely zero.

Bananas is full of hilarious comic ideas and lines, supplied by Allen and his collaborator Mickey Rose; then Allen, the director and actor, murders them. An American weakling gets involved in a Latin-American revolution—something like Harold Lloyd's *Why Worry?* (1923) up-to-date. There's a lot of smart satire of things worth satirizing, from TV coverage of serious events to facile libertarianism. There is some surprising corn, like Allen stepping out of a car and into an open manhole, or lisping before the word "pith," but generally the script is good. With Dustin Hoffman or Robert Morse, directed by any run-of-the-mill sitcom director from the Disney stable, this might have been a knockout. But see Allen trapped on an exercise machine or at a trial where he is both lawyer and witness, and you'll see the quintessence of Amateur Night. He confuses the ability to write comedy with the ability to perform it.

His directing is worse. He makes this clear in the first sequence where he wrecks a comic assassination; the shooting is too real for comedy. Incessantly he photographs from odd angles—once even through the corner of his eyeglasses—instead of relaxing, not worrying about proving he's intellectual, and just telling a story. On the rocks of his acting and direction *Bananas* splits.

La Collectionneuse

(*May 29, 1971*)

ERIC Rohmer may be an acquired taste, but I'm certainly acquiring it. Now we have the third of his *Six Moral Tales,* made in 1967 before *My Night at Maud's* and *Claire's Knee,* and I see by the papers that I'm not supposed to like it. Even those who like the later Rohmer (seen here earlier) have called *La Collectionneuse* a rough sketch or a parody of what was to come. I disagree. I think it's a good, fulfilled work in its own way.

Again Rohmer gives us a protagonist who becomes interested in a younger woman and ends up with an older woman to whom he was linked originally. Again passion is more examined and discussed than created. Rohmer is more interested in the effect of desire on thought and action than in the creation of heat.

For those who want only clear-cut drama and swift movement—and who doesn't like those things, too?—Rohmer will certainly seem static. For those willing to be engaged on a smaller scale, who like implications as well as statements, Rohmer is rewarding. He provides the extra dividend of all extraordinary film makers: the sense that an artist has made the medium his own, shaped it to his psyche and inquiries. In this case the tone is reflective and quiet—but only superficially quiet.

I would not suggest that Rohmer is on a level with the great Japanese director Yasujiro Ozu who, in a quiet film like *Tokyo Story,* plumbed the most profound reaches of contemporary life. I do suggest that Rohmer, like Ozu, understands that motion in film has more than one aspect.

Again Rohmer has put his film in a beautiful countryside during summer. Adrien, an antiques dealer, is sharing a house near St. Tropez with Daniel, a nonpainting painter. Haydée, a stunning girl of nineteen, is brought there by another young man who leaves her there. Adrien and Daniel dub Haydée "la collectionneuse," the collector, because of the number of (presumable) lovers who keep taking her out at night. She has nothing to do with either of the two principal men until well along in the story, and then only with Daniel.

There is a prologue in several short sections. The first shows Haydée walking on a beach in a bikini; then the camera roams over her, close-up, articulating her body. In *Claire's Knee,* a mature man's fancies about a nearly juvenile girl were distilled almost to disembodiment by his fantasy about her knee. Here the prologue tells us that Haydée's body is the figurative theater of this story and that intercourse, not fantasy, is the dynamics. I don't understand those who think that this difference between the two films is one of grossness.

After the components of the story have been set out, it begins, with Adrien narrating on the sound track. The film is in French, with subtitles; the narration is in English. This jars. Why not subtitles for the narration as well? Adrien, who is about ten years older than Haydée, imagines himself to be playing a sort of cat-and-mouse game with her, but, as in other Rohmer films, we see that the mouse is controlling the game. And we see that Adrien secretly knows this but cannot admit it to himself; or us. In time, with what he pretends is ironic dispensation, he makes a move toward her and is rudely rebuffed; but later she allows him to use her as bait for a rich American who is to subsidize a gallery for him. So she continues to dominate.

At the very end it seems that she is going to sleep with Adrien. They're driving back to the house when they meet a car with two men she knows, who are going to Rome. She gets out to speak to them, and declines their invitation to accompany them. Adrien has to move his waiting car out of the road. But when he starts, he just keeps going and leaves her with the other men. In the last scene he is making arrangements to join his mistress (whom we saw in the prologue) in London.

There is one brief shot of Haydée making love with a youth and there are a few caresses of her, but the film gets most of its sexual charge simply from her presence. Her being—her body, curves, breath, glance—is the constant mockery of the inner stances that Adrien thinks, or pretends, he is assuming toward her. At the end he flees; again pretending that he is disposing of her but really because he is afraid of being trapped by forces he can't control. Most of the film's tension comes from the contrast between the calm camaraderie of the trio in the villa, who are merely amiable much of the time, and the rationalized desires that are boiling in Adrien, particularly after the girl takes Daniel as a lover.

Haydée Politoff, the girl, is perfect: the personification of lithe young sex and airy sexual power. Patrick Bauchau is very attractive as Adrien. The American is played by Seymour Hertzberg, reportedly a pseudonym for Eugene Archer, a former film critic of *The New York Times*.

Again the clothes—such common items as shirts and sweaters—are chosen with exactness, so that their color and texture enrich the film. Nestor Almendros, again Rohmer's cinematographer, makes a seamless environment of people and things; Politoff's body (as seen by Adrien) is part of the same cosmos as the rounded pebbles shining under the sea. All the elements are distilled by Rohmer into what must again be called a classic style: a view of art in which form is not only the preserver of experience but the ultimate insight into it.

Une Femme Douce

(June 26, 1971)

IN some ways Robert Bresson is like Bergman. His films are manifests of his inner life. At this level he has, like Bergman, made some films that are successful artworks and some that are only finely wrought evidences of intent. Among the former are *A Man Escaped* and *Diary of a Country Priest*. Among the latter I would place his latest American release, *Une Femme Douce*.

Bresson's source is Dostoevsky's story *A Gentle Creature*. It begins with the suicide of a young wife, and the bereaved husband then recounts the events that led up to it. He is a pawnbroker, she was a young girl who patronized his shop and who, after a time, accepted his proposal. There was occasional joy in the marriage but never true union; she was distanced by his attempts at domination and by his worldliness. She was attracted to another man but didn't have an affair. A climax of illness and harassment led her almost to shoot her husband. Just when he thought matters had reached some peace, she jumped from a window.

Bresson transposes the story to modern Paris and films it with that beautiful selectivity of frame and shot that, at its best, is like the notes of a Handel aria falling into order. Here is the first sequence after the credits: a door; the maid going through into an empty bedroom; the balcony outside, with a table overturned and a rocking chair still rocking; then, from below the railing, a white shawl against the sky, floating down.

In the prosody of the film, there is scarcely a stroke out of place. Bresson is so discriminating that he uses a huge close-up only once: the wife's face as she steps out on the balcony at the end, just before she jumps. Because it's the only such close-up, the effect is like a great, simple cry.

The sound track is unusually and subtly important. Under the credits we drive up a busy Paris street at night, with crowds, neon signs, dense traffic. Then, throughout the picture, all through the scenes between this couple who are locked in a breast-to-breast struggle, the noise of Paris traffic flows by outside. (And the one meeting we see between the wife and her non-lover is in a car!) We become used to the traffic sounds as we become used to them in our own city lives, yet they are always subliminally present, an aural context of Now for a drama that is meant to be timeless.

But contexts—of various sorts—are really all that the film provides: the center is missing. Why does this film exist? To realize a drama (as the story does successfully) reported by someone who doesn't really understand it: the drama of an essentially religious soul driven by the imperfections of the world to suicide. But here, the religious center is only sketched. At the outset, when the girl comes to the shop, she pawns a crucifix. (One of Bresson's less happy touches: the pawnbroker separates the Christ from the gold cross; he wants only the latter.) At the end she glances at the crucifix in her drawer just before she jumps. There is no more than these hints. (And contradictorily, she is married in a civil ceremony.)

The sense of spiritual locus, which Bresson got so easily in *Mouchette,* is missing here. The conflict seems to have been changed from one between materialism and spirituality to one between materialism and culture sensibility. Bresson's pawnbroker is not presented as stupid or illiterate, but the contrast with his pawnshop world is effected more with visits to museums or to a performance of *Hamlet* than with otherworldliness.

Even this conflict is thinly drawn. The beautiful Dominique Sanda, the wife, could have provided the drama, but she is not given the material, however implicit, with which to work. She is further hampered by Guy Frangin who, as the husband, is a dead and deadpan loss. At one point Frangin is supposed to break down. He covers his face with his hand, and I'd bet that the sob we hear was dubbed by someone else. He's the blankest Bresson actor since Martin Lassalle in *Pickpocket,* whom he resembles.

Bresson's taciturn camera has delicately circumscribed a theater in which his intended spiritual drama does not take place. Still I hope that people who like Bresson will see the film. *Une Femme Douce* is the work of an artist—even if not one of his successes. Film artists of his caliber are not so common that we can afford to miss anything they do.

The Clowns

(July 3, 1971)

WELL, at least Federico Fellini has found something to do. In the past few years the Italian television network, RAI, has commissioned some directors to make films for broadcast. Fellini accepted a commission and made *The Clowns.* It's shorter and very much simpler than his previous picture, *Fellini Satyricon,* and at least it's something he did, not something that shows, however elaborately, that he had nothing to do.

From the title on, we're in familiar Fellini country. The idea of the human being as clown, seen affectionately as fellow grotesque, has always been central to Fellini's vision, even when the action was "straight." Giulietta Masina's persona is clownish. Mastroianni grappling with Ekberg in the Roman fountain of *La Dolce Vita* is clownish. Besides, the circus and clown, literally, have been in several Fellini films. He couldn't even do Petronius without including some circuslike performances. And now he has made a documentary-essay on the disappearance of the clown.

The European clown is a different breed from the American. There have been no great American circus clowns; our great clowns have been in vaudeville and films. Some U.S. circus clowns have been puffed as great, but I've seen most of them and I disagree. In our circuses the clowns, almost always, are mere wearers of make-ups and users of gadgets. With a few days' training, anyone could do any of the clown acts I saw in the Ringling Brothers circus last year. European clowns use make-up and gadgets but they also need talent. (The clown acts in Chaplin's *The Circus* are European in feeling.) Certain aspects of that talent are Fellini's principal subject.

He is tracing the modern history of the White Clown and the Auguste. The former was the authoritarian and the latter the miscreant, the slapper and the slapped. Fellini himself is in the film. (A wonderfully theatrical man, too, as anyone who has seen his TV interviews will know.) With his camera crew, whom he introduces to us, he goes off to interview the survivors of the old circuses: in Italy, in France, in Spain. Everything is framed in memory and fantasy; the film begins with the boy Federico being awakened in the middle of the night by the sounds of the men putting up a circus tent in the field next door, and it ends with a fantasy of departure. But the body of the film consists of interviews, explorations, and re-creations of the acts of long-gone clowns.

The happiest element is the free-flowing form, following impulse and nostalgia. *The Clowns* is not edited with the quasi-subliminal, shutter-clicking effect of some Fellini films. Its lines are cursive; visions flow in and past. Time and place are not strictly sequential, even characters shift: in the last sequence, reminiscent of the end of *8½*, two of the camera crew are among the clowns!

Many of the familiar Fellini hallmarks are present. First, the lighting—theatrical as ever. Often a character is first seen with his face completely shadowed before he "enters." Then there is Fellini's relating of the human face to Daumier caricature. After the boy Federico sees his first circus, he perceives how many of his fellow-townsmen look like clowns. And, as always, there is Fellini's eye for deep composition. Example: a stationmaster in that hometown is insulted by some schoolboys departing on a train. The pompous little official jumps up and down with rage. In a shot down the platform, Fellini shows us the hopping-mad midget in the foreground and, in various planes in the background, several fat men doubling up with laughter. The sanctification of memory touches this wonderful shot because it is silent: the sound under it is the narrator's voice, with music.

And this brings up a device I can't remember from previous Fellini. Often he plays dreamy music under a scene when the circus band, which may even be visible, is obviously playing something else.

Sometimes in the interviews he, quite deliberately, has the dialogue slightly out of sync with the speakers' mouths. This disjuncture of sound and image seems a way to remind us of time levels: the time past that is being commented on and the time present when the film was made.

Some of the music comes from *8½*, some of it comes from Chaplin. (The cabaret song from *Modern Times,* "Punkawalla Punkawa.") And there's another tribute to Chaplin. A magician in Paris has an assistant who is one of Chaplin's daughters. The slow shot in which the camera dollies up to her, as she takes off her clown nose and whirls paper streamers while soft music tinkles, is a bouquet.

Sentiment is both the strength and the weakness of the film. An unsentimental man could not have made it, which would have been a loss. A less sentimental one would have avoided things like the final trumpet duet in an empty circus hall. Possibly moments like this are Fellini's obeisance to explicit television.

Still I can't see why anyone wouldn't enjoy *The Clowns.* (A marvelous picture for children, and it won't bore the parents who take them.) It's a job that Fellini did and did well, employing both his strengths and his weaknesses. It's not an occasion for an essay on Fellini Today; it's a piece of work that he did in 1970, that's all. We'll have to wait for the next picture of his "own" for further comments on his progress. This is a valentine he contrived, while waiting.

Anyway, the film has its built-in warning against heavy comment. In one scene Fellini is seated with a serious young interviewer in a bank of otherwise empty circus seats. The interviewer asks him for the message of this picture; Fellini starts to reply heavily when the scene is suddenly truncated—I won't say how. It's an argument Against Interpretation much funnier than Susan Sontag's.

Carnal Knowledge

(August 21 & 28, 1971)

JULES Feiffer has half-done it again. His screenplay for *Carnal Knowledge* is acid satire, and it's written without superiority, almost with a confessional air: Gulliver as Yahoo, not as tourist. It's familiar Feiffer country, the American wars and truces of the sexes, man the vaginal raider, woman the castrator. And underneath it, of course, is American puritanism plus the latter-day reaction against it, both of them producing a piratical view of sex. The theme is hardly original, but Feiffer has been working with it for years and now takes it further, if not deeper.

Predictably, the script is witty, though less witty than some of his other writings; and there are banal patches that don't sound like satire. He tells the story of two friends, Jon and Sandy, from their college days just after World War II to the present, in terms of their sex lives. As a casebook of the American male "dating and scoring" mind, acquired in adolescence and inflicting psychic curses throughout life, it's clinically sharp.

But one of my feelings while watching it was, "I know all this." There's some pleasure in mere recognition, especially because—until recently—American films rendered American sex life about as realistically as the ballet does (and usually less imaginatively). But Feiffer only observes, he doesn't perceive. The characters are like his drawings, adroitly and economically sketched but two-dimensional— with two-dimensionality as their apparent reason for being.

Carnal Knowledge is not a drama or even a narrative in any generative sense, it's a chronological series of depositions. Even this might have a certain cumulative interest except that, once we know the premises, we can easily work out the rest for ourselves. There are absolutely no surprises—I don't mean plot twists, I mean enrichments or contradictions. Feiffer shows small sense of the paradoxes that lie beneath a seemingly consistent behavior pattern.

All the characters are stock. A handsome sexy hero. A less attractive pal whom the hero coaches on how to get a girl. (The hero gets her easily, of course, then later turns her back to the unwitting pal.) The nice girl who can't resist the hero but marries the pal. The vacuous but good-hearted show girl.

All four get their tags when they appear, then just go on displaying them. When Jon starts an affair with the show girl (out of TV), there isn't any doubt about every strophe that will follow. To sledge-hammer matters, there's a slide-photo reprise by Jon near the end, which adds zero. Through much of the film I sensed a slight invisible nodding in myself—not of drowsiness but agreement. And agreement is an insufficient reaction to purportedly serious work.

The chief reason that the film is never dull is that it was directed by Mike Nichols. He has made a good recovery after *Catch-22*, or to put it properly, he's again working with material whose tone and texture he can control. First, I note—as I've done often before—his ability to direct actors, which operates here against some rather odd casting. Jack Nicholson plays a man named Jonathan Fuerst from Evander Childs High School in the Bronx. Jonathan was evidently conceived as New York Jewish, and Nicholson neither looks nor sounds it; but Nichols has guided him to a performance so violently-defiantly wretched that the inappropriateness is muted, if never quite lost. Arthur Garfunkel, the Sandy, is not an actor at all. Nichols evidently thought his personality (which is apt enough) was worth the risk, and he has helped Garfunkel at least to behave credibly. I'd be perfectly willing never to see Garfunkel again, but Nichols makes him acceptable here.

There's been a great deal of gab about the miracles Nichols has wrought with Ann-Margret. I've never thought she was all that terrible—she's just had terrible parts. Here she has a showy, sure-fire part, and Nichols easily whips her up into various frenzies, just as he did with Elizabeth Taylor in *Who's Afraid of Virginia Woolf?* His much more subtle success here is with Candice Bergen in a quiet role. To my knowledge, Bergen has never before spoken a believable word. Nichols has rid her of her strain to *sound* credible, has told her something about thought process so that she knows what to do with her eyes (for a change). He has in short, sheared off her woolliness. Not exactly a memorable performance but not a phony one. I haven't seen much mention of this.

And I'm getting another considerable pain in the neck, to be frank but anatomically imprecise, from two other slights to Nichols. *Carnal Knowledge* is hailed as a watershed film in its candor by people who dismiss *The Graduate,* as if the new work were not the social-historical consequence of the earlier one, as if Nichols had not blazed the way for himself. Also, I've seen scant recognition of his increasing refinement in camera style. Compared with his previous films, the camera work here (managed by Guiseppe Rotunno) verges on the austere. Nichols is concentrating more and more on the frame—the held shot—as a source of power. Frequently there is a long take of one person, sometimes in close-up, who is motionless while bustle happens around him. It's a use of the camera as watcher, as *drainer,* rather than as participant—surely not the only way to use the camera but one that implies a growing stillness in the director, a sense of security, of serious fundamental decisions.

Carnal Knowledge has none of the arty angles of *Who's Afraid of Virginia Woolf?*, little of the cleverish cutting of *The Graduate,* none of the grandiloquence that spotted *Catch-22.* Nichols is simply bearing down, intently; but this simplicity apparently doesn't count for much at a time when Ken Russell and Bertolucci are being hailed as superb stylists.

Nichols is still a man who essentially looks for things to do, not a man who essentially *has* things he wants to do, which is why he is not (and may never be) a major artist. But he's a munificently gifted director who is clearly concerned to grow.

The Touch

(*August 21 & 28, 1971*)

INGMAR Bergman has made over thirty films so, naturally, some of them are not only not masterpieces, they're not even good. His latest, *The Touch,* is one of the latter. One reason for its failure is unique for Bergman: it has very small ambitions. Often he has reached for something large and missed it, as in *Hour of the Wolf.* Here he has reached for something smaller-scale—and has missed it by a wider margin.

Bibi Andersson has been married for fifteen years to a successful physician and devoted husband (Max von Sydow). She has a magazine-ad house and garden, complete with two children. An American archeologist (Elliott Gould) comes to work in the neighborhood and falls in love with her. She has an affair with him that shakes two years of her life and almost splits the marriage. At the end she and Gould part.

Bergman has said he wrote the film as the portrait of a woman whose safe enclosures are broken and who is eventually matured by dangers. We don't see this. She and her life are such stereotypes that the lover is more interesting, badly drawn as he is. He is (blatantly) different from her: homeless, unrooted, insecure—an unpleasant, almost irrational neurotic, and he comes across as sick and repellent, rather than anguished, but at least we can't foretell every move he's going to make. Some of *her* moves are shockingly cliché, like the scene where she changes her clothes four or five times before she goes to her first rendezvous and, to top the cuteness, finally selects the clothes with which she began.

At the film's end she says she can't go off with Gould because of her responsibilities; he says she's lying. Bergman maintains that the ending is ambiguous—maybe Gould is right and she's kidding herself out of cowardice. But that's not what we see. In the film she is patently telling the truth, and since Gould is pathologically selfish, we can all breathe a sigh of relief that she doesn't go with him—to inevitable disaster. What may have been intended as a drama of life-extension comes out as a sentimental tale of a lady with bad taste in lovers.

Max von Sydow could have played his part standing on his head, and I rather wish he had. Bibi Andersson could not give less than truth and appeal to anything she does, and she gives them here even in this dull role. Elliott Gould apparently doesn't know what he's doing or why. Most of the dialogue is in English—Bergman's English, presumably—and sounds like the dialogue used in dubbing. But the one who sounds clumsiest is Gould.

Something in this whole project seems to have thrown Bergman off from the beginning. The use of language is illogical; why do the Swedish couple speak English when alone although the doctor speaks Swedish to his assistants? There are more pretty-pretty shots than in any Bergman film since *All These Women*. The editing lacks confidence. One way to tell: I was *aware* of a lot of the cuts all through. The sound track is unsubtle: when Gould shows Andersson a newly rediscovered statue of the Virgin, a woman's voice sings medieval church music. Everything in this film is laid out, nothing is created; because, I think, there wasn't much to create.

Yankee, go home. Sweden for the Swedish. Bergman films for Bergman and his ensemble. The mistakes they have made up to now have been daring, have been *their* mistakes. *The Touch* is a detour up a bland alley.

The Hired Hand

(September 4, 1971)

The Hired Hand is seriously flawed but serious, and well worth seeing. It opens with a blurred-focus, slow-motion shot of a stream with one man fishing and another swimming naked. When a film opens with a "lyrical" shot, your heart has a right to sink. But the subject (two men) and the visual tenor turn out to be very much a part of this film.

Peter Fonda is one of a trio of foot-loose wanderers in the old West. One of them is murdered for his horse. Fonda and the other pal, Warren Oates, take some revenge, then head back to Fonda's long-abandoned wife and child on a farm—something Fonda had been planning to do anyway, because he's tired of drifting.

On the farm, through the sacraments of hard work, Fonda and his wife are reunited. Oates leaves; is captured by the murdering horse thief; and Fonda goes to rescue him. The rest is a kind of rite, in which a cycle of continuity is enacted.

Fonda directed, and it's a creditable debut, but the cinematic qualities of the film must be called a three-way job: done by him and Vilmos Zsigmond, the cinematographer, and Frank Mazzola, the editor. Zsigmond has tried to unite earth and sky and things and people as coinhabitors of space and time. Mazzola has used almost the whole contemporary editing vocabulary: very slow dissolves (*so* slow that they're not old-fashioned), occasional sequences with alternate frames removed (so that, briefly, the characters move like the astronauts in those early TV shots from the moon), occasional freeze-frames. And he has used this last device a bit differently: a sequence ends with a freeze-frame, which is then followed by another freeze-frame of the very same shot; or a sequence begins with a freeze-frame, which is then very gently urged into motion.

The object of all these techniques is, apparently, to refract realism into its essences, and through this visual enlargement, to let a large theme—larger than the story—speak. Trying for this, the film makers have not completely avoided preciousness. A lantern shines conveniently through Fonda's beard to frame him in gold; sunsets are always gorgeous; and there is some of that detestable focus-racking. (Changing focus in mid-shot. If the foreground is fuzzy and background clear—or vice versa—the foreground becomes clear and the background fuzzy—or vice versa.) But the richness of the pictures is not just a lot of loose syrup that flows off the screen and into your lap. It's contained by a purpose. Which I'll come to.

As actor, Fonda is earnest and intent, but he lacks substance. He is only quiet, not quietly forceful. He does nothing really wrong, he simply *isn't* enough. It's cruel, perhaps, but true to say that what his role needs is his father, at the son's present age. Oates is pleasing as the taciturn-trusty friend. Verna Bloom, who was the young Appalachian widow in *Medium Cool,* has a good deal of the grim earthy passion needed for the wife. The reticent score by Bruce Langhorne touches the film perfectly from time to time. The clothes by Lawrence G. Paull give homespun veracity.

(But why don't directors and designers watch actors' hands? Don't they know what farmers' hands look like? Not like Fonda's and Bloom's, I can tell them. Make-up and *acting* would help.)

The script by Alan Sharp is mostly straightforward and easy. Because it's so unconcerned with plot, two plotty elements stick out. How does the horse thief's messenger find Fonda? Why does Fonda ride into that town to face three men openly in a suicidal shoot-out? Both moments are meant to be ritual matters, I suppose: the messenger of fate and the union with that fate; but the mode of the film asks for more plausibility.

And the theme under it all? Nothing less than (let's call it) the Masculine Principle in a time of transition. That principle is the base of the myth of the frontier, the quintessence of the idea of new lands. The frontier is always concerned with men, as bearers of the myth, as adventurers and companions. The greatest American novel, *Moby Dick* (a kind of frontier epic), has an all-male cast. The generic American myth, the Western, is all-male. Women are only ornaments and rewards, never dynamic characters, in the classic Western; and marriage is usually where the story ends. Underneath the Western form is the idea of Natural Men, adventuring together, unbound by women and the society they represent. The wife in *The Hired Hand* tells the husband that his friend, with whom he has wandered for seven years, has had more of him than she has had. When the husband is shot, he whispers to his friend, "Hold me, Arch."

I'm not talking about latent homosexuality—at least not in any libidinous sense. This film is concerned with a theme that literary critics have often discerned in our novels: life as adventure versus life as service; self-love (either the Loner or the man with a human mirror) versus other-love. Essentially, the film is about the crossing, if not the passing, of a frontier. (Note that the wife lives on a farm, not a ranch.) One of the reasons we have all loved good Westerns, as John Ford understood, is their gesture of freedom, from place and possessions: not only the much-mooted triumph of plain Good over plain Evil but the idea that all your possessions are on your saddle and you can *go*—into great space—and make your way with or against men in much the same situation. (Women have loved Westerns, too, of course, which may indicate an old, deep-seated envy more valid than one of penises.)

But *The Hired Hand* is not about cribbing and confinement, but about maturing (Fonda *wants* to return); not about dimming and decline, but about civilization, which, if it still means anything, means increase through loss. In its small, imperfect, moving way, that's what this film celebrates.

McCabe and Mrs. Miller

(September 4, 1971)

VILMOS Zsigmond, who photographed *The Hired Hand,* also did *McCabe and Mrs. Miller,* in a different, somewhat misty, less spectacular vein, with lots of smoky interiors. But his fine work here is almost irritating, like hearing a good orchestra play trash. *McCabe* is glittery trash—"liberated," but still trash.

Warren Beatty (McCabe) is a supposed gunman who wanders into a Washington State frontier town, c. 1900, and takes over everything, including brothels. Julie Christie (Mrs. M.) is a cockney madam, for whom he flips but who remains cool. Beatty goes through a lot of self-indulgent clowning and through three unexplained stages of bravado, fluster, and bravery before he's killed in a dumb shoot-out. Christie continues her vacuous career in a part that is launched portentously to nowhere.

The script by Robert Altman and Brian McKay, from a novel by Edmund Naughton, evidently assumes that mere candor and eccentricity will tell us what the West was really like. Altman directed *M*A*S*H*,* which wandered and was often funny; then *Brewster*

McCloud, which wandered and was not funny; now this, which wanders and is repulsive.

I thought the camera would never stop zooming in and out, or italicizing the obvious (a whore's cashbox, a floating dead body). Some of the dialogue is literally inaudible, so casually do the stars act and the recordist record; and the cutting is generally freakish—I suppose to display freedom. (And in this "realistic" film, there is a Negro barber with a pretty wife; the wife is never molested by the drunken, randy miners.)

The thesis seems to be that if you take a corny story, fuzz up the exposition, vitiate the action, use a childishly ironic ending, and put in lots of profanity and nudity, you have Marched On with Time. But what *McCabe* remains is a corny story, badly told.

There are overblown songs by Leonard Cohen, the hip Oscar Hammerstein.

The Go-Between

(September 11, 1971)

SOME novels are remembered chiefly for their opening lines. Muriel Spark's *The Girls of Slender Means:* "Long ago in 1945 all the nice people in England were poor, allowing for exceptions." Even more memorable, L. P. Hartley's *The Go-Between:* "The past is a foreign country: they do things differently there." (Note that both these lines are nostalgic!) The latter is also the opening utterance, by an unseen speaker, in Joseph Losey's film of Hartley's novel.

And this is the most rewarding aspect of the film, its visit to a foreign country in which "we" once lived. That country is the summer of 1900—the time is the real geography. But the physical locality is a stately home in the English countryside near Norwich. Losey exploits so many details of costume and custom so well that we are plunged into the scale and rhythm and airiness of that home's upper-class life, so eternally secure for such a short eternity.

The story is of a doomed love affair as witnessed by a thirteen-year-old boy whose experience conveys the requisite information to us but who doesn't himself understand the matter until much later. The boy goes to stay with a school chum in the great house and is employed as a secret "postman" between the chum's older sister and a young farmer. The two grownups are having an affair, despite the fact that the sister is engaged to a lord.

Losey, like Visconti whom he evidently admires, is good at crystallizing detail: the croquet, the hammock, the Sunday bell ringers, the Sunday prayers in the household with the servants, the village cricket match, the Norwich market. It's an almost palpable re-creation of a past environment, and that environment is the film's real achievement, not the drama enacted within it. In fact, the "feel" is so fine that it increases our eventual disappointment: the picture comes at last to so little that we become a bit resentful of (let's call it) the build-up. If style and form are to be the content, very well; but then why pretend to content?

A great deal of nonsense has been written about Harold Pinter's screenplay. As a Pinter admirer, I deplore his getting praise—as well as blame—that he doesn't deserve. The dialogue has been garlanded with compliments for its rhythmic sensitivity, lyricism, and flavor. By my estimate, about 98 percent of the dialogue comes directly from Hartley's book. Pinter's job has been principally to select and compress, in a manner no better or worse than several dozen other professionals might have done. The one exceptional touch is the way he has handled the narrator—the adult "today" who was the boy then. Hartley begins and ends with him; Pinter begins with the man's voice only, then slips in quick flashes of him, in the present, on a pilgrimage to his past. These flashes gradually become longer and more explicit, the man's face eventually becomes visible (Michael Redgrave), and at the end, he has a brief scene with the heroine, now very old.

This is hardly an original device. Just one instance: Griffith used something like it in *Way Down East* (1920) to fix the point toward which his story was traveling before it got there. But Pinter uses it dexterously, making sure that all stops are pulled out for the *temps perdu* diapason.

Yet this dexterity, too, only adds to the ultimate thinness. What is this film about? Are we to be wrung by the stupidity of class barriers? Today? If the novel had been written by Henry Green or I. Compton-Burnett—let alone Lawrence or James—the resonance might have been immense; here it is shallow. Is it the *frisson* of the schoolboy "curse"? (The boy has a passion for witchcraft and concocts a curse. At the end the aged heroine says that her grandson, who is also the grandson of the farmer, seems to think he's under a curse.) But that's just a cheap vaudeville "snapper"—third-rate Saki.

There is only one small resolution for the story. The narrator is today an emotionally withered man, unmarried, presumably because of the events he witnessed as a child. ("You flew too near the sun and you were scorched.") Here Losey italicizes what Hartley left implicit. In the film the discovery of the lovers *in flagrante delicto* is flagrant indeed. But what does *that* come to? Is this whole intricate story simply the explanation of the narrator's trauma? This gives it the gravity of any Hitchcock psychopathic film about a Liebes-trauma.

Most of the time, Losey has directed it well, with much of his characteristic feline rhythm. He succumbs to the old pastoral cliché-shots through waving grass in the foreground, but generally the camera moves and perceives with a kind of easy tension. Gerry Fisher's cinematography appreciates the materials, except for the sunny skies, which sometimes come out white, as in amateur snapshots.

Margaret Leighton is first-class as the lady of the great house, filled with well-bred suspicion of her daughter, then with ire. As the father, Michael Gough is amusingly Olympian. Dominic Guard, the boy, has a nice homely face and is engaging. Alan Bates has sturdy composure as the farmer, though not much character. Also, he wears side whiskers and sometimes looks like Ringo Starr.

Julie Christie is the heroine and fails to supply the needed magic. First, she is prematurely losing her looks. Second, unlike Gough and Leighton and others in the film, she gives no conviction of gentility— that subject so dear to the working-class Pinter and the American Losey. If Leighton were still young enough to play her own daughter, it would have been a more satisfactory film. (Leighton was originally scheduled for the role when the film was first planned by others, back in the mid-fifties.) And if Leighton had played the daughter, in her last scene as her aged self she would not have needed to have her voice dubbed by someone else, which I assume is what they had to do with Christie.

Still I wouldn't want to leave a last impression that this film is not worth looking at and listening to. At his best, in such films as *The Servant* and *Accident* and this one, Losey makes all the right artistic decisions except the fundamental ones. As the old joke has it, don't expect much and it won't disappoint you.

The Devils

(September 11, 1971)

KEN Russell is the victim of a fallacy. He thinks that in order to make a film about hysteria, one must be hysterical. His version of *The Devils* makes his frenzies about the frenzied Tchaikovsky in *The Music Lovers* look like relative stasis.

The story is about the "possessed" nuns of Loudun in the 1630s whose visions, as whipped by the frustrations of Mother Jeanne and by political interests of the time, ended in the torture and execution of a priest, Urbain Grandier, a man worldly enough but completely innocent of the charges that were used by the state against him as a means of squelching a political opponent.

Russell has based his script on Aldous Huxley's historical work *The Devils of Loudun* and on John Whiting's *The Devils,* a very good play. (The play has also been made into an opera by Penderecki, which I haven't heard.) Seeing the film made me glad, for the first time, that both Huxley and Whiting are dead, so that they are spared this farrago of witless exhibitionism.

Russell has insured that, through every moment of the picture, we are paying attention not to the great themes of spirit and truth, morality and immorality, but to him. The camera whirls, the smoke wafts in and out, the lights flicker, the music whoops up the frequent climaxes, the editing palpitates, the angles of vision are mostly eccentric. Mr. Partridge in *Tom Jones* said he preferred the actor playing Claudius to Garrick in *Hamlet* because Garrick merely behaved like a man but, as for Claudius, "Anybody may see he is an actor." Russell is a director for the Partridges of this world.

And what is the self that Russell is so proud of? Part misunderstood German expressionism, part diluted Bergman (out of *The Seventh Seal*), part diluted Eisenstein (out of *Alexander Nevsky* and *Ivan the Terrible*), among other derivations. The only elements that seem *echt* Russell are the sadism posing as ruthless candor and the anxiety to be taken seriously.

But it should not be lost that, in this mess, Vanessa Redgrave, grotesquely directed, gives a good grotesque performance as Mother Jeanne; and that Oliver Reed, the Grandier, grows very respectably as an actor. Especially in the scenes where he addresses large crowds,

Reed shows a real power to take and to hold. Throughout, one feels him struggling to reach the reality of this man, against the tinselly asininities of Russell.

Nine years ago the U.S. saw—very briefly—a Polish film called *Joan of the Angels,* directed by Jerzy Kawalerowicz. It treated the same subject with understanding, with severe black-and-white beauty. The only compliment I can pay Russell's swirling multicolored puddle is that it made me hungry to see the Polish film again.

Desperate Characters

(September 25, 1971)

ANY white person who owns anything is under siege. Particularly if he's not young. A mansion or a one-room apartment, a Mercedes or a secondhand compact, if he owns anything, he is hated. The class war seems to be coming to the knife edge, but as Marx didn't quite foresee, it's not only a war between haves and have-nots, it's also a war between generations and races. The white poor hate the white nonpoor. (How many city people have had their country places broken into lately? Friends of mine, with a small house on a remote mountain road, have arrived three times in the last six months to discover thefts.) The young rob the nonyoung, and justify this "ripping off" on moral, almost evangelist grounds. And as for races, the brute fact—in New York, at least—is that every white person is an animal in a game preserve whom nonwhites can hunt at their pleasure.

I'm *not* forgetting historical reasons for all these matters. I *have* read *Soledad Brother.* I *have* read Proudhon on property. (And I know that many nonwhite people, too, are robbed daily.) But I'm not talking about causes and guilts, just about the facts of living day to day in this country as the white nonyoung owner of *anything.* You are a target. That's not Minuteman scare-talk. I don't think that anyone who lives in (say) New York today can honestly deny these conditions, no matter what his social-political beliefs.

This is the climate of *Desperate Characters,* the feeling that grips a couple in their late thirties—people who have a house in Brooklyn and another in the country, well-disposed people of the now-despised liberal persuasion, who feel they are living in a state of siege. But this state of physical siege is simply the locus for a state of moral and spiritual siege. What they feel within and between themselves is derived, fundamentally, from the same causes as what they see around them. Their physical unease—setting the burglar alarm before they go out for the evening, watching the new slovenly neighbors corrupt the community—is ultimately tied to the causes of their deepest unhappiness.

He is a lawyer whose partner, a lifelong friend, has just left for a more socially responsive practice, and the split is a tacit agony. She is a translator of French when she works, childless ("I've got a uterus like a pinball machine"), who has had one love affair and may have more. Brightness has fallen from their air. Hope is a question that has to be thought about.

The chief metaphor of the story is a cat bite. The wife feeds a stray cat outside the door, and it bites her. There is some question as to whether the cat is rabid. It must be caught, and presumably killed, for examination. The wife is bitten on a Friday night and won't know till Monday whether she's been infected. (It all takes place on one weekend.) At the end, on Sunday night, the question is still open. The symbolism is a trifle blatant because it's so clear: the stranger outside repays help with viciousness, may have poisoned the life inside just because he was outside and had to accept help, and may be killed in order to protect the life inside. Still it's used without verbal underscoring, except for one moment near the end.

Paula Fox's novel *Desperate Characters* (1970) fixed all this with comprehension and incisiveness. Now Frank D. Gilroy has made the book into a film. That's really the gist of the matter: he's made a good novel into a good film—has written, directed, and produced it himself.

This is the same Gilroy who wrote *The Subject Was Roses,* a Pulitzer-prize play that did nothing to raise the status of that prize and was later a film that did less. He has written other plays and films, with spots of interest in them, but even the best in his best work did not prepare me for the quiet authority, the *accepted* realism (unflaunted), the subtlety of performance, and the visual vitality of this picture. In making a film about the doubtfulness of hope, Gilroy himself has shown why it still springs.

He has adapted the novel with a sure sense of the filmable, the expandable, the contractable. For instance, the whole account of the wife's affair, instead of a substantial flashback as in the book, is handled in one long slow pan in the lover's office while an unanswered telephone rings and rings. He enriches the essences of the book: he has put in a scene in a subway car, in which we hear a man conversing amiably; the camera moves over the wife's face and other silent faces till it reaches the chatting man who is talking to himself, while everyone else in the car sits silently, not even looking at him. As the man continues to talk and they continue to ignore him, the scene cuts off. And Gilroy has given us a party scene that, for once, doesn't try to be the epitome of the Rotten and Superficial, it's just a party. (Out of which two young hips stride disgustedly.)

The dialogue is acute and self-conscious—the characters' self-consciousness: people who, like so many today, do not merely live their lives, they see themselves as characters. Much of this dialogue is from Fox, but a good deal has been tempered by Gilroy or is new.

The director's theater experience is apparent and valuable. What he does with his actors within the confines of any one scene, any one take, contributes tremendously to the integrity of the whole. Timing is precise, never hurried, never limp, inflections are sharp; voices and eyes work in relation to other voices and eyes.

In a rather daring move Gilroy has cast Kenneth Mars as the husband. My only previous knowledge of Mars is as the comic Nazi playwright in The Producers, not a memory I treasure. But Gilroy obviously knew something that nobody else knew, because Mars produces exactly the right performance, an intelligent man turning sour, which frightens him even as he masochistically enjoys it, a man fighting for a chance to remain decently, creatively cynical. All through the role Mars touches it with tiny sparks of imagination. For instance, he and his wife are discussing a friend called Tanya. Mars says thoughtfully, "I hate Tanya," then clears his throat—after he makes the remark! This tiny inversion—another actor might have cleared his throat before the line—turns comic cliché into comic truth.

Shirley MacLaine is the wife. I've never thought much of her abilities and have never thought her very attractive (outside of her first appearance in The Trouble with Harry). Even now she doesn't exactly suggest that she's a repository of profound secrets, and her face is not precisely the modern tragic mask, but this is easily the best performance of hers that I've seen. Gilroy has at least put her in touch with reality.

In his one long sequence Gerald O'Loughlin is excellent as the soberly drunken ex-partner who calls at midnight and takes Mac-Laine out for coffee. As an aging divorcée, Sada Thompson is brittle and barbed and piteous. Jack Somack, her friendly ex-husband, is the one actor who contends with his role a bit; it isn't quite digested.

Gilroy has done a good job of *seeing* his story. His very first shot, under the titles, pulls back from a Brooklyn street to the backs of some houses, then down to the back of our couple's house—one long slow declining arc. Then we see them, but don't hear them, conversing behind a window. (Only street noises through this opening. There are music credits, but I can't remember a note of music.) This first sight of them through the glass, as we are outside watching and not hearing, sets the right opening mood.

Sometimes Gilroy strains: there are too many overhead shots. But he's looked at Hopper paintings and knows how to tell us something about Brooklyn dawn; he's looked at Bergman films and knows how to suspend two people in an agar-agar jelly of deadened love. And he knows how to make his film reinforce itself, as when he uses a duplicate composition for irony. The first time we see the couple's pleasant country house, it's on the right side of the screen and, after a moment, they drive in from the left. When we first see their caretaker's dowdy house, it, too, is on the right side of the screen and, again after a moment, the couple drive in from the left. The repetition, with a different, cheaper subject, is a shrewd comment.

The end of the story leaves us where we started, outside their Brooklyn home. A lot of pain has been shown and implied, and is by no means cured, but now it's quiet again. End of the picture, but only an intermission in the drama of the bourgeois.

This is a film of authenticity, of delicately realized intangibles: small-scale about large issues, truthful without settling for honest-to-God TV fact. All the more credit to Gilroy—and to MacLaine, without whom it would probably not have been made—because there was small reason to expect this work from them. I submit, too, that the year that sees two such first films as this and Barbara Loden's *Wanda,* not to mention Fonda's somewhat lesser *The Hired Hand,* is not the year to be despondent about the future of film in this country.

Millhouse

(October 2, 1971)

EMILE de Antonio, who made the pungeñt *In the Year of the Pig* about Vietnam, has now made a documentary about President Nixon called *Millhouse*. From the deliberate misspelling of the President's middle name right to the end, de Antonio makes no pretense of objectivity. The film misses few chances to show Nixon at his worst. I wouldn't want to suggest that this is a difficult job, still there are lots of methods in the picture that could be used equally against de Antonio's heroes, whoever they may be. The first sequence is in Madame Tussaud's as they fit the waxen head on the Nixon dummy; it could have been Lincoln or Saint Francis. When Nixon is in trouble on his South American good-will tour, we get a snatch of *Chiquita Banana* on the sound track. When he's making TV tapes for his '68 campaign, we get his off-the-record comments and his fluffs in discarded material. What do they prove?

But then if one made the most highly objective film about Nixon and did it with completeness, it would have to include the "Checkers" speech of '52, the calculated scurrility of his previous California campaigns against Jerry Voorhis and Helen Gahagan Douglas, his farewell to the press after his '62 defeat in California, and the "let's-win-this-one-for-Ike" acceptance speech in '68. Also, between the time I saw *Millhouse* and the writing of this review, I saw the one annual TV show I never miss, the Miss America competition; and after looking at Bert Parks and listening to his sincerity. . . .

Millhouse is a good political cartoon (figuratively). Besides, it brings out several points. It highlights the blatant newness of the "new" Nixon, with wide smile and upstretched arms. (Who decided on the change and coached him?) Second, Mrs. Nixon. Repeatedly, one sees her sitting absolutely rigid as her husband speaks, her face slightly smiling. I couldn't escape the feeling that she looked frightened—of what might happen to her later, in private, if she moved an inch or smiled a fraction more or less. That's an unprovable impression, of course; but it reminded me of the impression I used to get from Mrs. Thomas E. Dewey in photographs and newsreels. She always stood close to Dewey (a sort of Nixon forebear) with a forced little smile on her face, and I always imagined he was twisting her arm behind her back.

The most revealing moment in the film for me was a statement by a former California neighbor of the boy Nixon, who tells us that the future President's mother, after a long day's work or early in the morning, used to bake forty or fifty pies for sale. That kind of grinding hard work around a child tends to produce one of two kinds of reaction: money-hate or money-worship. I mean worship, not necessarily itch for acquisition: veneration of money and of those who have it.

That memory of his mother, slaving at her pies, is very possibly part of the foundation of Nixon's world view: money is the best good and anything that stands in the way of your getting it legally is the Antichrist. Imagine how much more dangerous the present U.S. economic situation must be than he has admitted—or his view of it, anyway. If he is forced to interfere even slightly with a laissez-faire system, how very frightened he must be. His new economic policy, flabby and biased as it is, denies the aspirations and acceptances he learned from his mother's pie-baking.

Sunday Bloody Sunday

(October 9, 1971)

THE press handout says that John Schlesinger had the original idea for this picture and then selected Penelope Gilliatt as the "right writer." She was; or rather, she would have been, if it had really been the right idea. The milieu—of English art-and-intellect society, of minutiae as the tactics of contemporary internal crisis—is something that she has handled admirably in some of her stories. But where was the idea? Essentially *Sunday Bloody Sunday* is a situation, not a dramatic idea, and although there are many subtle touches in it, they don't grow toward anything much.

It's a triangle story, except that this time the triangle consists of a middle-aged man and a woman in love with the same young man. The youth is a successful London sculptor (Murray Head), the older man is a doctor (Peter Finch), the woman an ex-married employment counselor (Glenda Jackson). The theme—and I have to do some inventing here where I should only be inferring—is the tension among three people who are directly and indirectly involved with one another, tension arising out of differing modern attitudes toward involvement itself. Head wants to be free to concentrate on the moment, and then move on; Jackson eventually says she wants committed love though most of the time she is gallant about sharing; Finch is a happy man, interested mainly in possessions. (In the picture's last moments, he says that he will miss the youth, who has gone to America leaving both his lovers, but will be quite happy except for missing him.)

Now this is the *beginning* of a film of quiet, nerve-baring drama, but this script merely states its positions and then, for the most part, keeps moving around the triangle again and again, restating them. We know who these people are fairly quickly and there isn't much more that we know about them much later. Jackson is made to resign from her job quite arbitrarily, just so that she will have some outward sign of motion; her outbreak near the end, in which she tells Head she won't see him on his return from the U.S. because she wants all or nothing, seems like a "last scene" speech out of another picture. (If Head hadn't gone abroad, presumably she would have gone right on sharing him.) And she is the only one who is given even some trumped-up change. Nothing really alters in these people through the film; and they don't really do anything to one another. It's just one long situation.

About an hour into the story there's a scene in which Jackson drives past Head's flat at night and looks up at the lighted window. As she drives out of the shot, Finch drives in from the opposite direction, without seeing her, and he too goes past looking at the lighted window. I thought that this, in outer symmetry and inner design, was the end of the picture. It *is*, really, but the picture goes on for almost another hour. In fact the single best sequence comes later on, and it's very much to my point that this sequence has little to do with the triangle. (Jackson spends an evening, bed and all, with a quietly frightened fifty-five-year-old executive who has lost his job and whom she is trying to place. The man is played by Tony Britton, who helps give the whole episode tenderness and dignity.)

Much of the dialogue is sharply engraved—in that sequence, in a party scene, in a scene between Jackson and her mother (Peggy Ashcroft), as well as all the scenes with some small children of friends, who are delightful. But the script lacks a mainspring—not of plot contrivance, which would be foreign to its nature, but of boiling chemistries. Instead, we are asked to make assumptions about catch-all modern themes. Byron once described a certain kind of poetry as "O, glory, etc." These modern themes might be called "O, alienation, etc."

For some of the script's defects Schlesinger is presumably responsible since the press handout makes a point of noting that he had many discussions with Gilliatt while she was writing. He is certainly responsible for all the defects in execution and, sad to say, there are many. The virtues are few. Some scenes, like Britton's, are well controlled, and here and there—the party scene is one place—motion and meaning intertwine the way they have in Schlesinger's best work. And he gets a fine performance from Glenda Jackson: beautifully modulated, with humor and sharp slivers of pain and little catlike enjoyments.

On the other hand, watching Peter Finch is like watching a bolt of velour being unrolled before you, smooth smooth smooth. He's been selling that velour for so long that he's lost the actor's absolute requisite: credibility. When he ends a phone call with a silly patient, gets up, and says, "Jesus Christ, I need a drink," I saw the typed words on a page and heard the director telling him to move. As for Murray Head, Schlesinger's new find, he is simply a disaster. I couldn't believe, first, that he was so overwhelmingly attractive to these two tasteful people, and, second, his behavior cannot be called a performance. An actor who really fulfilled the role wouldn't have erased the film's faults but at least wouldn't have underlined them.

Schlesinger has worked throughout with a great many huge close-ups and slow dissolves so that, though the colors are generally muted, the film has a mushy texture that contradicts its air of understatement. He has never been an original director, but in his best work—A Kind of Loving, Billy Liar, Midnight Cowboy—he has synthesized intelligently and affectingly. Here I was chiefly conscious of bits and pieces and sources. The blue-filtered scene in the all-night drugstore is like the blue-filtered supermarket in Petulia. The youthful skaters in the nighttime streets seem out of Blow-Up. Schlesinger even lifts a bit from himself: the clergyman on TV while the couple copulate is like the scene with Jon Voight and Sylvia Miles in Midnight Cowboy.

Self-indulgence: a Bar Mitzvah that Finch attends (he's Jewish) goes on long past its use. Mechanical build-up: there's so much joy on an outing in a park with the children that we know there must be some disaster ahead. (There is.) Explication: every time we might be imagining something, Schlesinger spells it out for us—Finch at his nephew's Bar Mitzvah, flashing back to his own, Jackson, after a dog is run over, imagining that it might have been a child; Finch, just come from a hospital call (another good *peripheral* scene) envisioning that it might have been Head who was near death. Muzzy viewpoint: why does Schlesinger give us bits from the viewpoint of minor characters? (The parents of the children, for instance, as they drive off.) The *Elvira Madigan* syndrome: Schlesinger leans on Mozart, a heavenly trio from *Così fan tutte*. (Two women and a man, but a trio!)

There is some attempt to "situate" the film in our society. Love thrives by telephone these days so we watch calls move along telephone circuits. (An idea used some ten years ago by two USC film students, Stuart Hanisch and Russ McGregor, in a well-known short called *Have I Told You Lately That I Love You?*) We are told often, on car radios and in headlines, that this is a time of economic crisis. But these things, and others, seem only ritual obeisance to import; they don't resonate against anything the characters are or do, as cognate materials did in *Midnight Cowboy*.

And then there's the title. I thought it meant something about weekend boredom, but the film story begins on a Friday, ends a week from Sunday, thus includes two Sundays. I don't know why the ten days have to be labeled with subtitles or why the picture is called what it is.

There's some acuteness in the film and the chance for pleasant recognitions of human quirk. But mostly it seems to want credit for what it does *not* do: it does not have any worked-up plot, does not spell out all its motivations, does not end on any high dramatic or low ironic note. In fact, it does *not* do so much that it made me think of Roy Campbell's famous quatrain about some South African novelists:

> You praise the firm restraint with which they write—
> I'm with you there, of course.
> They use the snaffle and the curb all right;
> But where's the bloody horse?

The Last Picture Show

(October 16, 1971)

So many things in Peter Bogdanovich's second film are so good that I wish I liked it more. Worse, I feel ungrateful. I complained that his first film *Targets* showed considerable skill but was trapped in Movieland, in more than subject matter. That's not true here: he's addressed better material and shows even more skill; and, caddishly, I'm unsatisfied.

The script is by Larry McMurtry and Bogdanovich, from the former's novel. McMurtry also wrote the novel on which *Hud* was based. (And wrote a funny article about visiting the film company on location. I wish he'd write another, from another perspective, now that he's been actively involved.) Once again we're in sunbaked, freezing, sex-strangulated, power-pent Texas, the landscape as flat as the outlook of most of the young inhabitants. It's 1951, a small town, and the first thing we see is the "picture show" (film theater), then the camera pans up the quite unspectacular main street. The very last shot reverses this movement, ending on the picture show, now closed forever. (TV has replaced movies as the dream-stuffing of empty lives. Free, too.) Between those shots, we've seen the hero move from late adolescence to the beginnings of manhood.

That's the first trouble. The script is framed just as neatly as the film is with those two shots. In order to define the end of a period in the hero's life, things are *made* to happen. Toward the close, an older man who has befriended the hero suddenly drops dead, the boy's long infatuation is exploded by a trick marriage, his best friend goes off to Korea, his affair with an older woman dissolves, and as if all that weren't enough, a mute mentally retarded kid he likes is run over by a truck. Heavy hands are making the calendar turn over. There's personal observation, possibly autobiography, in the script, and I suspect that McMurtry's justification might be, "But that's the way it really happened." If so, it only proves again that life is no artist.

However, there's much in the film to be praised. First, Bogdanovich "saw" it in black and white and then made it in black and white. Hurrah for that. The demands of future TV sales didn't bully him into the color he thought inappropriate, as it bullies so many. Behind this choice and behind the gray tonalities of the picture, looms the loomable figure of Orson Welles. Bogdanovich wrote an adulatory monograph about Welles ten years ago, and this film is surely another homage—particularly to *Touch of Evil*. With Robert Surtees's fine photography, he has rendered a Texas with every gradation of light except cheery sunshine, as elegiac as his master's southern California. Also, there are bows to George Stevens: a long shot of a lonely house (*Giant*) and a burial on a hill (*Shane*). From a couple of dozen lesser figures, he has borrowed the Big Object shot: something huge in the foreground toward which characters move from far off. He uses it twice—a garbage can, a pair of feet sticking out of a car—which is twice too often. But generally Bogdanovich's own eye is lively, and so is his sense of flow.

And he has greatly improved with actors—both in his casting and his direction. Ben Johnson, belatedly coming into his own, is gentle and strong as the aging friend. Ellen Burstyn, a frustrated rich wife, Cybill Shepherd, her spoiled pretty daughter, and Cloris Leachman, a desperate and doomed woman, are all vivid and truthful. There are lots of scenes in which the texture of conventions is nicely inscribed. (When the hero parks with his steady girl after a movie, she takes off her blouse and bra as routinely as for a medical exam.)

But a big trouble is Timothy Bottoms as the hero. There's nothing drastically wrong with him—other than that it takes about twenty minutes to sort him out, in appearance and language, from his best friend (Jeff Bridges). Bottoms is genuine enough; he's simply not good enough. He never opens up anything, never surprises, is never really touching. The best I could feel about him was that he was never false. Which is not enough for a film that's situated exactly in the middle of its protagonist.

And that's a model of what's finally dim about the whole picture. It all seems true enough, but almost every scene reminds us vaguely of something we've seen before and generally have seen better. Ben Johnson's speech about time passing him by, the chronicles of social snobberies and sexual hang-ups, the bareness of the life, and the hunger for breaking out—all of these are credible but not illuminated by anything that makes them more than familiar. For long decades American films spent most of their time cramming American life into movie molds (often very entertainingly); now many American films, like this one, are trying to deal with American life as it is and was. But not falsifying is not enough.

Bogdanovich has real abilities and has progressed happily in most ways—except the central matter: self, being, style. I still don't know much more about him from his work than that he loves films and can make them. But who *is* he? That's a question which all really good directors answer about themselves, sooner rather than later. Bogdan-ovich's answer is yet to come.

The French Connection

(October 30, 1971)

Go see it—and take your viscera along. This thriller was made to grab your insides, and it does. It's the most exciting picture I've seen since *Z,* and it's not burdened with any ambition except to excite. Made with razor skills and a good sardonic sense of the film tradition it comes out of, it jets off from the beginning and, since in a way it's open-ended, it may still be going. You know while you're watching that it's just another cops-and-robbers but that it's not just another because it's so well done.

This time it's heroin smugglers out of Marseilles versus New York City detectives. The European and American settings are milked for contrasts, by the camera and the casting and the dialogue. Old-world streets, polished manners, and the sound of French versus Brooklyn bars, grimy cops, and broken-bottle dialogue. Near the end we get a chase—a car underneath the Brooklyn el, racing to catch an express train at the next station—that's the best since *Bullitt* (produced by the same producer) and more gaspy because there are some narrow escapes, so the incredibility is more credible. And the chase is exactly what we want at that point, it's the obligatory scene, just as we want the final shoot-out that follows shortly.

Why does this thriller outrun the run-of-the-mill? First, Ernest Tidyman's script (from a book by Robin Moore) is lean, hard, and knowledgeable about characters who are knowledgeable about them-selves. No bad guys against good guys, just black against gray. It's a script about cool modern professionals, each one good at his trade: pushing drugs, murdering people, or hunting people who push drugs. Without a lot of psychologizing about it, the script tells us that people have their pride: the pusher likes his cleverness, the chaser likes the chase.

William Friedkin cast and directed it to the (tightly clenched) teeth. I've disliked Friedkin's previous work, such as *The Birthday Party* and *The Boys in the Band,* because he seemed to be hopping all over his material so that we could see his footprints. The odd thing here is that, with material of small specific gravity, merely clever stuff, he is much less ostentatiously clever himself. One is never conscious of Friedkin sticking his face around the corner to grin at the camera, only of the story being whipped along.

Friedkin and Tidyman have a neat appreciation of the gangster-film tradition behind them. The mature ringleader has a young tootsie. (Louis Calhern and Marilyn Monroe in *The Asphalt Jungle.*) And there's lots of thirties gangster-film wryness. A Marseilles detective gets shot in his hallway on his return from shopping; the killer steps over his body, breaks off the end of the loaf that the dead man was carrying, and chews it as he departs. While two of the dope ring are lunching in a *luxe* New York restaurant, with vintage wines, two detectives are watching outside in the cold, stamping their feet and chewing pizza. When there's a fistfight between the detectives themselves, it takes place against the background of a bloody car accident on a freeway where the detectives have gone to see their captain.

And the cynical ending—using a device that echoes *Z*—is exactly right for a film that wants the surprises of recognition, not of fantasy.

Of course, as in all thrillers, even the most realistic of them, there are unbelievable things. Apart from the chase, how can we believe that a fleeing sniper would run down the middle of a street where he's most likely to be seen? Or that a car, stripped to pieces by searching police, could be reassembled so perfectly that its very sharp owners would never suspect? (And so quickly!) The answer is that when the price is right, we're willing to pay it. We want to believe the far-fetched when we want to be fetched.

One very big reason that we believe is the acting. Fernando Rey, of Buñuel's *Tristana,* as the drug chief; Marcel Bozzuffi, who was the homosexual thug of *Z,* as his assistant; Gene Hackman, who was Clyde's brother in *Bonnie and C.,* as the principal detective, all endow their by-now conventional characters with life, because these actors know that conventional characters have lives. (By the way, there's a cat-and-mouse game in the Times Square shuttle station between Rey and Hackman that is worth the price of admission.)

And a bow to the editor, Jerry Greenberg. No slouch, he.

Some people, alas, are bound to take this picture as a demonic but profound statement of contemporary morality, as a manifestation of "true" cinema, etc., etc. Don't let all this prevent you from enjoying this spin-off from truly serious work. The Golden Age of Hollywood, like that of TV, was largely gilt, and *The French Connection* is as slick and shiny and enjoyable as much of the best of it.

Fiddler on the Roof

(November 20, 1971)

ABOUT forty-five seconds into the picture, Tevye the milkman starts his famous number "Tradition," and as he sings there are a number of quick cuts of the interior of a synagogue, featuring the Mogen David (Star of David). That's what this show is really about. Not Sholom Aleichem, not *shtetl* life in East Europe; it's about quick heart-tug shots of the Mogen David while a man sings a catchy Harnick-Bock song. No wonder it's been a world-wide theater success: its universalizing sentimentalities defy parochialism. Well, folks, here it comes again—bigger, wider, softer.

Joseph Stein's book for the Broadway musical was an adulteration of Sholom Aleichem, but, once it was adulterated, Jerome Robbins made a marvelous production out of it, ingeniously staged and choreographed. Robbins's direction is of course now gone, his choreography is "adapted" (some of the good wedding dances are retained), and Boris Aronson's endearing sets have been replaced by a banal "real" village of Anatevka.

Norman Jewison hasn't so much directed a film as prepared a product for world consumption, trying to pet and wheedle this material into the shapes and curlicues of the "classic" movie musical. On a lower scale, this is *Seven Brides for Seven Brothers,* give or take a few brides and allowing for change of venue.

Critically, in fact, that's the most interesting aspect of the film—the way Jewison has carefully balanced two widely disparate elements, the extremely Jewish and the extremely gentile, no middle ground whatsoever, to serve everyone. Molly Picon, the marriage broker, and Zvee Scooler, the rabbi, wallow in Yiddishness as Second Avenue never dared. (Can one call a Yiddish actor a ham?) But when Tzeitel and Motel get Tevye's consent to marry, the young lovers race joyfully through the woods as if their names were Debbie and Tim. I don't contend that young Jewish lovers in Eastern Europe never raced through the woods hand in hand; I do contend that Jewison is saying, "See? Jewish lovers race hand in hand just like other people." This just-like-other-people quality runs all through the film, to make the Jewish audience feel integrated and to bring the gentile audience inside. The Friday night services, the dancing by the stream, the defense of the home, are all given a cosmopolitanizing lacquer of Norman Rockwell.

The score stands or wobbles as it always has, the book comes off somewhat worse. The film runs three hours, plus a fifteen-minute intermission, and during that intermission, you begin to count the matings of Tevye's daughters that are yet to come and the worked-up expulsion that you have to go through; and you realize that there's no drama, only a series of set pieces. And since Jewison doesn't have much gift for pathos, some of the set pieces fall flat: the parting with the radical daughter at the railroad, the parting with the renegade daughter who married a gentile. (Girl Meets Goy.) The best touch in the latter scene is that, as the Russian boy walks away, we see a chessboard dangling from the pack on his back.

Zero Mostel, who was the first Tevye, is not in the film. Whatever else one has to say of Zero (who can call him Mostel?), he's ineradicable. Those who never saw him are at an advantage with Topol, the Israeli actor who plays it here. Topol is vigorous and professional, but he's not funny, not deft, not moving, not out-rageous, not really a confidant of God—in short, not Zero. When Zero sang "If I Were a Rich Man," we watched the Pentateuch waddle. When Topol sings it, Israeli though he is, it's like Dean Jagger with wig and beard and accent.

Paul Mann, as the butcher, looks good, but his voice is too thin for his bulk and his hands, as usual, work in simultaneous gestures, two doing the work of one or, sometimes, what ought to be none. Rosalind Harris, the very Semitic-looking Tzeitel, is charming. But by far the best performance is that of Leonard Frey as her lover Motel. He's an *actor*. He was the ugly birthday boy in *The Boys in the Band,* on stage and screen, and I've also seen him as Harry the Hoofer in the Beaumont Theater's production of *The Time of Your Life.* Frey is an *actor*. Adjectives have become so stale in this business that, for him, I italicize the noun.

A Clockwork Orange

(January 1 & 8, 1972)

IN one way Stanley Kubrick's new film is cheering. This time, as in all his work before *2001,* he sticks to a narrative, depicts character, opts for "literary humanism"—does all the things that some critics claimed he had deliberately abandoned, in the space picture, for a new esthetics. Perhaps the new esthetics *was* only a wobble? Revised editions of various pronunciamentos may now be in order.

But there isn't a great deal more to celebrate in *A Clockwork Orange.* Certainly there are some striking images; certainly there is some impudent wit, some adroitness. But the worst flaw in the film is its air of cool intelligence and ruthless moral inquiry, because those elements are least fulfilled. Very early there are hints of triteness and insecurity, and before the picture is a half-hour old, it begins to slip into tedium. Sharp and glittery though it continues to be, it never quite shakes that tedium.

The screenplay, by Kubrick, follows Anthony Burgess's novel fairly closely in story, but that's not much of an advantage. This novel of the near future hasn't got much of a story, as such; Burgess relies principally on an odd language he has devised—a mixture of current English, archaic English, and anglicized Russian (today, yesterday, and the future). This language, more than any other element, is asked to hold the reader, indicate social change, and suggest moral quandaries. The effects are limited; it's not my favorite Burgess by any means.

Kubrick's first mistake may have been to select a book whose very being is in its words. The film is inevitably much weaker. Kubrick uses the verbal texture as far as possible, which cannot be far. The language cannot create a world for him as it does for Burgess. The modest moral resonance of the book is reduced: partly because of certain small changes, like converting a murder victim from an old woman to a sexy broad and killing her with a giant ceramic phallus (thus changing sheer heartlessness into sex sensation); mostly because Kubrick has to replace Burgess's linguistic ingenuity with cinematic ingenuity, and he doesn't. The story as such is thin, so the picture thins. In *2001,* the longueurs came from Kubrick's neglect of narrative to revel in gadgetry, but at least some of the gadgets and images were extraordinary. Here he doesn't neglect story for display, he depends on display to *make* his story, but his invention this time is weak.

The scene is England. Alex, a young ruffian, leads a quartet of young ruffians whose hobby is "ultra violence"—binges of rape and assault. Alex's one contradictory quality is his love of classical music, particularly Beethoven, particularly the Ninth. One night Alex goes too far, accidentally kills a woman, is caught, and is sentenced to forty years. A new psychological process for rehabilitating criminals has been devised and, by agreeing to be a guinea pig, Alex has his sentence commuted.

The process is plain Pavlovism: he is strapped in a chair with eyelids clamped open and electrodes on his head, is shown films of violence and sex along with a Beethoven sound track, and has shocks administered to sicken him as he watches. Later, when he attempts violence—or hears Beethoven!—he feels violently ill and must stop.

His case has been kicked around in the press as a political football. The Opposition party roars that a human being has been dehumanized, etc. Some Opposition people abduct him after his release, closet him with an endless recording of the Ninth to make him sick and raving, to drive him to suicide—for their advantage. But he is salvaged by the Government. At the end the Pavlovian cure is reversed: Beethoven once again brings on fantasies of sex and violence, and Alex is once again ready to ravage.

Much of the dialogue, and all of Alex's narration, is in Burgess's newspeak. Kubrick, like Burgess, relies on context to make unknown words clear. This is more difficult for the ear than for the eye, but, in the main, it happens, though slowly.

Inexplicably the script leaves out Burgess's reference to the title: it's the title of a book being written by a character in the novel, with an excerpt provided to clarify. That author's book-inside-the-book is a protest against "the attempt to impose upon man, a creature of growth and capable of sweetness . . . laws and conditions appropriate to a mechanical creation," the attempt to make a growing thing into a mechanism, even—as Stanley Edgar Hyman said—to eliminate his freedom to sin.

Now this is hardly a staggeringly new concept or protest, but Burgess makes it mildly interesting because of the linguistic acrobatics he can perform while expounding it. Kubrick is stuck with the message and, for this work, the wrong medium. We simply see the working-out of the design, the spelling of the lesson, with very little esthetic increment along the 137-minute way.

A few sequences are striking, such as the opening in a milk bar with plaster nudes as tables. There's a good gang rumble in a gutted theater, the hollowed-out place reflecting the combatants' spirits. But a great deal of the film is banal or reminiscent. The four ruffians stand before a streetlamp when they batter a tramp, so that the light streams out around them—one of the hoariest of arty poses. A speeded-up porno sequence is like the one in *Greetings,* a slow-motion fight is like several in *The Wild Bunch.*

The camera use is stale: the hand-held camera in the murder scene, the distorting lens on the author (Patrick Magee) when he realizes that Alex is his wife's murderer. Supposed frankness is flat or strained: Alex peeing, the prison guard examining his anus, two girls sucking penile ice cream sticks. Kubrick echoes his own past musical tricks: Rossini as humorously inappropriate comment, instead of the Johann Strauss in *2001;* Gene Kelly and "Singin' in the Rain" at the end, instead of the Vera Lynn and "We'll Meet Again" of *Dr. Strangelove.* A few of Alex's fantasies are witty, like the sex fantasy he gets from the Bible while in jail, but mostly they are hand-me-down silent-film dreams with fewer clothes and more violence.

Malcolm McDowell is Alex. This is the third time I've seen him, and although he hasn't yet shown great range, he does have energy and threat. Among the rest only Michael Bates, the guard, is outstanding. I've seen Bates do his shiny-cheeked popinjay twice before —comically—on the London stage. Here he does it less comically but efficiently.

Something has gone seriously wrong with the talented Kubrick. I won't hazard guesses as to what it is. But the one thing that, two films ago, I'd never have thought possible to say about a Kubrick film is true of *A Clockwork Orange:* it's boring.

Macbeth

(January 1 & 8, 1972)

SOMETHING has gone right with Roman Polanski, for a change. Not completely, still surprisingly right. The advance publicity on his

Macbeth led me to expect—I don't know what. The film turns out to be absolutely straight, a serious attempt to make the play a film, its only unorthodoxy that the hero and heroine are much younger than usual. Even the flacked-up nudity in the sleepwalking scene is very restrained.

Polanski and his co-adapter Kenneth Tynan have worked out some good ideas, chiefly toward the theme of power-hunger. Ross is used as the mysterious Third Murderer of Banquo; then after Ross comforts Lady Macduff, it is he who betrays her to Macbeth's killers; then of course he flees to Malcolm, so is on the side that crushes Macbeth, and comes out on top. At the very end there is an added (silent) twist. After Malcolm has been crowned, we see his brother, Donalbain, returning from exile and encountering the witches as Macbeth once did when they prophesied he would be king. And we know that the opportunist Ross is waiting to back another winner, if the witches prophesy the same destiny to Donalbain.

Some of the pictorial elements are breath-taking—shot in Wales (by Gil Taylor) in a climate into which rain comes and goes as breezes do elsewhere. But we expect stunning pictures these days. Where Polanski has really made film is, for instance, in the first scene: the three witches on a wide stretch of dismal beach, going about their witchy business in a nontheatrical mundane way, as if they were digging clams instead of burying a severed hand with an incantation. (One of the three is young and doesn't speak.) I never expect to believe the witches, I hope only to have them credible as symbols (which they aren't often), but I nearly believed in these three, and in the naked coven to whom Macbeth resorts after he is king.

Polanski has worked in a lot of helpful life-style touches of the time, and the editing—of sound and picture—is generally agile. The gory stuff is hardly exceptional in these days of Clint Eastwood. There is only one visual device I really regretted: the visible airborne dagger, which is supposed to be "of the mind." (It looked like a TV airlines commercial: Kill Now, Pay Later.) And several of the actors are very good, notably Martin Shaw as Banquo and Nicholas Selby as Duncan.

But the whole enterprise never really gets to be *Macbeth,* to be a tragedy—for two reasons. First, the leading actors are inadequate. Terence Bayler, the Macduff, sounds like a South Kensington dude. Francesca Annis, the Lady, is a zero. Jon Finch, the Macbeth, begins very well, and is genuinely interesting up through Duncan's murder, but he doesn't deepen. Hell is not entered; lines are painted on his face. (And since Polanski insists on young leads, why doesn't he make more use of the traditional sex motivation by which Lady M. rekindles M. after he has faltered in his intent to kill? To play this scene, Polanski even moves them out of privacy, on a balcony, into a room full of other people. For the most private and most sex-charged dialogue of the drama!)

Second, the old inescapable complaint about Shakespeare films. The text is slashed, to make time for the pictures. But the tragedy is in the words. Those words *cannot* (repeat: CANNOT) be transmuted into pictures, no matter how gorgeous, nor into action, no matter how exciting.

Still I got some moments of real pleasure from the film. And its general seriousness restored some respect—and expectation—for Polanski.

The Hospital

(January 22, 1972)

THIS is one of the rare films that bills its writer big—Paddy Chayefsky. I can't call myself a close student of his work: I tuned out somewhere around *The Americanization of Emily*. If a dilettante may be permitted an opinion on the Chayefsky canon, his dialogue seems to have changed considerably since the *Marty* days. Back there he seemed to think that the whole of art was to convey the attar of underarm odor; now his writing has some flourish and verve. Rather like a latter-day Ben Hecht, Chayefsky is not serious enough to be serious, just serious enough to be entertaining.

The basic idea—and if he had stuck to it, the film might have been a real zinger—is that American hospitals are now potential killers. They're so big and so compartmentalized that, if you want to kill a perfectly healthy man, all you have to do is feed him into an inappropriate channel of treatment and hospital care will murder him for you. But this muscular idea is flabbed up with considerable tripe and is then corseted into an ending that would have made Philco Playhouse happy.

George C. Scott plays the chief of medicine in a big New York hospital, a middle-aged man in the middle of male menopause, whose self-doubts and professional zeal make a good sardonic foil for the theme. Scott is a tornado, creating his own 3-D as he goes. An authentic actor-star. (When *auteur* critics are sorting things out, do they ever consider an actor like Scott as co-creator of a film like this one and *Patton*? How can he be overlooked? Most of what is valid in *The Hospital* comes from Scott.) Diana Rigg, the girl, is nicely cool, but her face always affects me oddly. It's insufficient. There just isn't enough of it.

In sum, this is the mod version of the old Hollywood-and-TV truth game: "Allow us our cop-outs and we'll give you some sham-true fun." OK.

Straw Dogs

(February 19, 1972)

I went from the theater where I saw Sam Peckinpah's new film *Straw Dogs* to another theater that was running his earlier film *The Wild Bunch.* I'm glad I did, because it elevated my high opinion of the earlier picture and helped to clarify some things about the new one.

Peckinpah is the 007 of film makers, licensed to kill. He earned this license in *The Wild Bunch,* a Western that enlarged the form esthetically, thematically, demonically. But now he endangers his license because he's getting qualms, he's moralizing—in *Straw Dogs* even more than in the less violent *Ballad of Cable Hogue* (1970), a sticky and ill-made whimsical Western. Moralizing is the enemy of his talent.

For the new film, Peckinpah and David Z. Goodman have adapted a novel by Gordon M. Williams set in Cornwall. Space has always been a Peckinpah theme, and plainly he was interested in the idea of big space contained in a small space, Cornish moors within a small island, instead of the seemingly limitless West. (We feel this as we watch: over the horizon here is London or the sea, but who can imagine the end of Texas?) Peckinpah was also presumably interested in the idea of violence in an ancient village instead of on the raw frontier. It may even have been in his mind to comment on the Western by showing that its basic elements are universal. If he had made his film without didactic theme, true to his own nature, it might have been another quasi-Artaudian experience. But he labors a cozy, trite, and questionable point this time, so the violence goes quickly from the frightening to the tedious to the irritating. A real 007 never explains. His life is what he is.

The story concerns a young American mathematician (Dustin Hoffman), with a sexy Cornish wife (Susan George), who goes to live in his wife's old home to work on a book. The wife is restless but not breastless, both of which facts are noted by the men who work around the place—particularly one who presumably had once slept with her. The men concoct a scheme to get Hoffman out of the house one day while two of them ravish the wife, in tandem. She complains a bit to them but not to her husband.

The lines of brain versus balls-and-brawn are quickly drawn, of moral courage against strength and swagger. The point, clumsily made, is that the former cannot exist in a vacuum; Hoffman, who has his own kind of guts from the start, has to cross over. The last twenty minutes (hours?) are crammed with assaults and batterings and shootings as Hoffman battles to protect a loony child-murderer from a lynch mob that includes his wife's ravishers.

The trouble is double, and comes from the script. First, heavy heavy hangs over our head in a corny way right from the start. An early scene of petty violence in a pub—crushing a man's hand on a glass—is a seed that grows into the last holocaust. A man-trap (literally), once used for poachers, is borne in at the beginning, obviously to be used at the end. Hoffman says early to his wife, "If that cat gets into my study, I'll kill it"—and guess what the first death is. Etcetera —including the wife's moronically blatant sexual teasings of the workmen.

The second trouble is the miasma of apologetics and justifications, the working-out of a parable: even a mathematician has killer instincts and will, presumably, be a more courageous mathematician after killing a few beasts in defense of principle. Coupled with this is the coupling theme. As a 1930 film once told us, Ladies Love Brutes; or rape is not rape that bends with the remover to remove. Long before the parabolic conclusion, the picture has acquired the air of a blacker Stanley Kramer, a savage sanctimoniousness. Peckinpah becomes Pecksniff.

His directing is still the work of a born director: he knows what to look at and how to look at it. But there are flaws in the direction, too. Susan George has the right sulky hot schoolgirl quality, but Peckinpah lets Hoffman give his only dull screen performance so far. Most of Hoffman's lines seem caught between his molars, like shreds of meat. And some of the editing is worse than the weakest moments in *The Wild Bunch:* crude referential shots (the wife remembering the rape during a church social) or crude contrasts (the child's murder intercut with a choir singing). Peckinpah even reuses a device that was not new in *Wait Until Dark,* where I last saw it: after the melee, a supposedly dead man suddenly revives for a last attack.

The subject of violence has been occupying film critics ever since there was film, and I'm not about to settle the matter here; but I suggest that we all lie about this matter as much as about pornography. If a violent picture is entertaining (or better), we may tsk-tsk later but we enjoy it while it's on. If it's not well done, we deplore it because we don't enjoy it. Surely there are more killings in *The Wild Bunch* than in *Straw Dogs,* but the former flays open the viewer to reveal his own neural system and the latter lacks real conviction. *The French Connection* is exciting, *Dirty Harry* is disgusting; the difference is not in numbers or methods of murders but in our involvement with characters and story. Possibly there's an inference here. If we put aside the question of the juvenile audience, about which no one really seems to know much, the way to solve the Violence Problem in films is to make violent films *well.*

The Garden of the Finzi-Continis

(February 19, 1972)

I love Vittorio De Sica's films of his best period, from the end of World War II to 1952, preeminently *The Bicycle Thief* and *Miracle in Milan.* I love the best film of his subsequent career, *Two Women* (1961). And I'm very fond of some of his marinara-sauce films like

Marriage Italian Style (1965). But I don't like *The Garden of the Finzi-Continis*. It attempts a serious theme and is neither good art nor good show biz.

The script, based on Giorgio Bassani's novel, deals with the Italian Jews of Ferrara between 1938 and 1943 as the Fascists increasingly ape Nazi anti-Semitism. The Finzi-Continis are rich and cultivated Jews; their immense, beautiful estate is a haven from the world, rendered insecure. The film ends with their being gathered up with other Jews for shipment to camps.

The subject of the Jews under Mussolini has never been the main matter of a film, as far as I know; it's an interesting idea and I wish the result had been better. The fundamental flaw is the script.

The story is about the love of a middle-class Jewish youth for the Finzi-Contini daughter and her inability to return anything but sisterly love. So the chief motions of the plot are utterly divorced from the theme. There are plenty of peripheral incidents that deal with growing Fascist oppression, but the plot is simply not an engine of the idea; it's only a time-filler, to plug the gap between the seeming safety of 1938 and the inevitabilities of 1943. The boy-girl story, as such, could have been between Catholics in Brazil.

De Sica has lavishly contributed shortcomings of his own. Nothing that can be sugared is left plain. The camera zooms as if this were the first time he had directed and he couldn't get over his delight with lenses. The colors are like endless boxes of candied fruit. The editing flutters with nervousness, and that weariest of pastoral shots, the camera looking upward as it moves along under trees, is used repeatedly. De Sica is weeping right along with his sad story, and his tears get very much in the way of ours.

The post-recording is bad. Helmut Berger and (the beauiful) Dominique Sanda are very noticeably dubbed by other actors. The rest have been rerecorded in studios with a poor sense of aural equivalence to the settings and planes.

A dozen years ago De Sica played the title role—excellently—in *General della Rovere* for Roberto Rossellini. In the last episode, before his execution by Germans, he waits with a group of condemned Italians, among whom are some Jews. I'm still moved by remembering them. I wasn't moved by the Finzi-Continis, and will forget them.

Cabaret

(March 4, 1972)

THE changes in Sally Bowles are the stuff of cultural history. Originally she was the title character of a story in Christopher Isherwood's *Goodbye to Berlin* (1939); then she was in John van Druten's dramatization, called *I Am a Camera* (1951), which was filmed (1955); then she was in the musical version of the play, *Cabaret* (1966); and now that musical is on the screen. Not to detail all the changes en route, she began as a bed-free English girl of good family, a quite conscious Noel Coward high-stepper of the late twenties in the boiling Berlin of the early thirties, a frenzied hedonist, deliberately ignoring the dark political environment of her cabaret-performing life. In this latest embodiment, she is American, much more like a cabaret star than a mere performer, and she sleeps around like mad because she's in love with her diplomat father who rejects her. When she became American, she had to be "explained," and the explanation had to be Freudian.

The changes in the narrator are revealing, too. He began as Isherwood, the "camera," which he remained in the play. His role as observer was itself part of the theme. His warm nonsexual friendship with Sally gave the story a poignant *Bruderschaft;* the tacit homosexual reason for it underscored the disjunctures of the time. In the musical, his name was changed, and he shifted from "camera" to activist, a young hero who had an affair with Sally. A doomed affair, of course, but only by romantic declension. This change hurt the original idea very much; it battered a unique and crystallizing story into one more set of heart tugs. Now, the screenplay by Jay Allen, sleek butcher of *The Prime of Miss Jean Brodie,* trades on the New Liberation of film. The hero still has his affair with Sally but also has a homosexual fling with one of her lovers! Thus the script gobbles up all stages of the story's changes and makes the hero all things to all men—and women.

The Isherwood original is incomparably the best; but the film musical is very much better than the stage musical, is much better cast than it was on Broadway, and uses the political atmosphere as much more than a first-act curtain.

Bob Fosse, who directed, is a justly celebrated choreographer and musical director in the theater, and did one previous film, *Sweet Charity*. (I missed it.) He has handled *Cabaret* like a smart Broadway musical director: always bright, always intent—not on authenticity but on keeping one step ahead of the audience's jadedness. He can do it. He whips along from one clever camera angle to another, with a fusillade of "shock" lighting effects. (Camera work by Geoffrey Unsworth of *2001*.) Film journals will feast for years on shots from this picture; as it rolled along, I saw page after illustrated page from a not-too-distant book called *The Cinema of Bob Fosse*.

When the curtain went up on the Broadway show, the audience saw themselves in a huge mirror. Fosse adapts this device here, opening (and closing) with a mirror in which the Berlin cabaret audience see themselves. Unlike the Broadway version, the musical elements are split off from the rest: almost all the songs occur on the cabaret stage, the rest of the picture is "straight." I suppose this is in aid of realism, but it doesn't quite succeed. First, as usual in movie musicals, the numbers are much too lavish and complex for the theater in which they're supposed to be done. Second, Fosse is much more comfortable with the musical numbers than with "life." But one clever non-number is more than clever. A sequence in a country beer garden begins with a close-up of an appealing youth singing a pleasant *heimisch* song. Slowly the camera pulls back and reveals his Nazi armband. The refrain becomes fervent, the camera keeps pulling back, more and more people join with Nazi fervor, and what started out as schmaltz ends as scare. Overly neat, perhaps, but so is most symbolic action.

Liza Minnelli, the Sally, sings somewhat like her mother Judy Garland and looks somewhat like her father Vincente Minnelli. Apparently there's an industry-wide agreement to make her the Star of Sickdom, to exploit what the public knows of her mother's life, to treat the daughter as a dark-eyed bundle of quick-giggling neurotic heartbreak. In her first starring film *The Sterile Cuckoo,* Minnelli affected me like David Warner in *Morgan*. All my sympathy went to the person who was trying to get away from her; my only impulse was to rush out and call a psychiatric ambulance. Now the Isherwood Sally has been tailored to the Cuckoo image, and the songs have been styled in the Garland manner. It's hard to like or dislike the result. I'm conscious of some talent and a lot of managerial synthesis. If ever Liza Minnelli actually exists, not peddling souvenirs of her mother as woman and singer, she may be good.

The success of the film is Michael York as the quasi-Isherwood hero. In his previous films—*Accident, The Guru,* and others—he's been interesting but hampered by script or direction. In *Cabaret,* right from his arrival in Berlin in 1930 broad-brimmed fedora, he strikes the center of the role and holds it. Pride, abashed eroticism, civilized intelligence, humaneness, fear and strength, all come to him easily and with charm.

As the master of ceremonies, Joel Grey repeats the good death's-head performance that he gave on Broadway. One curious point in casting is the use of two German actors, Helmut Griem and Fritz Wepper, who are both good but who resemble each other so closely that there's confusion. Of all the actors in Germany (where the picture was made), why two who look so much alike?

The gritty songs—by John Kander and Fred Ebb—are belted home; the film looks continuously chic; the grimness and gaiety are adroitly interwoven. *Cabaret* is far better than most movie musicals; but Fosse's smartness, Minnelli's professional unhealth, and the script's chrome-plated carpentry keep it from being as moving as it wanted to be.

Bartleby

(March 4, 1972)

I suppose *Bartleby* is one of my lost causes, like *Brotherly Love* (Peter O'Toole's picture). A poor film with superb acting in it. Who cares? Well, I do, very much; and there may be others.

In this English import, Herman Melville's story is transposed to London today, is attenuated, is directed with cloddish preciosity. But there are two jewels in it. John McEnery in the title role achieves such intense inner concentration that his immobility, amidst a rushing world, is perfectly convincing; and Paul Scofield, as the employer, is simply brilliant. Delicately and deeply, Scofield cuts the portrait of a businessman who has built a role for himself in life the way an actor does in rehearsals and who feels it being punctured by the very existence of this nonconformist.

Scofield couldn't be as good, in his more varied part, if McEnery weren't so good in his monochrome one. In fact, one could argue that McEnery's job is harder because less varied. But Scofield, catalyzed by this Bartleby, seems to make his thoughts speak, articulates with pause and rhythm, renders a whole man with his inflections of the commonplace. On balance, it's more impressive than his Lear in Peter Brook's film.

Anthony Friedmann, the director, doesn't yet know much about making films, but at least he appreciates acting. Thanks to him for that—from me and, I hope, others.

Tokyo Story

(March 18, 1972)

THE British film journal *Sight and Sound* conducted an international poll last fall asking critics to list their ten favorite films of all time. On my list—and on four others—was *Tokyo Story* by Yasujiro Ozu, made in 1953. I first saw it last spring in the Japanese retrospective at the New York Museum of Modern Art. Now *Tokyo Story* is having its first theatrical release in the U.S. I've seen it again, and I'm happy that it was on my list.

Ozu made fifty-four films, of which only a handful have been released in this country. I have seen only three besides this one. He was born in 1903, died in 1963, and is one of the two best Japanese directors I know, the other being Akira Kurosawa (*Rashomon, Ikiru,* etc.). In his own country Ozu is called the most Japanese of directors, and a Westerner can see at least a little of why this is so. But that is a defining, not a limiting comment. (Who is more Swedish than Bergman?) There is treasure for everyone in *Tokyo Story*—and shame that we have all had to wait so long for it.

The films of Ozu's last period, the ones I know, tend toward a *largo* tempo, and are crystallized in loving but austere simplicity. Kurosawa, a fine artist, is an immediately exciting director; Ozu, a fine artist, is not. Kurosawa is essentially a dramatist, Ozu a lyric poet whose lyrics swell quietly into the epic. Of his four late films, all of which have beauty, *Tokyo Story* is the most successful.

The reader may find it hard to believe that a wonderful work could be made from this story. An elderly couple who live in the south of Japan, with their unmarried schoolteacher daughter, go to visit their married children and their grandchildren in Tokyo. During their visit they also see their widowed daughter-in-law, whose husband was killed in the war eight years before. Then the old couple return home, and the old lady sickens, badly. The children gather at her deathbed. After her death, they go home, and the old man is alone.

This material makes a film of two hours and twenty minutes. It also makes a film that encompasses so much of the viewer's life that you are convinced you have been in the presence of someone who knew you very well. Students of mine were asked recently to write papers on what they know about Chaplin. One of them began: "I don't know how much I know about Chaplin, but he certainly knows a lot about me." That seems to me one excellent definition of superior art, and it applies to Ozu. As for his societal remoteness, the most obvious and fundamentally the truest point about Ozu is that by being "most Japanese," he has been universal.

The beauty begins with the script, written by Ozu and Kogo Noda, who collaborated with him through most of his career. Chishu Ryu, who plays the old man and who acted in very many Ozu films, said (*Sight and Sound,* Spring 1964):

Mr. Ozu looked happiest when he was engaged in writing a scenario with Mr. Kogo Noda, at the latter's cottage. . . . By the time he had finished writing a script . . . he had already made up every image in every shot, so that he never changed the scenario after we went on the set. The words were so polished up that he would not allow us even a single mistake.

Other good directors often work otherwise. With Ozu the result is not mechanical execution of a blueprint but the fulfillment of a design. He knows that when a passing neighbor wishes the old couple bon voyage at the beginning, the same neighbor will speak to the lonely old man at the end. He knows that, when he shows us a baseball uniform hanging on a clothesline outside a son's window, it will later tie in thematically with the daughter's class of children singing Japanese words to a Stephen Foster tune.

The subjects dealt with in this film are the subjects of soap opera—with one crucial difference. As the film starts, as we "locate" its components and its movement—the trip to Tokyo—we expect that there will be dramatic developments. *There are none,* except for the death of the old woman very near the end. A lesser film maker would have thought: "Now what complications must I devise to keep things interesting?" Ozu, with Noda, thinks only: "What are these lives like?

Really like?" And by holding to truth, much more than to naturalism, he gives us a process of mutual discovery, the characters' and ours.

In Tokyo the old couple learn that their doctor son is not quite the success, nor quite the man, they imagined; and that their married daughter has been coarsened into a penny-biting, suspicious shop-keeper. The breath of love they did not expect is from the daughter-in-law, who is still bound to her dead husband's memory, although both she and his parents know that he wasn't the most admirable of men. In responsive concern, it is they, the dead husband's parents, who urge her to remarry.

Three instrumentalities give this film its exquisite cinematic texture. First, the acting. Ryu, the bent, faintly ludicrous, somewhat egocentric, truly dignified old man. (With a partiality for drink—Ozu understands contradictions.) Chieko Higashiyama, his wife, quite homely, who—like Eleanor Roosevelt—becomes *facially* beautiful as her spirit is manifested. Setsuko Hara, the daughter-in-law, tall, ungainly, humane (one feels) partly out of fear to be selfish, out of fear of desire, but nevertheless humane.

Then there is Ozu's punctuation. As a composer uses rests or holds a chord, he puts in a shot of an empty street after a busy scene, or a railroad track, or a small ship passing, or an empty corridor in a house. This gives us time to let what has just happened sink in even further and helps to place it. The world, imperturbable, surrounds the perturbations of its people.

Third, inevitably, Ozu's eye. His famous characteristic is the "Ozu shot," the camera placed at the eye level of a person seated on a *tatami,* the Japanese floor mat. Much of the film is seen from this "national" viewpoint, even when characters are standing. That's perhaps as much a matter of psychology as of vision. Ozu's vision gives us such compositions as the stout old woman and her little grandson silhouetted on a hilltop; the old couple seated on a curved sea wall at a resort outside Tokyo, seen from behind, tiny but together against the illimitable sea; or the camera moving slowly past a pavilion in a Tokyo park until, around the corner, we see, again from behind, the old couple seated, eating their lunch—a moment of inexplicable, deep poignancy. In these scenes and many others, Ozu seems to be saying: "These are atoms. In any one atom is the universe. My task is not to dishonor the universe by honoring these atoms."

Symmetry is important to him but never becomes tiresome. Two

pairs of sandals outside a hotel bedroom door, precisely placed, show
that two people, en route through their lives together, are spending
this particular night behind that door. On a larger scale, he balances
sequences. At the beginning, the parents travel to the children; at the
end, the children travel to the parents. In Tokyo the old woman and
the daughter-in-law have a scene alone together, a very moving one in
which the old woman spends the night in the younger woman's small
apartment while the old man is out drinking with some pals. At the
end it is the old man who has a scene alone with the daughter-in-law,
after his wife's death. He tells her that his wife said her night in the
apartment was her happiest time in Tokyo, and he gives the girl the
old woman's watch as a keepsake.

Which raises the subject of scale. Everything in the film is cali-
brated with such refinement that feelings are always restrained but
never lost; so that when, near the end, the girl takes the watch and
cries quietly, the effect is of a tremendous emotional climax.

If I had to choose one word as the theme of *Tokyo Story,* it would
be "passage." Time passing, life passing, with the ache and (if we
admit it) the relief that this implies. Out of the loins of these two
people whom we see sleeping quietly side by side came the children
who are now turned away from them, and we know it will happen to
the children with their children; and the old people know it and,
without saying so, are content to have had what they have had and to
have been part of the process.

If I had to choose one word to describe Ozu himself, it would be
"purity." Like the Dreyer of *Joan of Arc,* the Bresson of *Diary of a
Country Priest,* Ozu gives us the sense that questions of talent and
ambition have been settled or forgotten, that he is now self-centered
in what can be called a selfless way. In *Tokyo Story* he is placing on
the screen the very least that will fulfill the truth of what he has seen.
There is no brave consciousness of integrity. He is simply consecrated
to serving life simply, and proudly.

The Godfather

(April 1, 1972)

HURRICANE Marlon is sweeping the country, and I wish it were more than hot air. A tornado of praise—cover stories and huzzahs—blasts out the news that Brando is giving a marvelous performance as Don Corleone in *The Godfather,* the lapsed Great Actor has regained himself, and so on. As a Brando-watcher for almost thirty years, I'd like to agree.

But from his opening line, with his back toward us, Brando betrays that he hasn't even got the man's voice under control. (Listen to the word "first." Pure Brando, not Corleone.) Insecurity and assumption streak the job from then on. They have put padding in his cheeks and dirtied his teeth, he speaks hoarsely and moves stiffly, and these combined mechanics are hailed as great acting. I don't see how any gifted actor could have done less than Brando does here.

His resident power, his sheer innate force, has rarely seemed weaker. His gift of mental transformation, the conviction that the changes are interior and that the externals merely reflect them, is not nearly so strong here as in, say, *The Young Lions* or *Viva Zapata* or *On the Waterfront* or *Teahouse of the August Moon.* He is handicapped by poor make-up: his hair is not gray enough and his hairline ought to have been altered so that he doesn't constantly suggest Brando. But the real fault is his own: his laxness, sloth. He has become so lazy in recent years that he is willing to take intent for deed. Corleone has no moments of outburst—the Brando trademark, the leap of flame out of menacing quiet—so his dominance has to come from imagination; muscled by concentration. What Brando manufactures is surface—studied but easy effects.

A few moments ring true. When he hears of the death of his son, an ache starts deep in him and works to the surface through the fissures in the old man's emotional armor. But generally, as they say at the Actors Studio that he used to frequent, he gives us mere indication. It's only the superficial contrast with the "standard" Brando that is making people gasp.

Compare Brando's performance with Jean Gabin in virtually the same role in a recent French film called *The Sicilian Clan.* What authority Gabin had, how the waters of the world parted before him.

If it's argued that Gabin had a headstart by reason of age and temperament, that only proves my point: Brando is being praised because of the difference between him and this role, not because of his achievement in it. The magnificent talent that dozed off some years ago is not fully awakened yet.

Like star, like film. The keynote is inflation. Because the picture has so much of the commonplace, it escapes being called commonplace. In no important way is it any better than *The Brotherhood* (1968), on the same subject. (The word Mafia is never mentioned, but it doesn't need to be.) *The Godfather* was made from a big best seller, a lot of money was spent on it, and it runs over three hours. Therefore it's significant.

We're getting the usual flood of comments that the Mafia is only mirror-image corporate capitalism. (All the killings in the film are said to be "business, not personal.") These high-school analogies ignore, among other things, the origins of the Mafia and its blood bonds of loyalty, which have nothing to do with capitalism. Almost every one in *The Godfather* is either a murderer or an accessory, so its moral center depends on inner consistency and on implicit contrast with non-murdering citizens around it. As the picture winds on and on, episode after episode, its only real change is the Mafia's shift from "nice" gambling and prostitution to take on "dirty" narcotics. (Time, the late 1940s.) Well, I suppose everything's going to hell, even the morality of the Mafia, but the picture certainly takes a long, long time to get there.

Al Pacino, as Brando's heir, rattles around in a part too demanding for him. James Caan is adequate as his older brother. The surprisingly wretched score by Nino Rota contains a quotation from "Manhattan Serenade" as a plane lands in Los Angeles. Francis Ford Coppola, the director and co-adapter (with Mario Puzo), has saved all his limited ingenuity for the shootings and stranglings, which are among the most vicious I can remember on film.

What's Up, Doc?

(April 1, 1972)

PETER Bogdanovich has now made his third imitation. *Targets* was derived from Hollywood's prewar horror file. *The Last Picture Show* suggested the Southern sex-and-sweat film of the fifties and sixties. With *What's Up, Doc?*, he's back to the thirties for a screwball comedy. It's Bogdanovich's original story, with screenplay by Buck Henry, David Newman, and Robert Benton, but it's really a quick trip through the archives.

There's an absent-minded professor hero and a madcap heroine who gets him away from his stuffy fiancée. There's a mix-up with four identical suitcases, hotel detectives, crooks, a bathtub-and-underwear sequence, and a prolonged auto chase including the fresh-asphalt bit, the stepladder bit, and the two men with the sheet of plate glass. And there's the climactic courtroom scene in which the whole mix-up is synopsized and recapitulated for its effect on a long-suffering judge.

So Bogdanovich tries to have it two ways. For those who don't know the comedies of Howard Hawks, Gregory LaCava, etc., it may—just possibly—seem fresh. For initiates, it's a series of "in" jokes—beginning with the deliberately corny opening, in which the credits are presented on the turning pages of a huge book.

It's all rather like a nineteenth-century imitation of Elizabethan blank-verse drama. Apart from differences in talent, the trouble is anachronism. I couldn't believe that our age produced this film; this decade's gaiety, such as it is, is less physical, for one thing. I laughed occasionally—some of the lines are formula-funny. (Even though they have dredged up the world's oldest auto joke. When she's driving, he says excitedly: "This is a one-way street." She says: "I'm only going one way.") But I didn't laugh at anything that *happened*—and this in a fast-moving farce.

Partly this is because the film doesn't have any thirties stars. Ryan O'Neal is not Cary Grant, he's a somewhat livelier Tab Hunter. Barbra Streisand is not Jean Arthur or Rosalind Russell. When Streisand chases a man, my heart goes out to the fugitive. And her idea of farce-acting is vulgar stridency. She's a pro (especially as singer), which O'Neal is not, but to me, an unattractive one. Millions, I know, think otherwise.

Where will Bogdanovich strike next? Which archive shelf? The
Western? The thriller? The zombie flick? In a very few years he has
established himself as our leading mockingbird—with a considerable
gift for imitation. His career seems assured. The one thing we don't
have to fear from him is originality.

The Sorrow and the Pity

(*April 15, 1972*)

LAST year, a four-and-a-half-hour documentary from Argentina, *The
Hour of the Furnaces,* a fine work. This year a four-and-a-half-hour
documentary from France, *The Sorrow and the Pity,* another fine
work. *Furnaces* is revolutionary propaganda, *Sorrow* is historical
inquiry. The first film looks at the past to make people behave
differently in future. The second one looks at the past and, rather
chillingly, leaves the future up to us.

The subject is the German occupation of France, the only occupied
country in the Second World War that collaborated with Germany.
The director, Marcel Ophuls (son of the director of *Lola Montes*),
has not tried to explain France's behavior; he has put a great deal of
varied evidence in front of us, while a lot of the people who were
involved are still around to talk of it, and has juxtaposed it with
newsclips from the past. A literary critic, intending to praise this
picture, called it "a fascinating hodgepodge." I've rarely read a less
accurate description of anything. At the furthest remove from a
hodgepodge, this film is an extraordinarily well-wrought work, which
makes part of its point through its being.

It begins with a wedding in Germany in 1969. The father of the
bride, interviewed at the banquet table, surrounded by his wife and
the young couple, is a former *Wehrmacht* captain who was stationed
in Clermont-Ferrand, near Vichy, during the Occupation. His comments about the present and the past take us to Clermont-Ferrand, on
which city the whole film is based. A series of interviews is threaded
through the film; and earlier film material about the people interviewed, or the matters they describe, is interwoven. The subjects are
residents of the city and vicinity, other people whose comments bear
on what happened there, and well-known people whose careers were
involved with all of Europe.

Among the well-known people are Albert Speer, Walter Warlimont of the *Wehrmacht* Supreme Command, Lord Avon (Anthony Eden), General Sir Edward Spears, Jacques Duclos, the French Communist, and, thank heaven, Pierre Mendès-France, surely one of the few great men in politics in our time, shamefully wasted, who predictably reveals himself as thoughtful, witty, modest, resolute, and sad.

Lesser-known figures are no less fascinating: an aristocratic French rightist who fought with the forgotten Charlemagne Division of the *Waffen SS* on the Russian front; two stout old farmer-brothers who were in the Resistance; a pharmacist; an English musical-comedy performer who had been a secret agent; a former *Wehrmacht* soldier who had been a prisoner of the *maquis* in 1944; a pair of old French schoolmasters. Others, many others.

The film is in two parts, one about the fall of France, the other about events under the Germans until the Liberation. Ophuls has worked for balance in his materials, believing—quite rightly—that the best balance he could make would be the best case he could make. Certain matters are skimped, the role of the Church, for instance; otherwise, Ophuls shows us that Anglophobia and anti-Semitism are sometimes latent but always chronic in France, that venality exists there as everywhere, and so does heroism; but that, for all the seeming explanations, the reason for difference between France and, say, Denmark is like quicksilver in the cracks. Honor the heroes, Ophuls seems to say, we have to cling to the fact that they existed; but be careful of feeling superior to the others.

Some of the news clips Ophuls has found are absorbing: Hitler touring the almost-deserted early morning streets of Paris; Hitler being (if you can believe it) almost attractive in a laughing conversation in his railroad car. And besides the preordained contrasts between past and present, Ophuls has worked out some nice harmonies in the present: for instance, Mendès-France's account of his trial by the Vichy government alongside his lawyer's comments on the trial.

One talent that is often skimped in discussing this kind of film is the ability to interview. I assume that lots of subjects were cut out because they didn't respond well, but lots of material is cut from any picture. Ophuls and André Harris, who worked with him, asked the kinds of questions that drew genuine answers, not interviewese, from much-interviewed people: as when Spears speaks of seeing French

sailors in London with English girls on the day that the British fleet
was to bombard the French fleet at Mers-el-Kebir.

Another reason for the interviews' success is preparation. When
the smarmy Comte de Chambrun, professional apologist for his
father-in-law Pierre Laval, cites statistics in support of Vichy's
humanitarianism, Ophuls interrupts to say that he knows those statistics, and knows that they are partial and misleading. Then he holds
the camera for a moment on Chambrun's silence.

Small keen revelations abound. Mendès-France recalls his nighttime escape from a Vichy prison into a tree-lined street (something
like Bresson's *A Man Escapes*) and how he had to linger on top of
the wall until a pair of lovers below decided to go home to bed. The
English secret agent says that one reason for his (very courageous)
service was that he is a homosexual and wanted to prove himself. The
Grave brothers (like farmers out of Rouquier's *Farrebique*) take us
down into their old wine cellar for a glass, commenting that they've
been down those steps a good many times in their long lives; and
Louis Grave tells us that he refused to revenge himself after the war
on the neighbor whose denunciation sent him to Buchenwald.
("What for?" he asks with quiet acceptance of more than we will ever
see.) La Vigerie, a founder of the Liberation movement, tells us with
humorous candor that he thinks most people who came into the
Resistance were maladjusted. (Something like Koestler's theory
about radicals.) The German ex-soldier says that it's just as well his
country lost the war or else they'd all now be doing Occupation
service in Africa and America; and in his *Lederhosen* he takes
another sip of beer. (On the other hand, I've met veterans of the
Wehrmacht and *Luftwaffe* who hold views of their service very different from those of any German in this film.)

Another technique has to be praised highly: the dubbing. In a
picture of this kind, where there is so much talk and where there is no
acting, probably dubbing was the best solution to the language
problem. The English is presented as translation, not as lip-sync
replacement. A speaker starts in his own language, and then his voice
is faded under an English-language translation. Not a novel device,
but it's used very carefully here, with voices that sound apt.

One more production point. This film was sponsored by three television networks, French, Swiss, and German. Switzerland is not
mentioned in the film. France and Germany are often shown unflat-

teringly. The film has been broadcast on German TV, not French TV. (Although it has played in French theaters.)

The Sorrow and the Pity is, first, a record. It was important that these statements, from chiefs to a hairdresser who served fifteen years for collaboration, should be preserved, both as they support and contradict what is generally believed.

Second, it is a reminder. History consists, for the most part, of material we never knew or material we have forgotten: no one can keep the whole past on the leading edge of his mind. (I had completely forgotten Mers-el-Kebir, in which the British killed 1600 French sailors. Lord Avon makes clear the hard decision his government had to make, to keep the French ships out of German hands; still, those were 1600 people, too.) Without the maximum possible knowledge of the past, especially the immediately antecedent past, we know little of who we are and even less of what we ought to do.

Third, most important from any view, *The Sorrow and the Pity* is a fine film. This "hodgepodge" is so well made that its very existence is a statement about its subject. Frank interviews and ironic contrasts are not new. But to put all the elements of this picture in reciprocating balance, moved by internal rhythms, framed by a sharp pictorial eye, guided by a good political intelligence, is to make history into art. Through the richness of the work, through the experiencing of it *as film,* the facts deepen. When we see the Grave brothers in their fields, with the exquisite Auvergne hills behind them, we understand a little more of both the sorrow and the pity.

There is no neat lesson to be drawn, no high-hearted resolve with which to leave the theater. Frenchmen are not Martians, they are our kinsmen—the heroes and the collaborators and the great mass of the apathetic. We all remember Stephen Dedalus saying, "History is a nightmare from which I am trying to awake." Ophuls implies that Dedalus was wasting his time; there is no awakening. One is more sensible to try for a little decency within the nightmare.

Pocket Money

(May 13, 1972)

IT takes a lot of nerve to make a pleasant picture, one that's not intended to excite or scare or stir us or even make us laugh aloud much, one that's just intended to be easy to watch. *The Flim-Flam Man,* with George C. Scott, started that way but lost its nerve and got dramatic. The Czech film, *Intimate Lighting,* did not lose its nerve and was pleasant throughout. A new one, quite different, is *Pocket Money.* It ambles and rambles, there are sections in it that almost audibly ask to be overlooked, it doesn't arrive anywhere much or deliver any great thump while getting there, but I certainly was pleased to be sitting in front of it.

It's a contemporary Western—a Southwestern, really. Paul Newman is a rancher who runs into money trouble. He takes a job buying rodeo cattle in Mexico, knowing that his boss is a sharper, but he has no alternative. In Mexico he looks up an old pal, Lee Marvin, who helps him. Like the boy on the bicycle who heads for the tree, these two head slowly but inevitably toward the reaming that they know their employer has in store for them.

This comedy has two principal aims. The first is to parody the conventional Western by breezily side-stepping all its conventions— the shoot-out, the chase, and so on. The film behaves like a steeple-chase horse that walks around all the jumps, which is funny. We know, because of our moviegoing education, when the moment has come for the big fight: so do the characters. They deliberately tease around the edge of it, and then don't have anything like a real fight. It's a genuinely comic concept, and it works.

The second aim is the characterization of the two principals. These are good, largely successful attempts at American rural comedy. Newman is determined and not very bright, good-hearted and knowingly gullible, hot-tempered and quickly repentant. In his last previous film, *Sometimes a Great Notion,* which he directed and which was one of the muzziest films in years, he gave a perfect performance as a stiff-necked, rugged-individualist lumberman. Here he is simply and completely transformed. No make-up, no limp or tic. His accent has changed but that is merely part of his complete conversion to this other man. Newman found himself a model or models, fashioned this man in his mind, and *is* that man, from his first on-screen breath. To see these two Newman films in a row is to learn a little of what acting is really about (and, incidentally, to see what has gone wrong with Brando in *The Godfather*).

Marvin, one of the few effortlessly compelling American screen actors, plays a man shrewd within severe limits, smooth except when he is jumpy, a great relisher of situations, a man in perfect control of very little. Marvin has waded through a lot of bad pictures lately, but here he gives his best comic performance since *Cat Ballou*.

Some favorite moments: Newman, in a fit of frustration, stops his car, gets out, picks up a bottle from a garbage dump, smashes it against a wall, then gets back in his car, and drives on. Marvin, badly hung over, comes out of his dowdy Mexican hotel room to wash up on the balcony, reaches blindly for the soap, and touches a pigeon that has roosted on the shelf. That, friends, is comic reacting.

The script is by Terry Malick, from a novel by J. P. S. Brown, adapted by John Gay. The dialogue is excellent, flavorful, dotted with those florid locutions that are the mark of a writer who knows his people and knows that they sometimes use surprising words. The direction is by Stuart Rosenberg, not the world's greatest master of camera placement. The action is, incomprehensibly, sometimes placed at a distance or behind a distracting object, like a parked car full of irrelevant people. But at least Rosenberg understood his stars. The cinematographer is Laszlo Kovacs (*Five Easy Pieces,* among others). Kovacs is overfond of sunspots on the lens and halation from white shirts, but some of the picture, like the last sequence in front of a dilapidated lonely railroad station, is stunning.

I could have done without such episodes as the one with the Mexican girl or with the nonexistent rustlers, but, in complete contradiction, I wish the film had gone on. In further contradiction, I liked the casual way it ended. People sometimes say that they are hungry for valid Americana in American films. Here is an American folk comedy, today. Expect little; get lots.

Slaughterhouse-Five

(May 13, 1972)

CONGRATULATIONS to Stephen Geller, Dede Allen, Miroslav Ondricek, and George Roy Hill for their work on *Slaughterhouse-Five*. Geller made a cohesive, dramatized script from Kurt Vonnegut's novel; Allen, one of the best film editors alive, dexterously braided the three-part story; Ondricek, the cinematographer, fixed quintessences—the gravy of suburbia, the grayness of bombed Dresden; and Hill directed with some compassion and humor.

The Vonnegut novel is an example of that much overrated author at his best: facile wryness, sophomoric rue, mousetrack implications of cosmic mysteries. His huge success in college dormitories—and with those faculty members who wish they could be living in them—is easily explicable: his philosophy could hardly be more accessibly ironic, his style more glibly implicative, his humor more nudgingly collusive, his humanism less demanding or more flattering. Like many inferior novelists, he films better than he reads; film supplies what he doesn't. But Geller, his adapter, could not—or at any rate, did not—supply the fundamental omission: a theme.

The book travels back and forth in time so constantly that one hardly knows whether it is written "now" and flashing back or "then" and flashing forward. That's fine, that fluid time-locus, in itself. The three main stories are the hero's wartime experience in the bombing of Dresden; his postwar well-upholstered married life with a well-upholstered wife; and his dream(?) life on the planet Tralfamadore, where a Hollywood starlet is brought to mate with him in a large plastic dome.

The war stuff, in book and film, is nicely balanced: German soldiers and U.S. soldiers are all victims of power madness. The suburban stuff, in both, is trite cartoon. The planetary stuff, in both, is Arthur C. Clarke warmed over: the wise spacefolk who look down pityingly on infantile earthlings and try to enlighten them. Outside of Vonnegut's cleverness in weaving these three strands, what is the point of it all? Is it that the war was fought only to return to a materialist society and that Out There people know better? All this cinematic apparatus just for that? And so banally expressed? Geller has given the film script a wholeness of form, but it still leaves us with an unfed feeling. After all the table-setting and headwaiter's flourishes, where was the meal?

Michael Sacks plays the hero, Billy Pilgrim. (*There's* a modest name to give your hero.) Sacks is so obviously intended to be Everyman that he ends up No-man, undistinguished and uninteresting. Sharon Gans plays the fat wife with porky devotion. Eugene Roche is good as a G.I. who was a Boston trade-school teacher. Ron Liebman, the violently vindictive Lazzaro, is more of a self-flagellant than an actor, but here he whips up some useful furies. Valerie Perrine, the starlet, becomes sexier as the picture goes on; maybe that's because I couldn't hear her dialogue in her first scenes.

A lot of good makings in this picture; but very little is made.

A Day in the Death of Joe Egg

(May 20, 1972)

"SITTING about like Joe Egg" is an English phrase which, in American, is "sitting around like a bump on a log." A young English couple have a helpless, mute, spastic daughter of ten named Josephine, or Jo. They call her Joe Egg.

The English playwright Peter Nichols began with an overwhelming situation in his play, *A Day in the Death of Joe Egg*. The manner in which the parents treat their vegetable child is utterly anti-heartbreak: jokes, irreverences, improvised conversations, with reactions and thoughts supplied by them for the inanimate, putty-like child whose only signs of life are occasional epileptic fits. The horror, the irrationality of the horror, is slashed into us through the breezy jokes and flippancies, and memories and sexiness of the young parents.

But, as noted, it is a situation. Not a play. The first half, when I saw it on Broadway a few years ago, was harrowing in a pleasurably painful way; the second half was padded to make the play full-length, and strained to make a drama grow where none had been predicated. A painful situation is not necessarily a dramatic one. So Nichols brought in the husband's mother and another married couple and tried to work up an attempt by the young father to let the child die and added some other stuff about the young mother's possible infidelity. It ended with the child's recovery from near-death, yet again, and the father's departure because he felt he had no chance against the child in the mother's life.

I've described the play because, allowing for suitable changes, it is also Nichols's screenplay. He brings in the mother-in-law and the other couple somewhat earlier, but the immediate iron grip of the work, the loosening, the patent attempts to tighten it, and the unpredicated ending are still there. (No slightest hint at the beginning that the husband's marital situation is so desperate he may leave. His wife even promises him the sex that he wants when he comes home from work.) At least two things are true about this picture: it's unsatisfying, and it's not to be missed. Nichols writes springy, stabbing dialogue, and the first hour or so is unforgettable.

The performance of Alan Bates as the young father is a mixed matter, too. Bates is very certainly growing as an actor. He has more variety in his voice, attack in his speech, vitality in his face—his eyes are much more use to him than they were when he began. None of this is mechanical, all of it is a matter of improved technique as an instrument of imagination. His upper lip is still distractingly immobile, and it keeps his speech from complete incisiveness, neither of which is a small point, particularly in a film actor; but he is serious, hard-working, and in this film, sometimes moving. Compared with Albert Finney, who played it on Broadway, Bates is straitened and somewhat shallow. This is especially notable when he slips into the flashback imaginary roles of a German physician or a hearty clergyman. Compared with Finney, Bates is a reputable road-company replacement. Uncompared with Finney, he has a pretty good grip on the part's humanity.

Janet Suzman, who played half the title role of *Nicholas and Alexandra,* is somewhat more in command as the mother. (She does have bad luck with her screen children. First a hemophiliac, now a spastic.) If she lacks a strong personality, she is still a very competent actress.

Peter Medak, the director, made a first picture called *Negatives* (1968) which was an artily busy disaster. *Joe Egg,* in its camerawork and editing, errs at the other extreme, on the edge of stodginess. In some scenes we are conscious of theater set-ups, arbitrarily interrupted with close-ups or reverse shots. And Medak's direction of Bates's irritating mother is much too heavy-handed. Overall, however, he has placed the story before us with care and sympathy, if not with brilliance.

The trouble with criticizing an unusual work, when one must, is that it may get to sound like a usual one. *Joe Egg* is not a run-of-anyone's-mill film. It's a faulty but intelligent and interesting picture, like the play from which it came. Inevitably it raises the question of Divine Will and, in general, raises it fairly delicately. The mother believes that the fact the child is "just alive" is itself a miracle. The father thinks of God, when he thinks of him, as a "manic-depressive rugby player." It is the parents, of course, who are the footballs, not the insensate child. The film's familiar arguments, pro and con euthanasia, add nothing. No, that's not true. They add to the immediacy of a situation in which the entrapped people happen to have wit and humor, and therefore feel the pain more sharply.

Uncle Vanya

(*June 17, 1972*)

THE question—again—is: What is supposed to satisfy us in films of great plays? An approximation of atmosphere, a synopsis of the text, some evidence that the actors would be well cast if only they had the full roles to play? Are we supposed to forget that the play exists, and to judge the film as an independent creation?

The problem is not new, and I'm not the only one who has written about it before. It persists, and it comes up again with a Soviet film of *Uncle Vanya* about which there has been critical joy. When a film is made from a minor play, all we ask is that it be a good film: because the only reason for making it was to produce a good film. But the film of a Chekhov play is made because of Chekhov. It ought to be good as film, but how can we separate the source-motive from the result? How can we excuse adulteration on the ground that now we are in a different medium? Isn't that, in fact, just one more patronizing derogation of film? (A common implicit practice among those who claim to be "real" film critics.)

Three of the actors in this version are excellently cast. Innokenti Smoktunovsky, as Vanya, is a well-bred man with overripe insides going to seed. Irina Kupchenko, as Sonia his niece, has lovely reticence, affection, and an air of untapped sexuality that will never be realized. Irina Miroschnichenko, as Yelena, is a delicate golden dream, lightweight but with the self-assurance that a lightweight person has a right to exist, too.

Sergei Bondarchuk, probably the best-known contemporary Soviet film figure, plays Dr. Astrov. (Bondarchuk directed *War and Peace* and played Pierre.) His Astrov—not Bondarchuk himself but Astrov —seems conscious of being a character in a Chekhov play. Bondarchuk has presence, but he trades heavily on the conventional symbology of mood and suffering that has become the cliché of Chekhov acting.

The young director, Andrei Mikhalkov-Konchalovsky, also made the adaptation. Of course the play had to be adapted for the screen; the issue is, how much license is there in that phrase "of course"? Even judging by subtitles, anyone who knows the play will know that subtleties and developments have been sliced, emphases have been altered.

In 1951 André Bazin wrote a long two-part essay called "Theater and Cinema." I would argue with some of this essay but certainly not with the section in which he wrote:

However one approaches it, a play whether classic or modern is unassailably protected by its text. There is no way of adapting the text without disposing of it and substituting something else, which may be better but is not the play. This is a practice, for that matter, restricted of necessity to second-class authors or to those still living, since the masterpieces that time has hallowed demand, as a postulate, that we respect their texts.

Bazin might agree that this *Uncle Vanya* is "something else," and not something better. Fundamentally, anyone who sets out to make a version of *Vanya* that runs an hour and fifty minutes has set out on an esthetic fraud, whatever his visual approach or cinematic injunctions. The camera dollying through empty rooms, the insertion of socially significant still photographs, the final (dreadful) helicopter shot do not compensate for the omissions, nor "convert" them into cinema. And what was the purpose of the numerous switches from black-and-white to color? (Soviet color, by the way, is far behind American. If the missile gap were as decisively in our favor as the color-film gap, Nixon would not have needed to go to Moscow.) The switching makes no more sense than in Lindsay Anderson's *If* . . . and the silhouette fade-outs to close scenes are technically below the work done in some U.S. film schools.

Further, the film distorts. When Vanya loses control of himself and takes a couple of shots at the Professor, Chekhov specifies that the latter is frightened. Here the camera looks past the Professor standing defiantly statuesque, a Russian Wyatt Earp, allowing Vanya to take a second shot, which misses. This is nonsense.

Much has been said of the "Russianness" of this Chekhov. Unfortunately, national origin guarantees nothing, as the Moscow Art Theater productions proved in New York. The best *Uncle Vanya* I have seen was done by the National Theater in London in 1964, directed by Olivier, with himself as Astrov, even better than when he did it in New York with the Old Vic in 1946. To protest that the Olivier production is gone and the Soviet film is available is to argue expediency, not art.

But the film did highlight one point about Chekhov for me. Here are some people merely living their lives, seen in such a way that the sheaths are rubbed off *by themselves* and we see the deepest currents that make them what they are. Yet, in this play as in *The Sea Gull,* much of the spiritual agony and social waste comes from the simple fact of unrequited love. If Astrov loved Sonia, if Nina loved Treplev, those two plays would have entirely different endings. At first, this may seem like plot mechanics: girl does not get boy or vice versa, the author decrees, so that we can have a play about suffering. But one sees that what this master is really saying is: a society in which the caprice of love, the roulette of sexual attraction, is the determinant of one's fulfillment, is specious.

La Salamandre; Charles, Dead or Alive

(July 1, 1972)

WALKING in Berne, in the early sixties, I passed a café full of hippies. A Swiss hippie! The idea was something like a Swiss sailor. Well, there *are* Swiss sailors (they have a merchant marine), and there are young Swiss rebels. And there is a new Swiss film maker—new to this country, at least—who has been a Swiss sailor and is now a rebel.

But he is not particularly young. Alain Tanner was born in Geneva in 1929, took a degree in economics, went to sea for a time, went to England in 1955, worked at the British Film Institute and for BBC-TV, returned (after some film work in Paris) to Switzerland, and made numerous documentaries for Swiss TV. In 1969 he made his first fiction feature, in 1971 his second. Both these pictures are now being shown here, and are welcome. Let's begin with the second.

La Salamandre is named for that mythical creature, the sala-mander, which can survive fire. It concerns two young Swiss men, both writers, and a girl. Pierre is a journalist who is commissioned to write a TV documentary about Rosemonde, who had been involved a year earlier in a shooting in which her uncle was wounded. Pierre needs help and calls in Paul, a more imaginative type, who supports himself as a housepainter and writes only when he pleases.

Pierre interviews Rosemonde and her uncle, and makes all the right intelligent, sympathetic journalistic moves. Paul at first refuses to meet Rosemonde, goes off to his suburban house outside Geneva, and works on his version of the script with some facts and much intuition. Eventually he does meet her at Pierre's place after she has spent a night with the latter.

Rosemonde is the focus of Tanner's story as she is of Pierre-Paul's. She is the seventh of ten children, in her early twenties, had an illegitimate child when she was seventeen, was sent to live with the uncle who used her as a drudge, and now works in a sausage factory. (She soon quits for a shoe shop; and she soon gets fired there for a peculiar but quite credible prankishness.)

She first appears as a commonplace girl. She is revealed gradually, in a different sense, as even more commonplace than we thought: she is baffled, shrewd, scared, libidinous, hungry for something she can't define—a thoroughly contemporary young human being, teased by a consumer society into aspirations she can't fulfill, into standards without resonance or sanity, into emotional complications without the possibility of complete investment. Near the end Paul asks her whether she really did shoot her uncle. (She has maintained for a year that her uncle did it himself by accident.) Slowly she smiles, and confesses it. That smile—the bleakness, the silly pride in at least one small accomplished private act—is terrible.

The film shows her moving, something like an older version of Antoine in Truffaut's *The 400 Blows,* from clumsy efforts at conformity to a break-out, with her future uncertain and unpromising. Equally important is the effect she has on the two men. After spending much time with her, sleeping with her, visiting her village with her, finding out more and more about her, the two men are unable to write the TV script. They become aware that, through her, they have touched more than they are able to deal with. They pass on from her life; she has no options, she has to remain in her life.

Tanner wrote the screenplay in collaboration with John Berger—I assume it is the same John Berger who is the English Marxist art critic and novelist. It is written as a film, to be fulfilled by faces and places and spaces, and yet, to judge by subtitles from the French, it is *written:* literate and pointed. Like Rosemonde herself, the story is ingeniously commonplace—it is made out of common events in such a way that they dramatize the forces beneath them.

The main influence on Tanner, obviously, is Godard, of the "bourgeois-revolutionary" period. The tone and intent of the piece are conceived as if to catch the characters and the film form itself by surprise, yet with an overall artistic discrimination. The root effect is of newsreel that is allowed to stray past its conventional boundaries so that we can see behind the figures, so to speak. There are lesser Godardian doodlings: Tanner calls the picture "a black-and-white film in color," for instance. And I'm aware that *La Salamandre* might be somewhat less interesting if it were French, might seem "one more," though better. The fact of its being Swiss, of its seeing a tiny prosperous country as a cage instead of a haven, increases its interest, as a kind of spiritual-esthetic-political travelogue.

But it would have real virtues if it were the hundredth Swiss film I'd seen instead of the first since *The Eternal Mask* (1937). Tanner's compositions and camera angles have a sense of concern, of a human attempt to look freshly but not freakishly. His editing is sharp, tart. He has a way, somewhat reminiscent of Antonioni, of deepening certain scenes simply by pressing on them. One day Rosemonde comes home from her routine job at the factory feeling empty and dehumanized. She puts on a rock record and begins to swing her head to it as if recharging batteries. Her roommate comes in, stops the record angrily, and leaves. The scene should end or change, no? But Tanner keeps the camera on Rosemonde as she continues to swing her head, smiling, in the silence, and her pleasure shifts to the edge of hysteria.

Bulle Ogier, who plays Rosemonde, looks like a mousy cross between Monica Vitti and Julie Harris, with sulks and insects crawling around inside her and with the ability to become very sexy when she chooses. Jean-Luc Bideau is attractively clumsy as the journalist. Jacques Denis is high-spirited and sensitive as the poetic housepainter.

Tanner's first feature, *Charles, Dead or Alive,* is again unfortunately labeled: "A Small Historical Fresco." Why "fresco"? Why anything? He wrote this script alone, possibly without a thought of Tolstoy's play *The Living Corpse,* but it's like an up-to-date Geneva version of that work. A successful middle-aged businessman, married, with two grown children, is discontented with his life and, instead of going to live with the gypsies like Tolstoy's hero, he goes to live with a couple of dropouts. The only one he informs of his whereabouts is his daughter, a student-rebel. His money-grubbing son hires a detective to find him, and in the end Charles is carted away out of his new happiness to an asylum, because he didn't want his old plump life.

This film is just as well-made as *La Salamandre*—both were acutely photographed by Renato Berta in brusque but understanding black-and-white—but *Charles* relies somewhat glibly on the audi-

ence's acceptance of certain assumptions, on pat symbols of alienation and the virtues of youthful revolution. A lesser facet of Godard
mars the script, a barrage of quotations like the Paris graffiti of May
'68. ("Be realistic. Ask the impossible.") These quotations, unlike
those from the Little Red Book, stoke the spirit of revolution without
providing a politics.

No question, however, that Tanner is a discovery. (Thanks, yet
once more, to New Yorker Films, who imported him, and *Tokyo
Story,* and many, many others.) Certainly he is a scion of the French
cinema of the sixties, but he has taken what suits him and has made it
his own. He knows what has happened in film and in himself; he not
only has the means to express himself, he has private experience to
explore. Character fascinates him, and he has the cinematic skill to
investigate it. Also, he has humor, compassion, and, to judge by two
films, a growing ability for ingratiating understatement. He is not so
far an innovator of any kind; he is a creative absorber—a gifted,
humane, observant film maker with a fine chance for a fine career.

Like Antonioni, Tanner did not make his first fiction feature until
he was almost forty. I draw no conclusion from the parallel; I merely
note it.

Frenzy

(July 8, 1972)

"THE old boy has come back." The word is already being buzzed
about the new Hitchcock film, *Frenzy,* and it certainly is his best in a
long time—since *North by Northwest* (1963). But the fact of the
matter is that it's Anthony Shaffer who has made the comeback for
him. Hitchcock hadn't much deteriorated as director in his recent
films; he merely had poor scripts. Now he has a fairly good one,
adapted by Shaffer (who wrote *Sleuth*) from a novel by Arthur La
Bern, and lo, it's the director who has come back.

Some critics and Hitchcock himself keep telling us that content
doesn't matter, style is all. In plotty suspense pictures! Hitchcock said
recently, "Too many films are looked at for their content. What's
more important is their treatment." Robin Wood begins his (gase-

ous) book on Hitchcock with the antique plaint that people are unable to *see* films, that they reduce them to literature instead of concentrating on the images. But then—to reply with another antique plaint—why aren't all films by a good image maker equally good? Or relatively so?

Arguably there are some directors who have made good films with mediocre material, but Hitchcock is surely not one of them. Look at *Marnie* and *Topaz* again, if you can, and see how sterile all the Hitchcockery is when it is used on stupid material. On the other hand, look again at *The Thirty-nine Steps* and see how the film lives, not because of the (very good) direction but basically because of the script by Alma Reville and Charles Bennett from John Buchan's novel. All of Hitchcock's successes are primarily writers' films—expertly directed, but overwhelmingly dependent on their scripts. How could it possibly be otherwise in the Hitchcock field?

Shaffer's script is not in the Reville-Bennett class, but it has some good forward motion, some thrills, and some good reworking of familiar facile Hitchcock ironies. Again there is a protagonist who, we soon learn, is innocent, although we see him being wrapped tighter and tighter in circumstantial evidence. (François Truffaut said to Hitchcock, "While your hero is generally innocent of the crime for which he's under suspicion, he is generally guilty of intentions before the fact," with which Hitchcock agreed.) Again there are sardonic juxtapositions: a (presumably) guilty man sits, background, in a pub while two men in the foreground discuss the murder. Again there are the false clues: we see a cut from a necktie around the neck of a strangled woman to a man putting on a similar necktie, but he is not the guilty man. (I spill few beans. We learn of his innocence early. The story is built on counterpoint between the seemingly guilty man and a seemingly innocent one.) Again the highly realistic texture is fractured by arrant movie mechanics: the hero's friend just happens to spot him in a park at a crucial moment and gives him shelter. Again there is a running gag: instead of the cricket enthusiasts of *The Lady Vanishes,* we get some skits on gourmet cooking. The police inspector's wife has culinary ambitions and, instead of feeding him the steak and veg for which he longs, inflicts fancy inedibles on him, as in recent Alka-Seltzer commercials. (The subtlest satire in the book is the inspector's "secret" meal in the office. His sausages and egg, which he relishes, look just as inedible as his wife's specialties.)

After a somewhat slow start, the story gets going, and makes us itch with the right frustration as we see the wrong man being cornered. Then just as he is tried and found guilty, as we might be willing to think that we are getting a full view of the dark side of the mirror, Hitchcock does a typical copout. The inspector who caught the hero remains transfixed by the latter's protestation as he is led from the dock—the cry that he will some day get the really guilty man. Then the inspector sets out to prove the innocence of the very man he has brought to book. *Why* the inspector should have been so readily changed is not really a matter of psychology but of box office.

But the familiar Hitchcock battery of cinematic devices has a generally good ground for operation in *Frenzy.* There is the razzle-dazzle murder editing, as in the *Psycho* shower, this time dealing with a rape and strangling—a sequence that will doubtless become a "classic" in editing classes for the easily impressed. There is the familiar quiet moment of murder-discovery, during which the camera waits outside while someone goes in and discovers the body we know is there. There is the weaving of locale into the fabric of the story—in this case, the Covent Garden market and what look like the actual premises of the Duckworth publishing company in that district.

This, in fact, is the first picture Hitchcock has made in London since the (abominable) *Stage Fright,* over twenty years ago, and we can be sure that Hitchcockians will sing about the opening helicopter shots—a long slow ride over the Thames and under Tower Bridge while we see the credits. A Return to Nativity, and so on. To me, it was just a distended travelogue shot, out of key with the film, upholstered with pompous music, not even a good contrast—as presumably intended—to the shock that soon follows. Hitchcock ends this shot with a politician speaking about pollution on the river-side: unfunny padding. If this long slow helicopter ride had ended smack on the floating corpse, which doesn't appear until after the pollution speech, the air ride might have been worthwhile.

I realize that I'm fluctuating in this review, between pros and cons, and I suppose that's because, even though I recognize that this is better than Hitchcock's latest work, sometimes genuinely exciting, and a film only an extremely skilled and experienced director could have made, still there is someting faintly loathsome about the film and about Hitchcock himself to me. He has said that his love of film is far more important to him than any considerations of morality, which might be an interesting statement from the Peckinpah of *The Wild Bunch* or the Polanski of *Repulsion.* But it has a tinny ring from

Hitchcock because his amorality is so suspect, his cynicism so pop, his explorations of evil so patently show biz. He turns his back on morality so coyly, so venally, that his lack of conviction becomes a lack rather than a conviction.

His voyeurism—the appeal to the Peeping Tom that he says has always been important to him—is more than faintly loathsome when it is sexual. Of course he gives us a glimpse of female pubic hair; he wasn't *not* going to take advantage of the new freedom. But he also gives us a sequence in a moving truck in which the murderer has to recover something from the grip of a naked dead female victim whom he had put in a sack of potatoes. First, diving into the sack amidst potatoes and legs, the murderer seems to perform parodic cunnilingus on the dead body. Then when he finds the object in her now-rigid hand, he takes out a knife and, as we are plainly shown, hacks and breaks her fingers. All this seems to me cheap sensationalism posing as sophisticated *frisson*.

The level of acting is higher than Hitchcock has had lately. Jon Finch, who was Polanski's Macbeth, is strong and angry and attractive as the hero. Barbara Leigh-Hunt and Anna Massey are, respectively, nicely smooth and nicely pathetic. Alec McCowen is amusingly clerkish as the inspector, and Vivien Merchant—Mrs. Very Harold Pinter of *The Homecoming* and the London *Old Times*—does a good breathy cartoon as his gastronomic wife. Barry Foster has a dodgy shiny-toothed gleam as the hero's false friend but not quite enough force. Hitchcock says, "The more successful the villain, the more successful the picture. That's a cardinal rule. . . ." Middling villain, middling success.

The Candidate

(August 5 & 12, 1972)

I came back from abroad to find one magazine's weekly list warning me against this political film, because the star, Robert Redford, has a likeness to the Kennedy brothers that is vulgarly exploited. I can't see why Redford suggests the Kennedys any more than he suggests John Lindsay or John Tunney. The character is modeled, not on individuals, I would say, but on the new political persona of the sixties:

slim, sexy, smartly dressed, intelligently humorous, socially concerned, and philosophically bland, young in feeling if not in fact. Why
in the world shouldn't this American phenomenon, of which there are
certainly more examples, be treated in American film?

It would be a small pity if this picture were ignored. The script is
by Jeremy Larner, a novelist, a contributor to *Dissent,* and a man
with experience of politicking. The director is Michael Ritchie, out of
TV, whose first film was *The Downhill Racer* (with Redford).
Ritchie has skill, if not much flavor. There are too many predictable
strophes in the camera movement and composition, particularly in
the crowd scenes, but on the whole the picture is seen neatly and
assembled briskly. It's fast and hip without bragging too much about
it.

Redford is a California lawyer, rich but working for the poor, son
of a former governor, who is invited by the Democratic Party to run
for senator against the white-haired incumbent. The campaign manager—Peter Boyle of *Joe,* who is easy and quiet—tells Redford his
job is to lose; the party simply needs a lamb for this particular
slaughter. What Redford will get out of it personally is some publicity
and a lift in his career. They hire a TV-spot producer, Allen Garfield,
that comic white grub, and what happens is unforeseen—by everyone
but us: Redford's personality begins to catch on and, as a personality, he gets elected. The last line of the film, which he speaks to
Boyle after he gets the news, is: "What do we do now?"

Most of the performers are adequate, including Melvyn Douglas as
the grudgingly helpful pa, and there is a good textural feel in the
picture, particularly in Ritchie's contrasts with coarse-grained TV
clips. Peripheral characters are used amusingly, particularly one of
those girls who gets turned on by good-looking politicians and who
pursues Redford tactfully until, we infer, she gets what she wants.

The Candidate has only one important trouble, but it's a big one. It
verges on the superfluous. After all the books about making and
selling presidents, all the inside views in press and on TV, can there
be anyone left in this country who does *not* know that large-scale
electoral success in this country is dependent on personality and
money and advertising skill, not on political conviction or states-
manly ability? All through *The Candidate* we keep thinking, "Yes,
that's how it is, all right." It is never boring, but it is never enlarging,
informationally or emotionally or thematically.

And it spotlights a vacancy. Political film usually means film about

126   LIVING IMAGES

elections. We very, very rarely get a film about a man or woman actually working in government. We get party bossing (*The Last Hurrah*) or comic grafting (*The Great McGinty*) but almost never a film about a person working in politics as a doctor works in medicine. The last one I can remember was British: *No Love for Johnnie* (1961) with Peter Finch. Law-enforcing, for much too obvious reasons, is incessantly treated; lawmaking, equally subject to human foible and infinitely more important, almost never.

Still, *The Candidate* is decent entertainment.

Deliverance

(August 5 & 12, 1972)

ON the second try, I managed to get through James Dickey's novel and wasn't particularly glad that I had bothered. The occasional glints in the prose didn't compensate for the labor of plodding after the parable. I kept thinking of Borges and his library of comment on unwritten books. If you can summarize a book very adequately in a paragraph, why bother to write it? Or read it?

The film, with screenplay by Dickey, is considerably worse. The novel takes us on a familiar journey through the thin ice of civilization to the dangerous black waters beneath—dangers from nature and from primitive man. The film starts out with heavy emphasis on nature, on its hidden savagery, and the despoilment of nature by technology. The first thing we see is a lumpy editorial, intercuts of bulldozers and sylvan beauty. But the only real drama comes from the encounter with two bestial mountaineers, who would have been what they are if bulldozers had never been invented. The four city men who foolhardily embark down a rushing river in two canoes and are warned against Ol' Man River could have had the same basic trouble on a highway in two cars if they had camped for the night.

Beyond the unfulfilled theme, the moral parallelisms of the script are intolerable. Burt Reynolds, who looks like a successor to Victor Mature, boasts at the beginning that he doesn't believe in insurance because he is proof against risk, so we know he's in for trouble. Jon Voight trembles at the beginning when he tries to shoot a deer with bow-and-arrow, so we know he's going to have to kill with that bow later.

No performance deserves comment. Voight's talent is wasted in a nondescript role. Next time I hope he has something better to do than rock climbing.

The director, John Boorman, is an Englishman who began his career impressively with *Having a Wild Weekend* (1965). Since then, although some have rhapsodized about *Point Blank,* I think his career has declined steadily. *Deliverance* seems to me even worse than *Leo the Last.* There is fundamentally no view of the material, just a lot of painful grasping and groping. The beauty-of-nature shots are trite, the drama is clumsy, and the editing clanks. It's difficult for a film that is not very tightly knit to unravel, but this one does.

And keeps on unraveling. Long after the picture is over, it continues, having shifted to a sort of police thriller. Dickey himself plays a sheriff. He's big, and he leans into cars very well.

Late Spring

(August 19 & 26, 1972)

ANOTHER film by Yasujiro Ozu, who made *Tokyo Story,* gets its U.S. premiere—a mere twenty-three years late. This 1949 work, *Late Spring,* antedates *Tokyo Story* by four years, and one can see, with the pleasures of hindsight, the developing techniques and film language that made the later picture a masterpiece.

It is possibly risky to say, but the chief reward in *Late Spring* is not in its materials, gratifying though they are. The highest benefit—as in *Tokyo Story,* though less strong—is appreciation of the artist himself. One is moved by a great deal in the film, but the ultimate and most moving of responses is one's regard for Ozu. This is in no way due to exhibitionism; most certainly it's not because of virtuosity à la Fellini. It's because everything in an Ozu film derives from his utter subscription to a view of life as infinitely sacred and of art as the most sacred exercise in life. He serves, rather than making anything serve him.

Late Spring is the story of a father and daughter in postwar Japan.

(Evidences of the American occupation are glimpsed, not underscored.) They are played by Chishu Ryu, the old man in *Tokyo Story,* and Setsuko Hara, who was his daughter-in-law in that film. Other members of the Ozu "company" can be seen, and the script is, as usual, a collaboration between Ozu and Kogo Noda.

The motion of this quiet-motion picture is in the effort by which the widowed father, a professor, turns his daughter away from the security-and-resentment ambivalence of her life with him toward a life of her own, gently urging her toward a marriage which she both wants and dreads. Ozu's touch is so implicative that we never even see the fiancé; our last sight of the girl is in her traditional wedding dress. Our last sight of the father, which is the end of the film, is when he sits alone after the ceremony, peeling an apple, in one long peel; and by his daring in ending here, Ozu crystallizes retrospectively the design of his film. Another way to put it: we don't know how good the picture is until it finishes. When we see Ryu sitting there alone, we comprehend how much Ozu has staked on a simple design to contain a great deal, what courage he has, what indifference to conventional demands.

His method is one of non-drama, but not in any prosy, naturalistic, flattened sense. He believes, with many Japanese painters and draftsmen, that if you select the right details and present them realistically, you have created an abstraction that signifies a great deal more than detailed realism. The drama, for Ozu, is in life itself, and his task is not to contrive but to reveal.

I hope that viewers will see *Late Spring* after *Tokyo Story,* as I did. The lesser work benefits from a knowledge of the larger one. *Late Spring* is lesser because of one specific and one general matter: the daughter's character is not as sharply drawn as it might have been, her contradictory impulses to go and to stay are not well enough understood (at least to a Westerner), and she becomes a generalized representative of emotional complexes, rather than a clarified person. Hara plays her well, but cannot supply motivations and contradictions that are not in the script. Second, the compass of the film is simply not as great as the later one, and could not be even if the character of the daughter were deeper. *Tokyo Story,* to put it vulgarly, seems to be about everything; *Late Spring* is about one sector of experience.

To see such Ozu hallmarks here as the *tatami* shot and the punctuation-with-empty-places after seeing *Tokyo Story* is to delight in the friendship of a friend; to see *Late Spring* first, because it is not as overwhelming as the other picture, might cause some feeling of disproportion, for a time, between film and method.

But, first or second or in any order, an Ozu work is an opportunity, not a film only.

Junior Bonner

(September 2, 1972)

SAM Peckinpah's ill wind is at least blowing Steve McQueen some good. Peckinpah's career gets increasingly worrisome, but in *Junior Bonner* McQueen gives the first non-merely-star performance of his that I've seen. As usual with a Peckinpah Western, this script (by Jeb Rosebrook) has a hero who is aging—in this case a rodeo rider who already has a limp and is on his way over the hill. McQueen is quiet, concentrated, true: the only really valid element in the film. Even Lucien Ballard's camerawork contributes less than usual.

No one could ever have doubted that McQueen was star material, with his taut Milt Caniff face, polite menace, lean stomach. He has long been an international smash; eight summers ago I woke up one morning in a small French town to read the banner headline on the local daily: *STEVE MCQUEEN A PARIS!* As Junior Bonner he has lost none of his star-light, but this time he has focused it on something. Instead of lolling on his assets, he is using what he has to understand and present someone else, a man who was (*was*) a young hellion. Stacy Keach, the Shakespeare and Chekhov actor, might take a look at movie star McQueen's work here to see the kind of central generative imagination that was missing in Keach's *Fat City* pug.

But Peckinpah, with his actors as with his film, is erratic. Ida Lupino is miscast as an Arizona mother; she looks and sounds wrong from beginning to end. (And of course she is hailed with critical rapture: she is English and an old-timer, therefore, this *must* be good acting.) Robert Preston is a likable man whose likableness let him give one of the best phony performances of the postwar era, in that phony musical *The Music Man;* but the phoniness swamps the likableness in the rapscallion old man Bonner. Every Preston inflection sounds like a song cue.

We're awash with rodeo films these days: a few months ago, *J. W. Coop* (poor); soon to appear, *When the Legends Die* (poor, but with a pleasant actor named Frederic Forrest as an Indian). In *Junior Bonner* Peckinpah has his own view. He brings his aging hero home for a rodeo in his hometown at the same time that Junior's wandering father returns to raise money in order to leave again. Meanwhile, Junior's brother is prospering here as a real estate developer. Peckinpah is once more rubbing maleness and male mythology against a constricting society. The idea is interesting, but was more effectively, if imperfectly, treated in *The Hired Hand*. Peckinpah has pasted on it all the empty apparatus of the cliché Western: clipped, taciturn, man-to-man dialogue; the sock on the jaw to end a conversation, and the sock later repaid with no hard feelings; and that last infirmity of noble-savage minds, the barroom brawl that everyone just simply loves. Peckinpah even stoops to the cliché of having four old men playing cards in the back of the saloon during the brawl, undisturbed by the fracas around them. All that's missing is a close-up of someone being crowned with a bottle and crossing his eyes before he sinks. I don't know how that bit got left out.

The worst thing about a debacle like this film is that it makes a mockery of some of the same methods that the director used well previously. I have seen *The Wild Bunch* again since seeing *The Ballad of Cable Hogue* and *Straw Dogs,* and it keeps its head well above those subsequent flops, but I don't want to see it again for a long, long time after *Junior Bonner.* Peckinpah's eclecticism I could live with. (He has previously borrowed overtly from John Huston; here he borrows from John Ford—the bulldozing scene in *The Grapes of Wrath*.) But the techniques used hollowly here cast a hollow ring backward. I don't want the vapidness of the prismatic cutting and the slow-motion violence here to affect their fine use in the earlier film.

Do we need still another argument in the style-content debate? Willy-nilly, Peckinpah supplies it. Style needs content. The opera world proves it over and over again: the surviving works of any one composer are usually those with the best books, even though he may have composed equally well for other books. Peckinpah has been good when his scripts were simple, mythic rather than moral. He was preachy and fancy, and therefore tedious, in *Cable Hogue.* He was pietistic in *Straw Dogs,* which was essentially a remake of Harold

Lloyd's *Grandma's Boy* without the laughs but with lashings of sex and gore.

It looks as if Peckinpah has been listening to his critics. I wish he'd listen to this critic and get back to Laurentian blood. He doesn't have much range, but at least he's at home on it. He looks silly with conventional moral frameworks; they make his violence look like sadistic decadence instead of feral outburst. And he's too unruly to make the neat sentimental film that *Junior Bonner* might have been in other hands.

Marjoe

(*September 2, 1972*)

Is *cinéma-vérité* as easy as it looks? Is it as unveracious as it looks? From *Marjoe,* at least, both questions get a ringing yes. This is a "documentary" about an evangelist named Marjoe Gortner who started as a California child and has been hell-raising most of the time since then. I put quotations around documentary because some of the prayer meetings we see were held especially to be filmed. The material is utterly familiar from fiction films on the same subject. Marjoe's frankness, off-pulpit, is occasioned by the fact that he is quitting evangelism. Both the evangelism and the frankness are interwoven with facile sophomoric smartness by the film makers, Howard Smith and Sarah Kernochan.

The film is very repetitious. We get the point long before they stop intercutting shots of people in religious ecstasy with shots of Marjoe counting the take. Further, the film is blind. It tells us, clearly enough, that there is some truth in Marjoe as well as hypocrisy; but, much more important, it is blind to the fact that he didn't cheat his congregations. (This film, if those people see it, will make them feel cheated, not the prayer meetings themselves.) Marjoe didn't cheat his congregations any more than Mick Jagger cheats his audiences when he sends them into comparable ecstasies by shouting and moaning about his broken heart when, in fact, his heart may not be broken and he, too, is doing it for the money. The function of revivalist religion in America, much discussed by historians, is close to that of the

Stones and the Beatles, even somewhat related to Sinatra and Vallee before them. While I was watching *Marjoe,* I thought of Bernard Shaw's remark that, come the revolution, he would make theaters free and would charge admission to churches.

I thought of something else, too. In the "interlude" scenes we get behind-the-camera shots of hip New Yorkers, those involved in making the film, sitting around Marjoe laughing wisely at his reminiscences. They seemed a good deal more silly and superficial, more antihuman, than Marjoe's ecstasists. I don't see the moral grandeur that automatically attaches to any pot-smoking Village type as against someone in Texas trying to find reason and relief in his life through "testimony." (And this is an atheist speaking.)

The Ruling Class

(September 16, 1972)

LATELY I've been getting adverse comments from some readers because, they say, I'm not adverse enough. They think I'm soft because I insist on discerning virtues in such patently imperfect films as *The Hired Hand* and *Pocket Money;* they would like more straight, uncomplicated guillotining. I'm afraid I'm incorrigible. For many American decades, approximately since the heyday of Mencken, the chief hallmark of critics on "journals of opinion" and quarterlies has been nay-saying. For this, much of the time, we can be grateful. But out of it has grown a wretched rule-of-thumb: the critic who says "no" *must* be more perceptive than the one who says "yes" or even "no, but"; and the critic who says the flat "no" most frequently— and most violently—is the best. Inarguably, most of what is produced in any art, particularly the audience arts of theater and film, is junk; and obviously the nay-saying is a reaction against the even more persistent yea-saying of the mass-circulation press. Still, through the decades, the nay-saying has become almost as much of a reflex as the mass yea-saying. What's worse, that nay-saying has sometimes been a cover for a lack of esthetic sensibility as abysmal as that in most of the booster mass reviewers. The diction and the air differ; but on each side a gallery is being played to, by critics who are not much more than players to their respective galleries.

I deplore both sides, and especially deplore the sort of mind which suspects that the critic who pans a work is, self-evidently, sounder than the one who finds merit in it. I've done my share of panning and hope to do plenty more, but where an imperfect, even failed work has merits in it, I hope to exercise what discrimination I have to point them out, as pertinent to my own *bona fides,* the artists' due, and the reader's possible interest in coming along.

All this is apropos of Peter O'Toole's new film, *The Ruling Class.* This picture is, finally, a mess; and it would be easy to write it off in a quick and (naturally) witty paragraph, scoring its ridiculous aspects. But this would be dereliction. There are fascinations and accomplishments in this mess, and I intend, with your patience, to say why.

The script, by the English playwright Peter Barnes from his play of the same name, is about a religious schizophrenic who succeeds to an earldom. His father, a beef-and-blood type (Harry Andrews), has a private little sport of stripping to his underwear, putting on a ballet tutu and a cocked hat, and hanging himself, partially. One day the stepladder slips, and the hanging is full.

His will is read, and to the horror of the earl's half brother and the latter's wife, the estate—except for 30,000 pounds to the butler—passes to the sole surviving son, Jack, who has spent the last eight years in an asylum, where he imagines that he is the Holy Trinity all in one. (Someone asks Jack how he knows he is God. "Simple," he says. "When I pray to Him, I find I'm talking to myself.") Jack (O'Toole) arrives, in monk's robes, long-haired and bearded, seemingly sane, and takes over. His behavior then fluctuates between the lucid and the (often comically) hallucinated. What usually takes him over the edge is mere talking. He starts to answer a question quite rationally, then just takes off into coruscating religious rhetoric about loving kindness, with himself as the center of the religion. For most of the film he declines to be called Jack: he prefers J. C. And he installs a huge cross in the immense drawing room of this Stately Home, on which he spends hours, standing with his outstretched arms resting on nails.

The plot is concerned with the efforts (again comic) of Jack's uncle and aunt to disinherit him—by having him marry, produce an heir, and then having themselves declared legal guardians. They succeed partway; but on the night of the heir's birth, the head of the asylum shows up with another religious maniac who shocks Jack out of his own religious mania: into another schizophrenia. Now he is "normal," except that his private fantasies are not of Jesus but of Jack the Ripper.

This is Barnes's point: as soon as Jack forsakes the preachment of love and starts his father's preachment of force and blood and privileged cruelty, everyone heaves a sigh of relief. Shaved and shorn, he takes his seat in the House of Lords, where his maiden speech, in favor of capital punishment, wins an ovation. In his canted mind, his public bloodthirstiness extends to private murder, and he commits his first. Suspicion does not touch him because of his rank. The film ends with the implications that his new kind of lunacy is compatible with society and that more murder is to come, now that he is behaving truly like a lord.

Now, the first, basic objection to this script is that it is philosophically puerile. It says that what is wrong with Britain (read "the world") is its aristocracy (read "oligarchs"). This is about as profound as the thirties belief that war is made by munitions makers. If Barnes really thinks that, for instance, hunger for the gallows back again is the monopoly of lords, he ought to have been at dinner with me in London two months ago when I heard a prominent newspaper editor, certainly no lord, fulminate against opponents of capital punishment as enemies of mankind. If only things *were* as simple as Barnes says, how much easier solutions would be—if only all the evil *were* concentrated in the powerful and privileged and all the rest of us were good.

Further, the script is grotesquely distended. (The picture runs almost two and a half hours.) Numerous scenes—like one with a Master in Lunacy who comes to examine Jack—are good and funny in themselves but stop the picture cold. And there is a disconcerting mixture of styles. I sometimes like mixed styles, including conscious theatricality, but then the mixture of styles has itself to be a successful style, and it isn't here. Jack's bride, on her wedding night, does a striptease number for the camera which she knows is there. Two very proper ladies of the village arrive and do a vaudeville number with Jack before they leave in a huff at his unorthodox behavior. The effect is chaos, not freedom.

And the ends of the script are too neatly tucked in. The asylum chief is made, incredibly, to go crazy. The butler turns out to be a secret Red—incredible even in fantastic comedy. (Shaw said, rightly, that the lords would be revolutionaries long before their valets.)

Peter Medak, who directed *A Day in the Death of Joe Egg,* a mixed bag, has mixed another bag here. He begins very well, nice straight storytelling, with only a few traces of *Joe Egg* theater staging—that is, stage "pictures" in which people who are not in the dialogue or action of the moment are kept on screen just because they happen to be in the room. As the script gets frenetic, Medak outdistances it. He slides from straight narrative into stop-frames, expressionist tradition, and subjective views. At the end we see the House of Lords through Jack's eyes, as a bunch of dusty skeletons.

But there's a good deal of good to be said about *The Ruling Class*. First, even when the structure wobbles and the ideas falter, the writing itself is sharp. The dialogue as such is much above the ordinary. And one of the ways it is extraordinary is in its wit.

This connects, through Medak, to the cast. Almost every one of them is first-rate. There is pleasure merely in hearing them speak the words, watching them play and interplay. Harry Andrews, the kinky earl, chews his bile with great clean snaps. William Mervyn, his shifty brother, Coral Browne, Mervyn's lickerish wife, James Villiers, their silly-ass son, Carolyn Seymour, Mervyn's mistress who is made Jack's wife, Nigel Green as a Scottish religious nut, Michael Bryant, the asylum head, all supply prodigally what's wanted in their respective roles. Alastair Sim, Mervyn's bishop brother, is the exception: this heavy-handed mechanic does not improve with age.

Two performances are even better than the general excellence. Arthur Lowe, the butler who inherits a bundle, then becomes tipsy and truculent, is beyond praise. And there's O'Toole.

I don't understand his make-up. He looks painted the whole time, even after his descent from the cross—one of the most artificial looks since Orson Welles in *Mr. Arkadin*. Outside of that, only hosannas. He has few equals among English-language screen actors, in romance, comedy, wildness. He has no equal in—lame word—the poetic: the sense that he has pushed to the furthest frontiers of sensitivity, where few of us could endure the heat. Or cold.

His performance in *Brotherly Love,* as another unbalanced lord, was more successful because the role was more organically built, although the picture was pedestrian. (Another film I declined to decapitate.) But here he gets absolutely everything out of what's given him—the "arias," the vaudeville, the piteousness, the regality.

In sum, this irritating and unsatisfying film is worth being irritated and unsatisfied by. A simple "no" to *The Ruling Class* would be easy; but wasteful.

Greaser's Palace

(September 23, 1972)

LAST year we had *El Topo,* by and with a Pole named Alexander Jodorowsky who works in Mexico, a mythic fantasy set in Mexican desert country, distinguished by a self-apotheosizing adolescent mentality (the director played a savior with mystical powers), a Buñuel-derived addiction to infantile cruelty, and a superb eye for images. Several times I tried to get up and leave *El Topo* because, in sum, it is insultingly juvenile. But part of that sum is a picture eye, and each time I thought I might go, I stayed to look at some more of the pictures. To me, a film with nothing more than good pictures is a species of porno, a bit like what Wallace Stevens says about sex:

> If sex were all, then every trembling hand
> Could make us squeak, like dolls, the wished-for-words.

Still, sex porno has some limited appeal, and so has esthetic porno like *El Topo.*

Now comes *Son of El Topo,* as it might as well be called, a film actually titled *Greaser's Palace* by the American Robert Downey, who once showed some wit in his scripts though none in his direction. I did leave *Greaser's Palace* about halfway; then a few days later, passing the theater a little before half time, I succumbed to conscience, unluckily, went in, and saw the rest.

This is another Christ allegory, this time in the American West, with a sort of Pilate (named Greaser), a sort of Jesus (in a zoot suit), a sort of Holy Ghost (in a white sheet), a sort of God (in a beard). There is a good deal of Beautiful photography.

But the art of photography is debased here as symphonic playing would be debased by putting the Concertgebouw Orchestra in the pit of *Jesus Christ Superstar.* The allegory is absolutely sterile, the profanities and sex jokes are of a kind that any good college humor magazine would throw out, and the deliberate discontinuities are a parody of both caprice and surrealism.

El Topo at least had overweening immature conviction. Downey's derivative is part cynical, part vacuous, and wholly sickening to anyone who wants film to be adventurous, witty, irreverent, and cinematically resourceful.

The Emigrants

(September 30, 1972)

How happily clear it was from Jan Troell's first film *Here's Your Life* that he had large talents and large ambitions. His second film has not yet been released here. Now we get his third, which is self-contained but is Part One of a two-part work. Troell's largeness pushes him toward the epic. *Here's Your Life,* now reduced to 110 minutes, was originally the longest Swedish film ever made. *The Emigrants* runs something over two hours; the sequel, already completed, is about the same length, I'm told.

This work is based on Vilhelm Moberg's four-volume novel, *Unto a Good Land,* a story of people leaving Sweden in the 1840s and coming to the U.S. Emigration to the U.S. in the nineteenth century, probably the most significant movement of peoples since the Moorish invasion of Europe, has been scanted in films. The only other serious attempt to deal with it that I know is Kazan's *America, America.*

Troell is a most extraordinary man: he writes, directs, photographs, and edits his own films. (Bengt Forslund, the Swedish critic, is his highly collaborative producer.) His direction is rich in empathy, stated delicately: the very first shot of *The Emigrants* is a close-up of a Bible open on a pulpit, then Troell pans up gently to show us the congregation listening to the preacher. In one small movement of a few seconds, Troell has established a place and time, the religious basis of the society, and the quality of relation between this church and its communicants. His photography is more than adequate to his ideas: his colors are gentle, only occasionally pretty-pretty, and his lighting always seems to draw the substance *out* of the composition instead of coming in and smacking it. (See the first sunlit shot of the "young" Liv Ullmann on the swing.) His editing is generally tart, helpfully elliptical.

He is weakest, relatively, as writer, but perhaps that's not the right way to put it. The script is the least impressive part of *The Emi-*

grants, but that's more a matter of a difficult concept than, say, faulty scene structure. Troell has deliberately opted for a novelistic approach, not in the Antonioni or Bergman sense in which the cinema does cinematically what the novel does novelistically, but the sense in which the cinema tries absolutely to reproduce the effect of reading a novel. Now this is dangerous ground and has been posted as such almost since the beginnings of film. Troell evidently knows the risks he has taken and has not escaped scot-free; but his talent and his calmness bring it off a good part of the way.

He wants, first of all, to take time. Not the way Antonioni did in his trilogy, by occasional magnification of a moment. The prime thing that a long novel does is to take a great chunk of our time, and that taking of our time, if the author is good, is itself a pleasant part of the experience. Troell wants to achieve the same sense of time transpiring, *our* time, *our* living through some experiences. Coupled with this, of course, is our sense of the characters' time. Seasons change, hopes alter, lives arrive and depart. Troell wants the same sense of this parallel journey, ours and theirs.

He achieves it, with us and them, but he pays a price. We are all theatrically conditioned, whether by theater or film, to certain expectations when sitting in a theater seat. That conditioning is primarily one of expectation: ranging from the level of "Will he arrive in time to get her off the railroad tracks?" to an interest in a character's physical or spiritual adventure, but always presented in a way to lead us forward. The serial consideration, though certainly part of the novel, is lesser (or can be) and is esthetically different. (For instance, I don't care whether I. Compton-Burnett's novels progress or not; I just like reading them.) I can't conceive of a fiction film in which texture itself would be sufficient. Troell's texture is always fine, and his picture never bores. "Boredom" is a facile, stupid term to use in connection with work of this quality. But there are moments that call for patience, willingly given, as we are patient with people we like and respect.

The title tells us a good deal before the picture starts. The conditions in which the farmer-hero and his wife live, in which his indentured brother suffers, in which his religious uncle is persecuted, all are shown with the knowledge that we know what they will lead to. The sea voyage is presented, in all its squalor, to make us feel its sheer duration. Soon the film almost takes on the quality of a historical rite, as if we were following motions and events that we know quite well, in essence, but which we are honoring and celebrating.

The very last shot of the film is one of its best. The farmer has pushed on past the other settlers in Minnesota, reaches good land on the edge of a lake, blazes his name on a tree to stake his claim, then sinks down with his back against the tree, pulls his hat over his eyes, and smiles. After all that has gone before, it is a lovely moment, that smile; an end and, of course, a beginning.

That moment is beautifully fulfilled because the farmer is played by Max von Sydow, one of my heroes in contemporary film, an actor superbly equipped to *be* a hero, a protagonist of an epic. (Which is far from all of his talent; see him as a filling-station attendant in *Wild Strawberries*.) He has an extraordinary range of sympathies and strengths, and like many fine actors (not all; some of them delight in visible virtuosity) he makes it look easy.

So does his screen wife, Liv Ullmann. See how both of them handle the simple-difficult matter of youth. They begin as a young affianced couple, with no trick lights or make-ups, just hair styles that are different from ones they wear later. They simply believe in the truth and worth of what they are pretending to be, so we take the pretense as truth. Women have more of a problem in demonstrating their range as actors than men because they generally wear less varied make-ups. If an audience could see a clip of Ullmann from *Persona* right after *The Emigrants,* they would see the same face, but they would get some idea of why acting at its best is creation, as well as interpretation. (She even sleeps differently in the two pictures.)

Eddie Axberg, who was merely a satisfactory figure as the hero of *Here's Your Life* and who plays von Sydow's younger brother here, has now become capable of filling in many of the deeper points of a character. Some of the best scenes in the film are between him and his fat fellow serf (Pierre Lindstedt), in their barn bunks, finding brotherhood in their mutual misery.

The costumes by Ulla-Britt Soderlund are first-rate, and I want to draw special attention to the make-up by Cecilia Drott. Skin looks like skin—grimy, worn, sweaty, blood-flecked. Hands look like hands that have spent years with tools and dirt and buckets. U.S. directors of Westerns and farm pictures, please copy.

The conflict and the virtues in *The Emigrants* come, fundamentally, from the dialectic between a traditional old-style narrative and

Troell's contemporary sensibilities. The synthesis of that opposition is not complete, but it's often fine. I mean it positively when I say that I can't remember many films that I have been less excited by that I have enjoyed as much. I look forward to Part Two.*

The Assassination of Trotsky

(October 7, 1972)

JOSEPH Losey's picture about Trotsky is atrocious. When the project was first announced, I had a small hope for it, despite the preening, torpid estheticism of Losey's recent films, because he has some knowledge of radical politics (and suffered from it in the McCarthy days, which is how he became an "English" director). But this film is the work of a man who went back to something that had once been vital to him and converted it all into tritely psychologized, pretty-pasteboard nonsense. It is almost an act of revenge.

Screen writers are complaining these days, with great justice, that their work is being scanted in all the uproar about directors. Let's give this script the attention it deserves. Nicholas Mosley is an English novelist, author of the book from which Pinter made the screenplay of *Accident* for Losey. Here, surely with Losey's guidance, Mosley has made a script in which old Trotsky, puttering around his Mexican garden, spends equal time feeding his rabbits, patting his companion Natalya, and quoting from his own works; in which the assassin uses his Trotskyite girl friend as a means of access to his victim but becomes impotent and rabid as the murder-moment approaches; in which the only possible point is the contrast between two couples, victim and woman, assassin and woman. Losey-Mosley must have had some reason for making this picture. The facts in themselves, so far as I can check them, seem accurate, but all I can get out of the use of them in this script is that Trotskyism shows people how to love and relate and that Stalinism is the result of psychosis, keeps people from good sex relations, and drives them to murder. That theme is either far, far deeper than anything that Mosley shows, or else it is a sickening, superficial joke.

The structure, full of inserted character-building touches and obvi-

* See p. 222.

ous parallels and spring-driven data, is about as valid as a Hollywood bio-pic of the thirties. The dialogue, outside of Trotsky's quotations, which are hardly his best, is incredible in two senses. Example:

> "I can't believe you're going."
> "All good things come to an end."

In the past Losey at his worst—no, except at his very worst like *Boom!* or *Secret Ceremony*—has usually provided some scraps of cinematic pleasure. Here there are none—only platitudes like the freeze-frames, or dreadful underscoring like the intercutting of bullfight clips as Jacson's moment of truth approaches. The murder-moment itself deserves to be called decadent. Jacson stands behind the seated Trotsky and takes the pickaxe from under his folded raincoat. Then Losey gives us a shot of the back of Trotsky's head as Jacson looks at it, a really terrifying moment—vulnerability in essence. An artist would then have shown us Jacson swinging and Trotsky bleeding. But Losey has to make Trotsky rise and turn to Jacson and has to give us a shot of both standing, Jacson holding the pickaxe whose point is fixed in Trotsky's skull. What could have been the horror of the act becomes the horror of the film. That shot crystallizes the putrefaction of Losey.

Richard Burton, the Trotsky, has no character to play, which is what he plays. Valentina Cortese, the Natalya, is herself lovely and gracious, which helps a bit. Romy Schneider, Jacson's girl, reminds me a little less than usual of a saccharine Fritz Kreisler encore, which is also a help. And there is a glimpse of Simone Valere, the best Ophelia I ever saw (with Barrault in New York twenty years ago), as a visiting Frenchwoman.

The only substantive reward in the picture, however, is Alain Delon as Jacson. Never mind the writing of the part, in which there seem to be two characters, one cool and the other crazy, with no believable schizophrenia. In the first part (as in Jean-Pierre Melville's idiotically retitled *The Godson*) Delon does the icy killer perfectly. He is a real film star. We make our own films while we watch his impassive face. When you add his powers of *expressed* acting, as shown for instance in *Eclipse* and the raving passages here, the sum is impressive. I always like to see Delon. The first shot of him here, bespectacled, shaving, is the best in the film.

Trotsky has been used as the center of fiction before this, for instance in Peter Weiss's play *Trotsky in Exile*. That play is not exactly a lithe and limber work, but at least it recognizes, from its title on, a certain function and view. Trotsky is the one great political figure of this century who continued to be a great political figure after he lost power. He spent nine years in office but almost fourteen years in exile before his death. He functioned by being alive and by writing—he was a great man of letters. His life and his writing were so potent that, though he had no temporal power, Stalin had to have him killed.

In one of the sad scandals of film history, Eisenstein eliminated Trotsky almost completely from *October* while he was editing his film of the 1917 revolution in late 1927, because Stalin had won the contest with Trotsky and wanted him obliterated. Eisenstein's action was at least one of omission. Losey and friends have committed their atrocity in public view.

Chloe in the Afternoon

(October 14, 1972)

WHAT Eric Rohmer has done in his films is to recalibrate the scale of responses between men and women. This is important work, and his new film continues and concludes it. His latest is the last of his *Six Moral Tales*. The first two, relatively short and shot in 16 mm, have not been shown here. The other three, in order of making, are *La Collectionneuse, My Night at Maud's,* and *Claire's Knee.* All four that I have seen deal with a man who gets involved with one woman and ends up with another. All are "classic" in tone, with a sense of design-as-meaning, of distilled emotion rather than immersion in heat. The atmosphere is Catholic, though in only one film, *My Night at Maud's,* is this explicit; and the Catholicism is Jansenist. The characters reach conclusions that seem predestined, though not predictable.

Contemporary attitudes in sexual relations tend to drive those relations toward one issue: to bed or not to bed—with a prejudice to bed because it is stodgy *not* to. The latest sexual revolution, women's lib, bases part of its beliefs on the physical locus of the orgasm in women. The latest cultural revolution, the widespread acceptance of film pornography, posits sexual athleticism in males as an ideal to which we are all to be consecrated. Into this superheated atmosphere comes Rohmer's work. He tells us, in effect, that God wants us to be happy and unhappy (a thesis I can support after a change of nouns); that sexual relations are the greatest source of both the happiness and the unhappiness; and that the question of whether to bed or not is, for mature people, subtly and infinitely reverberant.

In sum, Rohmer says that new knowledges and freedoms are blessings insofar as they magnify our sensibilities but are hurtful and silly if we are reduced by them.

Chloe in the Afternoon is about a young husband. (The better French title is *Love in the Afternoon,* but it was preempted in the U.S. by a Billy Wilder film of 1957.) He has a loved and loving wife who teaches in the suburbs, a good job in Paris, a young child, and another en route. It's clear, as we see him moving through the patterns of his life, telling us his thoughts on the sound track, that he is in the best kind of happiness: full of curiosity about each day. His married life has made him more male. ("Since I've been married, I find all women beautiful.") He relishes the looks of the women who pass in the streets; he dreams of magical powers over them. (In the fantasy sequence Rohmer uses some of the women from his previous films. This sequence is the only really banal passage in any of his films.) He goes home to his wife, uneasy, but conscious that his uneasiness is part of the riches that marriage has given him.

Then a girl named Chloe returns to Paris, someone he knew slightly, the girl friend of a former man friend. She is a drifter around the world, the sort of girl who gets into a lot of beds by exercising what she considers discrimination. She is not attractive to the husband—or to me, for that matter—but she is desperately needful, the sort of girl one meets so often these days who is free of encumbrances *and* roots. She needs the husband; he doesn't need her. She is proud and touchy, but nonetheless she manages to weave herself into his life. She comes to his office a good deal, he gets her a job in a boutique, he frequently sees her, nonsexually, in the afternoon. (One of the reasons I like this film so much is that Rohmer shares one of my dislikes, for the afternoon between the end of lunch and, say, 4:00—in city life, that is, and particularly in office life. Rohmer thinks of it as a specially vulnerable time of day.)

In most modern fiction and film, not to say modern life, there would be some relatively quick hopping-into-bed, with a proper decorum of *tristesse* and with a lot of "grown-up" talk to rationalize the glandular opportunism. But Rohmer takes things a moment, a day, a week at a time, and shows how the absence or presence of Chloe affects the outlook and insight of the young husband, how the fact of her existence is summoning complex responses in him.

He goes to her apartment one afternoon (!) as he has done before, in sheer friendship, and finds her coming out of the shower. She goes to her bed and waits for him. As he pulls his sweater over his head, he glances in the mirror and sees his face poking out in a way that has previously amused his child. He pulls the sweater back on, picks up his jacket, and goes quietly out the back door.

He phones his wife, then goes home in the afternoon—something he rarely does. She breaks an appointment to stay with him. They have a last scene on a sofa, beautifully played, in which she suddenly bursts into tears. The implication—to us, if not to him—is that she might have had a similar rendezvous planned for herself and is relieved not to go to it. Instead they go to their own bed.

The key move in the making of this film was the casting of a Parisian performer named Zouzou as Chloe. She embodies the idea of availability becoming attraction where there was no attraction to start with, of social competence covering tremendous vulnerability, of a pride that does its own sort of begging. When the husband puts his sweater back on and goes home, we feel it is only partly out of a recognition of where his love-making belongs: partly it is out of fright, despite Chloe's cool disclaimers, of acquiring even more responsibility with her.

An actual married couple, Bernard and Françoise Verley, play the husband and wife. He is adequate. She was unimpressive until that last scene, when great portals seemed to open within this mousy girl.

Except for the fantasy sequence, Rohmer has made this film as discreetly as ever. He ruthlessly excludes what doesn't interest him, and has no qualms about lingering a few seconds past conventional theatrical requirements when he feels there is more in front of us than has so far met the eye. His ability to leave things out helps to deepen what he includes. For instance, the lives of the two secretaries in the husband's office are well-drawn for us although we see very little of them. Rohmer's idea of camera technique, something like Bresson's, is not to have much of it. That last scene on the sofa consists of one medium close-up shot (as I recall), simply held while the husband

and wife live before us. He uses the camera as a watcher, not a manipulator.

One reason he succeeds with this approach is that, again, his cinematographer is Nestor Almendros. In these days when most films come out dripping with syrupy colors, like a child let loose in a soda fountain, Almendros is helping to remind us what colors really are. As Rohmer wants to remind us that there is more to sex than coupling, Almendros wants to remind us that there is more to red than Red. His control is as exact here as ever. I noted, in discussing past Rohmer films, how Almendros gets the most out of textile designs. Here the husband goes shopping—in the afternoon—and buys a green checked shirt that, through Almendros, becomes part of the story's texture. One of the most stunning shots that I have seen lately is not a sunset or a battle or a prairie but the young husband sitting in a café, his back to the street, with the street life teeming, plane on plane, far into the distance.

Throughout the picture Rohmer uses street sounds and next-door sounds to complement the planar levels of the camera.

Certainly Rohmer's films have been male-oriented; but so is his church, as its pope reminded us again recently. Certainly there is a certain smugness in the Jansenist comfort at being one of the elect: I left the theater wondering about poor Chloe, still waiting, naked and alone, on that bed. But Rohmer doesn't pretend that any of his protagonists are noble and altruistic; they are trying to understand themselves, trying to serve the best in themselves. Only for saints does the best for one's self mean losing the self in service of another. I knew a man who married a Chloe, and I have always thought of him as saintly and myself as merely mortal because, some years later, I was glad—for him—when the wife died. For non-saints (Rohmer is possibly saying) unhappiness is part of what we know and what we cause.

He has announced that he is not going to make another film until 1975. Whatever lies ahead of him, he has already made a substantial contribution to the cinema of our time, to the connection of cinema with our time.

The King of Marvin Gardens

(October 28, 1972)

GLUM news from the people who made *Five Easy Pieces,* which had a lot of good work in it along with some pretentious flab. In their new picture the flab has taken over. *The King of Marvin Gardens* hasn't been running two minutes before hope begins to shiver.

The very first shot is a fairly tight close-up of Jack Nicholson, wearing glasses, his face half in shadow as he looks at us. His first line: "I promised to tell you why I never eat fish." This is a doubly daring start. Pictorially, it deliberately puts us nowhere; textually, it assumes a level of sophisticated engagement, willing to begin in the middle of things. The unspoken message is: "Have faith. Clarification, enrichment, justification will come." They don't, and it doesn't take us long to find that out.

Nicholson goes into a story about a boyhood experience with his brother and his grandfather that utterly lacks the weight to justify the *misterioso* opening, a story of very little resonance. Pictorially, the opening tease fizzles just as dismally: after a while a red light flashes on Nicholson's face, then we cut back and see that he is in a radio studio, talking into a mike, and that the red light is a signal from the control booth. The opening shot is nothing more than the sort of cuteness that, say, Jerzy Skolimowski uses, beginning a sequence close to an unrecognizable object, then pulling back until we see that it is merely a detail of something familiar. For both the eye and the ear, this Nicholson opening trickles into mere trickery.

Nothing gets much better. Those same techniques are repeated often. Sequences begin abruptly, in their contextual "middle," straining always toward the bizarre for eye and ear, like a shot of Nicholson and Bruce Dern on horseback on the Atlantic City beach. The device is used so often that, with almost every new sequence, we spend a good deal of time merely trying to find out where we are and who is who. This elliptical method might have some point, even if things never became entirely clear, if the result were a rewarding ambiguity; as it is, portentous methods have been imposed on thin material.

Nicholson is a radio monologist in Philadelphia who is summoned to Atlantic City by his wild-dreaming brother, Dern. (Marvin Gardens, I gather, is a name on the Monopoly board.) Dern, who lives with a woman and her stepdaughter, has a scheme to develop a resort center on an island off Hawaii—not his first get-rich-quick fantasy—and wants his brother to join him. There is an extremely complicated counterpoint of black bosses, Japanese investors, and sexual hijinks. It ends with a sudden murder and with Nicholson back at his Philadelphia job.

The theme is good old Arthur Miller territory—dreams-of-success as the American narcotic, with one member of a family trying to persuade another to kick the narcotic and enjoy the life he has. The setting is a rundown resort paradise, so the dream is of a new resort paradise. None of this is arbitrarily unusable, but all of it is irritating when the apparatus turns out to be just apparatus. If Jacob Brackman, who wrote the script from a story by himself and Bob Rafelson, had been content to tell the story, had confronted the banalities of subject and symbolism with honesty, it might have been effective. But Brackman is much more concerned with showing himself a sage of gnomic rue, worldly wise and weary of film-script conventions. Brackman is more interested in Brackman than in his story or characters; since they are at his mercy, they suffer.

He is not the only distorter. The director, Rafelson, who shaped so much of *Five Easy Pieces* so well, seems to have lost the map of his directorial mind—temporarily, I hope. He seems not to know when he is being shallowly imitative (the tacky band at the station, to greet Nicholson, is fourth-rate Fellini), or when he is casting badly (a girl named Julia Anne Robinson could hardly be less interesting), or when he is shoving in irrelevant atmosphere (a high school band on the boardwalk) and unearned melancholy (a sad overhead long shot of the same band dispersing in the afternoon light). Connected with this is Laszlo Kovacs's photography, conceived generally in a palette of autumnal farewell that might have been a touch too much for Chekhov, let alone for this script.

As the brother, Bruce Dern works energetically, but since the principal question we keep asking of him is who the hell he is, his performance is doomed to flounder. Ellen Burstyn tries to give realistic pathos to a thirtyish doxy, but the part was never *seen* by the writer or director. (She's rather like Rayette of *Five Easy Pieces* after a trip through a Waring blender.) The sharpest performance comes from John Ryan in the brief, defined role of a hotel manager.

My biggest grievance against Brackman-Rafelson is that they have wasted Jack Nicholson. Melancholic resignation is not his strongest suit. He needs strong tensions, not necessarily loud (though he's good when loud) but deep and certainly tense. When he's being quiet *about* something—which means the threat of explosion even if he never explodes (like Gabin)—he's arresting. Here he simply stands around most of the time, observing and reflecting, occasionally wrinkling his nose bunny-style to adjust his glasses. It's quite a negative achievement to flatten Nicholson, but this picture does it.

BBS Productions, which produced *Marvin Gardens* and *Easy Rider* and *Five Easy Pieces* and *The Last Picture Show,* is trying, with varying success, to contribute to the growth of the American "personal" film. Fine and necessary and high time. But because the U.S. film world has almost no tradition of "personal" films (despite some isolated instances), the belated effort to compensate often produces an effect of dutiful strain, guilty heaviness, esthetic hernia. Hence the BBS production of Jaglom's *A Safe Place* last year, utter nonsense, and now *Marvin Gardens.*

I'm not saying, obviously, that other countries never make emptily pretentious films. (It's more the rule than otherwise in Poland and Czechoslovakia.) But new American film makers sometimes seem to worry overmuch about being mistaken for old Hollywood factory hands. If only Rafelson would stop proving that he is not Henry Hathaway or Robert Z. Leonard, if only he would realize that seriousness comes from fundamental sincerity—even in the best of the most baroque Fellini—then his gifts might flower. I suggest an example to him for study: the whole final filling-station sequence of *Five Easy Pieces.*

Fellini's Roma

(November 4, 1972)

THE public agony of Federico Fellini continues, and continues to be extremely sad. He is metamorphosing from an artist whose works can be judged into an invalid whose symptoms must be diagnosed. All that talent, swirling around in that big man, grasping frantically and (still) futilely at connection.

Since *Juliet of the Spirits* (1965), which itself had stumbled down from *8½*, he has made *Toby Dammit,* an enjoyable episode in an anthology film, *Fellini Satyricon,* a coruscating junk pile, and *The Clowns,* an avowedly sentimental, often moving quasi-documentary about circuses. Now *Roma,* another quasi-documentary: of what the city meant to him as a provincial youth, how it seemed when he arrived, what it seems to him today.

Not a bad commission for a picture, and anyone who has never seen a Fellini film might be struck by the fertility and easy skill of this one. Unfortunately not many of us have the requisite ignorance of Fellini. We keep seeing remakes here of what he has done before. The scenes of youthful longing are varied only slightly from those in *The Clowns,* which even then were not as good as in *I Vitelloni.* The burst of outdoor communal eating in Rome is only a domesticated modern version of the feasts in *Satyricon.* Fellini's "typage" (Eisenstein's term)—the ability to select unusual faces that are self-explaining, that serve their functions without dossier—used to be a kind of wonderful caricature; here the method caricatures itself because it is so repetitious and because there is no main substance to which it can contribute. The brothel scenes are the nadir in this matter; the use of raddled faces of cheap whores is always the last infirmity of a social commentator's art. Besides, after La Saraghina in *8½,* Fellini has said everything he has to say on the subject—which is precisely his problem on most subjects.

He hasn't even enough resource and observation to fulfill his own commission for this film. Desperate for material, he tacks on a long parodic ecclesiastical fashion show near the end, saying that he and his camera crew are going to visit an old lonely princess who lives in a huge palazzo. The fashion show is her dream. Why *her* dream in this picture?—except that it gives Fellini one more chance for clerical mockery, complete with drifting mist, and dramatically shifting lights? Besides, why would a pious woman have dreamed this satirical dream?

He pads the picture with some rainy-day traffic sequences—blurred auto lights in the mist, for heaven's sake, from Fellini! (Together with a brief recap of the traffic jam from the beginning of *8½.*) And things are so low with him that the only way he can think to finish is to follow a bunch of nighttime motorcyclists as they vroom through the city.

But I don't want to go on about it. Fellini has given me and millions much of the best pleasure we've had from films in the last twenty years. He is a victim of this age's gravest disease for artists: the inability to synthesize new subject matter out of experience, the shattering of creative confidence by the immensity of modern consciousness. I and, I'm sure, those millions hope for the best.

Two English Girls

(November 18, 1972)

FRANÇOIS Truffaut's new film is based on the second novel by Henri-Pierre Roché, author of *Jules and Jim*. The second novel, we're told, was an attempt to explore truthfully the experiences from which the first novel was fabricated. To judge by the film, it doesn't do any such thing; but it produces the best Truffaut picture since the other Roché adaptation in 1961.

Again with Jean Gruault as his script collaborator, Truffaut uses the rhythms, lifts, delays, and ellipses that constitute his now-familiar style. The story begins at about the same time as the first film but ends much sooner. Claude, a young, fairly well-to-do art critic and novelist, meets an English girl named Anne in Paris, then visits her and her sister Muriel and their mother in Wales. An engagement is almost maneuvered between Claude and Muriel, but not quite. During the next seven years, with settings in Paris and Switzerland, Claude deflowers both sisters; Anne dies and Muriel marries someone else. In an epilogue fifteen years later, Claude wanders through a group of schoolchildren in Paris, wondering whether one of them is Muriel's daughter.

The main resemblance between the scripts of the two related films is the use of narration (spoken by Truffaut?). It's spoken rapidly and impersonally—mere reporting—to cover time lapses, to describe hidden feelings, sometimes even to condense the very scene at which we are looking and whose dialogue we can't hear. Truffaut thus uses words as a species of montage—a device that in the visual sense he often used earlier, here hardly at all. But once again he builds his story in separated blocks, fading to black after a number of scenes—sometimes in the middle of scenes—as a means of punctuation. It's all pleasant enough and moderately stimulating. Only his persistent use of the iris is an annoying affectation.

The general tone is much like the earlier film: a surface of restraint through which flames of passion are sometimes allowed to leap; decorum and amity as a medium for sex; character stated, rather than developed; and the characters very conscious of being "characters" in the Victorian sense. This method works only if arbitrary actions add up to understanding. But here, as in so many *New Yorker* stories, they do not. Characters simply *behave:* unexpectedly, quietly; and are understood only by other characters, not by us. If action-as-flourish is done with enough bravado, it sometimes cows the viewer or reader into believing that the author has deep psychological penetration. Most of the time, as here, it seems mere precious four-flushing. For instance, how does Claude know, when at last he goes to bed with the virgin Muriel, that she intends this as a one-night matter only? The "deepness" of insight everywhere is pretty shallow.

Nor is this film credible as a "source" for *Jules and Jim*. Yes, it's about a trio (though differently composed), but the real point of the earlier film—confirmed for me by repeated viewings—is that Catherine is a psychopathic destroyer who kills one man and ravages the life of another, a female revenging herself on the brutally domineering world of men with the only means at her disposal, and doing it with the spirit and caprice that men seem to want in their destroyers. Claude bears no such reverse relation to the two English girls: he is as much the victim as victimizer. Anne dies of tuberculosis, he doesn't kill her. And Muriel, though she suffers a good deal, principally through her own romanticism, ends up better off than the finally lonely Claude.

Then what *is* the film about? Contrast of national customs and mores? Nothing new here, too weak a subject. Change of male-female attitudes through the era? Too oblique; unavoidable in any film covering these years. Maturation of a French mother's-boy? Claude is pretty much the same at the end as at the beginning.

No, none of these nor the fabricated "deepness" of the psychology is the subject; the real subject is charm. This has always been Truffaut's best accomplishment, with the arguable exception of *The 400 Blows;* and since *Jules and Jim,* charm has moved from being his method to his subject. He is now in the Charm Business. Period pictures are obviously best for that trade, and this is his first romantic period piece since *Jules and Jim;* thus it's his best film since that one, though not nearly as good.

Again he has Georges Delerue's music, again not nearly as good as before but apposite. (Delerue makes a brief appearance as a lawyer.) Speaking of sound, I can't recall another sound track that has made such insistent use of birdsong. Part of the Charm Business, of course, but Truffaut is good at his job. There are many lovely touches. One example: after Anne and Claude have gone to an island in a Swiss lake for their first bedding, the camera floats past their cabin in one long leisurely take as they busy themselves around the place and as the narrator explains how they are accommodating to one another. Their activity, poised against the camera's easy movement, with the narrator's voice above all, is cleverly appealing.

Some things are much less appealing. I never expected to see again a long shot of a house at night with a lamp going out as a symbol of death. Another example: there is a seemingly interminable and quite incredible sequence in which Muriel confesses to Claude by letter that she is addicted to masturbation. (Another example of Roché-Truffaut's false "deepness.")

But a good deal of the film is enjoyable. Jean-Pierre Léaud, familiar as Truffaut's Antoine Doinel, gives his usual formal, sensitive performance. The two sisters, Kika Markham (Anne) and Stacey Tendeter (Muriel), are nicely differentiated, and have the right kind of "discoverable" sex, instead of immediate pow. The two mothers, theirs (Sylvia Marriott) and his (Marie Mansart), are perfect. And Philippe Leotard is flavorful as a Slavic lover of Anne's.

Once more, in an age when we are drenched with pretty-pretty photography, Nestor Almendros helps to justify color. (As in *Chloe in the Afternoon*.) Of course Almendros is here photographing in a period and from a view in which everything is delicate and wistful, still the way he handles lamplight and gardens and such shots as one in which Claude, at a window, sees one of the girls take a letter from a postbox—it's all exquisite. And here's an example of what he does to make us happy it's in color: Claude is in his apartment before going to a sculpture studio to see Muriel for the first time in many years. The apartment is all rich reds and browns; the first shot of the studio is of gray walls, gray clay heads. It's like a transitional chord.

The Discreet Charm of the Bourgeoisie

(December 2, 1972)

THE child is father to the man, all right, but how often is the man father to another man? In art, not often. That's why Luis Buñuel, in the seventh and eighth decades of his life, is so extraordinary. In his later years, he has brought a minor strain in his temperament to maturity. And the "new" Buñuel is much better than the older, better-known one.

This early surrealist left that camp for a series of quasi-Marxist cinematic revenges on his Catholic upbringing, toward which he was nonetheless ambivalent, and for sexual fantasies, which were un-enlighteningly sadistic. *El, Los Olvidados,* and *Nazarin* are only three of his films that other people like more than I do. Then in 1965 he made the short, pungently witty *Simon of the Desert* and in 1968 *The Milky Way,* a delightful reflowering of his surrealist wit.

Both of these films were more interesting than *Viridiana* (1962) and *Tristana* (1970); the latter was well made, but both pictures suffered from his obsession that the macabre is automatically serious. Now, however, he goes back to the *new* older Buñuel—smooth, stiletto satire.

As with *The Milky Way,* the most important element is the script—by Buñuel and his usual collaborator in French, Jean-Claude Carrière. (He has other collaborators when he works in Spanish and English.) Buñuel's direction has the reticence of a man who needs to prove nothing, his casting is bull's-eye all the way, but it's the script that makes the film matter. His subject is the protocol of daily bourgeois life, how slavishly the members try to obey it, how easily it is wrecked, and how paltry the values are beneath it.

In and around Paris move the ambassador from Miranda (a mythical Latin-American country), the ambassador's mistress, her sister, her husband, and another married couple. En route the group acquires a bishop who likes to work as a gardener (a "worker-bishop") and a cavalry colonel. The repeated focus of the story is luncheon and dinner engagements, which are never fulfilled—for different reasons. The medium of the story is dream: sequences start as if they were actual, then become gradually and logically wild, violent or ridiculous, and end with the dreamer of the dream waking up with a start. Sometimes the dream *and* the dreamer are in the dream of a third party, who wakes up. The method is thus not strictly surrealist; there are no sharp juxtapositions of incongruities. Even more than in *The Milky Way,* it is the underlying philosophy that is surrealist, rather than any visible illogicality. Everything we see is familiar; it just gradually slides or melts away into the grotesque.

For instance, a casual dinner-party conversation changes into polite disagreement, then a guest pulls a pistol and shoots his host. Or, near the end, the seven friends sit down, at long last, to the dinner toward which the whole story has been moving. A gang of terrorists burst in (we know there are terrorists hunting the ambassador), and the ambassador hides under the table. The gang line up all the other guests and mow them down. For a moment we think this is the "real" irony that is to cap the film: the ambassador escapes his assassins, while his friends get killed. Then the gang chief sees a hand reaching up from under the table for a slice of meat! They discover the ambassador under the table, calmly chewing the meat as he awaits them, and we realize that what we are seeing is one more dream. The ambassador's greed, his aristocratic hauteur in the face of it all, have only been symbolized, in a neat comic action; and the slaughtered friends have not been killed "really" any more than a man hiding from assassins would "really" reach up for a slice of meat.

The business link between the ambassador and the two husbands in this circle is the cocaine trade. Some critics have objected that this element is too grim; since most of the audience do not push dope, it may distance them from identification with the other, bourgeois elements. But the cocaine-symbol doesn't seem to me any more distancing than the prostitution-symbol in *Belle de Jour* and is much less sentimental.

Another resemblance to *The Milky Way* is the recurring use of a journey along a road, as a sort of *basso ostinato.* Every once in a while, between sequences, we get a shot of the original six friends walking along a lonely country road in city dress. It's never explained, no destination is ever reached, it's not part of the story (as the road was in the earlier film). Journey or mystery or incongruity—the device essentially is just a pleasant metaphor in the sly comedy mystery.

Among the actors, Fernando Rey, Paul Frankeur, Delphine Seyrig, and Michel Piccoli are familiar from past Buñuel and elsewhere; Bulle Ogier was *La Salamandre* herself; Jean-Pierre Cassel, the

Pierrot of early de Broca films, is engagingly present. All of them, and others, give the film the effortless credibility it needs to make us twist our necks as we follow them from the dead center of behavior into the wildly eccentric. Finally this new film isn't quite as good as *The Milky Way* simply because the subject matter isn't as rich as the history of Catholicism and its heresies; still it's a delight.

Why?

(*December 2, 1972*)

THIS is the kind of quiet surprise we used to get from Italy in the fifties and early sixties, films like Comencini's *Bread, Love, and Dreams* and *Everybody Go Home*—"program" pictures which turned out to have unexpected substance. *Why?*, directed by Nanni Loy and starring Alberto Sordi, starts like one of those pleasant fictions about the fictitious Italy that we all love. An Italian engineer with a Swedish wife and two kids returns from Sweden, where he works, to his homeland for his first vacation in six years. As he drives out of France to the border station at Aosta, his heart leaps in song and our hearts leap with his. Alps, sunshine, Italian music—it's all there. Then, with a bow, an Italian customs guard arrests him, the police drag him off without an explanation or a word to his family waiting in the car, and a horror story begins, deepening as it goes.

Sordi learns, much later, that, during his absence, a viaduct on which he had worked had collapsed and a German tourist had been killed. The state needed a scapegoat and had issued a warrant for him on his return. *Very* much later, the charge is dismissed. In the interim Sordi is pulled down below the surface of smiling, song-filled Italy into lower and lower depths of petty officialdom, disregard of individual rights, insolence, torment, and, nearly, homosexual gang-rape. Near the end he is a shivering, wide-eyed shock case, strapped with restrainers to a hospital bed.

At last Sordi is released, a severely damaged man. The arbitrariness of the "happy" ending is right, because it matches the arbitrary beginning. That's exactly the point of the screenplay by Sergio Amidei and Emilio Sanna—the whim that hangs over an individual's head. Always below the beguiling landscape is the pit of power, greed, ego, and stupidity. The state shoots first and asks questions afterward. The beautiful border station looks different when Sordi and his family leave, precisely because he, and we, fell into the Sunny Italy snare at the beginning.

The theme is not exclusively Italian—to what country would it not apply?—but the locus is Italy, and Sordi is perfectly Italian. The authors and director do not make him a Noble Soul. The moment he gets in trouble, he gets slightly hysterical, nervously confident, compulsively obsequious—a transition that anyone who has lived in Italy has at some time observed. Sordi is not trying to be a hero in the abstract but the Italian average man in trouble. Under Loy's good hand, and with a very good supporting cast, he succeeds.

Play It As It Lays

(*December 9, 1972*)

THE consensus seems to be that the film of *Play It As It Lays* fails the novel. I disagree. The film is just as pretentious, posturing, empty, and, finally, commercially clever as the book. Nothing is so powerful as an idea whose time has come, said Victor Hugo, and nothing is so wretched as the cheap-jack exploitation of that idea. The vision of human life that was largely epitomized by Dostoevsky's Underground Man is now a signal part of our culture, even if we do not endorse it; but there's a lot of utilization going on, a lot of opportunism in the void-at-the-heart-of-the-universe business.

The argument is not that an author ought to believe what his characters believe and then act likewise (committing suicide, as one does here); nor is it even the old, respectable argument that nihilist art is a contradiction in terms. It is simply a question of *bona fides*. I felt from the first pages of Joan Didion's novel that the author thought she was on to a good thing, that Hollywood as absurdist hell hadn't been used in quite a while, and that she thought she could prove she wasn't just one more Hollywood debunker through the taciturn hyperthyroidism of her prose. Far from stating, or even watching herself state, a quantum of despair, she was watching me watch her. This effect takes writing past self-dramatization, which can sometimes be moving, to salesmanship.

Didion and her husband John Gregory Dunne wrote the screenplay and, it's said, selected Frank Perry to direct. Perfect. A phony serious novelist is naturally drawn to a phony serious director. To the mannered dialogue and understatement of the novel Perry has added a vast array of by-now conventional film devices, stolen (before he got around to it) from serious directors and already adulterated, so that he isn't even a bright magpie.

The heroine, Maria, is played, of course, by Tuesday Weld, who has become our leading phony serious actress. Maria is herself a film actress. She has a mentally retarded child. She has meaningless affairs. She has an abortion. She is upset by the abortion. Her husband, a director, is making a picture and has little time for her. Her only source of sympathy is her husband's producer (Anthony Perkins) who is a—guess!—homosexual. No conviction is ever struck in us as to why Maria got into the sorry spiritual state she is in from the start. We are supposed to recognize the standard code signs—tinsel values, a world of plastic, etc.—and just nod understandingly when she comes *on* nutsy. Like an archetype in a medieval pageant, she is not a person but a sign, except that, like the heroine of another Perry picture, *Diary of a Mad Housewife,* Maria is a self-performer acting herself for an unseen audience. At the end she even addresses us. All this is by now stale in modern theater and film—stale, that is, when it is merely exploited, as it is here; fresh and infinitely useful when it is rooted in validity, as it is not here.

The most ludicrous scene in this occasionally ludicrous picture (a relief when it *is* ludicrous, and not repellent) is Perkins's suicide. He invites Weld to take some Seconal with him. Wistfully, she declines. He says something like "Still think there's some point in living, do you?", swallows a handful, and lies down with his head pillowed on her lap to die. She cuddles his mortal coil as he shuffles it off in sleep. Two lost sheep, they are supposed to be. Two mutton-heads they are, poseurs even in a moment of death, making despair shallow and stripping suicide of mystery or nobility.

Desolation is an immense and immensely grave subject in our century, but American film makers seem unable to deal with it, unlike such others as Antonioni and Bergman and Kurosawa. Insofar as talent can be isolated from other factors, it seems to me not merely a matter of talent but of national temper. No nation in the Western world is less in touch with reality than the United States. If that seemed true in Henry James's day, the events of this century have intensified it. (Does one need more proof of the reality gap than the recent election?)* No nation has less of a tragic sense nor a greater saturation with the mythos of the TV commercial. Even if we don't actually believe that the new underarm deodorant will bring us happiness, our willingness to condone the myth, our tolerance of the mutual lie, is part of our reluctance to discard a life founded on fantasy. Those few who venture outside the fantasy frequently react like Virginia discovering that she has been lied to, that there is no Santa Claus; then they tend to convert the discovery into marketable goods, thus in their very disillusion supporting the illusion. (Compare Didion and Handke.)

The goal of good art is not solely to see who can make *angst* most convincing, but surely one essential of good art is, even under its comedy, some genuine acknowledgment of the shape, accidents, conditions, and limitations of living. One American film in recent years convinced me in this regard: *Wanda,* by and with Barbara Loden. But of course Wanda is not a self-dramatist, she simply *is;* she is a prole, so her story can be dismissed as a dated revival of thirties style; she doesn't live on Central Park West or in Malibu, so we don't "recognize" her furniture; and we can't get any yummy vicariousness from her trip down the Golden Slide because she isn't on one. Didion and Perry supply what the New Middle Class wants in this line: despair with a (figurative) percentage of the gross for the audience as well as the filmmakers.

Jeremiah Johnson

(January 6 & 13, 1973)

"THE strong silent man," wrote Lincoln Kirstein in 1932, "is the heir of the American pioneer, the brother of Daniel Boone whom James Fenimore Cooper immortalized as the American type for Europe." Although the type has since been metamorphosed occasionally into gangster or private eye or even hospital surgeon, the original remains a constant, and he gets a good reincarnation in *Jeremiah Johnson.* Robert Redford's new film is about the strongest and silentest of the lot, the mountain man of the Rockies in the first half of the nineteenth

* The re-election of President Nixon in November 1972.

century. He was strong or else he died; he was silent because, for months on end, he was alone.

The well-made script is by John Milius and Edward Anhalt, based on a Vardis Fisher novel and a story by Raymond W. Thorp and Robert Bunker. Redford, in the title role, is an ex-soldier of the Mexican War who is weary of the "civilized" world and wants a natural life. He arrives at a frontier post, buys some equipment, and, with minimal knowledge, rides west to trap for furs. In the mountains he meets an old-timer who gives him valuable advice; joins up for a while with another trapper; escorts the surviving son of a family butchered by Indians; and for a time has an Indian bride who is herself butchered by another tribe; yet, despite these companions, the effect is of a solo odyssey.

Through the last portion of the story, Redford tracks the Crows who murdered his wife and the boy, kills many of them, survives many fights, and becomes a quasi-legendary figure to the Crow tribe. The last moment is a weary truce between him and a Crow chief: they accept him as a figure apparently under divine protection, and he, his vengeance satisfied, accepts life as it is. That is the (tacit) bromidic resolution—a man can't escape the world by fleeing to the mountains. But the strength of *Jeremiah Johnson* is not in its homiletic theme but in its execution, which is its real theme. This is a gritty, weather-filled re-creation of the mountain man's life.

Photographed in Utah by Duke Callaghan, the film creates a sense of space so large that it is comfortable. (The interior of Madison Square Garden is impressive as space; the Rocky Mountains just exist.) The seasons are what you wear and live in, the ground is where you sleep. The transformation occurs early because of the way places are seen, the tempo that is struck, and because of the movement and address of Redford who, except for his modern-day speech, is very solid in his role.

Freeze is freeze, massacre is massacre. (A surviving maddened white wife is well done by Allyn Ann McLerie.) When Redford gets himself in a fix because of etiquette and has to accept the gift of an Indian wife, she really looks like an Indian girl, not a starlet done up brown by Max Factor.

Almost, this is a rock-hard picture. There are some soft spots. Sydney Pollack, who directed fairly well, insists on making his presence felt from time to time: a hand-held camera episode at the beginning, a "picturesque" pull-back from a burial on a hilltop, some zooming into and back from three trapped wagons. It takes austerity to make the camera "invisible," particularly in historical pictures, as Bergman did in *The Virgin Spring*. Will Geer, as the old trapper, is an arrantly professional sage; and (coincidence?) his dialogue contains the one pulp word, repeated often: he keeps calling Redford "pilgrim." Some of the incidents, like Redford's survival of a spear in the guts, take us to Movieland. And the songs on the sound track are terrible.

But there is much in this picture to relish, like a quiet ride through a Crow burial ground that profanes the place, like Redford's stumbling on a frozen-stiff trapper, like the daily business of trapping, like the spacious silence.

Traffic

(January 6 & 13, 1973)

I've never been a wild enthusiast of Jacques Tati, but *Traffic* is the best of his three films that I know. His Mr. Hulot (a name made differently famous by Balzac) is not a character but a clown-profile, so his films are arrangements in comic décor and observation rather than thoroughly engaging stories. But the arrangements are done with delicacy and wit, and *Traffic* has more sense of conclusiveness to it than his other pictures. Gags pay off better than they have usually done, and his customary anti-technology theme has more freshness.

This time Mr. Hulot is a Parisian auto designer. He takes his latest model to an international auto show in Amsterdam, accompanied by a mechanic and a swinging PR girl. Because of accidents, they arrive after the show has closed. Auto troubles dot this story of auto madness.

Many of the sequences are neatly funny. At the start, the huge exhibition hall is empty, with strings marking the rented spaces, and in a long shot, as men walk around the wide floor stepping over the (to us invisible) strings, they seem to be dancing. Two auto mechanics, who have just seen the moon-walking astronauts on TV, move around a garage in imitation of the heavy-floaty astronaut walk. A wheel rolls away from an accident and a Volkswagen rolls after it, its hood flapping up and down as if to snap up the wheel. White traffic markings on a highway flow past the camera in a delirious ballet. None of these sequences, you'll note, has Mr. Hulot in them, which may be why the net effect of the film is cool.

Yet it is a work proceeding from a central vision. Tati acknowledges the help of Jacques LaGrange and the noted Dutch film maker Bert Haanstra, but the best pleasure in the film is the sense of his control. Including the sound track which, in typical quirky Tati style, records only what it chooses to. I should mention, too, for parents that I saw *Traffic* in a theater full of children, who seemed to enjoy it.

The Heartbreak Kid

(January 6 & 13, 1973)

The Heartbreak Kid is the latest in a relatively new kind of American film—glittery trash. Many of these pictures, particularly the comedies, come from Neil Simon, who wrote this one, or his imitators. A previous example, *A New Leaf,* was directed by Elaine May, who directed this one. It glitters because there are some smart cracks in it and some facile observation of contemporary mores. It is trash because it betrays its subject matter, strains credibility, and swoons as sentimentally with "heart," in a hip manner, as any Victorian ever did in purple.

The original story by Bruce Jay Friedman, "A Change of Plan," is deft and astringent: a young man on his honeymoon is attracted by another girl; leaves his new wife and chases Girl Two to her Midwest home; eventually gets divorced and marries the new girl; and, at the wedding reception, finds himself attracted to the girl's mother. Simon's screenplay inflates and warps it all, changing a succinct story of a man without an emotional center into a fuzzy tale of a Feiffer-imitation fake go-getter. And Friedman's point is jettisoned for no point whatsoever.

On the honeymoon the film wife is made a ludicrous fool, who keeps asking during intercourse whether her husband thinks it's wonderful, who dribbles egg salad all over her chin, who gets herself severely sunburned in Miami (a patent set-up), and then smears herself repellently with cream. If the husband had *not* run away from her, it would have been a surprise. The sledgehammer writing and performance of the girl (by Jeannie Berlin, May's daughter) kills any chance for us to think the husband light-headed. (He is played by Charles Grodin in stock metropolitan-Jew revue-sketch manner.)

Here are some questions that this highly praised film left me with:

1) If Berlin insists on being such a boor, why did Grodin marry her?

2) If she doesn't know she's a boor, she must be staggeringly stupid. Again why did he marry her?

3) Why in the world did Girl Two, luscious Cybill Shepherd, pick up Grodin on the beach? *Him?*

4) When he chases Shepherd to her expensive Minneapolis home, how could her mother, unless she was an idiot, possibly be impressed by his moronic flattery at dinner? What insight does it show in the girl's father to tell Grodin privately that he has seen through the dinner-table talk and thinks it's a "crock of horseshit"? What infant would not have known as much?

5) How does this obvious phony finally persuade the very hard-headed father to let him marry the girl? This transition is simply omitted.

6) What in the world does the ending mean? In the last shot, Grodin is seen at his (second) wedding reception, after he has repeatedly mouthed platitudes to various guests, sitting alone on a sofa, deserted, "lost." Have we seen here the portrait of a rapidly degenerating psychotic? Is that what this comedy is all about?

Except for the refreshment of Shepherd's appearance and Eddie Albert's understated performance as her father, this film is meretricious, stone-fingered, and unbelievable, all done with a smart-aleck tone that is supposed to make us think it's comically candid. Simon and May have just found new tinsel wrappings for trash.

Pete 'n' Tillie

(January 20, 1973)

NINETEEN seventy-three is young, but already we can award Filmdom's Booby Prize of the Year to the person who titled this picture. It is not, as it sounds, the movie version of a dirty comic book nor a remake of a Wallace Beery-Marie Dressler oldie. It is, for the most part, an amusing, moving, sentimental comedy.

The script, based on a Peter De Vries novella, is by Julius J. Epstein, co-author of (to choose from a long list) *Casablanca*. The story, except for the last hoked-up turn, just attempts to let two people's lives run along before us. The dialogue is churlishly bright, and the wisecracks stay on this side of human possibility—that is, we don't feel, as we do so often with Neil Simon, that the characters have private gag writers in their homes.

Walter Matthau and Carol Burnett (no, that isn't a typographical error) are two mature "singles" who meet, have an affair, marry, have a son, and lose him at nine to leukemia. (De Vries's novel, *The Blood of the Lamb,* about losing a young daughter to leukemia, is a beauty, insufficiently recognized.) After the boy's death the script goes phony: a fight between Burnett and her friend Geraldine Page, an interlude with a swishy man, a split between husband and wife, and an arbitrary reunion. But up to that last fifteen minutes or so, it's a good laugh-and-cry film.

Matthau is by now Matthau, no more but—here at any rate—no less. The happy surprise is Carol Burnett. Under Martin Ritt's direction she gives a quiet, realized performance, with not a false moment in her, even when the script frazzles.

Ritt, a hot or very cold director, can't be said to redeem himself here after *Sounder:* his next picture may be just as slovenly and trite as that one was. (Even then he got a fine performance from Cicely Tyson.) Here he has worked with tight, discriminating control, with wit, and with an understatement that makes the sentiment effective. In her big scene, a set piece but a good one, Burnett walks out onto the lawn at night, as the time of her son's death approaches, and explodes in fury at God and Mary and Jesus. The scene could have been disastrous. But Ritt has lighted one upper bedroom of the house, from which comes the sound of a raucous comedy record, as Matthau entertains the dying boy. Against this counterpoint, with discreet lighting, with the camera gliding along gently and bearing down closer as Burnett moves, Ritt gives her a perfect "frame" for her big moment. And she fills it well.

Cries and Whispers

(February 3, 1973)

"IT'S the same old film every time," Ingmar Bergman said jokingly, while making *Cries and Whispers.* "The same actors. The same scenes. The same problems. The only thing that differentiates the film is that we're older. . . ." Though *Cries and Whispers* is one of his failures, his remark underscores its best aspect: it is further work by the only ensemble of quality in the film world today. Bergman and Company continue, respond, explore. The fact that the new film is not up to their best level is, in the long view, secondary.

Bergman begins his pictures not with a plan or a plot but with a sensation, a color, a glimpse—what Henry James called a *donnée.* The nucleus here seems to have been a vision of a big manor house, eighty or ninety years ago, with three sisters in it and a maid: an elegant isolated setting for some strong interrelated feelings among women. (He has generally been more interested in women than men.) The most beautiful moment in the film is one that sounds the original "note": it occurs in flashback near the end—the three sisters, in white, walk toward us across the great grounds, with the maid just a step behind, to the side, in dark dress. It is like a chord.

But unlike such wonderful works as *Persona* and *The Passion of Anna,* he does not proceed from *donnée* to articulation, even the articulation of ambiguity. He gives each of the three sisters a problem, and he links them in suffering and compassion (thus echoing Chekhov as well as his adored Strindberg). But the problems are all pat and patly affixed, like tags; the resonances in each and among all are stated, not created. One sister dies and the other two then leave the house; but these are only physical exterior facts as Bergman uses them. In terms of inner progress, catalysis, change, drama, the picture goes nowhere and accomplishes nothing.

Because one sister is dying, the other two are in the house, and we see something of their past lives in flashback as they wait. Ingrid Thulin, the oldest, is married to an elderly diplomat, a cold fish. In a flashback we see them having dinner in this house on a night in the past; then the diplomat withdraws to his bedroom to await her wifely services. In her boudoir, repelled and despondent, she calls her marriage "a tissue of lies." She takes a glass splinter and shoves it up her vagina, goes into his bedroom, lies on his bed, puts her hand between her legs, and wipes some of the blood on her mouth. I'm afraid that I thought this whole sequence was more or less what a contemporary Max Beerbohm might have done in parody of Bergman. The patently bad marriage, the phrase "tissue of lies," the extravagant actions, are all spin-offs from serious work done previously by Bergman. He has the courage for large dramatic gestures, but here the gesture doesn't represent or sum up anything that has really been generated, so it looks a bit silly.

Harriett Andersson, the next oldest, is a spinster dying of cancer of the uterus. Cancer is a facile device, artistically speaking, to rivet attention and establish horror, and Bergman doesn't shake suspicion of facileness. All that Andersson supplies here (powerfully) is physical suffering. And Bergman compounds the facileness of her death: later, the minister tells us that she had the strongest faith of the lot. It seems a sophomoric irony. What's worse dramatically, Bergman makes no pertinent *use* of her agony—on her sisters or anyone else.

Liv Ullmann, the youngest, is the least neatly tagged: her problem is a growing emptiness and indifference. She had an affair with the doctor who is now attending Andersson and would like to resume, but he declines, beautiful though she is, because she has changed too much. In one of the picture's good moments, he stands her before a mirror and shows her what has happened to her face; she says that he understands because the same thing has happened to him. A flashback shows that her infidelity has driven her husband to a suicide attempt, but this passage, too, is so arbitrary that it is almost like a cartoon of "Swedishness."

And there is the maid, Kari Sylwan, the one note of "health" in the film, but a rather stock figure, a heavy-breasted peasant type who accepts her lot. She accepted the death of her small daughter; after Andersson's death, she accepts the fact that she is to be turned out after years of service. She has even accepted, seemingly without any notion of wildness, the fact that Andersson liked the warmth of the naked body that the maid has often given her in bed. But again there is no enlivening touch: the maid is like a patient peasant out of a very old play.

In Bergman's long career there are two sorts of failures: the small-scale, rather petty ones like *The Devil's Eye* and *The Touch* and the ambitious ones like *The Hour of the Wolf* and *Shame*. At least *Cries and Whispers* is one of the latter: it aims at certain emotional chemistries that will interact in deep fire. But it misses. All through his mature films, Bergman has relied on us, the audience, as he relies on his company. This is always complimentary and is sometimes fruitful. Like any good artist, he has developed his own language, and now we can "converse" with him. But when he depends on us to supply virtually all the texture—for Thulin's wretched marriage or Andersson's crucifixion or Ullmann's spiritual atrophy—he moves from a dialogue with us to indolence. He is almost flashing cue cards, like a studio M.C., and asking us to react. He himself has not done enough work on this film, has not asked the script enough questions.

He has worked in period costumes before, most notably in *The Virgin Spring* and *The Magician* and *Smiles of a Summer Night,* and like the veteran theater director that he is, he understands them well. But the light in this new film is different, not just because it's in color—*Passion* was in color. He has not only moved backward in time, he has moved inland from the sea, and plays most of his film indoors, which he has not been doing lately. All is rich, overrich, lush. Even the bowl held up for Andersson to be sick in is too lovely. Predictably, Bergman has *seen* every shot exquisitely, and Sven Nykvist, his fine cinematographer, has doubtless added something of his own. But there's a lot of reveling in a fairly obvious color scheme. Red predominates; even the coverlet on the maid's modest bed is red. When sequences fade, they do not fade to black or white but to red. It is not a subtle chromatic scheme. Here, too, it looks as if Bergman has not thought hard enough.

I have omitted what I hope the reader takes for granted: no mature Bergman film could be edited prosaically or falter in rhythmic control. And it is acted perfectly, with Andersson particularly true.

Cries and Whispers doesn't reflect the bankruptcy one feels in the recent work of another master, Fellini. Bergman has plenty to "say": he simply hasn't said it very well in this instance. The writer—no, the conceiver—has failed the director. But, as I've said about previous Bergman misses, what of it? In Hollywood the law used to be— perhaps still is—that you're as good as your last picture. Bergman is as good as the best he has done, as the best he will surely do.

The Getaway

(February 10, 1973)

IF you could somehow weave a new leading actress into the master print of *The Getaway,* you would have a first-class crime thriller. All it needs is not to have Ali McGraw. Well, that's not quite all, still it would be so great an improvement that the other faults would diminish. The two leading characters are a bank robber and his wife—who are *not* characters, just stock figures. Steve McQueen, who was so good and complete in *Junior Bonner,* has no "internalizing" to do here. He is simply a commanding pro. McGraw is his wife. We never know who they are or why, but McQueen is enough of a star to silence our questions. McGraw is a zero, so she makes us question her all the time.

Outside of that (immense) flaw in casting, the picture is smashing. Sam Peckinpah directed, damn him. He is quite clearly a madman with, among other gifts, an extraordinary talent for murder, so powerful that he makes us enjoy blood. "Down, Peckinpah!" cries civilization. "Oh, yeah?" grins Sam, knowing the truth about us. Part of that truth is, if you have enough ability and enough conviction, you can make almost anything work in art.

This is his first film since *The Wild Bunch* about a man who kills as part of his profession, so it is his best since then. *The Ballad of Cable Hogue* was all wrong for him, from the title on. *Straw Dogs* was about an intellectual who is forced to prove manhood physically; the moralizing took the (cold) heart out of Peckinpah's amorality. *Junior Bonner* was about an aging rodeo rider—the "age" element of *The Wild Bunch* without killing. Now Peckinpah is back where he belongs: with killers whose only ethics is expediency.

At the opening McQueen has been in a Texas penitentiary for four years; we see him denied parole. He then asks his wife to visit a crooked big shot (who is on the parole board) and to say that he's up for sale. She sees the man and gets her husband released; together with two others, the pair then rob a bank for the big shot. (McQueen later learns that McGraw has slept with the big shot to help convince him.)

It begins to seem like one more Perfect Crime film. But the job goes wrong, for various reasons, and the pair find themselves on the lam, hunted not only by the police but by one of their gang and by the pals of the big shot. People get killed, dropping like leaves in a storm. Peckinpah insures that image with his familiar slow-motion for most of the deaths. The script is by Walter Hill, from a Jim Thompson novel, but it has a Peckinpah ring, including a salting of the salacious and a good deal of irony. The former is mostly supplied by the avenging robber (grotesquely well played by Al Lettieri) and the wife of a married couple whom he picks up as hostages. The irony runs all through.

For instance, in between the killings and escapades, McQueen and McGraw converse like just plain married folks, who might be having a spot of trouble and might just stop in at a marriage counselor on their way to the Mexican border. At the end they are driven across that border by an old junk dealer, Slim Pickens, whose principal concern is whether they are legally married and who befriends them knowing they are wanted by cops. He accepts a fat payoff, choking back a tear of love for these sweet kids (who have both killed people in pretty good quantity), and leaves, after saying *"Vaya con Dios"* to them as if they were Van Johnson and June Allyson en route to sachet-scented procreation. It's insane. And it's funny, because Peckinpah has forced us to enjoy their killings.

When he is right, as he is here most of the time, he is overwhelming. Take the very first sequence under the titles: McQueen goes for his parole hearing, is turned down, and goes back to his cell and his prison work, tight with frustration—a gem of a sequence, cut with subliminal memories of his wife. Lucien Ballard's photography is steely blue and soft, as needed, but it is Peckinpah's eye that pierces to the nerve of every shot, that edits it all together with crackling electric force. There's no sense in a lesser word: when he's in his element, Peckinpah is masterly. This includes a sequence on a crowded train where McQueen chases a petty thief who has stolen his valise with half a million dollars in it, not knowing what's in the bag; and the final shoot-out in a dingy hotel.

Another touch. My favorite moment in *Straw Dogs* was just after Dustin Hoffman discovered the hanged cat in his bedroom closet; immediately there was a jump cut to a long shot of the lonely house with only the bedroom window lighted, then a cut back to the room. In *The Getaway* McQueen and McGraw are quarreling by their parked car when we suddenly cut to a long shot of them, then suddenly back again. The effect in both cases is to *hit* the scene, to keep it moving, like a boy hitting a hoop.

Of course all the realistic apparatus is basically in aid of romance. When the pair tumble out of a garbage truck in which they've let themselves be packed so they could escape police, they look as if they had just been slightly wind-tossed. When their fleeing car rams several other cars, then skids up and shears the front railings off a porch, all they feel is exasperation. This is, literally and figuratively, an escape picture: escape into pure violence, which, like most qualities, rarely exists in pure form.

There have been comparisons with *Bonnie and Clyde*. Disregard. This pair have no mission or "meaning." As in all romances, *The Getaway* simply extracts one element of reality and dwells in it. Nor is the violence "American." Pictures like this don't fail overseas.

Avanti!

(February 24, 1973)

No word gets tossed around more freely in film criticism than "classic." Often it means only that the picture is no longer new but still enjoyable. But if we take the term to mean—as in one of its dictionary meanings—"adhering to an established set of artistic standards," then Billy Wilder's *Avanti!* is classic. It's one of his feebler works, but it's certainly modeled on good farce principles of the last two centuries.

The script, from a play by Samuel Taylor, is by Wilder and, as usual, I.A.L. Diamond. It could be diagrammed as a model structure for a scriptwriting class. This is not derogation. Farce lives or dies by technique—of all kinds; and Wilder-Diamond, as well as director Wilder, know a great deal about farce technique. After all, they made one of the best farces of this century—*Some Like It Hot*.

But *Avanti!* pumps and struggles, because it's not much more than technically good. An essential ingredient of farce, as these writers know, is physical motion; people must be under some kind of urgency to get somewhere or to do something and must run into obstacles that produce physical results—even if it's only diving under a bed to hide.

The initial urgency in *Avanti!* is weak. In *Some Like It Hot,* for prime instance, the two musicians are afraid of being killed; that's about as urgent an urgency as you can get. In *Avanti!* Jack Lemmon's urgency is to get his father's body home, from Ischia to Baltimore, by Tuesday in time for the funeral. Even though his father was a tycoon and the funeral will be big, it isn't enough of a mainspring. All through the film we see Lemmon and Wilder huffing and puffing to make us feel a duress that simply doesn't exist. They try so hard that it all runs twenty minutes longer than *Some Like It Hot;* length is a sign of insecurity in farce. Lemmon is—or can be, as here—an excellent *farceur.* But he's just never in enough trouble to make his agitation credible, thus funny.

And the plot complications smack of old-time viewpoints. Lemmon comes to Ischia because his father has been killed in a car crash with a woman. He discovers that, while the family thinks dad had been coming here every summer for ten years merely to rest, he had been having an annual rendezvous with that woman, who was English. (Lemmon meets the woman's daughter, who has come to claim her mother's body . . . you fill in the ending.) Lemmon's shock at his father's behavior seems dated, like his shock at the nude bathing by the daughter (Juliet Mills). Even today all these things might provide some embarrassment, but not enough for the comic anguish Lemmon goes through. And the ending, in which Mills sweetly accepts a life built around one month a year (like ma) at Ischia with Lemmon on leave from *his* wife, is much too slavish now even for women who are not libbed.

Wilder has often used a touch of the macabre in his farces—a very sound instinct, psychically—and often has digested it well into the comic mainstream, like the gang massacre in *Some Like It Hot.* But here the offstage killing of a valet merely makes us feel uncomfortable: first, because the man has been too well established as a character to be merely a body; second, because his death is not absolutely needed to fuel the comic machine.

But there are good things in the film: the way Wilder exploits the feeling of a lovely old hotel (as he did in *SLIH*); the way he uses vacationland light to make us feel high-spirited (as in *SLIH*); and, most particularly, the way he sculptures every scene, in script and direction. Every sequence has a sense of architecture and a final little polishing touch. For example, at the end of a mix-up at Italian passport control, Lemmon leans forward so anxiously that his nose presses against the glass of the official's booth; as Lemmon leaves, the official's hand reaches into the frame with a tissue to wipe the spot.

Wilder gets a good, sufficiently charming performance from Juliet Mills and a smooth, though rather unflavorful performance from Clive Revill, as the omniscient hotel manager. But he allows Edward Andrews to ham around as a State Department wheel. The dialogue is generally brisk, with touches of Wilder-Diamond political acidulousness, but they have lifted one line straight from Molnar's *The Play's the Thing*. Lemmon, exhausted at one point, asks the indefatigable manager when *he* sleeps. "In the winter," says Revill.

At least Wilder knows his formal sources (and he is a devout formalist). The structure is traditional farce. The body is in fine shape; it's the blood that's tired.

Under Milk Wood

(February 24, 1973)

LONG before you see *Under Milk Wood*, you know what's going to be said about it: it's not A Film. It's the kind of picture that's made once in a while (like the very different *Top Banana*) as if to provide an example of something that's not A Film.

All right, it's *not* A Film. It doesn't live by virtue of its being on the screen. It lived before it got to the screen, which is always dangerous for screen material (though of course this is a danger that's often overcome). The picture is an illustrated reading of Dylan Thomas's play for voices. As such, much of it is very enjoyable. The verse is beautifully spoken, for the most part; the film is nicely photographed and edited. The whole thing is marred here and there only when it worries about being cinematic.

I saw *Under Milk Wood* in the theater (London, 1956), and it fared better there for a quite simple reason. When the First Voice described the town, the hills, the sea, etc., we didn't have to look at the town, the hills, the sea. We simply listened. But there was no way that Andrew Sinclair, the director-adapter, could do this on the screen. He was damned if he did and damned if he didn't. Result: he did. So when the First Voice tells us about "the anthracite statues of the horses," we see the black outlines of horses on a nighttime hill.

But—granted that the picture was going to be made at all—what else could the camera have done at that moment?

What holds us during these passages is the speaking, by Richard Burton, who has been speaking these lines since 1954, when he was the First Voice in the first broadcast. We also see Burton wandering through the film with a pal—Ryan Davies, a Welsh comic—though they never speak on screen.

Inevitably the film functions best, as did the theater version, when the First Voice is silent and the many characters are speaking their own lines. Sinclair has cast the picture generally well; the citizens are quickly stamped, and when we return to them recurrently in the complex fabric, we recognize them instantly, by their individual colors and by the way Sinclair looks at them. Some of them are outstanding: Aubrey Richards as the Reverend Jenkins and Talfryn Thomas as Mr. Pugh the imaginary poisoner.

Sometimes Sinclair flubs. Presumably Elizabeth Taylor was part of the deal that included Burton. Cosmeticized and fineried, she looks less like a small-town Welsh whore than like part of the deal that included Burton. Peter O'Toole is miscast as gruff old Captain Cat. The poignancy of Cat's lines grows from the fact that the lyricism comes from a nonlyrical character.

And Sinclair has seriously marred the piece by putting in a pantomime section derived from another Thomas story. Burton and pal meet a girl in forties clothes, lead her to an abandoned wartime hut, and take turns with her. (Through much of this section Burton seemed to me slightly drunk. Not the character but Burton himself. His offscreen lines had been recorded earlier.) Sinclair has said that it's revealed that the girl is dead—I don't see how it's revealed—and that "these two visible spirits . . . have come back to relive their life in the timeless town and resurrect their lost love." Bull. It's just an attempt to keep the film visually interesting.

It doesn't. The episode is counterproductive because it's strained and out of place. But at least Sinclair has recognized the basic trouble with a play or film version of this work. It's not a drama, it's one long lyric, and two hours is a lot of lyric. *Under Milk Wood* is often compared with *Our Town*. Obviously, it's better written; Thomas is to Wilder as, say, Delius is to MacDowell. But in his (somewhat maligned) play, Wilder was at least conscious of theatrical imperatives.

Language is what we would go to this film for, as spoken by
Burton and most of the others, while our eyes are cheered by most of
the faces. OK, so it's not A Film; and I guess I shouldn't have
enjoyed as much of it as I did. Shame on me.

Last Tango in Paris

(March 3, 1973)

AND after all the advance fuss, what *is* Bernardo Bertolucci's film?
Three films. One is new Bertolucci, one is old Bertolucci, and one is
old New Wave. The first of these parts is what has been most loudly
touted, and, surprisingly enough, this touted part is the best in the
picture.

The "new Bertolucci" sections have an unexpected strength and
engagement. The good scenes in *Tango,* though never quite free of
attitudinizing, strike toward something black and truthful, something
deeper than the director's self-licking sleekness in the past (and elsewhere in this film). Those good scenes deal with Marlon Brando, an
American whose French wife, the owner of a small hotel, has just
committed suicide. He is forty-five, a battered soldier of fortune. We
see him at the start wandering dazedly in a Paris street. Maria
Schneider, a twenty-year-old girl, passes him, notes him briefly, then
goes on to look at an empty apartment that she is thinking of renting.
(Why? She and her widowed mother have a big apartment and a
country house. She doesn't need an apartment until her boy friend
proposes, much later.) She finds Brando slumped in a corner of the
apartment. (Why is he there? He doesn't need an apartment; he has a
whole hotel.) In this empty place, after some desultory conversation,
not overtly sexual, after some (presumably) symbolic stuff with telephones, he suddenly grabs her, she suddenly acquiesces, and they
make violent love.

They agree to go on meeting in this apartment, which he rents and
furnishes. He insists that they never tell each other their names. (Is
this why he doesn't take her to his hotel? Is this why he rents the
apartment? If so, it's a prodigal gesture, renting and furnishing a
rendezvous, for a man not shown to be rich.) He wants to make their

meetings something distinct from the daily traffic of their lives, a discrete pool of fornication into which they can plunge with, so to speak, disembodied bodies.

She is herself highly sensual, but she also seems to be aware that she is serving some desperate need of his. As the film progresses, we see that this need is for nerve-naked shock, a fierce gobbling of sensation to distract him from a new fear of mortality. His wife's death, unexplained and unexpected, has frightened him, and he devours this girl as nourishment against the cold.

She is slightly frightened by him, though she denies it, and very excited. The subtlest element in the film is her unspoken, possibly unconscious perception that, in this battling of their bodies, in which he sometimes abuses and degrades her, she is bound to emerge the winner.

The language of these scenes is frank, his in particular. (Brando speaks some French, which is subtitled, but most of their dialogue is in English.) As for the sex acts themselves, although some of them are graphically mimed, they are all simulated; and that simulation is much less graphic than in, say, *I Am Curious (Yellow)* or several Andy Warhol films. A lot has been written about the "breakthrough" in *Tango,* about how porno films have paved the way. Don't believe it. In explicit detail *Tango* does nothing that has not been done in past "program" films, and it is physically fake where porno is not. The only and obvious difference here is that a famous star is involved, more famous than Jeanne Moreau was when she made *The Lovers,* but what Brando does is not much more explicit than what Moreau did 'way back in 1959. The publicity has carefully suggested that you can actually see Brando "do it." You can't. You never even see him fully nude, though Schneider frisks about in her pelt. (When I told a lecture audience that they wouldn't see Brando's organ, the ladies groaned.)

But the *atmosphere* of hot hard sex is there and—for a time—gives these scenes a feeling of collision and relief. Then the tension begins to ebb: as Brando's autobiographical musings dribble into the commonplace, as his rue-laden background seems not particularly rueful, and as his bitter iconoclasm—on the subject of the family, for instance—sounds more and more undergraduate. The character, instead of deepening, dissolves into a patchwork of platitudes and actor's improvisations; and the power of the sex scenes dissolves, too. Until then, however, there is a new touch of iron in Bertolucci.

All the rest of the film, including the rest of the Brando-Schneider story, is poor, and there is a great deal of it outside that story. The old Bertolucci inflicts on us his familiar philosophical doodling with the idea of doubles (the dead wife's lover, who lives in the hotel, has a bathrobe identical with the one she gave Brando); the garishly melodramatic (a long scene with Brando and his wife's laid-out corpse, in which he reviles her, then breaks down and weeps); and an ultimately stupid obsession with photographic chic (the penultimate scene in a dance hall where a tango contest is going on). Vincent Storaro, who made *The Conformist* look like an issue of *Vogue* devoted to fascist Italy, is once more the obtrusive cinematographer.

Then there are the "old New Wave" sections. These include all the scenes between Schneider and her boy friend, Jean-Pierre Léaud, the hero of many a Godard and Truffaut film. These sequences, replete with the facile political radicalism of middle-period Godard, are also full of Godardian cinematic references. (The boy friend is a film maker.) For a time I hoped that Bertolucci was satirizing the New Wave elements he was so patently cribbing, but the edge is never turned, we never see *behind*. Apparently Bertolucci is seriously using these ten-year-old references to characterize the youth of the boy friend as against the maturity of Brando.

Toward the end the old New Wave merges with the old Bertolucci. Brando's character changes abruptly. For no reason given in the script—which is by Bertolucci and Franco Arcalli—the brute suddenly becomes a worm and crawls after the girl. Brando fails to keep a rendezvous with the girl; she breaks down and weeps; when he finally appears, she says it's over. Then, out of the blue, he begins to tease and whimper and plead (like a sclerotic Léaud). He tags along after her through the streets and into the (old-style Bertolucci) tango palace. When he later forces his way into her family's apartment, where she has fled, she shoots him with her father's pistol, which has been hammily "planted" beforehand. He dies on the balcony, curled up like a fetus—another elephantine Bertolucci touch. Brando's swift psychic regression and Schneider's urgency to kill him are pure theatrical hokum to make that fetus-finish possible.

The music by Gato Barbieri bleats banally. Along with the title credits Bertolucci uses two paintings by Francis Bacon—a man and a woman with corroded faces—the cheapest free ride on a superior artist's work since the use of Mozart in *Elvira Madigan*. The chromatic tones of the film are what Bertolucci is pleased to call "uterine," but what I would call corny golden-glow. The depth of his symbolism can be measured by his use of that tango contest as a figure of sexual emptiness and also as a hyper-clear source for the title.

That handsome and affecting actor, Massimo Girotti (of Antonioni's *Cronaca di un Amore*), is the quiet lodger-lover. Maria Schneider is a hip Raggedy Ann, pert and appealing, the kind of sexy puppy whose clothes always seem to be on the way off. But the film is built around Brando, and he is only partly satisfying. He still has a lot of his old hulky, door-punching power, his menace, his control that itself is a threat. Early in the picture he is a believable drowning man, screwing to keep afloat; and the role is tailored as close to him as possible, to give us the feeling of watching Brando himself in his own bedroom. (Those groaning ladies!) But some of the time he seems uncomfortable or silly, as in a bit of business with a dead rat that no actor could make either funny or even straightforwardly offensive. Some of the time in this capital-T Truthful picture, he is so patently made-up that he looks like an opera singer. And some of the time he mumbles his (English) dialogue like a night-club comic doing a Brando mumble. I've seen this film twice; the second time, by coincidence, was in Paris. It was only after I saw the French subtitle *"Nos enfants"* that I realized Brando says "Our children" after he is shot. The first time, in New York, without a French subtitle to help me with his English, I thought he said, "Ouch." In sum, his performance is a mixture: of the good things he always was and the good things he has not become.

Bertolucci is a mixture, too, but with him, it's an improvement. In *The Spider's Stratagem* and *The Conformist* he was like a Fifth Avenue window dresser gone political. Now, less political, he is also less flashy, at least some of the time. Usually actors profit by directors; but who would be paying so much attention to this director if Brando were not in his film? How many would be calling Bertolucci the genius of his generation? Also playing in Paris at the moment is a film called *In the Name of the Father,* by Bertolucci's countryman and contemporary, Marco Bellocchio. This generally brilliant film was shown in the U.S. only at the New York Film Festival two years ago. No Brando, no hot sex, so no news-magazine covers. That Bertolucci should be hailed over Bellocchio is only the latest of the sorry jokes with which the history of film criticism is strewn.*

* See p. 268.

Save the Tiger

(March 10, 1973)

IN one of those tandems that happen occasionally, here is another Jack Lemmon picture soon after *Avanti!* When an actor is as talented as Lemmon and as unreliable, it's nice to note that, in a two-picture cluster, he has done well. The first was a farce, and farce is the style in which he and Cary Grant have been our best performers—though he has wobbled much more during his career than Grant did. In the second film, *Save the Tiger,* he is, figuratively, the *farceur* offstage, as he was in *The Apartment* and *Days of Wine and Roses.*

This is the sort of script (written and produced by Steve Shagan) that in the desert of scripts available to actors probably looks like good truthful writing—as one reviewer said of it, in my favorite critical phrase so far in 1973, "deeply profound." But Lemmon is a very much better actor than Shagan is a writer, so, after accepting the script, Lemmon has come up with truths that are more "deeply profound" than anything Shagan gave him. In *Save the Tiger,* except for two flatly impossible scenes, you can see an actor improving a script by understanding it and going beneath it, coming close to the immanent moral anguish that is supposed to underlie the role, presenting his perceptions of his character with recognizable Lemmon style but without cliché, his or anyone else's. Like a good *farceur,* he knows how to use his whole body, and he doesn't let any of it go to sleep just because he has moved from farce to anguish.

He plays a middle-aged dress manufacturer in L.A., a high liver and high-pressure salesman, a financial juggler who, with his partner, did a "ballet with the books" the year before to keep their company afloat. Now they have a hit line of new dresses which will rescue everything if only they can find the capital to manufacture and deliver. The film deals with twenty-four crucial hours, when the firm has its fashion show for buyers, gets its orders, and has to find a way to fill them. The day is presented as a capsule of everything Lemmon is and has been; whatever validity there is in the picture—and there is some—comes mostly from his voice, rather than what he says, and from his tired terrier look. He leaps from crisis to crisis like a lumberjack on floating logs, and his sure inflections, crisp timing, and physical precision carve out some hints of truth *within* the script.

Shagan, as writer, has reshuffled a deck of cards worn out by the hands of Paddy Chayefsky, Robert Anderson, and many others. The formula is to posit a past in which the hero not only had the glow of youth but in which the world was, somehow, better; and to tug nostalgic heartstrings with old tunes, references to the Brooklyn Dodgers, and World War II. The cast is also full of stock ingredients mixed by a dull chef. If Lemmon is a sharpie, then his partner of course has to be humane—Jewish-humane, natch—played well enough by Jack Gilford. In his shop is a philosophic old Jewish cutter who is poorer than the boss but happier. Lemmon's wife is slightly tough and sexually aloof. She goes to New York, and he meets an uninhibited hippie girl on the Strip. There is no character who is not a stereotype, no dialogue that rises far enough above middlebrow drama to make the comment on middle-class life that it aspires to. And as heavily as Bertolucci in *Last Tango in Paris,* Shagan includes sequences to justify the title and make it ultra-clear—in this case, a man collecting funds in the street literally to save tigers.

We see Lemmon stooping. He has to pimp for a visiting buyer. He has to arrange with a professional arsonist to burn down a plant so that they can get the insurance money as capital. Gilford objects to both actions, Lemmon rationalizes. (Workers to keep employed, themselves to keep out of jail, etc.) The whole is presented as a drama of American corruption: how there is no ethics anymore—meaning since the days when they were young and those tunes were new.

This is nonsense, on two scores. First, there is not one item in this catalogue of decline that could/would not have been present thirty years before, except the hippie girl, who is herself by now a howling platitude. Second, more "deeply profound," there has been no moral decline from a Golden Age in this country, there was a seepage of corruption from the top down, and it didn't begin thirty years ago. For decades the middle and working classes behaved, generally, according to prescribed standards. The worker was "poor but honest," the clerk was thrifty and punctual and hard-working and eventually got to be manager. (See nineteenth-century fiction and drama.) Both of these patterns pleased the owners, the bosses, the power brokers, who were living by quite different ethics. (See nineteenth-century history.) Nothing pleased the robber barons more than the employees who would not have touched a penny of the firm's money or shaved a minute off office hours, while the tycoons juggled, swindled, and raped. All that has happened in this century is that the loci of power increased on a downward social graph, and the morality of power went along with them. In 1900 Lemmon would have been a manager for a huge manufacturer, scrupulously honest, with no real chance for ethical temptation, or he would have been a small manufacturer with the mentality of a manager. Now he is a small tycoon who—one may say perversely—is so crippled by his heritage of clerkdom that he doesn't have the brass to be a ruthless tycoon.

I suppose this dark view of American ethics is somewhat overstated, but at least it's a corrective to the dreadful sentimentality that this kind of script leans on—Things Used to Be Better—the sort of romance that Senator McGovern invoked last fall with his "Come home, America." Come home to what? The Indian Wars, Jay Gould, the Teapot Dome, Gastonia? Underneath the Currier and Ives trappings, just where *was* that lost Eden which we want again and which cheap-jack writers try to jerk tears with? There is, probably, some hope for morality in this country, but it doesn't lie in illusions about the past.

John G. Avildsen, who made a moderately impressive directing debut with *Joe* and then dimmed himself a bit with *Cry Uncle,* shows here again that he has skill, particularly in the use of camera movement within a shot. I wish he would forget telephoto lenses, and he overuses the device of a figure in close-up profile against whom background characters play, but he has some genuine gifts. The only paralyzed moments are those in the script that neither he nor Lemmon can lick: a speech at the fashion show in which Lemmon fancies he can see his dead wartime buddies and a word game with the hippie girl, which is supposed to widen the generation gap.

Tout Va Bien

(March 10, 1973)

JEAN-LUC Godard's new film *Tout Va Bien* begins with shots of checks being signed to pay for the production. Thus he tells us he knows he is back in the commercial fold after making several radical films (his most sincere) on shoestrings. His new picture has a nominal co-director, his political pal, Jean-Pierre Gorin, whose influence is invisible; and it has two stars, Jane Fonda and Yves Montand, very visible.

She is an American network correspondent in Paris, he is her French lover, a film maker now "temporarily" making TV commercials. They met during the troubles of May '68, and if the picture has a consistent theme, it is a probe into the heritance of May '68—in them and in France generally. The pair visit a food-processing plant that's on strike, and they get locked in with the boss—an Italian who speaks French with the foreign accent that Godard likes to mock. The conflict between the wildcat strikers and their union is a miniature of the Maoist versus Soviet schism that Godard often dwells on, itself an echo of '68. Montand and Fonda may be coming to the parting of the ways, as her feminine consciousness is being raised and his morale—about his work—is being lowered. After they get out of the factory we see him at his silly job, we see her attempts at candid reporting being hamstrung by her employers. She goes off on an assignment; when she returns and they meet in a café, they may or may not continue together.

Everything of any importance in this film has been seen in Godard's films many times before: in technique, antitechnique, and idea. In his earlier "commercial" period his politics served generally as stylistic apparatus; in his "outside" period his politics seemed much more genuine. They generated his esthetics—with great longueurs and clumsiness but with great conviction. Now he is back inside again, and again the politics is moving to the same pretty plane as Armand Marco's neat photography.

In the factory Godard uses a two-floor setting sheared off vertically so that we can see into rooms upstairs and down at the same time, a theatrical device dating at least from O'Neill's *Desire Under the Elms* (1924). His own familiar devices also stud the film: shots held very long, shots intercut subliminally, overlapping cutting (the same action seen from different angles), and, of course, the interview, in which a character faces the camera and answers questions that we don't hear. The one device of his that still has some juice is the very slow dolly shot, with which here he traverses the length of a Lille supermarket and back, several times, using the discoveries and returns for humorous observation and sometimes surprise.

Because of the food-plant sequences, *Tout Va Bien* reminded me of Tanner's *La Salamandre,* a much more mature work on—fundamentally—the same theme: the struggle to keep human beings human. Next to Tanner's picture, *Tout Va Bien* looks like cinematic graffiti: rhetoric full of bravado. Tanner, I'm sure, would acknowledge a debt to Godard, and it may be that Godard's chief gift to film will have been stimulation. Not a bad gift; but it doesn't make this latest picture stimulating in itself.

Payday

(*March 17, 1973*)

I don't know anything about country music but I know what I like—and it's not country music. Still, there are many millions of fans and they are by no means all out in the country: one of the largest New York AM stations has just converted to an exclusive policy of country music. Some people who know the field have just made a good film about it. In 1957 Elia Kazan and Budd Schulberg made *A Face in the Crowd,* which, with dull seriousness, missed the essence of the phenomenon by pasting political import on it; now *Payday* sticks to business and gets a lot done.

The story is another Day in the Life Of, but it turns out to be the last day. Rip Torn plays a thirtyish country-music singing star, traveling through the South in a chauffeur-driven Cadillac, with staff in another car. (They communicate by car phone.) Ralph J. Gleason, a familiar of the pop scene, was executive producer of the film; it was written and co-produced by Don Carpenter, the novelist. Carpenter has done the simple but daring act of not inventing a plot: he has observed the life and distilled it in a series of interrelated incidents. The only thing that might not have happened any day is an accidental killing. A drunken man comes at Torn with a knife, and Torn turns the knife on the attacker. Also—a once-in-a-lifetime event—Torn himself later dies of a heart attack. But both of these events are quite credible, and simply rack up as more items in "another" day. Given the Southern atmosphere of honey-covered hostility and Torn's regimen of pep pills and bourbon and no sleep and heavy wenching, both deaths seem mere steps along the way.

The dynamics of the film are, in their small scale, admirable. Carpenter starts his script with a gathering of forces that portend drama; then we see that it's the life of the protagonist that is making the drama, not a dramatist, that Carpenter is (in effect) more a selector and arranger than inventor. We have all been aching for "true" fiction films about the multifarious facets of American life; Carpenter has chosen a revealing facet, and has used it without hype or heating up.

We begin with the finish of a roadhouse date, Torn's quick back-seat bang with a blonde fan, the payoff with the house owner, and an all-night poker game. Next day Torn visits his mother, who is on pills herself (presumably his doing), goes hunting with another musician, fights with him and fires him, and acquires his girl. For a time Torn is traveling with her and his "steady" girl, and lays the new one in the back seat while the other snoozes next to them. (For sex, who needs *Last Tango in Paris*?) The "steady" makes trouble, he throws her out, then stops off to visit his estranged wife. Later he takes on a young songwriter—a witness to the killing who is hushed up by being hired—and when, still later, Torn's heart gives out, there is a hint that the young man will carry on. (A touch of *All About Eve*.)

Torn has always been a somewhat eccentric actor, choosing his roles oddly, sometimes foolishly, but always implying in a nutty way that there was something serious about him. His role here is perfect for him, and perfectly realized: a con man who knows it and likes it, overripening fast but damning it to hell, viciously egotistical but giving value for his money to his audiences, public and private. It's hardly a profound characterization, but it's a nicely paradoxical one: Torn holds our interest, yet we feel not a pang when he dies.

Whoever cast this picture did it superbly. I could single out Michael C. Gwynne, Torn's manager, but everyone from the estranged wife to a barber—one of the two blacks seen in this Southern picture—is exactly right.

The director is a Canadian named Daryl Duke who has made documentaries and done TV; this is his first fiction feature. He's smart. He gets a little fancy with crane and helicopter shots, giving grandiose emphasis to moments that are simply links in the narrative; but especially when he deals close and hot, he has skill. A surprising amount of the picture takes place in the back seat of that Cadillac—surprising in retrospect because Duke never gives us any plunkety-plunk routine of shot and reverse shot. He handles that back seat without any sense of cramp.

Easily, with no self-consciousness, *Payday* carries a good deal with it, just by being truthful about itself. It explores an entertainment tradition that is a commercial extension of folk song, brought to this country by Anglo-Saxons, now transmuted and exploited. It's a type of show biz based on its performers' false naïveté—"I'm jes' a country boy playing for you good country people"—and a public that still wants to think of rusticity as proof of virtue, even when they live (as many of them still do) in giant cities. It's one more version of the pastoral romance, giving fake simplicities and fake elemental emotions to people living quite otherwise. Torn's singer is an aging professional Tom Sawyer, now hip, hopped up, and horny.

Ludwig

(March 31, 1973)

Ludwig is about two mad kings, Ludwig II of Bavaria and Luchino Visconti, who made the picture. The latter is only figuratively true, of course, but along with Ludwig's disintegration, we can see Luchino's.

The first mad symptom is the choice of this mad subject. This is a historical epic without a hero (like *Nicholas and Alexandra*), a central figure but no protagonist. Two hours and fifty-three minutes, acres of scenery, brigades of actors, all to detail what is only a case history, not a drama, let alone a tragedy.

Visconti has lately been devoting himself to German sin. *The Damned* (1970) was an operatic and politically stupid account of a rotting family of Ruhr tycoons who embraced Nazism. *Death in Venice* (1971) reduced Thomas Mann's great novella about the survival of Pan to a sickly, bitter-centered bonbon. Now Visconti has found himself another Teutonic toboggan slide—the king (1846–86) who built fantastic castles, poured riches on Richard Wagner, was homosexual, became paranoiac, was dethroned, and committed suicide. Is Visconti wreaking one-man revenge for the Axis? Or is he, as an Italian friend of mine maintains, simply jealous of German grandeur?

The way of transgressors is hard, says the Old Testament, and Visconti doesn't make it any easier. We trudge along in a story without character or theme or narrative structure. Very obviously there has been a lot of chopping and patching of the film, which contributes to a general sense of lunacy. For instance, Wagner is present from time to time, naturally, but he just commutes in and out. His last appearance is on that famous Christmas morning in 1870 at Triebschen where he awakened Cosima with a performance of the newly composed *Siegfried Idyll*. Why that scene was retained in a film that lacks all sorts of other narrative links would be a mystery if it were interesting.

Or, another instance, a few minutes after the picture starts, a coup d'état is launched as a group of cabinet ministers leave for Ludwig's castle. Then it's dropped. I thought that Visconti had simply forgotten to snip that bit, and thought so for a couple of hours until the coup d'état story is picked up again and I realized that everything in between had been a flashback. Or, another puzzle, at the end of a scene with Elizabeth of Austria, Ludwig's near-mistress, she says something about being assassinated, then we suddenly see a shot of her laid out on a bed under a veil, covered with flowers like a corpse. She was in fact assassinated thirteen years after Ludwig's suicide, but how could we tell from this insert? Particularly since she comes in again later.

As Ludwig, Helmut Berger's teeth go progressively bad, but his performance beats him to it. Romy Schneider, the Elizabeth, is as repellently smirky as ever. Helmut Griem has a few fair moments as a military aide. Trevor Howard, as Wagner, is unwittingly funny. He's a fine actor and juices things up when he's on screen, but he so patently doesn't know what the character is or where it's heading, he's so patently impatient to get off and have a drink and pick up his check and head home to England, that he gives matters a certain breezy inattention.

So the whole film seems as mad as its subject—in every way but one. It is gorgeous. The photography, by Armando Nannuzzi, is good indeed, but it's the materials that make the splendor. Piero Tosi designed the costumes, and if I note that he did the same for Visconti's *The Leopard* and *Death in Venice,* you can foresee what opulence and sweep these clothes have. For uniforms, Tosi had only to be accurate; military tailors have always known what the purpose of a uniform is. With civilian clothes, Tosi has an unerring eye for the dramatic, the enviable. I could feel several of Ludwig's marvelous overcoats wrapping my body as I watched, which surely was the effect Tosi was after.

Under Visconti's direction. This former artist and latter-day mad charlatan understands the theater in an old-fashioned sweeping-entrance and delayed-exit way. (See how Ludwig leaves the all-night drinking party with the young men—pausing in the open door and looking back.) Visconti miscalculated badly in his choice of subject but he understands that he's dishing up what used to be called "servant-girl theater": thrills of luxury for the lowly. He lays it on with a mink-covered trowel. Not only palaces and châteaux—the film was shot on location—but small lake steamers and lamplit sleighs drawn by plumed horses. (The last is a lovely slow-motion moonlit shot.) And Visconti knows how to make "mere" incidents visually full, like the ministers coming up to the castle gate at night on foot in a pouring rain, each one carrying an umbrella.

Expect no sense. Shut your ears. (Besides the English, some Wagner gets murdered on the sound track.) Go to see a series of magnificent film clips, and you can have a good time. It doesn't matter in the least when you come or go or how long you stay.

Love

(April 7, 1973)

DECLARATION, first—and boast: Lili Darvas is one of my dearest friends. But I'm certainly not going to let that stop me from saying that she gives a beautiful performance in *Love* and that the film itself is a treasure. It was made in Budapest in 1971 (and won the Cannes Special Jury Prize that year). When Miss Darvas came back to New York, where she lives, and told me the title and story idea, I felt uneasy. How wrong I was.

The film *is* about love, and it *is,* as she told me, about a dying old woman in Budapest whose son is in prison for political activity although she believes he is in America; about the daughter-in-law who forges letters from the son describing his glorious American career as a film director, so that the old lady can die happy; and about the son, who is released from prison unexpectedly, but too late to see his mother. When you have heard those admittedly unimpressive facts, you know as little as I did when I first heard them. This is a film of depth and delicacy, small-scale but true. Basically it's a political film:

at least it's about the stubbornness of individual feeling, more than individual thought, in a society not designed to accommodate wide variations.

The director is Karoly Makk who is famous at home but virtually unknown here, although a film of his, *The House Under the Rocks,* won a San Francisco Festival Prize. The script was adapted by Tibor Déry from two of his own stories, the photography is by a wizard of black-and-white named János Tóth, and the light-fingered editor is György Sivó. Together, they have all focused sympathy and art on this slender story to make it not only moving but microcosmic. A good deal about a great deal is encompassed in this little film.

I mention another director only to suggest, by reference, a visual quality. Truffaut, the early free Truffaut, has possibly been an influence on the texture of this film and its lyric, imaginative editing. *Love* begins with some flashes of the old lady in her bedroom, rising from her bed, going slowly to her window—these flashes latticed with old photographs and details of her life, accompanied by a faint tinkle like the memory of a music box. Before the picture is two minutes old, you know you are in the hands of discriminating artists—one of them Miss Darvas—who are going to tell you a story of pathos without being pathetic. The very gentleness of the lyricism has a hard edge of selectivity about it, of restraint.

The daughter-in-law, Luca, is played by Mari Töröcsik, an actress of charm and wit, young but with long experience on stage and screen. Luca comes regularly to visit her bedridden mother-in-law (who has a devoted maid), and between the two there is a fabric of real affection, nicely and credibly tempered with impatience and jealousy on both sides. The old lady admires Luca's beauty and steadfastness but admires them less in themselves than as proof that her son chose well. Luca, very bright, knows this; likes it and resents it; and teases the old woman, who is Austrian by birth and apparently has a German accent in Hungarian.

Through these visits and little duels and meals shared and expenses deplored, we get much of the past of both, pivoted on the son. The omnipresent fact of his absence, Luca's deception of the old woman so that she can die proud, our knowledge of the political climate they all inhabit and that the son is a kind of hero—all these give the film an atmosphere of freighted quiet. There is more not heard in the picture than heard. Still the old woman and the young one love and tease one another; and, sprinkled through in quicksilver glimpses, we get the world of the old lady's youth—elegance and happy marriage and savor.

Luca loses her teaching job because of her husband's politics. She has to take lodgers in her small apartment, and she moves into a back room. She keeps up appearances for her mother-in-law with the maid's help. Then the old lady breaks her leg, develops pneumonia, and, after a last quasi-flirtation with a young doctor fond of music, she dies. (Something which, in the vein of this reticent film, we don't actually see.) And then, suddenly, inexplicably, the state releases the son.

This, clearly, is the second of the two Déry stories that are the sources of the script. Far from letting the seam show, Makk makes the most of the transition—to this central character whom we have not yet seen. At the end of the last "mother" sequence, the screen goes black. Then dots of light break the blackness as the grill on the son's cell door is opened.

He is in the film for only the last fifteen or twenty minutes, and what insures the picture against faltering is that he is played by Ivan Darvas (no relation to Lili). I saw him first in Budapest in 1964; he has made many films before and since. (His theater triumphs include *Hamlet* and *My Fair Lady*.) Darvas is an actor of very easy richness, and he fills this small but crucial role with every tonality you have been led to expect in the son. As he makes his way from his cell to the prison office to his home, he creates a man relieved but not free, glad but within limits, hopeful because—perhaps *only* because—he is alive.

Luca did not expect him and is not home. So you know there is going to be a scene where she walks in and finds him, and in a way you dread this moment. Will it spoil the film, with emotion too glibly tapped? The answer, resoundingly, is no. She comes into the kitchen and sees him—the husband who has been in prison a year and whom she expected to be away for another nine years—sitting quietly by the stove, eating a large slice of bread and butter. The camera holds her alone; and in that moment, this lovely girl grows old. Everything that she had fought off during the past year catches up with her as she looks at him. There are a few Truffaut-like flashes of their embrace before they embrace, and in fear of that embrace, she turns aside. Then he comes to her, and the film ends as it began: quietly. In love.

Bedridden, always feeble, Lili Darvas nevertheless creates an entire woman, tender, domineering, cultivated, silly, perceptive, frightened of dying without her son at her side. Miss Darvas made her debut in Budapest as Juliet in 1921, and in the late 1920s was engaged by Max Reinhardt to learn German and join his company. (Otto Preminger, a theater associate of hers then, once told me that she is the only non-German he knows who has learned to speak German without an accent.) She was thus a bilingual leading actress in the years before the Second World War, playing in the German-speaking theater and occasionally going back to Budapest. Among her other roles, for many years she did a new play written for her every year by her husband, Ferenc Molnár. She came to America when Hitler came to Vienna, and her career since then has not been what it would have been otherwise. But at least we now have this film.

To repeat: a treasure.

POSTSCRIPT. Lili Darvas died in New York on July 22, 1974. Once again, and never more so, I'm grateful that the medium of the sound film exists.

Brother Sun, Sister Moon

(April 7, 1973)

FRANCO Zeffirelli has made a film about St. Francis of Assisi, and if I were Pope, I would burn it. It's the twentieth-century cinematic equivalent of a nineteenth-century bleeding-heart religious chromo. The Church has enough troubles keeping its best minds and spirits, the true religious, without the added affliction of hollow religiosity on the screen.

Brother Sun, Sister Moon was made, apparently, because of the superficial resemblance between Francis and his Clowns of God in thirteenth-century Italy and the Jesus freaks today. Essentially Zeffirelli is up to the same game here as in his *Romeo and Juliet* (1968): flatter the young and swamp them in Beeyoodiful Color. And this time he has added songs composed and sung by Donovan— to prove that what Francis is about is today, man.

The picture *will* appeal to Jesus freaks, and to those who think that all religious lives take place in the land and light of an Italian Disney-land. The outlines of the script have some resemblance to the facts of Francis's life, but the film does not: it is an embodiment, in its swooning colors and sentimental dissolves and empty cinema rhet-oric, of everything that Francis forswore. When Francis visits the Pope in his gorgeous palace, he deplores the papal grandeur. Yet there he stands, in his bare feet and rags, possibly the most Christian man after Christ, the hero of a film that swims in visual oil.

The dialogue, in English, leaves something to be desired. (To put it with Franciscan charity.) For instance, humble Francis, kneeling before the Pope (played by poor Alec Guinness), shakes the Holy Father's composure by speaking a few words. What words? A few lines of the Sermon on the Mount. I got the feeling that the Pope thought Francis had just made them up and that he was greatly impressed.

The best performance is by Lee Montague, an actor of smashing vitality, as Francis's father. The pleasantest sight is the face of Judi Bowker, as Clare, another future saint. Graham Faulkner, the Francis, looks like Claire Bloom. When his beard grows, he looks like Claire Bloom with whiskers.

Such a Gorgeous Kid Like Me

(April 21, 1973)

ONWARD and Downward with François Truffaut. In his last film, *Two English Girls,* Truffaut showed a few revitalized touches, perhaps because he was dealing with another book by Roché, the author of *Jules and Jim.* Now, working from a crime novel, although a comic one, Truffaut makes his absolutely stupidest picture to date, enlivened only by one good performance, a brief scene with a child (he has a gift with children), and an occasional view of Bernadette Lafont's good breasts. (She was in Truffaut's second short film, *Les Mistons,* 1958.)

Lafont is a Naughty girl, interviewed in prison by a Good young sociologist with a tape recorder. OK, so you know the end already; you wouldn't mind that, if there were compensations. But every step of the way, most of which is flashback of the girl's life as she talks about it, the script is one more reworking of oo-la-la Frenchiness of the thirties. Essentially, it could have been made with Danielle Darrieux and Fernand Gravey, back then.

Truffaut, co-author of the screenplay taken from a novel by Henry Farrell, has never directed so badly. Over and over again he uses the device of starting a shot in medium distance, then moving in slowly for close-up—for no reason. Worse, he is apparently so conscious of losing the *brio* for which he was once justly famous that he arbitrarily inserts some filmic horseplay: one bit of trick camera work in which a farmer kicks his little girl up on to the top of a haystack; one rectangular iris-out; one stop-frame. Just so you'll get the *auteur* characteristics of the man who made *Shoot the Piano Player.* And there is Truffaut's usual homage to Hitchcock: two apparent corpses, left elsewhere, turn up in the criminal's bed.

Far from spicy immorality, the final effect of the film is nasty. The innocent sociologist is in jail for a long prison term, for a crime he didn't commit, while the guilty Lafont frisks outside. No poetic or supra-legal justice in it, not even irony. Just witless nastiness. The script needed a touch of Sacha Guitry, who really knew the charming-scoundrel business.

As director, Guitry would probably have approved the performance of Charles Denner. He plays an eccentric ratcatcher—puritanical, libidinous, physically as well as mentally askew—a sharp comic vignette by one of the very best French film actors.

The Mack

(*April 28, 1973*)

IF you haven't seen one of the spate of black action films that have been pouring out in the last few years, you've missed a significant contemporary experience. If you haven't seen such a film with a predominantly black, predominantly *young* black, audience, you haven't had the whole experience. I don't mean such a film as *The Learning Tree,* which was merely black mimesis of white *Entwicklungsroman.* I don't mean such a film as *Sounder,* which was like *The Corn Is Green,* transposed and adulterated in every way except for Cicely Tyson's performance. I mean the realistic fantasies, mostly in private-eye or crime-story form, which are simultaneously acts of revenge on whites and sublimations of frustration through violence, sex, and getting-rich-quick.

The first of the species, at least the first I can remember, was *Cotton Comes to Harlem* (1970). Then came, and I'm noting only those I have seen, a few among many, *Shaft, Super Fly,* and now *The Mack.* There has also been a line of black "horror" films, notably *Blacula.* In one genre or another, there is at least one such film a month.

Most of them seem to make money, and some of them make fortunes. The weekly list of top-grossing films in *Variety* for April 4 has four black films among the first fifteen. Every such film that I have seen has been a wretched piece of work, but none worse than *The Mack,* recently opened and already a big smash. (Number Five among all pictures in the country, according to that *Variety* list.)

"Mack," I hear, is a West Coast word for pimp, apparently derived from the French slang *mec.* Goldie is a black crook who serves five years in prison and, after release, is steered to Easy Street by a mysterious older adviser in shades. (This character appears subsequently from time to time, just at right moments, and warns Goldie of approaching dangers. I think he's blind and that the author, Robert J. Poole, has read about Teiresias.) Immediately Goldie meets a former girl friend turned tart, who immediately begs him to take her on as ward. Soon he has a string of girls—including the obligatory white girl who is mad about him—and he's rich. He is brutally persecuted by two white detectives who want a cut of his take (in the course of their shenanigans they kill an honest black detective), and the story ends as Goldie's social-revolutionary brother joins him in killings and counterkillings after their mother has been murdered.

The best thing to be said about this script is that it doesn't make any sense. Logic and connective tissue are avoided with a rigor that is awesome. We just see a series of episodes. Who is that Teiresias and how does he get his info? How does newcomer Goldie acquire his girls? And what is that sequence in which he lays down the law to his assembled girls in a planetarium, while he sits at the controls? The script so patently doesn't try to hold any water that I developed a kind of affection for its sievelike quality.

But for nothing else. Goldie, the lady-killer, is played by Max Julien, the least attractive male in the picture. The hatred of whites in the film caricatures the truth—and the true basis for black hatred of white oppression—by blaming every single setback that every black character has experienced on racial discrimination; and by making the two white detectives such cartoon heavies that genuine resentment of white vileness is cheapened as badly as anti-Nazi feelings in TV's *Hogan's Heroes*. The direction by Michael Campus took me back to Saturday-afternoon serials of the twenties, except for some symbolic sections which are like the worst musicals of the thirties—for instance, a moment in which Goldie stands in a spotlight looking up and dollar bills rain down on him from above.

The Mack has some strong resemblances to *Super Fly*. In both cases the hero is an outlaw (*Super Fly* was a cocaine pusher); in both cases the outlawry is shown as a triumph over ghetto conditions, the only way the hero could beat white oppression; in both cases there are doffs of the hat to sentimental proprieties—in *Super Fly* to the possibility of revolutionary action, in *The Mack* to Mother and the sanctity of small children. And in both the outlaw role—which is in fact socially damaging to black people themselves—is held up as a model.

Or certainly is taken as such by the audience of blacks, who are mostly young. That audience in effect completes the film; to see it otherwise is to see it incomplete. No audience of slum kids in the thirties cheered more loudly when gangsters machine-gunned cops than these black youths cheer—first, predictably, when whites are bested, but even more strongly when black heroes triumph over *circumstances*. At the first appearance of Goldie in his flashy new clothes, at the first appearance of his "pimpmobile" (his $35,000 car), at the mention of his weekly take, joy explodes from the audience; and the dialogue between them and the screen, which rarely quiets entirely, bursts into loud, happy obscenities. When the hero of *Super Fly* sniffed his cocaine, there were knowing and approving comments from the audience. Similar, knowing comments when Goldie mistreats his women. I don't want to commit the amateur sociological error of basing generalities on small samples, but what I've seen and heard, combined with what others have told me and have written, indicates that at least my experiences are not exceptional.

The first reaction is double: estrangement and shock. A white viewer gets the sensation of a separate nation within the country—not a new (or true) sensation but always a disquieting suggestion. Second is the shock that black film makers and actors, financed and industrially aided by whites, are willing to exploit their own people: to show a young black dope pusher and a pimp as examples, just because those examples will bring 'em in at the box office. (And the incidental homilies don't cover this up.) All that talk about Black Power and Black Is Beautiful, and when blacks finally get their long-delayed screen time, all they do is show that Black Is Ugly—just as ugly as everybody else.

That's the first reaction among a lot of black commentators and white ones, too. Whites allowed the protest to be registered first by blacks, lest they seem anti-black. But as despicable as these films intrinsically are and as disquieting as it is to see them with the audience they were made for, that reaction of dismay soon begins to seem sanctimonious and hypocritical. After all, Black Is Beautiful was just a pep-up slogan; the true slogan is, or ought to be, Black Is Human. And why in the world should we expect black film people, now empowered to make movie money, to behave differently or better than 99 percent of white film people behaved in the seventy years that they had full control of the screen?

Shaft and *Super Fly* and *The Mack* seem to me different from, for instance, the James Bond films principally in budget. For Bond, the sadism and sex fantasies are justified by anti-fascism and anti-communism; for the black protagonists, by anti-whitism. Both licenses are glib reductions of true dangers. Recently I saw the Coming Attractions of an all-white film called *The Crazies* that in three minutes managed to sicken me with its violence. I walked out of a film called *Sisters*—directed (to his disgrace) by Brian de Palma and scored (to *his* disgrace) by Bernard Herrmann, who did the music for *Citizen Kane*—after about thirty minutes of cretinous story and lavish bloodshed. Will there be equivalent protests about these two white films? You know the answer.

The protests about the new black films seem to me insubstantial. From blacks, they are unrealistic; from whites, they are patronizing. The whites seem to be saying: "Come, come, you blacks can do better than that. Now that we've given you your chance, you're not going to make this sort of thing, are you? Why don't you just turn out one masterwork after another and leave the crass moneymaking to white film people?" (Not to mention the fakery: white producers and distributors and theater owners are making a nice dollar out of black films.) If equality means anything, it means that one group is not judged by standards other than those applied to larger groups.

I'm not arguing, cynically or otherwise, that values are of no consequence. But only after this Pharisaism disappears can standards really begin to apply; only after there is a *body* of black films, as generally rotten as most white films, will there be a chance for the occasional good black film, as there is for the occasional good white one. To believe otherwise, to believe that black people will never make better films, is true racism; and so, by my argument, is the caterwauling about these present cheap films while similar white films are tolerated. And the way that black film makers, now that they have the chance, are rushing in to make money, as avidly as anyone else, has a kind of cold comfort in it. It shows that culturally speaking, Black Panthers and Black Muslims to the contrary notwithstanding, this is one nation indivisible.

State of Siege

(*May 5, 1973*)

State of Siege continues in the Costa-Gavras line—the fictional re-creation of turbulent political events. It's not a field that he monopolizes, as witness Francesco Rosi (with *The Mattei Affair*), Gillo Pontecorvo (*The Battle of Algiers*), and Nanni Loy (*The Four Days of Naples*). But Costa-Gavras is good at it. This time he is in Uruguay, dealing with the 1970 abduction and eventual murder of an American AID official, Dan A. Mitrione. (Under another name.) The director did the script with Franco Solinas, who wrote *The Battle of Algiers* for Pontecorvo. The fine, chromatically acute photography is by Pierre-William Glenn; most of the outdoor scenes, shot in Chile, seem to contain the climate. The one tune supplied by Mikis Theodorakis sounds like a theme from Grieg's piano concerto.

Costa-Gavras has said that it was a key decision to have the American played by Yves Montand, who has been in all his previous pictures. This was possible because the film is in French, and it was important because an American actor, however good, might have thrown the tonal elements out of whack. Montand's innate appeal is especially necessary to counterbalance that of the old German actor O. E. Hasse (dubbed?) who plays a journalist inimical to the government.

We're told before the film that all of it is factual, including the dialogues between Montand and his captors, based on tapes made by the Tupamaros. These dialogues are crucial. Montand is "tried" so that he can be justifiably executed, from the rebels' viewpoint, if his function as hostage fails—to get political prisoners released. (It does fail.) Montand finally admits that, contrary to appearances, his work in Latin American countries has been to train police in search-and-destroy missions against revolutionaries, that he does it to defend freedom and Christian civilization. He then asks his questioner what the revolutionaries want. Reply: A world that has no place for people like you. The exchange ends there, which is the most baldly incomplete moment in the film. Every dialogue has to end somewhere, but I was aching for Montand then to ask about the police in such states as Russia and China and Cuba. Also, though it's painfully clear that much of Latin America is a political sewer, it would help the film's credibility if every single policeman and government official were not portrayed as either sadistic or hypocritical. Surely even among oligarchs there is occasional sincerity?

Costa-Gavras has directed with less of the incessant camera movement that he used in *The Confession* to fight the static nature of a film about a prisoner. Here he intercuts frequently between the hunters and the hunted, but he avoids any feeling of flip-flop balance, and he stages such scenes as panoramic sweeps of police barricades and meetings of parliament with a good dramatic eye. His biggest triumph is the one that also distinguished *Z*—his ability to get excitement into a picture whose end is known beforehand. And again as in *Z*, he may be able to make some Americans think a bit more about this country's foreign policies.

Still, the best film by far about Latin-American politics is the four-and-a-half-hour Argentinian documentary *The Hour of The Furnaces*. Among its virtues, it doesn't pretend to be objective.

Scarecrow

(*May 5, 1973*)

HERE's a picture that manages to abuse two prime American myths at once—the Road and the Male Pair. The Road, apt for America because of its size, is in fact often linked with the Pair, as in *Huckleberry Finn* (where the river serves as the road) and *Of Mice and Men* and *Easy Rider* and *The Hired Hand* and even *Midnight Cowboy* which begins and ends with a journey. *Scarecrow* debases both of those classic concepts.

The script by Garry Michael White is about two men who meet on a road. Gene Hackman is just out of a Western prison, Al Pacino is a sailor just off a ship. Both are thumbing their way east. Hackman wants to visit a sister in Denver, then go on to Pittsburgh and start a car wash. Pacino wants to go to Detroit to see the child whom he has never seen (by a woman he presumably never married), then will become Hackman's partner in Pittsburgh.

The script is phony from Word One. Why are these two men, who evidently have a little money, thumbing their way? Only to shove them into the Road myth. Also, White seemingly wants to evoke some faint proletarian echoes of the thirties, which seem anachronistic in the seventies. This fake proletarianism is underscored when they stop in a bar and Hackman gets in a clumsily contrived brawl with a whore (gutsy, see?), which ends with their drunken roll in bed (gutsier, see?) while Pacino sort of looks the other way. (Pacino never beds anyone in the picture, though Hackman is fairly active; homage to Leslie Fiedler and the latent-homosexuality theme?)

There is no move missed toward fake symbolic realism. Hackman's Denver sister runs a junkyard (*oh*, boy). Her girl friend represents the dangers of domesticity for Hackman—and represents it by practically breaking into a striptease at her first sight of him. After Hackman and Pacino are jailed—a short term for another manufactured brawl—Pacino is befriended by a trusty who turns out, to the surprise of no one but Al, to be an aggressive homosexual. After the trusty assaults Pacino, Hackman beats the man up—in the prison hog farm. (Get *that?*)

A supposedly climactic scene is one of the worst I have seen in some time. In Detroit Pacino phones the mother of his child who tells him, falsely, that the baby is dead. He then goes dazedly to play with children in a park fountain, his heart just breaking the whole time. He ends up catatonic; catatonia never took so long to arrive.

Trust Jerry Schatzberg, who previously directed Pacino in the rotten *Panic in Needle Park,* to grab at every exaggerated fake-truthful close-up, every consciously pretty strophe that the script permits. His new film is particularly foul because it subverts a latter-day trend toward some truth about American life (example: *Payday*). This story is possibly supposed to be one of transformation—Hackman developing humanity, Pacino growing up—but Schatzberg's tasteless and untalented attempts to dramatize these matters only emphasize how White's script has muffled them.

Pacino proves, to those who needed proof, that he is good only for menace; and this role has no menace. Anything other than tense gutter-rattiness is beyond him. Hackman is a good actor, badly miscast as a physical brute (Lennie in *Of Mice and Men,* but sexy). And here he wallows in actorishness, rather than in acting. Simple instance: blowing cigar smoke in the face of a girl he's hugging. That's an incredible action even for the rough-tough he's playing. Empty actions, done for their own sake, equal ham.

Godspell

(May 12, 1973)

I went to *Godspell* with some distaste and left with some, but in between there were a few moments of real pleasure. I had missed the New York show, which has also been a hit elsewhere, and I dragged my feet about going to a film that sounded like a dehydrated (just add holy water) version of *Jesus Christ Superstar*. In effect this musical is just that: it works up bits of the Gospel (St. Matthew) in pop music, pop culture, and pop attitudes; but it's less offensive than *J.C.S.* because it transposes the story to the present, right to Manhattan, the characters are pop sketches of some of the originals, not the originals in pop dress, and there is no claim of one-to-one reproduction. There are only eight apostles, half of whom are girls and two of whom are black; John the Baptist also fulfills the functions of Judas; and all ten of them, including Jesus in a Superman shirt, are young.

In anything remotely resembling something that could begin to be called a religious sense, *Godspell* is a zero; it's just Age-of-Aquarius Love fed through a quasi-Gospel funnel, with a few half-hearted supernatural touches. Stephen Schwartz's music and lyrics sound like spin-offs of an era, not original works. (But at least they are not as abysmal as his score for the Broadway musical *Pippin*.) The film gets its occasional lifts from two elements. First, the sheer concerted

attack on us by the youth of the ten. Youth and freshness and freedom are what they are selling, much more than talent. As a general
rule, this tends to put my back up—not just because I'm not young
but because, in commercial theater and film, self-praise by the
untrammeled young has almost replaced self-praise by the trammeled
middle-class. However, this group cracks through from time to time,
like a child who comes on cute and then occasionally *is* cute.

But even more effective is the direction of David Greene, a new
name to me. Evidently Greene is no stranger to the *oeuvres* of Richard
Lester, but unlike those who mechanically imitate Lester, Greene has
found his own rhythms within the Lester style. His pattern of cuts
and angles and surprises—throughout but especially in musical numbers—is more than merely arbitrary action, it seems to be obeying a
genuine and high-spirited imagination. And he has airily preempted
the city of New York, using it as his property in a way that no other
musical director has done. He has not prettified, he has selected—
archways under bridges, fountains in parks, skylines and streets—
with light-fingered affection. In one splendid zoom-lens sequence, he
begins a musical number with one person on a rooftop, pulls back,
then zooms down to someone else on a rooftop blocks away who is
continuing the number, then has the pair join, then cuts to the conclusion of the number in front of an electric sign high above Broadway.
The only vaguely spiritual quality in the film is Greene's use of the
best of the Manhattan spirit.

Memories of Underdevelopment

(May 19, 1973)

Memories of Underdevelopment, made in Cuba in 1968, was to have
been shown in a festival of Cuban films in New York two years ago,
but the Treasury Department intervened—after the festival had actually opened—because of licensing irregularities, and the festival was
canceled. All the films, I'm told, are now licensed for import; the
irony is that *Memories* was the one film duly licensed at the time.

This is an extraordinarily sensitive piece of work—exactly the
opposite of the gung-ho stuff one might expect from a newly orga-
nized government. Like the Hungarian film *Love,* it's one of those

complex, self-questioning films that occasionally come from police states in their periods of planned relaxation.

Memories was directed by Tomas Gutierrez Alea, forty at the time and a graduate of the national Italian film school in Rome, who also wrote his own screenplay from a novel by Edmundo Desnoes. The period is 1961; refugees are leaving Havana for the U.S. Sergio, a well-to-do man in early middle age, sees his wife and parents off but is himself remaining, not out of revolutionary fervor, or any other fervor, but basically out of a kind of curiosity.

When he returns to his penthouse, he remembers (with the aid of a tape recorder) his quarrels with his wife; he fantasizes about his pretty cleaning woman; he plays at writing (he has an independent income); he watches the city with a telescope on his terrace; and he waits. He has always been "European" in temperament and interest, has always felt ambivalent shame and pity for Cuba; now he feels hopeless and fascinated by the revolution. Will this island get over its (to him) congenital underdevelopment?

Bored and sexy, he picks up a girl one day, a would-be actress, and soon he persuades her to have an affair. He tries to "Europeanize" her with visits to museums and a trip to Hemingway's former home (a sharp, double-edged sequence). The girl, frightened of her position with Sergio, tells her parents that he raped her. He is tried, and acquitted. Now it is 1962, the time of the Cuban missile crisis. Sergio goes back to his terrace: to wait, to watch, to wonder.

Gutierrez Alea has made the film with a tactful, confident skill that proves itself through reticence. The only effect that stands out in memory is the use of the hand-held camera in the opening airport scenes, to give the feeling of actuality—how nicely it slides into conventional camera use as Sergio goes home. There are a few other "real" touches, notably a symposium of Cuban writers that Sergio attends, including the author of the original novel Desnoes and the caustic comments of a visiting American, Jack Gelber.

But the picture rests on the vision and exploration of Sergio's character and the casting of Sergio Corrieri in the role. Corrieri's face and manner fix the delicacy, the intelligence, the faded strength, the stubborn curiosity that are needed. To put the matter in shorthand, what the film gives us is an Antonioni character in the middle of a political revolution, a man who comes out of 100 years of cultivation-as-refuge, now facing profound changes that may alter the reason for the refuge and the refuge itself. He is an anachronism who lives in quasi-fear that he may turn out *not* to be an anachronism, who has only a shaky faith in the revolution that may make him obsolescent.

Memories is memorable, primarily for the truth of Sergio's character and the tensions of his situation; but it's also noteworthy for an extrinsic fact—that Cuba made this non-caricature film about a non-revolutionary's questions. There is no alternative to this change, says the film, but will this finally change the alternatives? Out of a revolution bred on slogans comes a film without answers: thus lending some credibility to the revolution.

The Day of the Jackal

(*June 2, 1973*)

THE film form eats up certain kinds of material from other forms, takes them over completely. The Western, believe it or not, was once a kind of *play;* it never will be again, of course. (I can't remember any play in my time that could remotely be called a Western, in the genre sense.) The film also seems to be eating up the theater thriller. There used to be lots of thrillers on Broadway; in recent years, two— *Sleuth* and *Child's Play*. Will the film also eat up the thriller novel?

Many are still published, and some are big hits, like Frederick Forsyth's *The Day of the Jackal*. Despite their success, I still don't understand why one would want to read a thriller that one knows is going to be a film, even if it means waiting a year or so. Why bother to read those descriptions of cars, guns, planes, pursuits, girls' bodies, etc.? Prose is now too precious for that sort of sight-substitute. Film can do it swifter and better. The process of reading has, contrary to symposium fears, been elevated by film, I think. The entertainment branch of fiction is now outmoded by the entertainment branch of film; and prose fiction can concentrate on the upper realms that are unique to its powers.

Having said that, I must contradictorily report that the film of *The Day of the Jackal* is dull. I read about half the novel before the bother of reading it outweighed the excitement. But at least I could see the well-greased mechanisms working. In the film I see them again, except they don't work very well.

The chief trouble is the director, Fred Zinnemann, a competent man (*The Nun's Story*) who just doesn't seem to relish this job. Without such relish, this sort of picture is nothing. Before *Jackal* is five minutes old, you know it's just going to be told professionally, with no flavor and no zest. I am no Hitchcock helot, but I certainly wish he had been in charge—if only to make me queasy with his cleverness. Take for instance a scene in which a maid brings up a breakfast tray to the boudoir of the lady of a château. We know the lady has been murdered. Hitchcock would have figured that, since we already know about the death, the effect of the sequence must come from the discovery by those in the film itself who don't know; so he must devise some way to let us enjoy our superior knowledge. (There are comparable moments in *Frenzy* and *The Birds.*) Zinnemann completely flubs it, using neither confrontation nor implication but a muddle of both. The lack of tension is doubly damaging in a thriller about the assassination of Charles de Gaulle because, if you don't mind my tipping the end, de Gaulle was not assassinated.

Edward Fox, brother of the James Fox who was so good in *The Servant,* is breezily mad as the hired killer. The rest of the cast are all right except for the cloying Alan Badel as a cabinet minister and the lovely Cyril Cusack as an Italian—*Italian!*—gunsmith.

A Touch of Class

(*June 9, 1973*)

THIS comedy is set in the present, but it was written by two men who go pretty far back in pictures, Melvin Frank (who also directed) and Jack Rose, both of them around sixty. Each used to work with a different partner, Frank with Norman Panama, Rose with Melville Shavelson; both know their trade very well. That trade comes out of radio sketch-writing, down through the early (and funny) Bob Hope pictures, Danny Kaye pictures, and so on. Their field is not the easy, unstrenuous hip humor of some mod comedies. Frank and Rose are cause-and-effect men; unforeseen-complications men; running-gag men; architects of the pyramid build-up to the payoff. All these things can be dull routine in dull hands. Frank and Rose have not been unfailing masters in the past, but here they are almost entirely on the beam. They know how to write funny, and Frank knows how to direct lean. No flab, no fat. When the heroine describes an ugly view out of a Spanish hotel window, Frank doesn't flash an insert of the view, he stays with her and her description, which makes it funnier.

The basic plot idea has some relation to *The Facts of Life* (1960), of which Frank was co-author and which was probably Bob Hope's best picture (with Lucille Ball). It was about a husband and wife—but not each other's—who go away for an affair and, for various reasons, including moral inhibition, don't consummate it. Thirteen years later Frank and Rose have their lovers consummate their affair like crazy, but things sort out conventionally, by newer conventions, at the end. (In fact, the tone of the ending is too solemn for the tone throughout.)

George Segal is an American living in London with his wife and family. Glenda Jackson is a London divorcée with two children. They meet cute, as the old protocol demanded, they go to Spain for their first (harried) meeting, they set up a little love nest in Soho for further (harried) meetings; eventually they part. The dialogue is bright, the incidents are only occasionally labored (a bit too much trouble with that Spanish hotel), the pace is brisk. Segal gives a limber-taut performance, much like Jack Lemmon at his best. Paul Sorvino, who was good in the New York production of *That Championship Season,* is good here as Segal's friend. The delightful surprise is Glenda Jackson. The Charlotte Corday of *Marat/Sade,* the sensitive woman of the world in *Sunday Bloody Sunday*—in a Lucille Ball-Rosalind Russell-Claudette Colbert fast-and-funny light-comedy role; and she is absolutely first-class. Her body is hardly voluptuous, but her personality, her acting, her voice are so seductive that there's never a doubt that Segal would flip for her. The picture is good fluff, but fluff; the only serious thing about it is that it shows the astonishing range of this very fine actress.

Paper Moon

(*June 9, 1973*)

PETER Bogdanovich is the Miniver Cheevy of our time. "Born too late," he keeps using the film as a time machine to take him back to the movie days when he thinks he would have been happier. *What's*

Up, Doc? was set in the present but was made like a screwball comedy of the 1930s. His new film is set *in* the 1930s.

Paper Moon is heart-tugs about a young Kansas con man and a nine-year-old girl who may be his daughter. (She's played by Tatum O'Neal, daughter of Ryan O'Neal who plays the con man.) Alvin Sargent's script, from a novel by Joe David Brown, is a series of adventures by these gentle grafters (O. Henry's term). A setup like this man-and-child pair can be an agreeable contrivance if it's used agreeably, and part of the time that's true here.

O'Neal, a phony Bible salesman, visits the funeral of a former mistress while passing through a Kansas town, and some neighbors give him her child to take to an aunt in St. Joseph, Missouri. On the way the child hooks him into partnership, her wiles being orneriness, independence, cigarette-smoking, and a touch of profanity. Finally, he gets rid of her in St. Joseph, he thinks. (The best touch in the script is that the aunt to whom he delivers the child is a nice woman, not a witch.) But the child chases after him, and he is presumably stuck with her forever.

O'Neal is like a soft plastic imitation of Warren Beatty. He simply has no force, although he's flaccidly bearable. His daughter is a spunky little girl, quite appealing, who does exactly what she has been told to do by the director. Sometimes you can even see her responding to his requests, when she poses and makes faces, but she is likable in an anti-winsome way. One curious point: she has a Midwestern accent, but her real-life father's accent is quite wrong.

Bogdanovich mixes a collection of "influences" and hackwork with a few good touches. In the first shot of O'Neal, you see him scurrying across the cemetery, filching a bouquet from a grave to bring to the funeral, and you know the film has nowhere to go but up. It does, from time to time. Some of the con games are amusingly handled, particularly when focused on the child. Some of the incidents, like a wrestling match and a beating of O'Neal, are platitudes. A howling cliché of a cooch-dancer hustler is partly offset by the handling of her fifteen-year-old black maid. The occasional fresh use of detail—a country hotel still lighted by kerosene lamps in the thirties—is offset by heavy-handed attempts to use the landscape as better directors have done (a picnic on a hill with one bare tree; the long winding road at the very end, consciously corny but corny just the same).

The look of the film is all wrong. Bogdanovich has had Laszlo Kovacs shoot it in the black-and-white sententious tones that Orson

Welles impasted on *The Magnificent Ambersons* and *Touch of Evil,* quite inappropriate for this sentimental comedy. I've rarely seen a film that looked so unlike what it was about, doomed to this schism because this time Bogdanovich has imitated wrongly. He is still a modestly talented non-person.

O Lucky Man!

(June 16, 1973)

FOR a decade or so, there was promise that Lindsay Anderson might become a British analogue of Ingmar Bergman—a good theater director who went to films as a place where he could be creator more than interpreter. Now Anderson has made his third feature film. Like his two previous ones, *This Sporting Life* (1963) and *If . . .* (1969), it shows that—if we can consider talent apart from works— he is the most gifted director in British film history. But his first picture was flawed, his second more so, and *O Lucky Man!* is so much the worst of the three that it seems twisted by rancor—pickled in Anderson's bile because he wasn't called a genius for the first two. The film exudes conceit and pigheadedness, and is steeped in self-display and self-reference, a three-hour effort at self-canonization. (Even the title is an echo of an early Anderson short, *O Dreamland,* to give scholars of the future something to mull.)

There is no single moment that is not well directed, some moments much better than that. But what is supposed to be a work of radical daring, in method and matter, is only a laborious sophomoric dud. Its cinematic "originality" is out of Godard and Truffaut and others; its social criticism is a harvest of thematic and symbolic corn; and its complicated apparatus, which is supposed to produce the episodic history of a modern Candide in Brechtian clothing, is like a scattering of battered parcels dropped behind the hero as he goes.

The script is by David Sherwin, who wrote *If . . .*, and is said to be based on Malcolm McDowell's life as a coffee salesman before he became an actor. McDowell, of *If . . .* and *A Clockwork Orange,* plays the leading role, moderately well. The narrative is built in episodes, each labeled with a place-title (Brecht); these episodes are separated-linked by shots of Alan Price, a British pop star, recording some of his own songs in a studio (Godard). The film begins with an iris-in shot and silent-film sepia tones (Truffaut), then—and later—uses silent-film subtitles (*Tom Jones*).

After a pointless prologue, which is the only section in sepia, the main story begins with a satire on factories and sales training that might have seemed fresh sometime before René Clair and includes the predictable seduction of McDowell by the company psychologist (Rachel Roberts). Throughout the film there are many moves like this, telegraphed ahead more clearly than Western Union at its best. When McDowell is traveling for his firm and stops at a small hotel, his horny landlady is waiting in his bed when he comes home. When he calls on the manager of a posh hotel, he gets taken to a party and, by gum, they show porno films, which tell the Truth about sterile, seamy modern life. When he is innocently casing a military base in Scotland where he wants to sell coffee, he is arrested as a spy. How could he *not* be, in this Sherwin-Anderson tonality of the innocent among wolves?

When the film isn't being excruciatingly banal in its "exposure" of the ills of our time, it's being equally painful in its opposing glimpses of purity and the lost Eden. Escaping from the military base and inquisitional torture through a lucky accident (O *lucky* man), McDowell soon finds himself in an idyllic pastoral setting, complete with rustic church, where a vicar's buxom wife suckles him when she learns he's hungry and where her two children then guide him across great fields to a highway. Change of mood: he gets a lift straight into a science-fiction horror episode—a hospital where a mad doctor grafts human heads onto animal bodies. (Heartless Science.) Change of mood: McDowell escapes from science horror to a passing van with Alan Price and combo, and a girl who sleeps with him while they more or less watch. (Brave New World.) Change of mood: the girl's father is a world tycoon who takes McDowell on as an aide, only to make him the fall guy in a swindle. A trial (with a lift from Genêt in the judge's chambers), then prison, then purification . . . well, it ends up with McDowell going to an immense open audition for a Lindsay Anderson film, presumably *If.* . . . Anderson, with the sureness that has distinguished him throughout his film career, picks McDowell out of a great mob like *that,* tests him, and asks him for a smile. When McDowell (inexplicably) refuses, Anderson strikes him across the face with a script, and then there's a smile.

That moment is the crux. The picture is apparently intended as a picaresque account of a hero protected by innocence, whose good-heartedness sees him through. (I would have thought it was his good looks that made the happy ending, but no matter.) This is all shattered by the blow that Anderson smites. At that moment I had the feeling that the very long, heavily fraught enterprise had been created for just that blow, so that Anderson could strike someone else on screen, an actor, a creation of his, like a master, like a thaumaturge, like a demigod ordaining life. It revolted me. It was the single most sickening, self-indulgent, ego-drooling moment I've seen in a film since woozy Norman Mailer got down on his hands and knees and barked back at a barking dog in *Wild 90*.

Even without that slap, the arbitrary happy ending, which is supposed to carry the irony of the end of *The Threepenny Opera,* would fail: because what has gone before has been so pompous, so trite, so full of mannerism without matter. The film could have ended an hour sooner or gone on three hours more: the plain truth is that Anderson and Sherwin have *absolutely nothing to say*—and I use the word "say" in its widest possible sense.

As further evidence of his meaningless daring, Anderson casts some of his actors in a number of different roles, almost always without disguise. (Life is a play, you see, and one man in his time plays many parts, and characters and types repeat along life's journey, and oh my aching back.) Ralph Richardson is touching as a lonely old duffer in the small hotel, who gives McDowell gnomic advice and a symbolic golden suit that he's made for the young man which miraculously fits perfectly; but Richardson is quite wrong later as the ruthless tycoon. And the "doubling" pattern is toyed with. I kept wondering, dullard that I am, why McDowell didn't recognize Rachel Roberts or Dandy Nichols or Mona Washbourne when they popped up elsewhere again as other people; then he *did* recognize Helen Mirren, the girl in the van, when she popped up later in a different setting—only she was still the character she had been. So, because her name was still the same, I guess, McDowell knew he had seen her before.

Out of this mess of pretentiousness and egotism and aimless skill, what emerges finally? A great zero for this film and a hovering zero for Anderson's film future. How can one still hope that he is going to acquire the discipline—his own or someone else's—to make a whole, good film? He's now fifty years old, pretty well molded, and if this film seems a stubborn bad-tempered reaction to the response to his first two features, what will his reaction be to the response to this one? His work in the theater, serving projects defined by someone else, is extraordinary, as far as I have seen it: his production of Storey's *Home* and the American productions of Storey's *The Contractor* and *The Changing Room* which were presumably modeled on his London originals. In the theater I hope he keeps working and that I can see everything he does. But the line of his film career points drastically down.

Pat Garrett and Billy the Kid

(June 16, 1973)

WELL, this shows what Sam Peckinpah can do when he doesn't put his mind to it. He bought himself yet one more reworking of this much-chewed story, this time by Rudolph Wurlitzer, a young novelist whom some people esteem highly. Into this story of an outlaw who was a *kid*, Peckinpah has nevertheless managed to inject his usual autumnal colors, his theme of active men growing old; and on this story of mindless murders, he has even managed to impose some populist Robin Hood overlay. (If a man is poor, particularly if he's Mexican, he's Good.)

But this stale saga of the tracking and killing of the outlaw (Kris Kristofferson, husky-voiced and fat) by his former outlaw pal now turned lawman (James Coburn, the poor man's Lee Marvin) is dull, slow, and sillily portentous. What a lot of loutish, cretinous, degenerate layabouts they all are, supposed to be epic because once in a while, or oftener, they kill one another.

Bob Dylan is in the film, a sort of quizzical quiet knife-throwing pal of Billy's. I hope Dylan hasn't given up his singing career.

But, through all the crud, Peckinpah's film-making mastery still shines. His violence is still the most shaking on the screen (not the most gory). And, aided by his cameraman John Coquillon, he proves again his wonderful eye. In one sequence, a man rides alongside a pond, himself and horse swallowed in shadow but both visible as reflected in the water.

And a special note for Ted Haworth, the art director. Haworth, whose credits include *Some Like It Hot,* musicals, and Westerns, has designed saloons and trading posts which are much too good for the goings-on in them but which at least Peckinpah's eye appreciates.

(July 7 & 14, 1973)

"Der alte Sturm, die alte Müh'," says Wotan when Fricka comes in with her complaints in the second act of *Die Walküre.* Loosely translated: "The same old beefs, once again." I thought of Wotan when I read the inside stories about what happened to Sam Peckinpah's *Pat Garrett and Billy the Kid* before release, how the producers had snipped and altered it, and that what we're seeing is not the director's concept. Certainly it's a ghastly practice, but almost every American film director (and many a foreign one) knows that it can happen to him, that it usually does, and that he has to be judged by the film as released, not as he talks about it or shows it privately to friends. The right of last cut virtually doesn't exist for U.S. directors; and virtually every review ever published in this country that treats a film as the director's own is merely using a semantic convenience. But what's the critic's alternative? Chaos.

The change, of course, ought to be in the right of final cut; if a director is worth hiring, he's worth the right to finish the job, or should be. But until that change occurs, all the talk about the troubles of Peckinpah—and many others—is only painful, not useful. Anyway, the whole question of the textual integrity of films after release, even in those cases where the director has had final cut, is almost too sore to bear thinking about. In a New York theater recently I saw *Potemkin* with its single most famous shot—the woman with the broken eyeglasses—not even in it. (And like everyone who rents 16mm prints for classroom use, I'm continually appalled by missing snippets—not to mention filthy prints that are the rule rather than the exception. Complaints are always politely answered; nothing changes.) The situation is simply uncontrollable, like any complex matter that depends on voluntary honesty rather than enforceable prescription.

But whether it's first release or subsequent release, we can only deal with what we see. I have long and often urged viewers to complain when they see films that have been tampered with. I urge directors to complain about interference and to take what action they can against it, as a professional group, and would do whatever I could to support them. OK, now everyone is urged. Meanwhile, how can I review a Peckinpah picture that I and others will not see?

The Hireling

(*July 7 & 14, 1973*)

THE peasant-and-princess sex relation is one of the oldest themes in literature—from the *Arabian Nights* through Middleton and Strindberg and Hamsun and Lawrence to the English novelist L. P. Hartley who, in his own scale, dealt with it in *The Go-Between* (1953) and *The Hireling* (1957). The former was filmed two years ago by Joseph Losey, not really well; now a film of the latter comes along and is in almost every way much better. In my dissenting view (from most views I've read), it's a very good use of the very old theme.

We're in the past again, not 1900 as with the other Hartley but the early 1920s. No revenant boy, no mysticism, no "curse" as in the earlier film, just a small, implicative tragedy. Sarah Miles plays Lady Franklin, a recently bereaved young widow, grieved to the edge of mental derangement. When we first see her, she is being released from a (luxurious) mental hospital. Her mother has sent a rented limousine and liveried chauffeur to bring her home to Bath. As this first sequence unfolds, the neck and uniformed back of the chauffeur become a man named Leadbetter, played by Robert Shaw.

He is strong, resourceful, reserved, an ex-sergeant-major, very mindful of his place, giving and exacting respect. She is weak, pathetic, dignified, soft, very responsive to his male competence, yet without sexual reaction. That last point generates the drama. Subsequently she employs Shaw frequently, to drive her about, sometimes merely to the country on outings and picnics. She makes no sexual move toward him, and she's not restraining herself; she merely needs his strength and company. He makes no move toward her and, in the early stages, he isn't restraining himself either. He simply enjoys the use she is making of him, besides being glad to build up his car-hire business. His only courtship of her, quite oblique, is to tell her, in answer to questions, that he has a wife and children (we know he lives alone), because he thinks it's what she wants to hear.

Time brings her recovery, her rekindled interest in society; and brings him disaster. He has fallen in love with her, and seethes with rage and jealousy when she is attracted to a young politician of her set, particularly when Shaw knows that the young man has another woman. Chauffeuring Miles one day, Shaw kisses her and tells her he loves her. She is upset, frightened, grieved, unresponsive. Soon after, he gets drunk and bursts into her home one night; he confronts her and her fiancé in a melodramatic "exposure" scene (about the young man's affair). It fizzles, and not just because the facts are irrelevant. When Shaw sees how and why he has failed, he drives drunkenly home and in the courtyard of his garage, drives drunkenly back and forth, smashing into other cars with his Rolls-Royce. As he is smashing away, committing a form of suicide, the picture ends.

At least five elements make this film extraordinary. First, Wolf Mankowitz's screenplay. I won't detail the differences between Hartley's novel and his work, except to say that the screenplay is much more interesting, particularly the treatment of Lady Franklin and the elimination of Hartley's self-sacrificial ending. Mankowitz's script is remarkably simple, inevitable, compact.

Michael Reed's color photography is a relief in these lush Laszlo Kovacs–Vilmos Zsigmond days. Reed renders the English colors, the English mist on the skin; the lovely damp friendly feeling of the ride back from the hospital, the golden lights in doorways welcoming people out of the weather, all this and much more are very choicely and endearingly handled.

Alan Bridges, the director, newly out of British television, wants to serve the work, not aggrandize himself. There are no supposedly overwhelming effects, no drowning in period sauce à la Losey, although every legitimate detail is legitimately used. Bridges unfolds his story as cleanly as it is written, with a nice eye for peripheral action of minor characters and a tacit fulfillment of ideas. (A large cut stone on her doctor's desk fascinates Miles; no explanation. Later, just in passing, we see a collection of stones that had been made by her husband.) Bridges uses windows as a nice symbol of vision, distanced: the other patients are glimpsed through the hospital windows, and this is echoed by a figure in a window of Miles's house when she returns. Miles herself is glimpsed through windows by Shaw outside, as she descends the stairs of her great house. (Incidentally this is actually the house of J. Paul Getty, who lent it for the film.) And there is Bridges's work with his actors.

All the praise above, and more, is well deserved; but this picture would not exist without its two principal performances. I haven't seen Miles's recent films, *Ryan's Daughter* and *Lady Caroline Lamb,* but out of such past work as *The Servant* and *Blow-Up,* I've had very mixed feelings about her, a feeling of potentiality and also of affectation. Now, presumably with Bridges's help, she strikes a realized note from our very first sight of her as she stands on the lawn of the hospital gazing at a pond—the most wonderful first effect an actor can create, not that a character is going to be built for us (though of course it is) but that it *has* been built, that we are joining the created character at this moment. This shaken, groping young woman simply appears. I got the image that Miles saw this woman as lifted and held by the nape of her neck, dangling in air between the thumb and forefinger of a giant fate. Her whole being seems to hang physically from her nape, helplessly, like a puppy. As her feet figuratively reach the ground again, through the course of the film, the center of physicality seems to shift outward to her shoulders, once again squared, and the tonality of her character follows suit, still gentle but nevertheless stronger.

As for Shaw, I have long thought him one of the most gifted English actors on stage or screen, or both. He changed Pinter's *Old Times* for me almost singlehandedly. The London production had another actor in the one male role, but it wasn't until I saw the New York production with Shaw that I got an idea—in my own view, at least—of what the play was about. His film performance in Pinter's *The Birthday Party* was superb, characteristically underestimated by most critics because the film as a whole was poor. As Lord Randolph Churchill in *Young Winston,* he was good enough but miscast. Here he is perfectly cast, and plays perfectly.

Possibly excepting Albert Finney, Shaw is as close as British films have come to producing a Cagney or Brando or Gabin—a talented actor whose generative force is menace, lurking surprise. But, like them at their best (and unlike Richard Harris), he doesn't merely trade on this, he acts. His characterization of Leadbetter is a synapse in the social system of Britain. And the drunken scene in which he bursts in on Miles and her fiancé is a sustained explosion of outrage exacerbated by impotence, strength defeated by class calm. It is a crystalline moment which, inevitably, collapses his whole life.

Some have said that the film is flawed because it is built on a mere misunderstanding—Shaw's belief that Miles loves him and will respond. This seems to me a myopic view. The man's tragedy is that *whether or not* she reciprocates, he loves her and has finally to burst out with it—hopeful of course but without alternative. The essence of the catastrophe is that his contact with her has put him in a kind of iron cart—not a limousine—that cruelly and ineluctably takes him over a cliff. The social conditions of *The Hireling* may be past in Britain or almost past; but it is a well-shaped and excellently performed small historical tragedy.

Playtime

(*July 21, 1973*)

I always feel a little guilty about Jacques Tati. The man has so much of what one is always bemoaning the shortage of: taste, skill, personal vision. Yet his films leave me with something of the feeling I get from a Marcel Marceau performance—technique and talent employed in the pursuit of preciosity.

Playtime was made in 1967, before *Traffic* which was shown here earlier this year, and it deals with ultramodern Paris. Except for some reflections of the Arc de Triomphe and Sacre Coeur in swinging doors, all we see are high-rise glassy office buildings which could be on Park Avenue or Michigan Boulevard. No story: just an assembly of episodes built loosely around a busload of U.S. tourists who move through a day in Paris, one of whom is a quiet sympathetic girl who encounters Monsieur Hulot (Tati). Hulot, as usual, is only a prominent character, not the leading one. The point of the picture seems to be that people are still people, even if Paris is not still entirely Paree.

Once again, the sound track is a designed burble, rather than clear dialogue or clear silence. Once again, there are brilliant strokes, and strokes that *ought* to be brilliant.

And once again Tati is satirizing his old foes, technology and modern pace, and also trying to live with them. In both his satire and his peacemaking, we can get a look at where he succeeds and fumbles. Instance: Hulot goes to see someone in an immense office building and waits downstairs after being announced, sitting on a sofa. The man he has asked for appears at the far end of a long corridor, the sound of his heels approaching. Two or three times as we watch the man plodding along toward us, Hulot rises, and the hallman gestures for him to remain seated, there's plenty of time. The moment makes its point of contrast with human-size buildings. But the whole sequence comes to nothing. Hulot and the man get lost chasing one another around the building. That evening, quite by accident, they meet on a street corner and amble off to have a conversation. What about? We never learn. The contrast between the business-appointment atmosphere and the casual encounter is patent, but the sequence leaks away.

Or, during a very long sequence in a new restaurant on its opening night, a glass front door shatters, and the doorman simply moves the big brass doorknob as if the door were still there. Funny, because we see the idea working. Later, a waiter brings a fish on a serving table to a couple of diners, seasons it, and is drawn away on other business; another waiter comes by soon and repeats the seasoning without serving it; then later a third waiter seasons it and tries to serve it, but by now the first pair of diners have moved to another table. The fish is wheeled away to their new table and we never see the payoff. Worse, we later see the original pair leaving quite happily. Didn't they ever eat the trebly seasoned fish? We'll never know.

Besides, Tati cannot rest with observation, he has to arrange. A minister in a drugstore pauses in front of the neon sign "Drugstore" as the "o" lights up, giving him a halo. An overhead shot of a traffic jam going slowly around a circle is given carousel music, à la Disney, to suggest a merry-go-round. From sharp comment we decline through pointless points to cuteness.

Tati still seems the wrong distance from his audience: not so far that we cannot see his gifts, not close enough so that they really touch.

Blood of the Condor

(August 18 & 25, 1973)

A revolutionary film from Latin America. Jorge Sanjines, who was born in 1936, made the first Bolivian feature film in 1966. The second, and the first shown publicly here, is the *Blood of the Condor,* made in 1969. It's in neo-realist style—that is, a fiction film close to fact, made with non-actors, shot in actual locations. Sanjines wrote the script with Oscar Soria, and the anti-U.S. heat of the result makes Costa-Gavras's *Z* and *State of Siege* look comparatively temperate.

The picture contends that the Peace Corps is being used as an arm of Yankee imperialism. A maternity clinic up in the mountains outside La Paz helps Indian women give birth and also, without their knowledge, sterilizes them. (Recent doings in Alabama provide an unanticipated echo.) The charge is that, even though Bolivia is not overpopulated, the U.S. is cooperating with the government there to keep down elements of the population that may eventually prove dissident and troublesome.

The script is built fairly neatly, and the gravamen is worked in obliquely. An Indian couple are worried about their continuing childlessness although they have had children, who died. The police arrest the husband along with two other men, then while traveling, urge them to run. All are shot in this attempt to "escape"; two are killed, the husband is wounded. He is taken to La Paz but dies in the hospital because neither his wife nor his brother can raise the money to buy blood for a transfusion. The events leading up to his arrest are worked in, from time to time, through flashback.

Technically the film is mediocre. The photography is only passable—all skies are gray even on sunny days. The dubbing is not good (although I have heard worse sync-ing and matching of levels in much more lush productions). But Sanjines evidently has an eye and a feel for tart, incisive editing. One proof of his quality is our conviction that some of the rough texture, as in the joining of flashbacks, would be there if he had had a fortune to spend: that roughness is part of what the film is about.

Most of the dialogue is in Quechua, one of the two chief Indian languages of Bolivia; many of the people in La Paz can speak to these Indians only through a Spanish translator. This language barrier goes to the heart of the film, which is that the life-style of these Indians, their language, their religion, and their lore are badly disregarded, if not despised, by the Bolivian Establishment. Sanjines vividly dramatizes this Indian life. The mountain village finds out about the clinic's secret sterilizations, not by explicit information, but through the local shaman who casts coca leaves on the earth and reads them. And the Indians' revenge is direct and primitive: they storm into the clinic and castrate the two doctors. (Chronologically this flashback action precedes the arrest we saw at the beginning of the film.)

I and most who may see this film have no first-hand knowledge of the truth of the charges against the Peace Corps. Certainly the three Americans in the picture are cartoons. But cartoons are not necessarily false. And most of us are aware of U.S. influence in Latin-American affairs, including economic and political pressures (like ITT in Chile). Grant that Sanjines's charges are as yet unproved: his work is still a spurt of heat from a fire that is inarguably burning through Latin America. His film is not nearly as good as the Argentinian *Hour of the Furnaces;* but it's sharp and unsettling.

Bang the Drum Slowly

(*September 1, 1973*)

THE last time I went to a baseball game was ten years ago with a visiting Englishman. I rarely read sports pages any more. I thought my early affection for baseball was well behind me, and my biggest experience at *Bang the Drum Slowly* was to learn that it isn't.

In its feeling for the game, this is the best baseball film I can remember. Some forty years ago I loved Joe E. Brown, himself a ballplayer, in *Elmer the Great* and *Alibi Ike.* Earlier there was Babe Ruth in *The Babe Comes Home,* having a romance with Anna Q. Nilsson, the laundress who washed his uniforms that were stained with tobacco juice. I've seen a lot of others through the years but none that got more of baseball's unique kinetic qualities than this one—the alternation of plateau moments with lightning flashes of action (like the double play), the physical protocol (the careful cap-tugging, bat-weighing, mitt-pounding), and the superlative grace into which deliberately clumsy men can blossom (the base runner sliding under a tag with arms upraised).

John Hancock, the director, understands all this and more, and when I realized that fact, you could have knocked me over with a bean ball. The theater work of Hancock's that I've seen has been doggedly avant-garde. (I missed, as who wouldn't, his first film, *Let's Scare Jessica to Death.*) And I went to this picture dreading that I might be seeing baseball from the viewpoint of the bat or God knows what. But Hancock sees the game whole and renders it whole, with just enough slow motion scattered throughout to serve as humorous commentary and esthetic tease. He falls into cliché at the beginning of sequences—pulling back from objects like statues or flags to give us the whole scene—and in one sequence the team are wearing road uniforms in their home stadium, but by and large he's done a good job with atmosphere, actors and storytelling.

He's greatly helped by the fact that his leading actor, Michael

Moriarty, who plays a major-league pitcher, really has what they call "a good motion." When Moriarty winds up and throws the ball toward the camera, he's authentic. That good motion is as necessary for his character as a believable quick draw would be for a Western gunslinger.

This is Moriarty's first big film role. I've seen him in the theater, where he was pleasantly adequate, and that's what he is here. He resembles Jon Voight, which is just a tough coincidence, but his acting is like a good version of Voight's, which is more serious. At any given moment Moriarty delivers about 60 or 70 percent of what Voight could be doing. It's as if we were seeing a likable understudy.

His roommate, a catcher, is played by Robert De Niro of *Greetings* and *Hi, Mom*. This catcher is an amiable, unbright Georgian, a tobacco-chewer with a cornball haircut. De Niro does all right in outline and design, but he doesn't fill it out with sufficient flavor and body. Vincent Gardenia plays the manager (based on Casey Stengel?) and murders syntax with fierce authority. As he showed in *Little Murders,* Gardenia is a funny angry comedian, but I wish he could get the chance to show the range he has shown in the theater.

The script, by Mark Harris from his novel of the same name, is one more variation on the two-pals theme that preceded *Of Mice and Men* in American writing and has followed it as well—one pal smart, the other dumb, the two linked by brotherhood and by a tacit protectorate. The novelty here, as against Steinbeck, is that we know from the start that the dumb one is going to die (Hodgkin's disease). His disease is secret from everyone but Moriarty during most of the picture; the script works the counterpoint between a profession that depends on physicality and the presence of imminent unknown death.

Most of the time there is more sentiment than sentimentality. (There's an occasional dreadful line, like one that tells us everybody is dying and that's why we're all so nice to one another.) With the obeisance to Ring Lardner that every writer about baseball must pay, Harris keeps the texture pretty good, but there isn't much more to the script than the texture. Not much point or theme; the story simply winds to its foreseen end. The team used to rag the dumb catcher before they learned of his illness, and the last line is Moriarty's: "From now on, I rag nobody." *That's* the point? Pretty puny; and pretty false. What would sport be without ragging? Or what would American humor be in general?

I liked Hancock's work better than Harris's. The parting of the two friends, at an airport, is particularly good. The place is empty. De Niro, lugging his suitcase, waves to Moriarty and starts toward the plane, going home (as they both know) to die. The empty field, the steps leading up to the plane, the two stewardesses waiting at the top of the steps—all these are sheer fact, untampered with, converted by selection into symbol. Nice.

Cops and Robbers

(September 8, 1973)

IT's long been a paradox of our money society that it pays some men a few thousand a year to protect the property of others with many thousands a year and to stop the activities of criminals who make many more thousands a year. On every side the policeman is battered by consumerism, by advertising, by a society with only one really vital standard respected by all—mazuma; on every side he sees people who have more, whose "moreness" he is expected to protect for less; he sees criminals living like kings. And in the midst of all this, in a country where, to name only two among recent items, an ex-governor is sentenced for tax evasion and an incumbent President's reelection committee pressures big corporations for illegal campaign contributions, we have the naïveté to complain about police corruption.

Not Donald E. Westlake. He wrote the script of *Cops and Robbers,* and he based it on the assumption that it's ridiculous to expect policemen, as a group, to have higher morals than any other group, particularly when they have extraordinary authority and opportunities. He has devised a latter-day Runyonesque story of hoods being hoodwinked by two New York Cops who want to make a million apiece—just like everybody else—so that they can get out of the suburbs.

A lot of it is funny. All that I didn't believe was that the two cops could get away with it, that the Mafia leader would be gulled by their deal or that they would escape even if he was. But their anguish and their hunger, their discovery of their own daring, and Westlake's décor of radio commercials and TV interviews, are full of laughs.

The two cops are Cliff Gorman, who was good as Lenny in the toothless Broadway play of that name, and Joseph Bologna, whose previous films I've missed. Both of them underplay nicely, managing to be nondynamic without receding into the woodwork. It takes skill to be completely present without being too powerful for the tenor and the material, and these two men bring it off. John P. Ryan is powerful as the Mafia chief.

Aram Avakian, a gifted film editor, showed in his first directing job, *End of the Road,* that he knew a bit too much about film making. Here he relaxes, displays less, tells more, and produces a neat, neatly finished picture. When he needs a little bravura, like some zooming on garden apartments, he lays it in gently. His editing, particularly in a long robbery sequence and a couple of chase sequences, is keen. It all adds up to a picture placed crisply before us.

But, as I said, it's scary. This film is absolutely crooked, with a kind of puritan absoluteness. Even a robbed stockbroker manages to make a bundle crookedly out of the robbery. And so much of it is funny. Is it funny because we're beginning to whistle past a long, long graveyard?

American Graffiti

(September 15, 1973)

EVERYONE thinks his young years were fascinating, and everyone is right. For himself. But when artists use their young years as subject matter, which they frequently do, they have to prove that their young years can be fascinating to others. Broadly speaking, there are only two ways to do this: by showing that your young years were extraordinary or by finding depth and form that illuminate and preserve the commonplace.

The young American director George Lucas has tried for the latter. He has taken some familiar bull right by the horns and has wrestled it into a reasonably good film A couple of years ago Lucas made a "future" film called *THX 1138* in which he lavished impressive cinematic skills on material so trite that he made me feel he had "an arrogance toward the need to have a fresh idea." This new script—by himself, Gloria Katz and Willard Huyck—still has no new ideas as such. But working close to what is apparently his own youthful experience, Lucas has so integrated methods and material that he finds some of the depth and form mentioned above; and, to some degree, he transforms the banalities of TV situation comedy into a small epiphany of a period.

American Graffiti, a tart, apt title, is a dusk-to-dawn picture. Its only resemblance to *La Notte*! It deals with four high-school buddies, and chiefly with two of them, in a California town in the early 1960s. At the beginning those two boys are presumably bound east for college together, one reluctantly, the other eagerly. By morning, the roles are reversed: the first boy leaves, the second stays with his hometown girl. The reasons for the changes, plus other plot strands involving friends and enemies, make up the story.

But the story is not the film—only its means of coming into being. (Which is what Lucas attempted, less successfully, in *THX 1138.*) The weakest parts are those that try to beef up the script, in plot and literary "theme" terms, like the mysterious blonde in a white T-bird who weaves symbolically through the film, taunting one of the boys. The young performers are all passable, but the pleasures of the picture are in the way it was made. There is no mere springboard of accurate milieu, as in *Summer of '42,* which got all its details right, then wallowed ahead into syrup: the milieu, so to speak, *is* this film, or what is best about it.

Lucas has picked a moving medium for a moving picture. Most of it—seemingly—takes place in and around cruising automobiles in the town streets. I saw this phenomenon in the mid-sixties when I spent a weekend in Grand Rapids, Michigan: boys and girls driving slowly up and down the main street all night, couples in cars or all-boy and all-girl cars honking at one another, sometimes conversing as they passed or stopped at lights, just flowing and cruising for hours. It was like the classical promenade of the European village, motorized.

This mobility is of course fit for film, and it's an easy figure of sexual exploration and of social rite of passage to maturity. From dusk to dawn, yet. But Lucas sees the automobile as the focus of other cultural implosions: the broadcast music of the time, the eating of the time (drive-ins, with waitresses on roller skates), even the hoodlumism of the time. When some not-so-juvenile delinquents want to scare one of the boys, what do they do? They take him for a ride!

So we see a group of late adolescents pinned to a target for cultural barrage. The drive-in food has funny names ("a double Chubby Chuck") that seem to feed them as much as the food itself. They are followed everywhere by the voice of a disc jockey whom they adore.

And of course there's the force of the movies themselves, who modeled the gang of hoods and the styles of kissing and romance.

As the picture floated and intertwined, it reminded me of Twyla Tharp's recent ballet *Deuce Coupe*—the phrase occurs in the dialogue—which used early sixties music from one of the same sources, the Beach Boys. The more it resembles ballet, the better *American Graffiti* is. The more it tries to delve into character and build climaxes (like an unbelievable prank on a police car), the thinner and more sitcom it gets.

Haskell Wexler, the accomplished cinematographer who was "visual consultant" on the film, saw the need for realistic abstraction. For instance an all-night stand called Mel's Drive-in is an oval neon temple with suggestions of the War Room in *Dr. Strangelove*. When *American Graffiti* concentrates like this, on *being* what it's about, it succeeds.

Visions of Eight

(September 15, 1973)

Two winters ago I couldn't believe I was staying up until one-thirty or two in the morning to watch TV broadcasts of the Winter Olympics from Japan. But I was. The Japanese camerawork and color were so lovely that I forgot I was tired. Recently I didn't believe I could be held by a film about the Munich Olympics, not after Leni Riefenstahl's huge two-part film of the 1936 Olympiad and what I saw of Kon Ichikawa's *Tokyo Olympiad 1964*. And again, surprises—happy surprises—in *Visions of Eight*.

Eight directors from different countries went to Munich last summer, not to make a joint documentary of the games, but each one to respond to some part of them as individually as possible. Presumably this was the project of David Wolper, the producer, and, allowing for a couple of thuds, the results are remarkable.

The biggest disappointment is Ichikawa himself, the one who has treated this subject before. His episode on the 100-meter dash is facile and unstimulating; his Olympics imagination seems to have been drained eight years earlier. No disappointment at all, quite predictable, was Milos Forman's episode on the decathlon: hokey, full of tricky Disney musical effects and speed-up motion, so devoid of sympathy or insight that it quickly becomes a detestable bore. John Schlesinger, who does the closing episode, on the marathon, drags it out a bit. (He is the only one to include reference to the Arab terrorists.) Claude Lelouch, with "The Losers," has only a fair grip on what could have been a poignant section.

But the others go from good to better. Michael Pfleghar, a West German director unknown to me, deals subtly with "The Women." He shows how a German jumper becomes an athlete, competing and concentrated and sexless, then how, having won, she relaxes into personality and prettiness. And he adores—he knows *how* to adore—the petite, lovely and breathtaking Russian gymnast, Olga Korbut.

Two amusing paradoxes. The Soviet director Juri Ozerov, also unknown to me, does "The Beginning" and thus includes the various religious services attended by the athletes, including Catholic communion. And the one woman director of the eight, the Swedish Mai Zetterling, deals with the biggest men in the games, the weightlifters. She gets real drama, a sense of ancient Greek agon and (as she says) of obsessiveness from this unspectacular, exciting event.

But the most delightful, the one truly beautiful, episode is by Arthur Penn—about pole-vaulters. If there were nothing else of merit in this collection, and there is, it would be worth seeing just for this section: to appreciate how Penn used his head before he used his camera, how he saw why he was attracted to this subject, how he found the kinetic core of what he wanted to catch, how he presents it with neither affectation nor cliché, how he makes us perceive more in a subject that we may have thought exhausted. For example until Penn's tactful slow motion, I never saw how the pole-vaulter pauses —or seems to pause—as he twists and slips over the top of the bar, how delicately he tosses the pole back on the side he has left, how he seems to *decide* to come down. And Penn's use of his sound track is a paragon of the abstract use of sound, to help the abstract use of the camera draw out the essence of an action. An excellent short film in itself, and the peak of this anthology.

Heavy Traffic

(September 22, 1973)

I walked out of Ralph Bakshi's first cartoon feature *Fritz the Cat* because it was vulgar and dull. I didn't walk out of his second, *Heavy Traffic,* which is vulgar but often interesting.

It mixes animation with some live action as it tells the story of a young New York cartoonist who, while playing a pinball machine (ah, there, Saroyan), wanders off into a (cartoon) fantasy involving a stunning black bar hostess. Subsequently, in live film, he meets her and they "find" each other in Union Square.

The cartoonist is the virginal son of a low-level mafioso, who philanders, and a Jewish mother who strangulates with near-obscene doting. There are ghetto derelicts, drag queens, hookers, mafiosi, and other delectations of the New York scene; the ambience is grubbiness. Nothing is hinted at that can be shown, including genitals, and the story gets nowhere, not very fast; still some things are extraordinary. First, it's the best mixture of animation and live photography that I've seen—the only one I've seen that had some point. Second, which *is* the point, the texture, taking us from the real into the distorted real, makes it all a metropolitan *Walpurgisnacht.* Bakshi hasn't completely avoided tenement-poetry banalities, like the sensitivity of the hero and the hearts of gold in some derelicts he encounters, but in the main, and in the mainline, this is hell. Done with brio and pizazz, peopled with cartoons, but still hell. Which is just how one feels at times in New York and other big cities.

The New Land

(October 6, 1973)

INGMAR Bergman says that Jan Troell is the best thing that's happened to Swedish cinema in ten years. Too mild. Troell is one of the few really important things that's happened to world cinema in that time. This is sweepingly confirmed by the second half of his two-part work based on a series of novels by Vilhelm Moberg. The first part was *The Emigrants;* the second is *The New Land.* Each can be seen separately, but it would mock *The Emigrants,* and Troell, to deny that you enjoy Number Two more for having seen Number One. Like the first part the second has bumps and obvious surgical scars, but it is lovely. Together the two parts describe a long curve in the history of the nineteenth century. In story it is the most ordinary of emigrant-immigrant family chronicles. In realization it is—to use truly a much-battered word—an epic: large-spirited and fine-grained.

If an epic is a work that deals with the adventures of a national hero, then this double film is a double epic: because it has two heroes, the farmer Karl-Oskar and his wife Kristina, and it involves two nations, Sweden and the United States. *The Emigrants* showed us the couple, the farmer's brother, and their friends in a Sweden that enslaved and stifled them; then took them through a terrible sea voyage and across the country to Minnesota. The last, wonderful shot was of Karl-Oskar (Max von Sydow, blessed among actors) sinking to the ground with his back to a tree on which he has just blazed his mark and claimed his land, with a smile on his face that concluded Part One and promised Part Two.

The New Land begins in the same year, 1850, as Karl-Oskar brings his wife and children and his brother to the lakeshore he has claimed. The events that follow are, in the main, predictable—there are few narrative surprises. But in a work of this kind, whose principal purpose is to portray *time* absorbing and consuming human life, we don't want surprises any more than we want a growing plant to develop freakishly: we want the story to fulfill its nature. We want to see more children come, the farm expand, the brother grow discontented and set out with another young Swede for California gold. We know that husband or wife will die first and, in a way, we are looking forward to the death scene of the first because we care so much for both. In a work that has the old-fashioned daring to reach for the rhythms of earth and labor and growth and aging, those pulses are the core of the work, rather than dramatic tensions and conflicts.

Not that there is no drama. The danger of the Sioux on the periphery of their lives is constant and, after some years of mishandling by the U.S. government, finally erupts into slaughter. After the suppression of the uprising, almost forty of the Sioux are hanged, and in the long shot of the mass execution, Troell transfixes some American tragedy. And there is a sequence in a fierce blizzard (I have never seen snow and cold more graphically used than in both these films) that traps Karl-Oskar and his small son in their ox-drawn sled. Earlier we have seen, touchingly, how much the acquisition of that ox meant to him and his wife—a lovely silhouette shot when he brings it home and she meets him. Now, when his son begins to freeze, Karl-Oskar unharnesses the ox, kills it with an axe blow, splits it, eviscerates it, and snuggles the boy inside the warm carcass while he goes for help.

Yet the weakest sequence in the film—not short either—is the one that tries most explicitly for drama: the series of flashbacks that tell us, after the brother returns from California, what happened to him out there. This material had to be included to explain how the brother got the money and what his state of mind is, and it had to be differentiated in texture from the farm narrative; but the camera angles, choice of lenses, and editing show a strain for effect that never touches the body of the work. On the other hand, when the brother, who is suffering both from the California trip and an ear injury he acquired in Sweden, resigns himself mutely to die, the sequence in which he goes out in the forest to do so is a small discreet elegy for a man who will never be understood. (And underneath it we hear the flute music, by Bengt Ernyrd and George Oddner, that accompanied his departure on the Western trip.)

The brother is played by Eddie Axberg, who also worked on the film as a sound engineer. We've now had the chance to watch Axberg from Troell's exquisite first film *Here's Your Life* through this long film, and have seen him grow, literally and figuratively. Confidence in Troell is, I believe, the key to Axberg's growth as an actor. I have rarely seen a face so homely by objective standards become so touching, so winning.

With Max von Sydow, as Karl-Oskar, I have to restrain myself from gushing; I just feel gratitude that he exists, and acts. It's offensive to say that there are no false moments in his performance, but it's impossible to detail all the true ones. I note only two: the scene where he tries (unsuccessfully) to enlist in the Union Army and has to run around a table naked for the examining army doctor, a perfect blend of commonalty and wrenched privacy; and the long shot in which the aged widower crosses the barnyard, the last look at him before he dies (1890), a perfect crystallization of the finish of the story, of the long years of work, sharing, loneliness, and calm.

About Liv Ullmann, as Kristina, I *shall* gush. Her latest film *Forty Carats* (American, made subsequently to *The New Land*) put obstacles in our way, which we had to get past in order to love her. Here there are no obstacles, only enablements. She is irresistible. In the long spectrum of aging and experience through which this two-part film takes her, she is utterly and always a giver of life, her wonderful talent making her beauty more beautiful. In a fairly trite moment, like the one in which the hard-working farm woman suddenly tries on a very fancy hat, she tears it out of film triteness into experience because it really is happening to that woman. She does the same with her death scene, where she holds an apple from a now-mature tree that they brought as a sapling from Sweden. As written, her role has less variety and contrast than von Sydow's, but Kristina never becomes mawkish or consciously noble because *Ullmann* is aware of fallibility. After her death, worn and weak, we see a shot of her as her husband remembers their meeting—a girl walking toward us down a Swedish road, smiling, a bit nervous about her braids. The radiant simplicity, the simple radiance—well, I promised to gush, and I'm only sorry that space limits prevent me from going on.

Per Oscarsson, that fine mad actor of *Hunger,* makes a brief appearance as an itinerant preacher. The handling of his character and those of two religiously bigoted neighbors suggest that they were truncated in editing: subjects are started but not concluded. I don't know whether this happened in the original editing (1970) or in editing for the U.S. or in the script itself, but these, like similar bumps in the first part, are patent flaws in an ultimately majestic work.

The script is by Troell and his producer, Bengt Forslund. The direction, the photography, and the editing are by Troell. All honor to this beautifully gifted man. His color camera doesn't scrounge for calendar gorgeousness: it selects and harmonizes with an occasional chromatic crescendo. His editing—within any one sequence—is usually unnoticeable, discreetly helpful. His compositions, though his "ridge" shots show that he knows his Bergman, are usually tuned perfectly to the intensity of the scene. He uses a lot of close-ups. As with patriotism in public life, the close-up is often the last refuge of the artistic scoundrel. Troell, by the atmosphere he creates throughout and the immediate contexts, makes his close-ups "privileged moments." Examples: the close-ups of the Sioux as they await execution; or of Karl-Oskar and Kristina in bed as she confesses her homesickness for Sweden. (I should note, by the way, that much of this picture was shot in the U.S.)

Scenes like this last one show how, as a director of actors, Troell understands that in this long film of history, he is also celebrating a marriage. It is one of the most fully realized marriages I can remember in a film, excepting Ozu's *Tokyo Story,* and is helped greatly by Troell's now-familiar magic with children.

The New Land runs two hours and forty minutes; with *The Emigrants,* the total must be well over five hours. (The Swedish versions run longer; and I read that these films have been seen by more Swedes than any other film ever.) We now have, from a foreign director, the only adequate film statement of one of the great American historical phenomena, the mass movement of peoples to this country in the nineteenth century. Because of its occasional flaws, in fulfillment of plot strands and textural wandering, and because (unlike *Toyko Story,* for instance) its ultimate aim is commemoration rather than enlightenment, it cannot at the last be called an absolutely first-class work of art. But in its steadfastness, its sense of time shared and humanity known, in the warmth of the many talents with which it shines, it is the work of first-class spirits.

Day for Night

(October 13, 1973)

THE film world loves to love itself. Films about film making—its joys and heartbreaks but mostly its glamour—began almost with Edison. Well, why not? The theater has been writing about itself since Aristophanes, so egocentric films have a precedent, especially since many of the cultural elements that the film thinks are its own are really inheritances from the theater, technologically amplified. Lately, however, the self-loving film has taken on a new aspect: it concentrates on the director—the very director of a particular film. He puts himself in as biographical medium (Fellini in *The Clowns* and *Roma*) or as mock divinity (Anderson in *O Lucky Man!*). But I remember nothing quite like the way François Truffaut puts himself into his new film *Day for Night.* Just sufficiently modest to give himself a fictitious name, he plays the director of a film called *Meet Pamela,* the making of which is the subject of *Day for Night,* and there is only a scriptural phrase for the way Truffaut sees himself: he is the Just Man Made Perfect. He is always calm, courteous, competent. No problem is too large or trifling to get an immediate and correct decision. His voice-over narration breathes reason; his big heart handles actor crises and the family troubles of his crew. He dashes off good new dialogue for his film as needed, and he is even ready with an instant obituary when one of the cast is killed in a car smash.

More. The director wears a hearing aid, using it deftly in phone conversations. I couldn't remember any deafness in Truffaut the few times I've met him, so I checked with the distributors who say that his hearing has not been impaired. Apparently he's wearing the aid to show more equanimity under fire—and possibly as homage to Luis Buñuel, who *is* hard of hearing.

And that's not all. Truffaut has split himself in two. He wants to show us his earlier immature self, possibly to magnify his present maturity, so Jean-Pierre Léaud plays the leading young actor of *Meet Pamela* and plays that actor as a sort of early Truffaut—much as Léaud has done in the role of Antoine Doinel in several earlier Truffaut films. This actor has had a hard childhood, is emotionally starved and affection-greedy, and is obsessive about moviegoing, yet eccentrically winsome.

Still, the odd overall fact is that, despite Truffaut's blushless icon-making of his Before and After selves, I enjoyed *Day for Night*. He's so infatuated with everything filmic (this picture is dedicated to Dorothy and Lillian Gish), he's so clearly an *idiot savant* of film, that the subject brings out the best in him: his romance, his lyric lift, his combined wonder-and-shrug about sex, his humor, his melodramatic irony. Day for Night is itself a film-script term, which means that a scene takes place at night but will be shot in daylight with special lens filters. The French term for this, which is also the title of this film in France, is *la nuit américaine*. The English phrase is actually more suitable, because it implies a whole system of substitutions in film life: fake rooms for real rooms that somehow become more real than the real ones because of the intensity with which one looks at them; the hotted-up affection of actors in the same company that replaces (briefly) the lower-flame, longer-lasting affections of "civilian" life; and so on. Of course the very choice of this subject by Truffaut is a small confession of bankruptcy, like a writer writing a novel about a writer, but it has long been clear that not much is happening to Truffaut. He doesn't grow. So he turns his attention to a subject that is already within his small province—the film world; and though the material is hardly fresh, he can freshen it with his sentiment, even with his sentimentality and his egotism.

The very opening typifies the whole picture—a familiar trick used well. The scene is a Paris street, full of people. Léaud comes out of the Metro, walks along until he meets Jean-Pierre Aumont, then slaps him. Just as he slaps, a voice calls "cut!"—and the street turns out to be a set in a Nice studio. A counterpoint between the film and the film-within-it is nicely carried on throughout, with some easy but effective harmonics. (For instance the leading actress of the company is married to an older man and has a brief affair with Léaud: in *Meet Pamela* the heroine, played by that actress, leaves Léaud for an older man, his father.) Truffaut handles his camera and editing with that light insistent drive, that unperspiring dynamics, that mark his work at its best. Pierre-William Glenn's photography has the snapping-bright NBC-type color that Truffaut likes. And in Georges Delerue he has once more his ideal composer. Truffaut's hyperbolic view of the "classic" elements of film tradition ("classic" in Movieland can mean practically anything before World War II) is nicely supported by Delerue's Vivaldi-style score.

Some good performances, too. Valentina Cortese, as the actress who plays Léaud's mother in *Pamela,* is enchanting as always. Aumont, whose fan I am not, is surprisingly unaffected and taking as the actor who plays Léaud's father in the inner film. Jacqueline Bisset, a truly lovely girl who has had bad luck in her American films to date, does very well as the rather tense actress who comes to France to play Pamela. Jean Champion is highly agreeable as the producer; and there's a bit appearance, as an English insurance executive, by Graham Greene.

Of course there are lots of wipes and split screens and superimpositions, à la old Hollywood, and there are a lot of oblique references to earlier Truffaut pictures. And it's all too long. Still I thought I'd had my last dram of enjoyment out of the Pagliacci theme and studio magic, and Truffaut shows that there's life in the old whirl yet.

Mean Streets

(*October 27, 1973*)

MARTIN Scorsese grew up in New York's Little Italy and has made a film about his home neighborhood. This personal impulse, which would not exactly be hot news in any other art, is so unusual in American film that it has already knocked some people sideways. Scorsese is a graduate of the New York University film school, has taught there, and has made a previous feature set in lower Manhattan, *Who's That Knocking at My Door?* His new picture *Mean Streets* is very much better—more intense, better integrated. Nevertheless its intensity is often theatrical in the wrong way, it's both lumpy and discursive, and it ends up as only a fairly bright promissory note.

The screenplay by Scorsese and Mardik Martin centers on two young Italian-Americans, a hood with a conscience and a slightly demented drifter, played by Harvey Keitel and Robert De Niro. Keitel is seen—or is meant to be seen—through a prism of Catholic anguish as his *capo* uncle grooms him for Mafia success, as he writhes through an affair with the drifter's cousin (the girl is an epileptic!), and as he tries to look after the feckless but violent drifter, who is his best friend. De Niro, gleefully and savagely loony, blows up mailboxes and scares people with rooftop sniping, welches on a loan, manipulates Keitel's friendship, goes berserk toward the end, and brings death to Keitel and himself.

I think we're supposed to feel that the plot is not the point, that the film exists for its milieu and texture, but it doesn't come out that way. So much of the script gets mired in the tropes of gangster melodrama that plottiness intrudes; and, conversely, some scenes limp, so the very plottiness is bilked. As for texture the editing is jumpy and irresolute; for instance in the first church scene, there's a lot of leaping from long shots to close shots to reverse shots, revealing a lack of vision of the scene. The color is garish and flashy in barroom scenes, in the esthetic fallacy of trying to look like what it's about, but abandoning this idea elsewhere. (The idolaters of *The Godfather* told us that the wedding party looked faded in order to simulate home movies. But wasn't that sequence shot by the same people who shot the rest of the film?) Scorsese simply hasn't found the objective correlative in his very method that George Lucas, with Haskell Wexler's help, found in *American Graffiti* to lift banal material beyond itself. Scorsese gropes and stabs and lunges along.

Honesty of intent is rare in any nation's films, but it has been even rarer in U.S. films until the last decade or so. Most of our films, particularly the ones by talented men, compromised as best they could. So when we get an honest film, as this one wants to be—particularly when it's autobiographical in tenor—it overimpresses everybody. Worst of all it overimpresses the film maker himself who thinks his honesty will see him through his artistic problems. It won't. Recently we saw this in a play called *Moonchildren* by a young American named Michael Weller who was out to tell the truth about his generation but who was so insecure as a playwright that he fell into theatrical falsity on the way to his thematic truth. In filmic terms this happens to Scorsese.

We get the *Godfather* scenes, the stripteaser scenes, the good and the bad slum kids who are nevertheless pals (*Angels with Dirty Faces*), the ultimate gunning-down. I don't question the truth of the material, I question Scorsese's ability to lift it out of the movie gutters into which less truthful directors have trampled it.

And Keitel's religious remorse and aspiration, which could have been part of the paradox of Mafia Catholicism, wither into a tag. He is the only one in the film shown to have religious impulse or doubt, so instead of being generic, his spiritual questions become an obvious device to make Our Hero sensitive. The way that the hero of bad novels is the one guy in his gang who won't go to brothels and thus we know he's poetic, that's the way Keitel is the one guy in his gang who goes to church.

The incompleteness of every inner motion affects the film as a whole. When it's over we want to know what it was about. To tell us what life is like today in Little Italy? A twenty-minute documentary could have made the (implicit) point that these former slums have changed inwardly, if not outwardly, into middle-class centers. And is this all there is to life in Little Italy? Is he telling us that everyone there is like this, that there is no escape? If so, just to name one instance, how did Scorsese come out of it? The film gives us no hint.

Still, *Mean Streets* has some ragged, intermittent flashes of fire, particularly in a poolroom brawl triggered by De Niro and in his angry explosion at a usurer. In *Bang the Drum Slowly* De Niro understood what he wanted to do as the dumb doomed Southern catcher; he simply couldn't summon up enough of the juices and flavors. Here he is wild and strong. It's a flash part, and every actor who sees it will gnash his teeth because he'll know that anyone with any talent at all could score in it. The *part* is a success (it always has been); De Niro happens to be the actor who has it. He uses it very well, but, without putting him down, I note that he's had some good luck in casting lately: a sweet guy doomed to die and a loose, pathetic, obscene quasi-maniac. What actor could ask for more?

Keitel has a much less flashy and much more difficult part, not monochromatic, in fact rather scattered in conception. He works hard to pull it together and, in general, succeeds.

The Long Goodbye

(November 3, 1973)

THERE's nothing wrong with Robert Altman that a little regression won't cure. I liked his early film *M*A*S*H* and increasingly disliked the ones that followed, *Brewster McCloud, McCabe and Mrs. Miller* and *Images*. It's a pleasure—unexpected—to report that his new film is a pleasure. Evidently Altman has just been miscasting himself; he is neither a whimsical fantasist nor a poetic reviser of myths nor a prober of the psyche. He is, as he showed in his army film, a satirical comedian, and he just needed to go back to that early style. *The Long Goodbye,* made from a Raymond Chandler novel, is a good private-eye picture, but it's also a good satire on private eyes and their pictures.

The distributors have been nervous about the film, I hear—release was delayed while worrying went on. I would guess that the only real cause for worry was two names: Chandler's and his detective's Philip Marlowe. Altman had chosen to do his spoofery with a famous hard-boiled novelist whose private eye had been played by Humphrey Bogart, no less. (And also by Dick Powell and George Montgomery and James Garner, who were much less.) Without the burden of those names, the picture would have caused no sweat because in itself it's a generally amusing piece of bite-size cynicism.

The setting is Hollywood, mostly, replete with fungoid lushness, outside and in. Marlowe is played by Elliott Gould (who was in

M*A*S*H) as the opposite of Bogart. He slumps and slurps and slobbles along, usually unshaven, frequently cigaretted, making a distinct effort to seem well off the ball while, under his fog, he's well on it. The key is still anti-heroism, as with Bogart, but Bogart's tenor was consciously and competently anti-heroic. It's only retrospectively that we see Gould has been thinking-thinking-thinking the whole time under his muzziness, and it's a continual comic surprise that, in the tightest of spots, he is never frightened.

The novel has been updated in the screenplay by Leigh Brackett, who was co-author—with William Faulkner and Jules Furthman—of the Bogart film made from Chandler's *The Big Sleep* in 1946. A nice touch of sentiment, if that's the right word in Chandler context, to use Brackett here. Now there's plentiful profanity and the multiracial casting of cops and hoods. (The chief hood, a sly little brute, wears the Star of David around his neck. There's progress for you.) And the whole story is wrapped in mod-poppery. For instance four girls live in a apartment across from Marlowe and spend most of their time on their terrace, stoned on hash, doing yoga and other exercises. They are always seen only in passing, just bare-breasted décor.

The story holds because the crimes and consequences are credible (except for one sequence in which Marlowe chases a car on foot), because the developments keep developing, and because it's peopled with just the sort of superficially vivid characters one wants in a private-eye film. Sterling Hayden, the mad general of *Dr. Strangelove*, gives a somewhat better performance than is called for as a bearded author with writer's block, going out of his mind with drink and blustery fear. His wife is played by Nina van Pallandt, the Danish pastry of the Clifford Irving affair. Her frankly fortyish beauty, her poise and intelligence, and her quite respectable acting ability take her far out of the scandal-exploitation league. Irving's wind has blown some good.

Altman's hand wobbles a bit. He commits the thoughtlessness of having the camera linger with two other characters when the hero leaves, in a one-man's-vision picture. He leans hard on the use of animals throughout—a cat and numerous dogs—as if to give film students a Theme to write about. He quotes from other films with a heavy wink—an opportunely passing funeral out of *Greed*, an ending visually modeled on *The Third Man*. And he closes with a thirties tune, "Hooray for Hollywood," which he also used for openers, to make it ultraclear that he's saying something about movies in his movie. But the story finishes with a good snapper, keeps pretty snappy while getting there, and Gould is just right for the tone that Altman is after—it's all a joke but no less serious for that.

Andrei Rublev

(November 3, 1973)

ANDREI Tarkovsky (b. 1932) made *Andrei Rublev* in the USSR in 1966. Rublev was a monk and icon painter (c. 1360–1430) whose work is preeminent in Russian art. Tarkovsky's film ran into political trouble, presumably because it showed an individualist under authoritarianism. Its release was delayed, then its export. It was shown at the Cannes Festival in 1969 in a three-hour version, which was a condensation. The version shown at this year's New York Film Festival was a half-hour shorter than that.

Still, two things are evident, even in this lacerated version. Tarkovsky was not making a straight biographical film: he was presenting a series of historical panels, through which Rublev moves, to re-create the Russia of that day. Second, he re-creates it. *Andrei Rublev* contains some of the most authentic historical reality I have seen on screen, done with lavishness, intensity, and sweep. I don't expect ever to forget such episodes as the sacking of a town by Tartars or the casting of a giant bell. I'm not talking about capital-B Beauty of the sort that every Technicolor spy thriller has these days. (*Andrei Rublev* is in black-and-white, except for its last moments.) I mean historical-artistic imagination made manifest through cinematic talent.

The fate of this film must be one of the decade's major crimes in the film world, a world that does not lack for crimes.

I. F. Stone's Weekly

(November 10, 1973)

WHEN I. F. Stone started his independent weekly in 1953, because his newspaper career had been blasted by political blacklisting, he said to his wife, "Honey, I'm going to graduate from a pariah to a character, and then if I last long enough I'll be regarded as a national institution." A man who has that kind of humor about his courage at the same time that he's no-kidding courageous doesn't have to worry about praise or overpraise. He will outlast his garlands. But he's got a very good garland in *I. F. Stone's Weekly,* a sixty-two-minute documentary film by Jerry Bruck, Jr. It took three years and a lot of shoestrings to finish, and let us all just say thank you to Mr. Bruck for saying thank you to Mr. Stone.

Looking like a kindly bespectacled chipmunk, Stone squeaks his falsetto "hello" into telephones, burrows into files, talks, laughs, thinks with wrinkles, walks, proofreads, writes, and enjoys himself like crazy in this picture. Like every consumed man, he knows that he is lucky, that "the true joy in life," as Bernard Shaw said, is in "the being used for a purpose recognized by yourself as a mighty one." Bruck has wisely caught Stone at several informal talks in universities, so we get a painless conspectus of his views, with pointed instances. Bruck has also skillfully overlapped footage on Lyndon Johnson, Richard Nixon, and Spiro Agnew with Stone's comments made *at the time* that the public and most of the press were swallowing official lines.

Stone's thesis in political reporting is simple, as these examples show. Every government is run by liars, and nothing they say should be believed; but a government always reveals a good deal if you take the trouble to study what it says. The true court of last resort is an informed public—or, to put it properly, the informed segment of the public. Stone is no sentimentalist about the Peepul. He began as a Communist anarchist and is now (his term) a counterrevolutionary who insists to college audiences that their "revolution" without politics is just childish tantrum. "You talk about Power to the People," he says to them in this film. "If people ever came to power, we'd all be in jail!"

The narration, reticent and apt, is by Tom Wicker of *The New York Times.* Some other professional colleagues get a raking from Stone in the picture. We see a TV clip of Walter Cronkite in Vietnam in 1965, mouthing the then-current pap about Marshal Ky. Superimposed we see Stone's comments *at the time* exposing the real Ky. How could one lone man have known the truth when a huge news organization did not? Merely by reading, filing, researching, remembering and—the paramount matter—*wanting* to tell the truth. Then we see Stone and an altered Cronkite meeting in 1970 when they were both given Polk awards, with Cronkite suggesting amiably that they get together some time and Stone saying "Love to, love to."

At that Polk banquet the president of the Associated Press, Wes Gallagher, gives a windbag speech about objective reporting. ("The refuge of the journalist . . . is his professionalism.") We see Stone listening. When he's called on to speak, he reminds the assembly about George Polk, the man for whom the awards were named—"the first journalistic victim of the Cold War" who wanted to report the agony of the Greek people but was "murdered by the Greek police" who tried to blame it on the Left. My only real criticism of Bruck's film is that he didn't show us Gallagher's face at this point.

The *Weekly* has closed down now. Stone was editor, reporter, production manager, etc., and it all became too much for him when he reached sixty-four. The film's best sequence, in cinematic terms, is his last day at the printing plant two years ago. Typical of Stone is the way he walks out of the plant for the last time, obviously moved, but hurrying along to the next chapter of his journalistic life.

To show influence and inheritance, Bruck has included comments by two young journalists. Peter Osnos, now of *The Washington Post,* tells with wit and affection of the ten months in 1965–66 that he worked for Izzie Stone and how difficult it was to keep up with his boss. ("Generally it starts about 7:30 in the morning, when Izzie's on the phone, and he's saying, 'Pete!,' and you're beginning to shake already.") And Carl Bernstein, of *The Washington Post* team of Woodward and Bernstein that cracked Watergate, speaks simply, touchingly, of Stone's "incredible respect for knowledge and for truth."

Bruck is a Canadian, twenty-six, with a degree in history from Yale, who learned how to make films by making a documentary about Nixon's first inauguration called *Celebration,* which has been shown at some festivals. He began work on this second picture in 1970, making forays from Montreal on those occasions when Stone was doing something "shootable." Bruck's sense of balance and rhythm, his understatement, his editorial wit and keenness are all impressive. What could have been a gilded monument is a highly enjoyable film.

Your local theater manager is unlikely to book a sixty-two-minute picture, no matter how good it is. Pressure him. He can run it as the second half of a non-gargantuan double bill. *I. F. Stone's Weekly* is available in 16mm form so high schools and colleges can get it. If

you're an educator, do the next generation a favor and show them
this film. Show them that, despite what's all around them, human
beings *can* survive, possibilities *do* exist.

The Way We Were

(November 10, 1973)

OCCUPIED as he's been with politics, I. F. Stone has still kept open to
art and the position of artists.* (Note, for instance, his pieces on
Toscanini and Pasternak reprinted in *The Haunted Fifties*.) I wish he
could find time in his still-busy life to review *The Way We Were*.

The script by Arthur Laurents is a comedy-romance, going from the
late thirties to the early fifties, about a WASP man, apolitical, and a
Jewish girl, Communist. Say, that's a pretty good dramatic contrast
right there. And you just have no idea what hindrances anti-fascism
and anti-McCarthyism were to the course of true love. And it's even
worse, folks, because the fellow has writing talent, and his girl—
eventually his wife—tries to impose ideals on him in his work,
analogized from her puritanical idealism in politics. She is rigid; he
just wants to succeed. But they love each other, alas. Alas for us,
really, because that love drags on and on, taking them through splits
and reunions, until at last they manage to separate, just as we are
about to suffocate. At the end he is a Hollywood writer, she is protesting the H-bomb in front of the Plaza in New York. They meet
there and for one fearful moment I thought they were going to get
together again, that the picture would go on.

Glittery trash—a category that to me means New Truth pasted on
Old Cardboard. The script is fake-daring about political conflicts of
its period, priding itself on the fact that some formerly taboo political
words are now permissible for the heroine but utilizing its ideas in the
most offhand exploitative way. The dialogue is pseudo-bright. Not
one moment in the picture is anything but garbage under the gravy of
false honesty. Only the music is *frankly* awful.

The director, Sydney Pollack, makes sure that everything is worse
than it has to be. He handles his camera as if this were a Fonda-

* See p. 233.

Bennett valentine of the thirties, never missing a moment of *True Confessions* anguish in the girl or a chance to predict, by camera placement, what's going to happen in a shot. If a park scene opens with a wastepaper can looming big in the foreground, you know that the heroine coming toward us is going to stop at it, tear up some papers, and throw them in.

The girl is Barbra Streisand, who is still a monster. The first dictionary definition: "a fabled animal combining features of animal and human form." She's fabled, all right, and she can assume human form: that's one of her several unquestionable talents. But my image of her is of an egotistic animal gobbling the story, the audience, the very film stock on which her image is printed.

One thing she cannot devour is the man she plays opposite this time. Before, she ate up such weaklings as Omar Sharif, George Segal, and Ryan O'Neal. This time it's Robert Redford, a solid, subtle actor and a genuine star in his own right. He treats this spurious script seriously, and he handles every scene with an originality that comes from verity, not display. This, for me, is a Redford picture, in which the girl playing opposite him tries to gun him down and fails. If he could win out over Arthur Laurents, Streisand was no problem.

The Iceman Cometh

(November 17, 1973)

SOMETHING over two years ago Ely Landau, a film producer and former TV producer, formed a company called the American Film Theatre. The basic idea was to build a national subscription audience for a series of films to be made from noted plays with noted actors and directors. The prior commitment by subscription would subsidize these low-budget films; and the films would help to fill the gap left by the virtual disappearance of the "road," a gap not filled completely, or unfailingly well, by the more than forty resident theaters throughout the U.S.

The AFT plan, as Landau knew, ran counter to a federal decree against block booking (where a theater is asked to buy a group of films, with no option to buy individual items in the group). There was to be a court hearing to plead for an exception to the decree. I was asked by the AFT's lawyers to be a witness for them, and on the basis of the projects they were ready to produce, I agreed. I was aware of the esthetic risks in film transcriptions of good plays—I had adversely reviewed Landau's own production of O'Neill's *Long Day's Journey into Night*. Still, once in a long while a good film is made of a good play, like *Pygmalion* and *The Caretaker*. Most important, the subscription plan was essential to the financial security of the project, and I couldn't see why the law should arbitrarily prevent the addition of these eight projected films to the general mix available to the public. So I testified, along with witnesses on other aspects.

The legal exception was granted in May 1972, the AFT swung into action, and with the aid of a huge ad campaign, set up its subscription system while it was making its first films. About 500 theaters are selling subscriptions to the eight pictures, each of which will play for only two days in any one month in each locality. The country has been divided into seven zones, and the eight films will play in different sequence in different zones to obviate making 500 prints of each film.

Last summer the AFT invited the press to a program of excerpts from the films. I stayed away, unwilling to be prejudiced pro or con by a bill of Coming Attractions. Now the first three films have opened around the country. O'Neill's *The Iceman Cometh* is playing in two of the zones, Pinter's *The Homecoming* is in two others, and Albee's *A Delicate Balance* is in the remaining three. I have seen only the first.

Iceman runs four hours (two intermissions) and has therefore been cut. One character—Ed Mosher, the ex-circus man—has been eliminated, and a few of the longer speeches of others have been curtailed. I don't think that these changes hurt. I know that O'Neill said he wanted some things repeated eighteen times in the play, but that doesn't automatically mean he was right—in theater terms. Shakespeare wanted Voltimand and Cornelius in *Hamlet,* but I've never missed them in the theater.

The prime concession one has to make, almost before one goes, is that this is not going to be a film at all. At best it's going to be like a good TV version of the play—with the camera doing its best to move pointedly or unobtrusively around the one set—which is precisely what it turns out to be. And it's easy to make the concession because, within the first few minutes, it's apparent that the cast is extraordinary, the color is right, and John Frankenheimer, the director, is profiting by his previous TV experience. Plus one more important reason: Sidney Lumet's film of *Long Day's Journey into Night* seemed cramped because it's a realistic play and Lumet's efforts to make it more so only nagged at it; *Iceman,* for all its insistence on the seediness of the derelicts in this 1912 New York saloon, is a symbolic play, and film disturbs it less. On screen we miss the "whole place" visual effect that can make *Iceman* a modern equivalent of a medieval morality play, but the film medium becomes only a further abstraction of a work that is fundamentally an abstraction to begin with.

Anyway, questions about the medium fade beside the general quality of the acting. Some of it, admittedly, is poor. Tom Pedi, who was Rocky the bartender in the very first production (1946), is even more mechanical here. Clifton James, an inveterate bad actor, is down to his usual standard as Pat McGloin, the crooked ex-cop. The former British and Boer officers are tedious characters—they supply the same colors over and over again—and Martyn Green and George Voskovec give them little nuance.

But most of the principals are fine. Bradford Dillman, who has not before been especially impressive, makes a first-class Willie Oban, the tremorous son of a Wall Street swindler. Sorrell Booke, who has always been impressive, gives the best performance I have seen of Hugo Kalmar, the crazy radical. Moses Gunn is solid as the black gambler, Joe Mott. Jeff Bridges does very well as Don Parritt, the young anarchist renegade. No human being could possibly be convincing in those bursts of contrapuntal confession that O'Neill gives Parritt through Hickey's final speeches; it is flatly impossible. But until then Bridges plays with subtle shading and thorough conviction. The late Robert Ryan, who never became quite the actor he could have been, gives a sterling performance as Larry Slade, the embittered ex-anarchist. Inevitably his many lines about his desire to die now take on an added pang.

Beloved Fredric March, that handsome man, that excellent actor, plays the sodden old saloon keeper, Harry Hope. I never expected to see another Harry Hope as good as the first one, Dudley Digges. March is just as good—even better on points, perhaps, because Digges was Irish to begin with and not handsome. March is a wonderfully wise old film-theater animal, making his way surely through the mysteries of re-creation with all the skill of an old stalker, pouncing with secret glee—we can feel it!—on the core of truth in old Harry.

And to crown the work there is Lee Marvin, as Hickey, the salesman-apostle. To put it simply: Marvin was born to play Hickey. He has perfect understanding of the man and perfect equipment to deal with it. Hickey's first three acts (the first two-thirds of the film) are all uphill for an actor, as the reformed heller tries to brush away the "pipe dreams" of his former drinking pals, to make them face reality the way he has done and share his peace of mind—all without becoming an evangelical drag. Marvin understands the bumps and sags, and he lifts it all adroitly with gesture, with vaudevillian's *esprit,* to present both the man who was and who is. Then comes the payoff, the great last act. Marvin is wonderful. I have seen James Barton, the first Hickey, and Jason Robards (along with others), and though they were both unforgettably good, Marvin goes past them—so powerfully that he makes the crux of the play clearer than I have ever found it before, on stage or page.

A chief critical dispute about *Iceman* has been whether or not Hickey was sane when he murdered his wife. It can be argued that he was insane, is insane all through the play, and that the play therefore is about the madness of any hope to escape from illusion. Marvin's performance is the ultimate critical comment on the matter. He makes it beautifully clear, in the way he plays the tremendous narrative of Hickey's life, that the man was sane; that Hickey had worked out agonizingly, through a Dostoyevskian rationale, the need to kill his adored wife, to protect her from the pain he had caused and would continue to cause her and also to protect himself from the pain of causing her pain.

Hickey grabs frantically at the cover of insanity after he hears himself repeat the words he exclaimed over her body: "Well, you know what you can do with your pipe dreams now, you damned bitch!" At the moment of her death it had been a cry of frustration at her illusions about him, of transformed anguish at what he has done, an explosion of the shadow side that accompanies every love; but it was not, in any operative sense, insane. Now, however, the words sound horrible to him, and he says—pleads—that he must have been insane. Then, when he sees how his old friends perk up at this, how they *depend* on his having been insane all the time he was preaching at them, he performs his ultimate sacrifice for them. He insists he was insane the whole time he has been here so that they can write off his sermons as madness, so that their whiskey will get back its kick and they can slide back out of life into torpor.

Marvin, no doubt with Frankenheimer's help, illuminates all this dazzlingly. Early in his narrative he recalls how he told Evelyn, when they were young, how much he loved her. Between those lines and "You damned bitch!"—both exquisitely done, like everything in between—Marvin encloses much of the aspiration and inconsequence of our lives.

In my testimony at the AFT hearing I hoped that, in time, the AFT might use its subscription audience as a base for filming works created directly for the screen. I still hope so. But if they never do any more than to preserve, in uneasy filmic form, acting of the quality that Marvin and March and Ryan give us here, the whole project will be justified.

Charley Varrick

(*November 24, 1973*)

FICTIONAL killings are fun—when well done. All you need to do is integrate the violence into suspense and drama. If the film isn't intrinsically engaging, the violence seems egregious, possibly offensive. If the film engages, the violence is exciting. Most of the critics who bellyached about *Straw Dogs* were ecstatic about *The Godfather*.

Charley Varrick is a good one. It was directed by Don Siegel, a great favorite of the *auteur* critics, and it proves yet again that there's nothing wrong with an *auteur* director that a good script can't cure. When Siegel directs grotesque flapdoodle like *Two Mules for Sister Sara* or *Dirty Harry,* we are enjoined to watch his style. When he gets a good script like this one by Howard Rodman and Dean Riesner (from a novel by John Reese), we don't have to be enjoined to watch anything; we can't *help* watching. And the violence loses most of its moral discomfort as it becomes dramatic necessity.

This is the best crime thriller I've seen since *The French Connection.* It's about a middle-aged, thoughtful, but fast-moving bank robber who, with his wife and two pals, knocks off a rural New Mexico bank expecting to take some thousands. Wife and one pal are killed, along with some cops. Varrick and the other survivor escape with their haul, to find that they have taken over three-quarters of a million. Varrick is very worried.

He suspects—and it's confirmed by the bank's report of only a small loss—that this is Mafia money, dropped in a country bank en route to foreign investment. Varrick isn't worried about the police; he knows they can tire in time. He knows that the Mafia never gives up. His job is to make the Mafia think they've rubbed out the robbers before they reach him. How he does it is the gist of a fast and clever script whose surprises are retrospectively waterproof. Well, maybe not the very last scene—a duel between an automobile and an old biplane. (Varrick is an ex-pilot.) But we know there has to be a biggie for the climax, and Siegel shoots and edits it well; and the duel is capped with a snapper.

Siegel and the authors have a feeling for the odd settings so helpful in giving tangential zings to a thriller: a hideout in the basement of a Chinese restaurant, a cheaply *luxe* brothel in some trailers, a seedy photographer's studio. Along with these come the requisite oddball characters: a big quiet pipe-smoking killer, a crippled gunsmith, a sexy blonde passport forger.

But the key casting was Walter Matthau as Varrick. To make a bank robber and killer of this epitome of wry, undemonstrative, middle-class respectability, the king of second mortgages and six-packs, was a very wily move on Siegel's part: we're on Varrick's side almost before the picture begins, because of Matthau's previous pictures. Andy Robinson, who was a maniacal killer in *Dirty Harry,* plays Matthau's unstable pal. He is developing quite a line in instability: he was Prince Mishkin in Joseph Papp's production of Montgomery's *Subject to Fits.*

When gifted people who take this kind of film making seriously get the right material to be serious about, they make very good trifles. Which this is.

The Homecoming

(December 8, 1973)

THE second picture I've seen from the American Film Theatre, this film of Harold Pinter's play, is even better than the first, *The Iceman Cometh.* Ranking of Pinter and O'Neill is not involved; Pinter's play has been more sensitively directed, is at least equally well cast, and is much more comfortable on the screen. Both plays are in one set, but the set of *Iceman* is *meant* as a set—an abstract locale for an abstract work. In *The Homecoming* the set is a room. The quintessential Pinter mode is to fix an enclosed space, then have an outsider enter it. The power of enclosure, of making related series of enclosures, is native to film, and the motion of the camera itself counterpoints the idea of alien entry.

This Pinter room was designed by John Bury, who did the setting for the original Royal Shakespeare Company production, later seen on Broadway. Bury has scaled down his ideas for the intimacy of the camera, but the atmosphere is unchanged: the house of a family of men, cold, drab, patched but clean. The color camera is in the gifted hands of David Watkin, who did *The Charge of the Light Brigade* and *Catch-22,* who puts much of the film in the clerestory light of nineteenth century painting that makes the real look like a comment on the real.

Peter Hall, who directed the RSC production (and who has made several previous films), directed again here. Hall's theater production of this play stands out for me as a high example of the musician's art (so to speak) in the theater, exquisitely wrought and felt, perfectly *heard.* He has found ways to translate his directorial designs into a new syntax, to use camera placement and the composition of shots to refresh his original perceptions, not to trim them. He has been well helped by the editor, Rex Pike. Example: near the end the family proposes to set up Ruth as a prostitute in a Soho flat. She listens. Her first comment is to ask how many rooms there would be in the flat, and we get a quick glimpse of her husband's face before we go to the reply from his brother. That glimpse is not a banal reaction shot: it's like a beat before a leap.

And the actors, the actors. What a feast. Here is a play/film that lives by its ambiguity and ambivalence, by its ability at every moment to be more than what is being said or done, to encompass at every moment different, even conflicting views of what is happening. To say that these six actors, four of them from the original RSC production, are capable of encompassing all this is true but not enough: they are also able to give us pleasure in their ability to do it. This is a dangerous compliment because it sounds like praise of self-display; but with the best acting (as Stanislavsky knew), self-display is part of selfless art.

The best way to appreciate their work is to look at the play itself.

Max, a widower of seventy, lives in his North London house with his brother Sam and two of Max's sons, Lenny and Joey. Home on a surprise visit comes the third son, Teddy, a professor in America, bringing his wife Ruth, an Englishwoman whom he married before he left six years ago but whom the family has never met. The main movement of the play is toward Ruth's decision to remain here, by invitation, when Teddy returns to America and their children: her decision to be the sexual companion of Max and his sons and to be set up by them as a tart.

As with most good works, a synopsis of *The Homecoming* can be accurate but must be false. What this play is depends on how often one has seen (or read) it, how it is performed, even on the sequence in Pinter's work in which one sees it. Here are four responses to my latest viewing. First, it's a comedy, in two senses: in method, through the rude juxtaposition of irreverences and *non sequiturs;* in overview, through its vision of men and women furiously making their pygmy arrangements and pronouncements in the face of huge dark over-whelming forces. (In line with the play's irreverent method, I would sometime like to see it played in Marx Brothers style and tempo.)

Second, although the characters are individuals, they are used as mediums. Through them we get both their lives and relations as they are stipulated to be, but we also get their repressed thoughts and unconscious feelings—not as asides or implications, they are switched right on to the main tracks of their utterance. This is one of the sources of the comedy, as when remembrance of the dead mother abruptly switches from sentiment to vilification; but, more important, it gives chordal texture to the play as it progresses homophonically. This view of the characters as mediums transforms them into fissures through which we see not only their own psyches but their world battering at them.

Third, the power of the language. What a wizard of the vernacular Pinter is. How easily he transmutes the commonplace into splendid rhetoric simply by hearing sounds and rhythms, by building in rising arcs (Lenny's description of clumping the amorous woman) or by dropping in the perfect, unique, irreplaceable phrase: "You daft prat." "He'll be chuffed to his bollocks." Lenny savagely needles his father about what was in the old man's mind the night he begot Lenny. The father listens grimly, then after a pause, says: "You'll drown in your own blood." Try speaking that line aloud if you want an example of how to make six simple Anglo-Saxon words into a thick and terrible blast. That is theater mastery.

Fourth, sequence in Pinter's work. To see *The Homecoming* again, after seeing his subsequent, almost equally good *Old Times,* is to see the earlier play as part of a pair (whether consciously designed as such or not). *Old Times* deals with female space and one male intruder; *The Homecoming* views matters the other way round, male space and one female intruder. In both plays the female element finally dominates the male, more or less cruelly. The true homecoming referred to in that title, as has been observed, is Ruth's, not Teddy's: not just because she was born in this neighborhood but because she is like a queen of sexuality moving into a kingdom that has been waiting for her and for which she has been waiting, a life more complex and powerful than her American domestic existence. Of course there are literal explanations for the offer from Max and Lenny. Lenny is a pimp and there is a strong implication that Ruth was a tart before marriage. (Max's shocking denunciation of her the instant he sees her turns out to be true.) All the terse teasings of the play—with the water glass, with Ruth's lines about her underwear (prefiguring *Old Times*)—even the comic reduction of the bed-bout with Joey, are meant as part of the underlying mystery of sexual contest, more than the literal story of a seemingly conventional wife being revealed as a whore.

The actors are so strong in their shadowed roles that they make connections with darknesses in us. Paul Rogers, as Max, is a sly old mastiff, magnificent in his sibilance and growl. Ian Holm, as Lenny, is quietly vicious, with a streak of irate fear meant to suggest, I think, sexual impotence. Joey, the non-bright son, is hulkingly played by Terence Rigby. Ruth is Vivien Merchant (Mrs. Pinter), silken, secret, insolently strong.

The two newcomers to the cast are that lovely Irish actor Cyril Cusack, who plays Max's brother Sam with nervous vindictiveness, and Michael Jayston as Teddy, the professor. Jayston managed to be good as the czar in the flabby *Nicholas and Alexandra;* here he gets a better chance and makes the most of it.

A word, too, for the soundtrack recorded by Robert Allen with a sharp ear for levels. Sounds of plates and doors, the rustle of Ruth's stockinged legs as she crosses them, become part of the drama. Under the titles (there's no music except when Lenny plays a record) we hear the rummaging of Max in cabinet drawers for a pair of scissors. It's a wonderfully fitting, comic, bare overture.

Pinter wrote his own screenplay. So far as I can make out, this consisted principally of inserting a couple of silent scenes outside the house, one glimpse of Lenny in his room, and the transfer of parts of a few scenes to the kitchen. That's all that was needed.

A fine play is now a fine film. It's a safe bet that generations to come will be glad that it exists.

A King in New York

(December 29, 1973)

WHEN Charles Chaplin and his family were aboard the *Queen Elizabeth* in September 1952, en route to Europe, he got a message from Attorney General McGranery informing him that he would be barred from reentry into the U.S., that before he could reenter he would have to go before an Immigration Department board of inquiry to answer political and moral charges. This governmental action was the outgrowth of an atmosphere of McCarthyist redbaiting—not unexacerbated, it must be said, by Chaplin's windy political pronouncements and his much-publicized amorous career. But neither his political views nor his loves would have caused much governmental stir except for the temper of the times. Naturally Chaplin chose not to appear before an inquiry board. He and his family settled in Switzerland, and he returned to his country only twenty years later, by invitation, to receive honors.

In 1957 he made *A King in New York* in England, his comment on the matters sketched above. It has not been shown in the U.S. until now. King Shadhov (Chaplin), of Country X, flees just before a revolution and arrives in New York with money, he thinks, and with plans for the peaceful use of atomic energy which he hopes to sell. His money is stolen by his crooked minister, and the Atomic Energy Commission (when he finally sees them) isn't interested in his plans. He falls, or throws himself, into the clutches of a pretty advertising woman who uses various tricks to persuade him to make TV commercials and to endorse products. He's broke so he agrees. On a visit to a progressive school he meets a bright, politically minded boy, and after some adventures with the boy, whose radical parents are sub-poenaed by HUAC, and after a subpoena of his own, Shadhov leaves the U.S. He will join his estranged queen in Paris who, despite her announcement at the beginning, will not divorce him. He leaves the pretty young American adwoman, and the current American madness (which he hopes will end soon); he returns to Europe with American money.

The film is produced in typical Chaplin style—tackily. The light-ing, photography, settings, and editing are common and cheap. The music is music-hall. The concern for accuracy is so small that, in what is supposed to be New York, the doors to a theater orchestra are labeled "Stalls," an elevator is labeled "Lift," and in a street scene we see the office of a famous London bookmaker. The direc-tion is, as always, Chaplin-centered and theater-oriented. Most of the actors seem hardly to have been directed at all, and the predominant motions of the film are of actors' entrances and exits, rather than any intrinsic cinematic mode. The cast is generally execrable. Dawn Addams, the adwoman, is almost as disastrous as Marilyn Nash in *Monsieur Verdoux*. Chaplin's son Michael, then ten years old, as the precocious boy, shows he can memorize and imitate but has no talent. Only Maxine Audley as the queen and Oliver Johnston as Shadhov's faithful aide are adequate.

The script, by Chaplin, seems a series of ad hoc inventions with only the vaguest general plan. Whenever the phone rings or the door buzzer sounds in Shadhov's hotel suite, which is the story's "basic" set, you know that the sagging plot is going to get another boost. The satire on American witch-hunting is, surprisingly, more forbearing and avuncularly patient than vindictive. It ends, inexplicably, with a newspaper headline in which Shadhov is called a friendly witness—after his protests against repression and after some courtroom horse-play with a firehose. The script has much more effective satire on film violence, wide screens, and TV commercialism. The one consistency in this adventitious collection of bits is that most of the seeming disasters turn out to be advantageous. Shadhov is trapped by a hidden camera into making a TV spectacle of himself, and it transforms him into a celebrity. He "blows" a TV whiskey commercial by coughing, and it makes him a comedy hit. The implication—that nothing is too ridiculous for American success if only it's sufficiently "exposed"—is much better satire than any of the political stuff. And into the midst of all this topical satire Chaplin thrusts his inevitable Dickensian strand—the lonely misunderstood schoolboy who at one point is even shivering in the snow when Shadhov rescues him. (The script's one truly serious note is the fate of this boy, who is warped by government pressure.)

If this film were by and with anyone else—a stupidly impossible conjecture—it would simply be bad. But being Chaplin's, it has many fascinations, even in its faults. It's the last film in which he will ever appear—he subsequently directed the unfortunate *Countess from Hong Kong* (1966) but appeared only briefly in it—and it's one that makes ultra-clear what happened to his latter-day career. As political satire it's feeble; as cultural satire it's moderately keen; as self-revelation by Chaplin it's an essential work.

First, it shows most vividly how schizoid the later Chaplin had become. In all Chaplin films up to *The Great Dictator,* there was only one Chaplin, the Tramp. In the anti-Nazi film he played two roles which at least were tonally related; the real split came at the end when he launched into the long, controversial speech. There the "serious" Chaplin divorced himself from the clown, as if in fear that the clown, whose very persona had won him his claims to seriousness, was no longer serious enough—or not explicitly serious. That schism deepened in his three final pictures, *Monsieur Verdoux, Limelight* (Calvero is not the Tramp), and this one. In *A King in New York* the schism between comedy and seriousness is not only deepened but takes on another color. Shadhov represents not only Chaplin's politically and socially conscious self but Chaplin himself as King—the King that the Tramp has made him! The Tramp had brought to Chaplin all the perquisites and prerogatives that are here Shadhov's: the front-page attention, the press conferences, the dinner-party lionizing, the expertise in food and dress and nightclubs. Shadhov gives Chaplin the chance to show these personal attributes and acquisitions in public. True, strands of the Tramp-persona are intermittently woven through the King-persona: a fully clothed graceful leap into a bathtub (he was sixty-eight at the time), some fancy footwork in the hotel lobby evading a supposed process server, some pantomime in a noisy night club telling a waiter that he wants caviar and turtle soup (reminiscent of the Oceana Roll in *The Gold Rush*). But the integrated character of the great films is gone, split into a comedy person and the (very literally) self-conscious creator of that comedy.

This schism derives from the schism in film history: the advent of sound. The classy Chaplin, the speechmaking Chaplin, the intellectual parvenu, would have been inconceivable in silent films. He was worried by sound, and he resisted speech in the first two films he made in the sound era, *City Lights* and *Modern Times*—his last two great works. When he succumbed to speech, it took over and hagrode him; he overcompensated for his earlier resistance. He split his world-worshipped character in two and made the "serious" half a vehicle for talk; but sound also affected the comedy self, usually adversely. The moment here when he is fingerprinted by the Immigration Department at the airport as he talks about his joy at being in free America would have been funnier in dumb show with subtitles, without the limitations of Chaplin's limited voice and the *fact* of the words. Shadhov recites "To be or not to be" as a party entertainment—misquoting it, incidentally—but it's neither funny nor an effective instance of the classic clown-as-Hamlet idea which Chaplin wants us to admire.

So, under or above all, *A King in New York* shows how the coming of sound was a curse to Chaplin; how its freedoms dissipated his strengths; how his attempts to exploit it intellectually and ideologically played to his weaknesses; how, in short, he was much more grievously hurt by history in art than by history in politics.

But—obviously, I hope—all the above is comment, not advice to the reader. *A King in New York* must be seen by anyone interested in Chaplin, which is to say anyone interested in film or, for that matter, in the twentieth century. If you like Beethoven, you want to hear the Triple Concerto at least once in your life; no matter what you think of it, you can't *not* have heard it. If you admire this first towering genius of a new art, you must of course see his last work.

The Day of the Dolphin

(January 19, 1974)

THE worst aspect of Mike Nichols's new film is not that it's an utter failure but that it's a manifest of cynicism. I don't mean the professed cynicism that one can find in Lubitsch and Wilder and Hitchcock, which is often their subject matter; I mean cynicism toward the act of film making itself, the air of uncaring, exploitative facileness. This deterioration is possible only to a man of proven talent—I haven't seen anything like it since John Huston turned the corner about a decade ago—so its effect is disgusting.

I didn't read the original novel by Robert Merle, and shan't, but apparently it's based on zoological fact. Dolphins, which are mammals, are fantastically sensory and intelligent and can be taught to speak, in limited monosyllables. (But were the lines for Nichols's dolphins spoken or dubbed?) The footage devoted to the dolphins could be lovely, if extracted from this film that degrades them.

Dolphins can be, may have been, trained by naval people for scouting and planting mines, etc. This much may be in the book, as well as the dumb-ass plot in Buck Henry's screenplay; but the smart-ass wisecracks that occur from time to time are surely Henry's, so that the whole thing sounds as if a cabaret sketchwriter had been brought in to liven up a Saturday afternoon kids' spy serial. George C. Scott's performance is sententiously moronic and vice versa. (He's the dolphin-loving hero.) Georges Delerue, the French composer who has written lovely scores for Truffaut and De Broca and others, here applies his two chief modes—flute-over-strings and mock-Vivaldi—without a shred of aptness.

As for Nichols, whatever one may have thought of his previous four-film cinematic career, whether or not one thought (as I did) that it began well and improved and then wobbled, it showed throughout one constant: a jeweler's precision with his actors. Even that is absent here. The whole thing seems to have been shoved through the cameras as glibly as possible, so that everyone concerned could grab the money and run. I called the picture a failure, but that implies attempt. I felt a real effort only in the first four or five minutes.

The plot? Some Bad Guys steal Scott's dolphins and try to get them to fix a mine to the hull of the yacht of the President of the U.S. But the Bad Guys are hoist with their own dolphin-borne petard. (I hope I've given away the twist.)

Serpico

(January 19, 1974)

THERE'S nothing seriously wrong with *Serpico* except that it's unmemorable, not even terribly interesting while it's going on. And that *is* wrong, really, because it deals with something highly important. Frank Serpico was the New York City detective who, with Sergeant David Durk, testified to police corruption a few years ago and was subsequently shot in the head. He recovered and retired. The assumption, as filmed, is that his fellow officers allowed him to be shot (by criminals) during a drug raid.

Not long ago a comedy called *Cops and Robbers* dealt, fictitiously, with two New York cops who pull off a tremendous heist, and it all seemed uncomfortably possible, factually and morally. *Serpico* is a factual film (though everyone's name has been changed but his) about an honest cop on a police force that is mostly either corrupt or tolerant of corruption. It's a major subject, and it ought not to come off damp and limp. Some of the people actually involved have complained of the film's inaccuracy; what bothered me was its lack of impact.

Partly this is because the whole subject of cops is being beaten to death in films and on TV. Here comes a truthful, important aspect of the matter—essentially, is honesty possible in a capitalist society's police?—and it seems only a moderately clever switch in plotting. Additionally, the script by Waldo Salt and Norman Wexler (from the book that Peter Maas wrote with Serpico) is full of familiar strophes and unfamiliar gaps. The police routines and the girl-and-pad routines are humdrum; on the other hand we never know why Serpico is unusual, why he is anomalously honest. He seems as arbitrarily good as a prince in Grimm. Sidney Lumet directed, with less of his customary trickery but with no communicated verve. And two of the big supporting roles were given to two exceptionally unbelievable, even unpleasant actors—John Randolph and Tony Roberts.

But the picture is a box-office smash. This year's mini-*Godfather*. Obviously most people are not as tired of cop stuff as are some people. And a lot of the success is due to Al Pacino's hit in the title role—as clean-shaven cop, swinging lover, and bearded multi-disguised plainclothesman (hippie, rabbi, bum, etc.). Pacino, like Lumet, has at least rid himself of trickery. He thrived for a while on patently fabricated tensions that burst out occasionally; now he plays relatively straight, if monotonously. He relies on a mirror-image concept: heroes are usually taken to be impressive, strong, commanding, so he plays it slouchy, shuffling, and offhand. Thirty or forty years ago Cagney, no less plebeian, would have transformed such a role into a kinetic distillation of fact. Pacino plays the vernacular fact, graceless. This, like most cultural successes, tells us something about our times—like those currently fashionable high-platform shoes, for men and women, that destroy grace and make every wearer clumsy.

Incidental intelligence: shortly after this film smashed in, the N.Y. Police Department held its first qualifying exam since 1970, and 51,655 young men and women took the test for a possible 6000 vacancies.

The Sting

(February 2, 1974)

ABOUT an hour into *The Sting* I began to understand it. Not the plot, which is clear enough, but the raison d'être. This Paul Newman—Robert Redford vehicle is set in the thirties, and I couldn't really understand why. Unlike (say) *Bonnie and Clyde,* the story isn't tied to the period. Why do it that way? Then Newman and Redford appeared in dinner jackets—sorry, tuxedos: with those thirties lapels that would impale you if you fell on them and those ready-made bow ties with the ring and hook clearly visible in the black elastic. When I saw the ring and hook, it clicked. I had seen exactly the same bow ties on TV a few nights before, in some film made *in* the thirties. Audiences, I guess, aren't as nostalgic for the decade itself—most of them are too young to have known it—as they are for films of the decade. This isn't a film about the thirties as much as it's an attempt to make a thirties film. It's the Antiques Made to Order business. So were *Paper Moon* and *What's Up, Doc?,* both hits. And *The Sting* seems to be a hit.

Recurrently, to the point of galloping tedium, articles appear telling us how American films have lost the Golden Glow of the high Hollywood days, how the writer grew up in love with Gary Cooper or Myrna Loy, and how pictures may now be more mature and more serious and candid, but what happened to all the fun? When these articles don't make me yawn, they make me laugh. First, there's the implication that our film world is just bursting with maturity; second, there's the curious belief that "they don't make them like that anymore." The biggest hit last year, says *Variety,* was *The Poseidon*

Adventure—$40 million in domestic rentals alone for mildewed corn. When the Hollywood-regret articles go on long enough, I stop yawning and get sick. If there's anything worse than bad "serious" pictures it's condescension by people who feel they can save their brains and taste for something other than films.

The Sting probably won't make those people happy enough because it lacks romance in two senses. Girls play almost no part in the story, and myth-making glamour—star as Star—doesn't figure much, either. Everyone has compared the picture with *Butch Cassidy and the Sundance Kid,* with the same leads and the same director, George Roy Hill; but I would bet that the people involved also saw *Borsalino* (1970), with Jean-Paul Belmondo and Alain Delon, directed by Jacques Deray, an engaging French attempt to manufacture a Hollywood crook picture of the thirties. Those pictures were probably more what the buffs like; still *The Sting* may carry them back to the Bijou balcony again.

It's about two Chicago con men who take a big Irish racket boss from New York for a big bundle. There's a moral base—they are exacting revenge for a murder—but the bulk of the picture is con. The original script by David S. Ward has pretty good dialogue, but besides the fact that some of the surprises are phony, the weight is thrown largely on the mechanics of the complicated swindle that the two men set up to fool the wily racketeer. So much time is given to these details that the characters of the three leading men are thin, with occasional spoonfuls of "depth" ladled over. There's a lot of *bonhomie,* on the movie principle that criminals who don't hurt or kill are Good Guys (as in the recent pickpocket opus, *Harry in Your Pocket*). It's more than two hours long, but if you can edit out about twenty minutes in your mind as you watch, it's passably entertaining.

Three fine actors are wasted. Newman and Redford have, as actors, virtually nothing to do, although they are on screen a lot. Robert Shaw, the racketeer, hulks well, but tries too hard to find the center of a role that has none. Hill, the director, is mildly competent but has no style or flavor. (And is overly addicted to cute thirties tricks like iris-outs and "wipes" and to following feet or elevators as a way of bringing us into places.) Robert Surtees, the vastly experienced cinematographer, gets more out of the pictures than the director knows how to use; and Henry Bumstead, the art director, has given Surtees some good stuff to work with.

The Exorcist

(February 9, 1974)

I dragged my feet about going to *The Exorcist* because of the gimmicky subject, and the adverse reviews that I saw made me purr at my prevision. But this film about the diabolic possession of a twelve-year-old girl has become such a huge hit that I thought I ought to grit what's left of my teeth and investigate. I'm glad I did. In this case, anyway, *vox populi vox diaboli.*

This is the most scary picture I've seen in years—the *only* scary picture I've seen in years. (Though I admit I don't see many "horror" films. Too unhorrible.) I haven't been more scared by a film since Mary Philbin snatched the mask off Lon Chaney's face in *The Phantom of the Opera* in 1925. The reference to childhood is particularly apt because the point of *The Exorcist* is to cut through everything we've learned and cultivated, to get down to the talent for fright that we are virtually born with. I haven't felt so much like Robert Warshow's "man watching a movie," his *homme moyen,* since the same director, William Friedkin, did it the last time with his (quite different) *French Connection.*

Friedkin seems to have found his forte. He started serious (*The Birthday Party, The Boys in the Band*), but there he seemed strained, and obtrusive—like a tumbler in a ballet. Evidently what he needed was material where nothing mattered but the effects. *The French Connection* showed he had real gifts for gut punching; *The Exorcist* shows his gifts for chilling the spine. This new picture starts slowly: there's a lot of background material to be laid out and some of it is lingered on excessively; but when Friedkin centers on his main material—the possessed child in modern Washington, D.C.—he handles it with very exceptional skill. The cutting, the lighting, the sound track, and above all, the special effects have been ordered up carefully by the director and used precisely. Even the music is faultless—most of it by Krzysztof Penderecki, who at last is where he belongs. During most horror pictures that I see, I keep watching how it's done and waiting for it to be over. Here the directorial hand is quicker than the eye; and ear. Here I got frights and the pleasure of unmediated visceral response. Disbelief was canted, if not suspended, so that I could watch the story play out. And virtually all of this was Fried-kin's doing.

William Peter Blatty wrote the screenplay, from his own best seller, and produced the film. I haven't read the book and certainly won't now—I've *had* these jolts—but in the film script, anyway, there are some matters left unfinished. A prophecy that the possessed child makes about an astronaut: does it come true? What about the Washington detective (Lee J. Cobb)? Did he just quit investigating the case? The specific occasion for the satanic invasion is only vaguely hinted at, and then only at the end. It has something to do with a small silver religious medal that an archaeologist-priest dug up in Iraq; but why it's important and how it got to this Georgetown house is never clear. If I'm putting this together right, then a point of irony was muffed: because one of the exorcising priests is himself the archaeologist who dug up that medal.

The theme of possession is an old reliable: it's the basis of a chief work in the Yiddish theater, Anski's *The Dybbuk*. The idea of the doom-haunted object has worked for dozens of minor writers, includ-ing Lord Dunsany and W. W. Jacobs. Blatty has blended the two elements in this story of a film actress (Ellen Burstyn) and her twelve-year-old daughter (Linda Blair) living in a rented Georgetown house during the shooting of a picture in Washington. First, the house itself begins to act strangely—inexplicable noises, a shaking bed. Then the child begins to act strangely. Conventional medical procedures are explored; no help. Doctors themselves suggest exorcism. A psychiatrist priest is called (Jason Miller, the actor who is also the author of *That Championship Season*), and eventually an older priest who knows exorcism well (Max von Sydow). One reason I could go along with all this is that I know such things happen: a few years ago a rabbi told me he had recently been called on to perform an exorcism. Anyway, the ending of *this* exorcism is meant to provide a touch of Christian martyrdom, but it really doesn't carry much weight. The ending is a way out of the plot, that's all, and the plot is all that matters in this supernatural melodrama.

The moralistic critics—who invariably object when they happen not to like a current instance of horror or violence, although they may have been caroling the week before about Clint Eastwood or Hitch-cock—bemoan the fact that a child is called upon to mouth some obscenities, pretty foul ones, and to perform an obscene-profane action (shoving a crucifix up herself). I don't see how the child's satanic possession could have been shown by having her exclaim "Darn!" and by breaking Mom's favorite vase. And in a world where five-year-olds in TV commercials parrot stuff about detergents and cereals, with no point at all except selling goods, I'm not upset at Linda Blair's taking part in what she knew was a fiction. As for the horrors, the only time I had to avert my eyes was not for a demonic scene but for a "straight" scene in a hospital where doctors inserted long needles in the girl's neck in preparation for x-rays.

The Exorcist makes no sense. For instance why couldn't the devil have done earlier what he does right at the end? It makes no more sense than a musical, has no more ambition toward sense than a musical. In both cases we accept the non-sense for the sake of entertainment. The theater where I saw The Exorcist was crowded with people being entertained by horror; they giggled after most of the possession scenes (after, not during), a sure sign that they had been shaken and had to right themselves. If you want to be shaken—and I found out, while the picture was going on, that that's what I wanted—then The Exorcist will scare the hell out of you.

POSTSCRIPT. To avoid spoiling the shock, I didn't mention that Linda Blair's voice was dubbed in the possessed scenes; I equivocated by saying that she "mouthed" obscenities. While the review was on press, publicity told us that Mercedes McCambridge was the voice of Satan. Devilish good, too.

Partner

(February 9, 1974)

BERNARDO Bertolucci, who subsequently made Last Tango in Paris, made Partner in 1968. It's just released here. The script is by Bertolucci and Gianni Amico, derived from Dostoevsky's The Double. The "twin" leading roles are played by Pierre Clementi: a drama teacher in Rome and his double, a violent revolutionary. The story, such as it is, follows the efforts of the teacher to succeed in love and to bring off a revolutionary street "spectacle." While this is happening, the activities of the physically identical revolutionary, including a murder, counterpoint the teacher's life.

Already the picture is heavily dated. Cinematically it's redolent of high sixties Godard; politically it's full of late sixties rhetoric and gesture. But for all its imitations, its slavish obedience to mode that poses as bravery, it shows some talent and authenticity.

With Bertolucci's later work, *The Spider's Stratagem, The Conformist,* and much of *Last Tango,* I felt as if I were walking barefoot over rotten fruit. Here I felt it much less; and felt that, despite the clichés, there was some conviction. Although Bertolucci had enlisted in the Godardian ranks and was snapping to attention and executing orders, he was doing it as a zealous partisan. In later pictures he became an interior decorator in cinematic excelsis.

For me, the best whole Bertolucci is still his first film shown here, *Before the Revolution;* his best sequences are the early sex scenes in *Last Tango;* but *Partner* has some genuinely good things in it. Like the very first shot—Clementi in a café, sitting next to a plate-glass window in which we also see his reflection. Our very first glimpse of the film tells us quietly what it's about.

The Mother and the Whore

(February 16, 1974)

THE director of this film, Jean Eustache, is French, born 1938. Perfect. This put him in the right country at the right time for someone of his temperament (if one can fancy a whole potential person being dropped by the stork). Intellectually he came along after postwar existentialism, after the subsequent vogue of café existentialism, just in time for the current era that mocks existentialism. (Much of *The Mother and the Whore* takes place in the Café de Flore, Sartre's hangout, and Sartre comes in for a ribbing.) Cinematically Eustache is about a decade younger than his patent two chief influences, Jean-Luc Godard and Jacques Rivette, which allows him to lean carelessly back on their achievements just as he can lean carelessly on the Despair so painfully articulated by Camus and others.

This is not to accuse Eustache of exploitation—he has ability—it is simply to place him historically. *The Mother and the Whore,* one sees very soon, is a product of what has happened in French film and in Parisian conversation since the mid-1950s. The source of the work is film, not just because there are frequent mentions of pictures and directors but because the characters consciously live like film characters. One of the few utterly false moments occurs early. The hero declares love floridly to a girl, who then asks derisively, "What novel are you being a character in?" Obviously the operative word should have been "film."

Besides, Eustache makes every moment look and feel less like a film of life than like a film of a film. It's almost as if his lens were fixed to the borders of preexistent pictures. André Bazin said that the real esthetic division in film history is not between silent and sound films but between those directors who believe in image and those who believe in reality. By image Bazin meant "anything that can be added to a depicted object by its being depicted on the screen." Eustache seems superficially to be interested in reality, but he adds to his depicted objects (his people and their lives) his consciousness of the world of film experience that lies behind him and them.

So much is plain very soon. Still one asks what this "imaging" mode is being used *for.* Through the film's three and a half hours (*sic*) the answer seeps in.

The Mother and the Whore is Eustache's fourth film, the first one to be released here, and it won the Grand Special Jury Prize at Cannes last year. In blunt yet casual black and white, it fades in on a couple sleeping in a small Paris apartment. Morning. He rises. (It's Jean-Pierre Léaud!—hero of so many Godard and Truffaut films that we start to write the script at once.) He goes to see another young woman. He and Number Two have obviously been lovers, and he wants her back. She declines, thus virtually exiling herself from the film. (Exactly the sensation we get.) He immediately picks up another girl, a nurse, who bears some superficial resemblance to Number Two. The rest of the film is concerned with a newly formed triangle: the young man, who does no kind of work but is apparently an ex-student; the nurse, who is poor, Polish-born, programmatically promiscuous; and the first (sleeping) woman, who turns out to be about thirty, the owner of a boutique and also (since she is played by Bernadette Lafont) of a beautiful body, which we see completely for too few moments.

This triangle is explored in a very leisurely yet sometimes intense manner. The young man likes both women, they both like him, the nurse (Françoise Lebrun) even likes the boutique owner. He sleeps with both of them, often on the same day or night, and the three of them are in bed together on a couple of occasions, though not literally as a trio. Toward the end the nurse has a long drunken tearful soliloquy seated on the other woman's bed, telling the other two that fucking (the term that is used innumerable times in the subtitles) is no good without love. At the very end, we are in the nurse's room; she is off camera throwing up after her drunk while the young man, seated on the floor, watches her. He has just proposed to her and she has presumably accepted.

Now, even if we put aside the inescapable S. J. Perelman overtones of this synopsis, we still have to face the banality of a great deal of this script (by Eustache), epitomized in the soliloquy mentioned above. The banality is of course deliberate. But is that deliberateness a justification? For three and a half hours of boudoir chess and record playings and walks and drives and drinks, heightened only by occasional flashes of drama? (At one moment, for instance, Lafont suddenly swallows a handful of sleeping pills because the other two are busy in her bed. No explanation for this reaction after a good deal of sexual accommodation on her part.) The answer, at last, is yes, and it's an odd justification because one has seen it from the beginning without understanding it.

At first one toys with the idea of symbolism. The young man is young France today, the older woman (mother-mistress) is the intrinsically French past-present, the nurse (French by acculturation, "whore" as protection against feeling), is the possibly altering future. The period, as we are reminded several times, is post '68. Revolution is derided; Sartrean inquiry is derided. The choices for French youth are a (very Gallic) bourgeois life that is withering, or a day-to-day hedonist improvisation that does not want the burden of being called existentialist and has less in it to risk withering.

But that symbolism isn't really earned; it's just an easy amusement during the film's longueurs. Then one really sees what one has been looking at all along, and the perception puts the glib hopelessness of the film in another dimension and gives *The Mother and the Whore* some cultural validity and importance.

Here are all the familiar elements of latter-day French films by and about young people, including the anarchic editing and the gnomic dialogue rehashed from student graffiti. ("Phoniness is the hereafter."

"My dignity is my cowardliness.") Lafont's bedroom and the lighting and the camera movement go right back to Jean Seberg's apartment in *Breathless* (1960). But through all these familiar strophes, the film conveys at last that these strophes *themselves,* of cinematic method and of characters' behavior, are the subject. Everything these characters have in their lives, every way we are given of looking at them, is derived from films without which this film itself could not exist, films that once derived their material from life. Thus *The Mother and the Whore* is image, where its predecessors—to a greater degree anyway—were reality. In the lives of Eustache's three characters, attitudes and stances have replaced beliefs; trivial routines—like the protocol of ordering drinks in cafés—have replaced religious and secular rites; intellectual chat full of Wildean inversions and signals of despair has replaced crucifixes and uniforms. This cosmos of commonplaces supplies at least fragments to shore against ruin, these routines at least provide a world in which the young man and the nurse can marry and to which they can safely resign the older woman. And the language in which they collaborate on their cosmos is not French but the cinema of the last fifteen years. They are not like kids in an attic dressing up in adult clothes and imitating movie stars. From the chromosomes out, they are creations of a world created by film. Their lives, we feel, would be a film even if there were no camera present.

The Last Detail

(February 23, 1974)

THERE's a kind of film that reveals its entire shape very early, with an epitomic cleverness that makes us both interested and wary. During such a picture the main question isn't "What happens next?" It's "Are they going to muff it?" Some examples, differently successful: *The Gunfighter, The African Queen, The Informer, Lifeboat, The Lost Patrol, The Defiant Ones.* Latest example: *The Last Detail.*

The script by Robert Towne is based on, and better than, the novel by Darryl Ponicsan. Two U.S. Navy sailors, old pros, are assigned to escort a young sailor from the Norfolk, Virginia, naval base to the naval prison in Portsmouth, New Hampshire. The story deals with the three men in transit, and the moment you understand that, you see that this is going to be a symbolic film with overtones. The situation is far from new: innumerable Westerns have dealt with a marshal bringing back a prisoner to justice, the two men traveling through wilds and hostiles, facing danger together. But *The Last Detail* is better than most like it because the story is not so consciously abstracted and, chiefly, because the drama results from the struggle not to change, rather than building to some kind of rosy affirmation. This script ends exactly where it was headed from the beginning. Nothing is bettered. The real agon comes from the fact that, after temptations to go somewhere else, the script gets right back where it was heading—into reality, habit, fear, and compliance. The result is not ironic; it's flatly truthful.

Jack Nicholson, of *Five Easy Pieces* and *Carnal Knowledge,* is the senior of the Shore Patrol duo. The other is a black actor named Otis Young, previously unknown to me. Their prisoner is Randy Quaid, a big fellow who has been seen before in small parts. Quaid plays a kleptomaniacal eighteen-year-old boy, insecure, apathetic, uncomplaining. He tried to steal a collection box containing $40—he didn't even get away with it. The collection was for polio, the pet charity of the admiral's wife. Quaid got an eight-year sentence, with a possible two years off for good behavior. The two old toughies have to take the kid to the prison and turn him over to begin his sentence.

Nicholson's first plan is to hustle the kid up to Portsmouth as quickly as possible, so that he and Young can have the rest of the allotted five days on their own. But the boy's continuous presence, the enormity of his sentence, his incompetence to handle his life, his inexperience of practically everything, his puppylike regard for his guards, all of these have a foreseen but nicely handled effect. Instead of rushing, Nicholson dallies. He obviously wants to give the boy something, some fun, some pleasantness, before he gets shut away. This of course includes first sex, in a Boston brothel. Young argues with Nicholson about his sentimentality. (In other language. The dialogue is, justly, very raunchy.) They either have to let the kid escape or turn him over, and they're not going to let him escape because that would mean *their* asses; so why all this silk wrapping? Why not just get it over with, without sops to their own nobility? But Nicholson insists, and Young, who really wants to do the same thing, agrees.

"Don't let it go pulpy," we keep hoping. Except for a contrived encounter with some Greenwich Village types engaged in Nichiren Shoshu chanting and some fisticuffs with marines that are right out of Paramount service comedies of the thirties, the script hews to its line. No one short of a beast could have responded less than these escorts; no one but fictional characters would have let the boy escape as a result of that response. They deliver him to prison at the end and walk away, chatting about what they're going to do before they get back to Norfolk. (An improvement over the novel, which has a long tediously ironic coda.) Responsibility, the script implies, is always elsewhere; the lower man bucks it to the higher, and the highest bucks it back to the lowest, en masse. This last is called duty to the corps or the service or the People.

A strong undercurrent of the script is the implication, not new but still true, that the armed forces are the career for you if you want to remain a boy. Substitute Cokes for beer; eliminate sex, which is only one number on a program, an incidental chance for triumph or patronization; and you have three twelve-year-olds on an outing with overeating and dormitory hijinks. A uniform, particularly for the lower ranks, is armor against growing up.

Jack Nicholson, tattooed, comes back. He was figuratively away in *The King of Marvin Gardens* and *A Safe Place;* here he has a part that is exactly right for him—a rough romantic, innately furious, frequently gentle but knowingly cruel. To cavil, the only thing wrong with his taking over this picture is that his role has been built for him to take over the picture. Aside from the faint air of virtuoso occasion, he and the role are ideal for each other, and together they galvanize the film.

As his sidekick Young is less effective. He's passable, but I was always conscious of his working; he lacks that last access of confidence in the medium, confidence that the camera will reach in and *get* the performance from him. Quaid, I thought at first, was not going to be good. But physically he reminded me of so many big country boys that I used to know, with spaces between their teeth (I don't mean missing teeth), his very lack of appeal contributed so much to his pathos that my reaction soon became that of his guards. Michael Moriarty, now so fine on Broadway in *Find Your Way Home,* has a nice bit as an uppity marine lieutenant.

The director was Hal Ashby, who made *Harold and Maude* and *The Landlord.* I saw only the latter and disliked its inflated cinema rhetoric. Here his work is hard, businesslike, clean. (But he ought to have watched the fellow passengers on train and bus; they are strangely oblivious to the trio's broilings.) The opening credits are whipped past briskly to staccato drum rolls. (Military marches occasionally underpin matters—the one attempt at irony, and superfluous, I think.) At Portsmouth Quaid is whisked upstairs into prison without even a chance to say goodbye; it's just the effect that's needed, like the abrupt clanging of a steel door. And two other moments are especially well handled. Nicholson and Young take the boy on a detour to Camden to see his mother who lives there alone. The mother isn't home—another improvement over the novel, which has a trite scene with the mother and her seedy lover. After some chuffing and blowing on the wintry porch, Nicholson tries the door. It's open. We get just a quick look at the scruffy living room. The boy doesn't even step inside. Our look at the room and the boy's reaction to it tell us all we need to know about the past life that has put him where he is.

Then, during a childishly perverse picnic in a snowy Boston park, the boy makes a last-minute unplanned attempt to escape. The guards chase him. He slips; they catch him and subdue him. Ashby holds the camera back from the struggle in a long shot. It's an excellent touch. Ashby doesn't want to maul us with immediate violence; he wants us to see the three men, former friends, struggling in the middle of open space, three physically and humanely entangled items of humanity. Instead of being shocking or gory, which it might have been, the moment is perfectly sad.

Thieves Like Us

(March 2, 1974)

THE hero of *Thieves Like Us* is a young bank robber and murderer. At the end he is gunned down by the police in a Mississippi motel cabin, and they carry out his body in a blanket. Then, in a close-up, we see them setting the body down in a puddle in the yard. That close-up and the choice of the puddle are typical of the heaviness, the fundamentally mawkish fatalism with which Robert Altman has loaded this film.

Altman along with Calder Willingham and Joan Tewkesbury wrote the script from Edward Anderson's novel (1937). I read it in 1949 when it was reprinted by a paperback publisher for whom I was working, to tie in with the release of the first film made from it, Nicholas Ray's *They Live by Night.* I liked the novel as a reticent piece of pore-inspecting quasi-naturalism. It's just been reprinted again as a film tie-in, and I still like it, though now the purple metaphors jar the texture more than they did twenty-five years ago. Still, Anderson's book does exactly what Altman's film does not do: it fixes its hero and heroine, Bowie and his girl Keechie, as creatures of circumstance, helpless and overpowered, grasping frantically for some truth—a paradox of the possibility of spirit in a drastically degraded moral landscape. We accept Bowie's values, given his conditioning, and accept the fate of Bowie and his girl as Zola-Dreiser specks of human grit bursting into flower for a few moments before the juggernaut of society rolls over them.

Almost all of this is missing from Altman's film. His only attempts to connect Bowie with society are in terms of minutiae—a sound-track décor of contemporary radio programs (by now a painfully trite device), the drinking of Cokes, etc. Anderson's stimulus for his novel apparently came from the story of Bonnie Parker and Clyde Barrow. The script for the *Bonnie and Clyde* film by David Newman and Robert Benton leaned overexplicitly on social and Freudian motivations; Altman's script, possibly in reaction, leans so far the other way that we almost get two cleaned-off clinical specimens. We cannot feel that these two are products of the Depression or of environment, only that Bowie is a moral idiot and that Keechie is a mollusk clinging to him. Then Altman the director emphasizes the script's coldness and bareness by going exactly the opposite way in execution; he and his cinematographer Jean Boffety have worked with wistful visual sentiment from the opening shot. He misses few chances of any kind to blunder artily. A mirror cracks fortuitously and symbolically. When the young pair first make love, a radio gives us *Romeo and Juliet,* and keeps repeating the same bit, like a stuck phonograph. (It's the one purposely unreal touch.) Altman couldn't have been satirizing his lovers, so he must have thought he was embellishing the scene. And to pile on the art for us, he alters Anderson's ending. The novel has the lovers killed together, quickly. Altman has the girl trapped outside the cabin and made to witness the killing, at length. The blasting of the cabin is itself superfluous; there's no reason why the hidden cops couldn't have shot the boy the moment he stepped out of his car before he went inside. That wasn't done so we could have the protracted shooting in which the cabin is nearly blown apart, and he dies alone so we could have a fancy epilogue in which Keechie melts into the crowd. Art has rarely seemed longer, or life shorter.

Keith Carradine, the Bowie, looks right but has absolutely no appeal to make us supply, in empathy, what the part needs if it's going to rise out of the specimen jar. Shelley Duvall, the Keechie, at least manages a few flexible moments that hint at possible depth. But she is a big-toothed beanpole. The casting of Duvall is not only contrary to Anderson's description of her (as a sexy little piece); more important, it shows Altman's sentimental insistence on the very opposite, the unappealing. Bowie's two robber-pals, John Schuck and Bert Remsen, sound as if they came from other parts of the country. (And one of them commits a superfluous murder, not in the novel, at Altman's behest.) Ann Latham, as a coy temptress, is right out of the Southern-slattern pigeonhole. Only Louise Fletcher as a convict's waiting wife is completely valid.

Again Altman proves that he has little security except in satire like *M*A*S*H* and *The Long Goodbye*. He has no grip on the center of *Thieves Like Us,* so it never grips us. The glib invocation of Faulkner in relation to this picture, indulged in by some, apparently comes from the acceptance of similar data as similar accomplishment. By the same declension one could invoke Saul Bellow for *Save the Tiger*.

The Three Sisters

(March 2, 1974)

THE recent American Film Theatre releases have been poor, mainly because the choices of plays were poor. Albee's *A Delicate Balance,* in which a shriveling playwright tries to disguise that fact with swathings of fake mandarinese and fake metaphysics, is like spending three hours head-down in yards of velour. Ionesco's *Rhinoceros* is thin enough to begin with, but Tom O'Horgan stretched it past endurance with directorial clownishness. Osborne's *Luther* is an unsuccessful grab at a complex subject, susceptible of redemption by a good performance; but Stacy Keach simply showed more of his creeping paralysis.

Now a vault upward—Chekhov's *The Three Sisters*. This is, arguably, the best play since Shakespeare; so, inevitably, it's uncomfortable as a film. Laurence Olivier, who directed, knew this before he started, and has done his best to keep as many characters on screen at once as possible so that we can, in his words, observe "who is listening and who is thinking of something else." Given the impossibilities, his direction is generally good, except for some clumsy "touches" like a close-up of the bumptious Natasha's shoes when she first enters, so that we will identify her clatter thereafter, and some dream effects. Also this film is based on the British National Theater production and Olivier has retained his use of the *Internationale* at the end. As I noted in my review of the stage presentation four years ago, this idea is dreadful.

Otherwise the film is very much better than what I saw on stage—in Los Angeles, without Olivier in the cast and with a different Vershinin and Masha. Although we're always conscious that this is a theater work, the film has more flow and cohesion and tonal consistency/variety than the ragged touring production had. I don't know why Olivier wanted to retain Josef Svoboda's walls made of rods in the film; and some of the performances are poor. Louise Purnell is not beautiful, which Irina must be, and is sometimes incomprehensible, as she was on stage. Sheila Reid plays Natasha too heavily, though that's the director's fault. (I don't believe that Chekhov hated Natasha as much as most directors do. Her behavior is well motivated; and why is her affair ipso facto more reprehensible than Masha's?)

But many of the performances range from good to wonderful. As Masha, the married sister suspended in numbness until a lover comes along, Joan Plowright (Lady Olivier) is very much better than Maggie Smith was on stage, lacking final elegance but playing without cliché and with genuine inner life. Alan Bates, as Vershinin her lover, is better than Robert Stephens was: Bates needs weight and complexity, but he is straightforward and, well, appreciative. Olivier, as the drunken doctor Chebutykin, looks more like Lear than a seedy old self-hating boozer and he skims the part, but he's high heavens above the wretched actor I saw filling in for him on tour.

And there are three flawless performances. Ronald Pickup is the best Tusenbach I ever hope to see—fine-strung, modest, eagerly alive, sweet without begging for love. In the very difficult role of Solloni, the captain who is Tusenbach's Nemesis, Frank Wylie is self-doomed, knowingly crazy, marvelous. As Andrei, the adored brother of the three sisters, Derek Jacobi crystallizes the soul of a man who has really sought the shabby fate that he now blames on the world and on his wife.

This film, made in 1970, was released in Britain and elsewhere but could not find an American outlet. I'm told that this impasse is what gave Ely Landau his idea for the whole AFT project. Good enough. Despite its flaws, this picture is worth anybody's time.

Conrack

(March 16, 1974)

CONRACK's real name is Conroy—Pat Conroy, a young South Carolinian who went to teach black children on an island off Beaufort in 1969 (and wrote about it in a book called *The Water Is Wide*). The children heard and spoke his name as Conrack, and he accepted it that way as a means of being accepted by them. Conroy was raised a racist and, for unspecified reasons, became an egalitarian. He took on the task of "liberating" these small black children from the heavy hand of his white school superintendent and the dissimilar heavy hand of his black school principal.

This story, as you can see, is presold. (I'm not discussing its truth or worth, simply its effect as theatrical artifact.) Heroism, to be useful in theater or film, has to be based on resistance—to authority, if possible, and it's even better if the resistance is motivated by love. In *Conrack* we get a tiny portion of *William Tell* in a container of *The Corn Is Green,* and it's easy to take.

Martin Ritt, the director, worked with a black subject two pictures ago in *Sounder,* but there he had a hokey kid-picture producer named Robert Radnitz, who had previously made such things as *Misty* and *A Dog of Flanders,* and who showed it. (The producer's control of an American film is almost always underestimated.) On *Conrack* Ritt was working with Irving Ravetch and Harriet Frank, Jr., who also wrote the screenplay. These three had previously collaborated on *The Long Hot Summer* and *Hud,* pictures of at least some cinematic substance. As a result *Conrack* holds together where *Sounder,* except for Cicely Tyson, was just runnels of glop.

But it was Ritt alone who worked with the actors. He got Jon Voight to play Conrack, and Voight has suffused the role with vigorous, winning, mischievous sweetness. He commits his *body* to the role in a way that dramatizes mind and spirit. And Ritt did absolute wonders with the twenty-one local black children. (The film was shot mostly on the Georgia coast.) Ritt's sympathy, patience, and confidence are reflected through those children back into the camera. It's the single most beautiful element in the film.

When he has things under control, as he had in *Pete 'n' Tillie,* as he has here, Ritt is a good sentimental director, and good sentiment is always welcome. Conrack's breezy unconventionality, his playful but utter commitment are all very fetching. The picture is as enjoyable as it is predictable, except for the very finish. We know Conrack is going to win the kids over, but that's where his victory ends. Still, even the poignant fade-out helps to make the picture retrospectively more Edenic. When Conrack sails away, fired for insubordination, and the children line the dock, with their phonograph playing the Beethoven Fifth which he introduced them to, we know we are leaving a Never-Never Land, credible because the things really happened and because they ended.

In the Name of the Father

March 23, 1974)

A man and a youth come toward us through the arcades of an Italian city. Suddenly the man strikes the youth, forbidding him—his son, as we hear—to strike back. But the son does hit back. More silent walking. Another sudden assault by the father, another response by the son. End of sequence, which is never explained. We never even see the father again. We cut immediately to the boy's school.

This is the opening of Marco Bellocchio's *In the Name of the Father,* made 1971, just released here. Like many other openings, it tells a good deal about the picture that follows and about the maker's methods. The film begins as if it had already been going on for some time. True, under the credits we have previously seen some empty corridors of a school, so we can make inferences. Still, backed by Nicola Piovani's slashing music, Bellocchio plunges us in precipitously, warning us at once that we are only going to be presented with data from a continuum and will have to make our own narrative connections. His opening is a small, hard, almost tangible phenomenological sample. This method, to drive separate slivers of experience into us and let us make the inferences, is just right for Bellocchio's purpose: to contrast what seems to be with what is. It's only when he tries to do the inferential work for us that the film wobbles.

Almost all of it takes place in the boy's school, a Jesuit institution for the sons of wealthy fathers. Angelo is about sixteen (played by Yves Beneyton) so that's the group we stay with, though there are also younger boys. I shan't detail the events (script by Bellocchio) except to say that they deal with and juxtapose three groups: the (largely) clerical faculty; the waiters and servants, who are misfits, morons and ex-convicts, underpaid; and the students, who are all extreme examples of adolescent frustration under more than the usual stress that our society imposes on them. The high point is a school play prepared by and starring the handsome, bright, youthfully perverse Angelo, a play that is a subtly obscene and heretical horror comedy.

The themes are, inevitably, anti-clericalism, anti-traditionalism, anti-pedantry. The obvious reference point is Vigo's *Zéro de conduite,* along with its derivative, Anderson's *If.* . . . There are even some reminders of the school sequences in Fellini's *8½* and, because of the harassment of a nun and some insistence on ugly faces, some overtones of Buñuel. But all this is merely to say that Bellocchio, like most good artists, comes from prevous good artists as well as from himself. His film is original because it is his: his experiences of life and of art have fused through his talent into a unique temperament.

A school is always an apt setting for a drama of change, or of change defeated, because it's the most obvious place where the past/present tries to affect the future. Vigo's glorious forty-five-minute film is still the best work on the subject because it's the one in which fact and metaphor most confidently support one another, but it has one grievous, much-noted fault. All the boys are appealing, all the teachers are creepy or villainous except the young teacher who is on the boys' side. In Bellocchio's script the boys are a very mixed lot; many of *them* are creepy. And the vice-rector (Renato Scarpa), who is certainly not on their side, is a well-meaning, patient, abused man who sees matters differently from and, he believes, more clearly than even the brightest young Turk like Angelo. So it's not just because of fairness but also on the more important point of the reality of generational schism that Bellocchio's script is, in this one particular, better than Vigo's. (Not to mention the ludicrously lopsided *If*. . . .)

But the best strengths of the picture are in its being as a picture. Like Piovani's music, the color photography by Franco di Giacomo cuts at us from the first shots of the empty rooms. "Cut" and "slash" are the dominant figurative words for the film. Bellocchio moves his pictures across the screen vigorously, even harshly, striking at us with images, rhythmically controlled yet often disconcerting.

As was plain from his first two features, *Fist in the Pocket and China Is Near,* the mind behind it all is Marxist, but complexly so, not dogmatically rigid. The anti-clericalism is not presented as the unchallengeable Truth, only as the brightest boys' sole possible response; but Bellocchio also wants us to understand the works and intent of the Church, which in Italy means much more than religion. The vice-rector is a sincere man as much victimized by the system as are the boys. Angelo's last remarks about a society based on reason and science are surely enclosed in Bellocchio's irony. The perfect faith of the adolescent in perfectibility is to be seen as part of historical process, not a conclusion.

This director's sensibility is surgical, prying, sharp. Often the camera moves down the hall past the boys' rooms, peering through the engraved-glass portholes in their doors, revealing them as isolated near-maniacs, as might be the case in a prison (as was the case in Genêt's prison film *Chant d'Amour*). Some of the film is brilliant, like the school-play sequence, or a sequence in which the Madonna comes to life and approaches a boy who is masturbating during mass. Some of it is lurid and grotesque, like the sequence in which Angelo, wearing a dog costume from the play, drags the body of a dead priest upstairs and down, or one involving the neurotic mother of one of the boys. Some of it, after two viewings, I still don't understand, like the scenes of demolition of part of the building. Over it all the title with a double meaning, God and dad, arches like a threat.

The picture is uneven, exaggerated, unsatisfactory, and for all the emotion in it, cold. It is also the work of a born film maker who is overwhelmingly gifted, who is developing a style of his own—lean, harsh, and contemporary, yet streaked, almost nostalgically, with the Italianate. Bellocchio does not woo or seduce us or try to squeeze emotion out of us like milk from a teat. He strikes us across the face with the "facts" of his film, somewhat in the manner of Brecht's epic theater. We are deliberately distanced by a hand that *holds* us at that distance. He is not, or not yet, a sure master, but he is the best Italian director of his (mid-thirties) generation that I know.

Badlands

(April 13, 1974)

TERRENCE Malick wrote the screenplay of *Pocket Money,* one of my favorite films of 1972, an ambling humorous grainy modern Western. Now he has written, produced and directed *Badlands,* which is very different and which sets him high indeed among new American film makers. I have severe reservations about the concept of *Badlands,* but I have no doubt at all about Malick's ability to write dialogue, see scenes, direct actors, and knit a film.

This picture was apparently "inspired" by the story of Charles Starkweather, the nineteen-year-old who, in 1958, went on a killing spree in the Midwest with a fourteen-year-old girl friend. Ten people were murdered. Starkweather was executed, the girl got life. What has fascinated Malick, obviously, is the cool, almost accidental quality of the story and the figurative hand-in-hand innocence of the young pair strolling through it.

In his fictional re-creation he has made the boy twenty-five and the girl fifteen, which renders the coupling even more bizarre, but his intent has clearly been to preserve the quality that attracted him to the story in the first place: its smooth glassy surface covering so much horror. Malick says he put the story in the 1950s because it "had to be set in the past. It's meant to be a fairy tale or romance. . . ." My own sense is that the very unreality he's after would have been heightened by a present-day setting: the motivelessness would have contrasted more strongly with present pressures. But certainly, as he also says, he was not on a mere nostalgia trip.

Martin Sheen, familiar to New York theater audiences and lately the protagonist in the TV film *The Execution of Private Slovik,* plays a South Dakota garbageman who, as he likes to hear, resembles James Dean. The girl, Sissy Spacek, is a red-headed freckled passive child, no less and no more interested in sex than Sheen. Her attraction for him is in some sort of security that she provides; his for her is as an approximation of fictional romance. (She narrates the film, and her rhetoric is out of love stories much earlier than the 1950s.)

Their story begins as if it were going to be a tale of two unconventional lovers doomed by convention to trouble. Her father quite naturally warns Sheen off. When he finds Sheen in the house one day, he goes to call the police. Sheen shoots him, calmly, almost politely. Sheen feels no remorse or panic; the girl seems only very interested, like a held spectator. Then concern sets in. They set fire to the house and flee.

Hidden in a forest, they live like Paul and Virginia, except on guard. When they are discovered, he kills several of the posse; they escape, travel, and leave a trail of killings behind them. They finish up driving across the Badlands in a stolen Cadillac. As capriciously as she first joined him, Spacek decides not to play the rebel-killer game anymore. Sheen allows himself to be captured (after first marking the spot with a small cairn). He is taken away in chains, just as undismayed, reasonable and conversational as he was at the beginning.

If the object in casting the girl was nondistinction, Spacek fills the bill. Sheen gives a clean poured-plastic performance. He doesn't have much force, but he has a careful actor-intelligence. Malick's dialogue is idiosyncratically tight. The three-man camera team—Brian Probyn, Tak Fujimoto, and Stevan Larner—perceive landscapes exquisitely without snuggling up smarmily to Mother Nature.

But *Badlands* is disappointing because it accomplishes very little other than chronicle. To reverse the recent trend of Capote *et al.*, it is fiction as nonfiction. And at that it's not much more than the record of an aberrant. *Bonnie and Clyde* and *Breathless* used their killers as epitomes of their eras. This new film could have taken place practically any time, anywhere. It's not about a product of American society c. 1958; it simply tells the story of a psychic freak who could have freaked out c. 1858—with a weirdly impressionable child companion.

Malick has too easily accepted the aberrant as significant, too easily accepted mindless violence as a self-explanatory semantics. He provides a blank page on which we are to write, but unfortunately we don't feel much impulse to write anything. The mimetic fallacy oppresses him. He has drawn a hero who feels little, but he gets the wrong result: we feel little about the hero. Underneath all the quite sophisticated film making here, there is a somewhat sophomoric acceptance of Nothing as the equivalent of Nothingness.

The Great Gatsby

(April 13, 1974)

WHEN I saw the 1949 film of *The Great Gatsby,* the only other person in the screening room was Edmund Wilson (whom I didn't know). Afterward, as he left, a smiling Paramount publicity man asked him how he had liked the picture. "Not very much, I'm afraid," said Wilson, and kept walking to the elevator. The Paramount man looked less disappointed than betrayed, as if saying, "We've gone to the trouble of making a whole *movie* out of your friend's book and you don't even appreciate it!"

There are lots of reasons why I wish Wilson were still alive, and now one of them is to hear his comments on the new *Gatsby* film. It makes the 1949 version and the 1926 version before it (as far as I can remember it) look like twin pinnacles of art. Every single aspect of the new film is bad. Even Robert Redford, fine actor and attractive man, presents a Gatsby who is a dopey mooner instead of a subtle, large exponent of an American tragedy—a man for whom the romances of Money and Romance are inseparable, a compulsive feeder on illusions insisting that they must be true because the facts of his worldly accomplishments are true, and, saddest of all, a believer in "the green light, the orgiastic future that year by year recedes before us."

If Redford fails, then failure is too kind a term for Mia Farrow as Daisy, a skeleton in amour; or Bruce Dern as Tom, supposedly a well-bred gentleman who despises his parvenu neighbor but who looks and sounds like a nervous shoe clerk; or Lois Chiles as Jordan, another cover girl trying to be an actress; or Karen Black as Myrtle, a writhing gargoyle; or Sam Waterston who looks right enough as Nick but whose voice is stultifyingly boring. Since he does a great deal of voice-over narration, Waterston hurts the picture a great deal.

The script by Francis Ford Coppola turns Fitzgerald's suggestions into blatancies; for instance Nick is escorted into Gatsby's presence for their first meeting as if it were a scene out of *The Godfather* (by

Coppola) instead of the original casual surprising encounter. Nelson Riddle's music is even more heavy-handed—in fact ridiculous. Douglas Slocombe's color photography, last encountered in *Jesus Christ Superstar,* is equally subtle here.

Much of all this must be accountable to the producer, David Merrick, but at least as much is accountable to Jack Clayton, the director. Clayton accepted the above collection of incompetencies and inadequacies, and he directed the wretched performances. He once made a good picture—*Room at the Top,* in 1961. How his undistinguished career since then led him to this job is one of movieland's higher mysteries. Besides the tinniness of ear he shows, he insists on an utterly inappropriate atmosphere of quasi-expressionist grotesquerie—sweaty faces, fish-eye lenses, Gatsby's parties as somewhat degenerate debauches—an atmosphere that stupidly controverts the reticence of Fitzgerald's novel. To make it all just a little worse, Clayton slam-slam-slams an enormous number of enormous closeups at us, quite pointlessly, which is rather as if a composer worked steadily in loud chords.

In sum this picture is a total failure of every requisite sensibility. A long, slow, sickening bore. For me *Gatsby* on film is my memory of Warner Baxter in the 1926 version, floating on his deserted pool in a moment of lonely autumnal melancholy just before he is shot.

The Three Musketeers

(*April 27, 1974*)

The Three Musketeers is full of action, dash, and slapstick, and it depressed me very much. This is Richard Lester's first picture since *The Bed Sitting Room* (1969), a picture that showed a sad lapse in Lester's judgment of scripts though not in his unique and wonderful filmic style. *The Three Musketeers* has a sounder script, but it shows an absolute abandonment of the style that made Lester Lester. Such films as *A Hard Day's Night* and *The Knack* and *How I Won the War* overflow with imaginative pyrotechnics that manage to be brilliant and helpful at the same time. *The Three Musketeers* overflows with nothing but what must in Lester's case be called conventional ebullience. It tries to render the Dumas novel as action comedy and, if memory is serving, it takes that vein somewhat further than the Douglas Fairbanks version did. Here it's not only D'Artagnan who is a somewhat overheroic hero; virtually all the other characters except Richelieu are used for laughs, one way or another. But none of it is Lester comedy, cinematic eruption. Almost all of it is script-y, devised, derivative—and harmful to Dumas.

We can conjecture. No Lester films except the Beatles pictures made much money, if any. *The Bed Sitting Room,* from a Spike Milligan play, was a disaster. (And the disastrous Milligan is present again here.) It almost seems as if Lester were permitted to return on condition that he be un-Lesterly and stick to strictly linear slapstick.

But *The Three Musketeers* isn't very successful even in that vein. David Watkin, one of the best living cinematographers, has worked for Lester before, but here his recently developed style—the clerestory lighting of *The Homecoming*—is much too serious for what happens in it. The jocular seems out of place in these exquisite shots. The script, by George Macdonald Fraser, is a sequence of stunts and set pieces, rather than a strong sequential narrative. D'Artagnan and his three friends are stripped of character and become interchangeable brawlers—so Dumas is robbed of his nice touches of sentiment. And the conclusion is just a limp pageant.

There is an immense star-studded cast, but Charlton Heston, the Richelieu, is by far the most impressive because his role is the only one given a few tatters of characterization. Raquel Welch, the Constance, is asked to look sexy and play comedy; she succeeds at the first. Geraldine Chaplin is Anne of Austria, the woman whose beauty is supposed to be the keystone of the plot. No wonder it all collapses. Michael York, the D'Artagnan, is a good actor, but lightness is not his forte. There's no point in naming the actors of the musketeers. The roles are such faceless mechanisms that any three actors would have served.

It's one dragged-out forced laugh. No sweep, no romance, no convincing chivalric tradition to mock. And, worst of all, no Lester. Not the Lester who has been missing for too long.

The Conversation

(April 27, 1974)

THERE's hope. There always *is* hope in the film world, of course, even when there's no immediate reason to believe it, but Francis Ford Coppola's new film is an immediate reason. Coppola, now thirty-five, is a graduate of the UCLA film school who began his career in 1962; wrote and directed *You're a Big Boy Now* (1967) and *The Rain People* (1969); directed *Finian's Rainbow* (which I avoided); wrote the screenplay of *Patton* (1970); co-authored and directed *The Godfather* (1972). From all this—and the list is incomplete—I inferred that Coppola was a hypertypical film school graduate: a well-trained executant who began with a burst of Hollywood-type integrity and soon settled into smooth oiled-rail success. Well, at least he has not completely settled into it. The juvenile profundities and the neat manufactures have at least now been very pleasantly varied by an authentic script, authentically made. *The Conversation* is not an overwhelming film, but most of the time it's interesting in several ways, and it leaves one feeling, more than anything else, respect for the man who made it.

This film has some resemblance to Haskell Wexler's *Medium Cool:* in both pictures a man who thinks of himself simply as a technician becomes aware of the power of his technology and moves out of mere efficiency into moral concern. With Wexler it was a technology of the eye—the motion-picture camera. With Coppola, it's the ear—his protagonist is a specialist in bugging, or, as they prefer to say, electronic surveillance. This man, played by Gene Hackman, is hired to bug a man and a woman walking in a crowded park, and he devises clever means of doing it. The recorded conversation seems to portend one result; then as Hackman plays the tape over and over (something like the way the photographer magnifies the picture in *Blow-Up*), he suspects an intensification of that portent; gets involved personally to stave off that portent; and finds a different though equally dreadful ending. Because his moral concern has got him personally involved in this case, he is now himself the subject of bugging. He strips his apartment to find the bug—without success—and at the end sits in the middle of his (doubly) self-created desolation, tootling on the saxophone that was the only "human" element in his make-up. The last vision is something like Miró crossed with Munch.

Coppola's script stacks the deck. Hackman's character is made flavorless and monomaniacal, a man without a "personal" life even with the woman he sleeps with, a lifeless figure set up so that life can visibly invade him. And Coppola suffers from the mimetic fallacy almost as much as Terrence Malick in *Badlands*: Malick's mindless killer left a mindless hole at the core of the picture; Coppola's flavorless technician oversupplies us with flavorless episodes. Some of *The Conversation* is hung with unpregnant pauses. Hackman does what he can with it all, which is considerable, but in some of it there is simply nothing for him to do but be single-minded about taping.

The phony camaraderie at an electronics convention is laid on a bit heavily. The Kafka's-castle feeling of the office building where Hackman has to report is, again, very convenient for Coppola's theme. And the whole work operates at what can be called Level One of art. That is, it proceeds predictably with its givens. The allegory, despite the plot surprises, is thematically pat, the fulfillments are mostly fulfillments of design, not of enlargement. It's hard to imagine anyone leaving this film with the feeling that his perceptions or consciousness had in any measure been deepened.

But, within its limitations and despite its sags, *The Conversation* is satisfying. A serious subject has been treated seriously—and with extraordinary cinematic skill. Bill Butler's photography and Walter Murch's editing are very effective instruments for Coppola, and, except as noted, he has held his film firmly to the edge of his allegoric knife.

For me there is something else here of importance. *The Conversation* is still more evidence—as were *Badlands* and a dozen pictures before it—of a fascinating phenomenon. New American film making of consequence is more strongly influenced by European films of the 1960s than by any other precedent. As the European films of the 1970s tend (with exceptions) to become less interesting, American films tend to become more "personal" and European in look and approach. Coppola's new film is surely the work of a man who has seen Antonioni—not just for the *Blow-Up* parallel but for the use of places as dramatis personae; who has seen Czech and Polish films of the 1960s and in them has seen men on earth seeming to float soundlessly through air, calling out voicelessly. Coppola is trying to assimilate such influences to the exploration of American experience.

REVIEWINGS

reviewings

WAY DOWN EAST

DAVID Wark Griffith was thirty-three when he moved into films in 1908. He had been both a theater actor and a playwright without much success, which was why he went to work for the Biograph film company in New York—then the center of production activity. When he left Biograph in 1913, he had made about four hundred and fifty films—most of them in one reel, ten minutes or so—and had clarified the new cinema language.

In the next seven years he made seventeen feature-length films. Some of them were very long and complex, possibly because Griffith was reacting against the early restrictions of the one-reeler, and some of them are still peaks of imaginative energy in the medium.

Among these feature films, *The Birth of a Nation* (1915) and *Intolerance* (1916) are the most famous and, justly, the most praised. Lower in this group is the status of *Way Down East* (1920), but for me it is a picture of persistent strength and of exceptional interest in American cultural history. *Way Down East* was made from a highly successful play of the same name that had its premiere at Newport, Rhode Island, on September 3, 1897, and that was performed around the United States for more than twenty years. William A. Brady, the producer, recounts in his autobiography how this play was brought to him by Lottie Blair Parker, how he thought it had the germ of something but was not in shape, how he engaged an actor-manager named Joseph R. Grismer to revise it (Grismer played the villain in the first production), and how they all wrestled with the script in several versions and through several cool receptions until it became a huge hit.

The Parker-Grismer-Brady play is a melodrama, and came at the end of a century in which the form had dominated the American theater. What is a melodrama? The term has often been defined—it is one of the easier dramatic terms to define—but for my purposes I will try one more definition. Melodrama is a dramatic form using monochrome characters and usually involving physical danger to the protagonist; its one essential ingredient is earthly justice. A "straight" drama may merely imply justice or may end in irony at the absence of justice; in tragedy, justice is often Hereafter. In melodrama, justice may be slow but it is sure, and it is always seen to be done.

By implication, then, melodrama is an artistic strategy designed, *and desired,* to reconcile its audience to the way things are. In the nineteenth century its chief aim was to support the economic-moral system: a great deal was made of the "poor but honest" theme. (Today, melodrama supports different conventional ideas, like *Mission Impossible* on television.) Many thousands of farmers saw the play *Way Down East* in the years that it toured the country, and they must have known that this Currier and Ives version of their lives was a long way from brute fact, but the fiction gave them two things: escape while in the theater, and roles to imagine themselves in outside it. As Eric Bentley says, "Melodrama is the Naturalism of the dream life."

Griffith apparently had a sense of these functions of melodrama in a bourgeois, mock-egalitarian society—terms he probably never used. He also must have had some sense of the pluralist nature of the public at any given time, the perception that new interests can coexist with old ones. (For instance, I don't think he would have been surprised that *Easy Rider* and *Airport* were successes simultaneously.) So in 1920, the year in which O'Neill wrote *Beyond the Horizon,* when Stravinsky and Satie were already known composers, when Picasso and Matisse were known painters, two years after the end of a world war that had altered certain traditions forever, Griffith paid around $175,000—much more than the entire cost of *The Birth of a Nation*—for the screen rights to a twenty-three-year-old rural melodrama.

Griffith made many bad decisions in his life, but this time his choice was sound. Lillian Gish, who was to play the heroine, says in *The Movies, Mr. Griffith, and Me:* "We all thought privately that Mr. Griffith had lost his mind . . . We didn't believe it would ever succeed . . . After I had read the play I wondered how I was going to make Anna convincing." It did succeed, tremendously, and in large part because Griffith showed her how to make Anna convincing. Before shooting, he rehearsed his cast for eight weeks in New York. (His studio was then in Mamaroneck, just outside the city.) He had had plenty of experience in the theater, a theater that was full of plays like this: he had begun acting in 1897, at the age of twenty-two, with a stock company in his native Kentucky, had struggled in a number of other stock and road companies, and had written a melodrama that had been produced, unsuccessfully, in Washington, D.C., in 1907. Out of this experience, evidently, came the conviction that he knew how to make *Way Down East* "work" and that the postwar public had not shed all its old affinities. And, very clearly, he also understood how film was taking over the form and function of melodrama from the theater, expanding it in the directions toward which it had been moving.

That's the last point to note before we discuss the picture itself. Inventions don't happen at random in human history. They are the result of scientific progress, of course, but also—which is less often recognized—they are often the result of intense cultural pressure. In an invaluable book called *Stage to Screen* A. Nicholas Vardac has shown that "a cinematic approach" was increasingly evident in the popular theater of the nineteenth century. One can say, not too fancifully, that cultural dynamics foretold the arrival of the film, that the nineteenth-century audience *demanded* that the film be invented.

Griffith was not the only director to understand how the film could satisfy certain hungers in the theater audience, but he was exceptionally well equipped to take advantage of the metamorphosis. *Way Down East* was not the first, or last, theater melodrama to be filmed, but, through it, one can almost hear Griffith saying to the audiences of twenty-five years before, "Here! This is what you *really* wanted."

Today it may be necessary to explain the title. "Down East" is an old phrase used to describe the farthest reaches of New England, particularly Maine, which at its tip is considerably east of Boston. The picture tells the story of Anna Moore, a poor and innocent country girl who goes to visit rich relatives in Boston and is there seduced by a wealthy womanizer, Lennox Sanderson. He has his way by tricking her with a false marriage. He asks her to keep their marriage secret for a while, but when she becomes pregnant, she asks to be recognized publicly as Mrs. Sanderson. He reveals his trickery; she goes off in solitude to have her baby, who dies soon after birth.

Anna is turned out by her censorious landlady, takes to the road, and eventually comes to Squire Bartlett's farm. She asks for work. The squire is at first reluctant to hire her because she is unknown and may be immoral; but, persuaded by his wife and son, he engages her. Anna proves her virtue by hard work (how else?), and the squire's son, David, falls in love with her. When he declares himself, she tells him, without disclosing the reason, that nothing will ever be possible between them.

Sanderson's country estate is nearby, as it happens (as it *has* to happen). He discovers that Anna is on the Bartlett place, and he urges her to move on. She tries to obey—he still has "male" power over her, evidently—but the Bartletts, who know nothing of the Sanderson matter, although they know him, persuade Anna to remain.

Some months later, at the end of winter, the secret of her past comes out. She is sent forth into the night by Bartlett, but not before she reveals that Sanderson, who is an honored guest at the squire's table, is the guilty man. She wanders through a snowstorm, faints on the ice of the river just as it is breaking up, and is almost carried over a falls, but is rescued by David. Sanderson then offers to marry her authentically; she refuses. She is forgiven by the squire, because she was tricked into immorality, and in the end she marries David.

Many have noted the resemblance of this story to Hardy's *Tess of the D'Urbervilles*. Whether the authors of the original play knew *Tess*, I don't know. It would not have been necessary: the materials were not all that original, even for *Tess*. The difference with Hardy lay, among other reasons, in the fact that he was not interested in demonstrating justice. But Griffith knew Hardy's work, at least in filmed form. In a 1917 interview he said: "Somehow, most of the stars who come to us from the regular stage lack sincerity. . . . Mrs. Fiske, in *Tess*, was a notable exception. I know she drew from me the tribute of tears." It may be that three years later he was remembering that "tribute," and it helped him to decide to film this somewhat similar story.

There are a number of subplots involving other characters, and it is worth noting that, in the original typescript of the play, each character has a casting tag: "Martha Perkins, Comedy Spinster; Hi Holler, Toby Comedy," and so on. (A Toby was a rustic clown who usually bested smarter city folks. Until quite recently Toby shows toured the Midwest.) *All* the characters are theater stock, both in the sense of platitude and of availability, a method of show making at least as old as the *commedia dell'arte*. Griffith used actors for each role who were experienced in that "line of business" and gave each of them at least a few chances to work in close-up that were the equivalents of a few moments center stage. Qualitative judgments aside, all those minor roles form a museum of nineteenth-century theater routines.

Griffith engaged a playwright named Anthony Paul Kelly to do the screenplay and paid him $10,000, but, says Gish, Griffith retained only one thing from the Kelly script: a bit of comic business with her gloves and elastic tapes that always got a laugh and so, to Griffith, was worth Kelly's entire fee. The screenplay that was used, presumably Griffith's own, is a model of the film adaptation of plays, in the sheerly technical sense. Much of the formal beauty of play design arises from limitation: the necessity to limit action and to arrange necessary combinations of characters on stage. The skill with which these matters are handled can be a pleasure in itself, as well as a positive enrichment of the drama. But this skill is not essential to the screenplay, which has infinitely greater freedom of physical and temporal movement, can unfold intertwined material into serial form, and can run virtually parallel actions. These contrasts can be seen in the Parker-Grismer script and in Griffith's screenplay—in principle. (I don't want to magnify in the slightest the literary worth of either.)

Griffith tells his story chronologically, beginning with Anna's visit to Boston. This gives him several advantages: he can show the homes of the rich, thus visibly dramatizing the difference between sophisticated city life and country simplicity; he can give Anna the experience of betrayal and loss of her child "onstage"; and he can make her a differently seen character by the time she reaches the point of what was her first entrance in the play. When she first appears in Squire Bartlett's farmyard in the play, a wanderer looking for work, we soon understand that she has some sort of secret; but at that same point in the film, we know her history—we are already her confidants and she is already a heroine. However, Griffith had the problem of establishing the Bartlett home and his male star before Anna reaches them— about half an hour into the story. He solved the problem with a device deliberately borrowed from Dickens. He inserts the title "Chapter Two . . . Bartlett Village" at an early point and gives us glimpses of the farm and David (Richard Barthelmess), relying on our assumption that if the director is not insane, he's showing us these scenes for a purpose that will become clear. In fact, the lack of clarity is itself an enticement.

Griffith links the two strands before Anna and David meet with mystic prescience; for instance, when Sanderson drops the wedding ring during the mock marriage, David starts suddenly from sleep in his bedroom. (No explanation of why David is in bed during the bright day of the mock marriage not so many miles away!) This mystic device, sentimental as it is, simultaneously draws on three kinds of design protocol: that of the theater, of the novel, and of the purely cinematic, fusing them into a new form that we can call the film.

The most obvious physical expansion is in the storm scenes at the end, which were filmed over a considerable period of time outdoors in Mamaroneck, New York, and in Vermont. There is also a shot of Niagara Falls. (In one Mamaroneck blizzard we can see snow gathering on Gish's eyelashes. And in her autobiography she tells of floating on a Vermont ice floe so long that her hair froze and her hand; trailing in the icy water, felt as if it "were in a flame.") The advantage in excitement of this physical expansion is self-evident; it is the realism, or purported realism, that, as Vardac shows, the Victorian theater was aching for. But also, on the thematic level, it gives us a much more engrossing way of sharing Anna's purgation.

Still, in recognizing the advantages provided by the film form, we mustn't lose sight of what theater practice meant to *Way Down East*. As a result of his own stage experience and viewpoint, Griffith patently relied on verity of acting to sustain the picture, and indeed the best acting moments are the film's anchor points today. The truth of those moments, in a script that is beneath serious regard, stands out like the best arias in a trumpery old opera.

The remarkable fusion of new film elements and old theater heritage is why *Way Down East* is still effective and why it is historically important. On the one hand, we see Griffith using sheerly cinematic language to fulfill his drama. When Sanderson (Lowell Sherman) is introduced, there is a quick succession of cuts—close-ups and medium shots—so that his first appearance sparkles prismatically, dangerously. When he and Anna first meet, we see him over her shoulder before we see them together, as Griffith uses the film's power to shift the audience and thus increase the feeling of encounter. When the camera comes in for close-ups of Anna in her baby's birth-and-death room, Griffith vignettes her against a black background to underscore the icon effect. When Anna is thrown out by her landlady after her baby's death, there is a lovely long shot of her starting down a country road, her few possessions in a box under her arm—a shot that bitterly contrasts the beauty of the scene with her sorry condition. (Usually Griffith uses nature shots to endorse a character's feelings; this contrast is an exception.) She arrives at the Bartlett gate on foot, and Griffith intercuts a shot of Sanderson on horseback, at his estate nearby, thus commenting sardonically and at the same time knitting his plot. When the spinster Martha Perkins discovers the facts of Anna's past and hurries to spread the gossip, we get one of the film's few tracking shots: the camera trundles eagerly ahead of her on the snowy path, and its very motion becomes part of the idea of the scene.

Further, the seminal influence of Griffith on other directors can be traced to this film as well as to the usual sources, *The Birth of a Nation* and *Intolerance*. The early Soviet masters, in particular, responded to it. Sergei Eisenstein writes at length of the background of *Way Down East* in his essay "Dickens, Griffith, and the Film Today." V. I. Pudovkin writes in *Film Technique* that in the storm sequence the harmony between the blizzard and Anna's feelings "is one of the most powerful achievements of the American genius." Pudovkin adapted the metaphor to his own purposes in his film *Mother* (1926): the breakup of the ice is used there as a larger symbol—of revolutionary turbulence—but it clearly owes a great deal to *Way Down East* in vocabulary and technique.

On the other hand, we can also discern Griffith's purely theatrical gifts. Some instances: the handling of Barthelmess so that, quite soon, his very movements articulate the poetic qualities of his personality and quicken his trite role; Anna's face, as Sanderson tells her that their marriage was fake; Anna in the discovery of her baby's death; and, an even keener theatrical touch, the very next scene in that bedroom, where the bereft Anna is sitting on a stool next to the rocker in which she had baptized her child and gently rocks the now-empty chair. Talk about the "tribute of tears!"

Possibly Griffith's highest achievement here as director of actors is the ballet he created with Lillian Gish's body. If there were no titles of any kind, one could "read" her body: the butterfly dance around her little parlor as she awaits her supposed husband; the crushed figure who trudges the road after her baby's death; the recovery of some self as she works at the Bartletts—a medium between the joy of the beginning and the desolation of the abyss. She tells us, simply by the way she moves around the Bartlett place, that she will never again be as happy as she once was but at least she is once more breathing. Since Gish did her best acting for Griffith, it seems fair to assume that her fine performance closely reflects his direction.

No appreciation of *Way Down East* should lead us to the film-buff silliness of hailing it as a transcendent artwork. It is a mechanical and saccharine story, with dialogue to match, full of glaring moral signals (for example, only bad or frivolous people smoke cigarettes), and Griffith's heavy editorial comments. What is more, the best print of the film I have seen contains errors of editing (overlapping action, repeated in successive shots), and the light in the storm scenes varies widely. (Some sequences in the original prints were hand-tinted; the absence of that color now may cause those variations of light.) There is even a split second in which an actor seemingly gets a hint from off-camera: the charming Mary Hay catches her heel in her hem and someone, unseen, tells her so.

Still, the empirical fact is that, despite all we know about the film as we watch it, it grips us. Substantially this is because of the elements analyzed here, all underwritten by the utter seriousness with which Griffith took the whole project.

And that seriousness is rooted, consciously or not, in the myth that underlies much of melodrama: moral redemption by bourgeois standards. It has been suggested* that Anna is a secular saint, truly good, suffering for the sins and blindness of her fellows, finally undergoing an agony that reveals her purity. She is betrayed in her trust, she goes through travail, she labors in humility, she declines happiness because she is unworthy (refusing David's love), and she shows that death holds no terror for her. At last she achieves heaven—on earth.

To extend the analogy, the God in the story is the squire (the owner of the Eden)! It is he who at first is about to expel Anna from the Garden, who finds largeness in his heart to let her remain on trust, who at last provides the crucial forgiveness—because when she sinned, she did not know it; she thought she was behaving rightly. Not only is she forgiven, but when she marries David, she wears white; her virginity has been restored by dispensation of the squire. Here, in capsule, is sainthood founded on respectability, which was possibly the chief criterion in nineteenth-century society.

Scoff as we may, the possibility that there *is* earthly justice is the fundamental appeal of *Way Down East,* as it is in our contemporary melodramas. Other old melodramas of stage and screen have died because their claptrap dates and strangles them; this film lives because, beneath and through its claptrap, it makes the possibility of justice poignant still.

And it lives, too, because it is one of the most lucid instances of a tremendous historical change: the theater culture of the last century being transformed into the theater-film culture of this century. *Way Down East* feeds on the earlier culture and seeds the later one. In chronology it came fairly late in that historical process; but in crystallizing that process, it is a landmark.

* By Michael Annand, a former student of mine at Yale, in a paper contrasting Anna with Dreyer's Joan of Arc.

POTEMKIN

SOMETIMES one imagines that there is a small but constant supply of genius throughout the world and that a particular juncture of circumstances in any one place touches the local supply to life. Otherwise, how explain the sudden flowering of Athenian architecture or Elizabethan drama or Italian Renaissance painting? Can one believe that there had been no previous talent and that geniuses were born on cue? It almost seems that the right confluence of events brings dormant omnipresent genius awake; without those events, nothing. Possibly the man with the greatest potential genius for symphonic composition lived in New Guinea five hundred years ago, but there was nothing in his world to make him know it.

This theory, admittedly fanciful, gets some support from what happened in Soviet Russia in the 1920s. A new revolutionary state was born as a new revolutionary art emerged, and that combination brought forth at least three superb creators in the new art: Vsevolod Pudovkin, Alexander Dovzhenko, and—the most important because the most influential—Sergei M. Eisenstein. Conjecturally, all of them might have had outstanding careers in other fields, but the Soviet Revolution and its need for film, one may say, made geniuses of them.

For all the joy and ebullience that attended the birth of Soviet film and Eisenstein's entrance into it, his career as a whole is a sad story, and it puts my comments on *Potemkin* in true, cruelly ironic light to have some of the biographical facts first. Sergei Mikhailovich Eisenstein was born in Riga in 1898, studied engineering in St. Petersburg, and entered the Red Army in 1918 to fight in the civil war. While in the army, says Yon Barna in his recent biography, Eisenstein became involved in amateur theatricals, which intensified an interest in the theater he had felt since he was a boy. He decided to abandon an engineering future for a theatrical career. In 1920 he was demobilized, got himself to Moscow, and found a job at one of the new workers' theaters as a scene designer. He went on to do some designing for the renowned theater director Vsevolod Meyerhold, whose anti-psychological, anti-"internalizing" views influenced him greatly; then in 1922–24 Eisenstein himself directed plays, including one called *Gas Masks*. But his impulse toward direction, as he later wrote himself, was much more cinematic than theatrical: he staged *Gas Masks* in a gasworks!

From there he moved quickly into film. He had already done a short film interlude for a theatrical production, and in 1924 he made his first feature, *Strike.* In 1925 he made *Potemkin,* which is sometimes known as *Battleship Potemkin* or *Armored Cruiser Potemkin.*

Absolutely congruent with his bursting film energies was his fervor for the Communist Revolution and the establishment of the Soviet state. These factors are integral in any talk of Eisenstein. To think of him as a director who just happened to be Russian or who (in those early days) was subservient to a state-controlled industry and managed to slip some good art into his films despite this subservience, is to miss the core of Eisenstein. His works in those days were cinematic exponents of his beliefs.

With his next completed film *October,* released in 1928, the complications begin. Originally the film had sequences showing Trotsky's part in the revolution of 1917, but while Eisenstein was finishing it, Trotsky went into disrepute and then into exile as Stalin ascended. Eisenstein had to revise his film to take account of this rewriting of history.

His troubles increased as time went on. The Stalin era was not exactly a continuation of the high, shining Bolshevik days. To sum it up: the rest of his career, until his death in 1948, is a story of frustration and frequent abortion. Out of numerous projects he completed only four more films. Even an expedition he made to the West ended abortively. He was allowed to go to America in 1930, discussed several projects with a Hollywood studio, made none, and then shot a lot of footage in Mexico for a film he never edited, although others have arranged versions of it.

He spent much of his time in his later years teaching at the Institute of Cinematography in Moscow, writing (most of these writings are not yet in English), and not complaining about the state. Still the facts speak for themselves: this furiously imaginative and energetic man left a total of only six completed films. One virtually completed film, *Bezhin Meadow,* was apparently destroyed by the Soviet government in 1938, although the official line is that it was destroyed by German bombs in World War II. (Isaac Babel worked on the final script of *Bezhin Meadow,* which was based on a Turgenev story that echoes the ideological difference between Eisenstein and his conservative father.) The USSR's waste of Eisenstein, melancholy in any view, is especially grim when seen in the light that blazes off the screen from *Potemkin.*

When it was first shown abroad in 1926, it was hailed by many, including such disparate figures as Max Reinhardt and Douglas Fairbanks, as the best film that had yet been made anywhere. Agree with that opinion or not; few can see this relatively short picture—five reels, eighty-six minutes—without being catapulted into an experience that is stunning in itself and illuminating of much that followed in film history.

During the mid-1920s the Soviets were busy trying to consolidate ideologically their political and military victories, and they called on the arts to help. Eisenstein was assigned to make a huge film called *The Year 1905,* dealing with the events of the earlier, failed, but momentous outbreak against Czarism. He and his script collaborator Nina Agadzhanova-Shutko wrote a scenario in which, says Barna, "the *Potemkin* mutiny took up a relatively tiny part." When Eisenstein went to Odessa to shoot that part, he decided to limit the film to that single *Potemkin* episode.

Here is the episode, as he presents it. While the warship is anchored in the Black Sea near Odessa in June 1905, the restive crew protest against the maggoty meat that they are served. The captain orders the execution of the dissenters. Instead of obeying orders, the firing squad joins the crew in mutiny, and they take over the ship. One of the leaders is killed; his body is taken ashore so that it may lie "in state." The sympathetic citizens of Odessa pay homage to him and support the sailors on the anchored vessel with gifts of food. When a mass of these citizens gathers on a huge flight of steps overlooking the harbor to cheer the *Potemkin,* the Czar's troops appear and march down the steps, scattering the crowd and killing some of them. The government sends a naval squadron to retake the *Potemkin,* which sails to meet them in battle. At the moment of encounter, the fleet allows the mutineers to pass through. In fact, the ship sailed to Constanta in Rumania, where the crew opened her seacocks, then sought refuge inland; however, Eisenstein leaves the story open-ended, with the *Potemkin* sailing onward through the friendly squadron, bearing the seed of revolution that was to bloom twelve years later.

Now, irrespective of the viewer's political beliefs, this story is a natural thriller. Nothing has more wide or direct theatrical appeal than resistance to tyranny, whether it is Spartacus or William Tell or the Boston Tea Party. Any competent Soviet director could have made the *Potemkin* story into an exciting film. But Eisenstein—and, to repeat, this is the core of his importance—was an *artist of revolution,* not merely a good director, not merely a gifted propagandist. That revolution was as central and generative for his art as, to cite a lofty precedent, Christianity was for Giotto. There are acres and acres of fourteenth-century Italian frescoes and canvases that present Christian ideas more or less affectingly, but the Arena Chapel in Padua is the work of a Christian genius and a genius that was Christian. In proportion, the same relation exists between Eisenstein's genius and Soviet communism.

The dynamics behind the particularity of his art can be traced to Marxist concepts and, I think, to none more clearly than to some in the *Communist Manifesto* of 1848 by Marx and Engels. I do not maintain that Eisenstein used the *Manifesto* as an explicit text, but he certainly knew it well and its ideas were certainly part of his intellectual resources. One idea in the *Manifesto* seems outstandingly relevant. In the second section, where the authors anticipate objections to their arguments, they write:

Does it require deep intuition to comprehend that man's ideas, views, and conceptions—in one word, man's consciousness—changes with every change in the conditions of his material existence, in his social relations and in his social life?

Straight to this profound concept, that a changed world means a changed awareness of the world, Eisenstein struck in his film making, and never more deeply than in *Potemkin.* That he was following Marx preceptively I cannot say, but clearly he felt that a new society meant a new kind of *vision;* that the way people saw things must be altered; that it was insufficient to put new material before, so to speak, old eyes. Anyone anywhere could tell a story of heroic resistance in traditional style; it was his duty as a revolutionary artist, Eisenstein felt (and later wrote), to find an esthetically revolutionary way to tell a politically revolutionary story.

The prime decision was in the visual texture. He wanted to avoid historical drama; he wanted to make a drama of history. He and his lifelong cameraman, Édouard Tissé, aimed at a kind of newsreel look: not coarse graininess (there is, indeed, a good deal of subtle black-and-white gradation), but not painterly chiaroscuro either, no imitation museum-look. He wanted the feeling, essentially, of extraordinary eavesdropping.

A recent scion of this approach was Pontecorvo's *The Battle of Algiers,* except for the difference that, in these earlier days, Eisenstein relied very much less than Pontecorvo on individual performances. That was Eisenstein's second decision; he used very few actors. Mostly, he used ordinary people whose faces and bodies he liked for particular roles—a furnace man as the ship's doctor, a gardener as the ship's priest—and each one was used for a relatively short performance that the director could control easily and heighten with camera angles and editing, in a kind of mosaic process. Eisenstein called this approach "typage," the casting of parts with such striking faces— often introduced in close-up, sometimes intense close-up—that our very first glimpse tells us most of what we need to know about him or her as an element in the mosaic. In his subsequent films *Alexander Nevsky* and both parts of *Ivan the Terrible,* Eisenstein blended the use of "typage" with large roles for professional actors, but in *Potemkin* human depths come from the combination of pieces rather than the exploration of any one piece.

The "typage" idea leads directly to the cinematic technique most closely associated with Eisenstein: montage. Basically, montage is editing: the selection and arrangement of bits of film to produce certain effects. Every film ever made, from *Potemkin* to TV commercials, literally contains montage. But Eisenstein's use of montage was different from any use of it before him, including the work of his acknowledged master D. W. Griffith, is immediately recognizable as Eisenstein's, and is the source of much that followed after him.

He wrote often on the subject, which for him was the heart of cinema. For him, there were five kinds of montage. Briefly put, these are: metric montage, which is simply a relation between the lengths of the various pieces; rhythmic montage, which is based on the contents, in movement and composition, of the various pieces; tonal montage, based on the emotional colors of the pieces; overtonal montage, which is the conflict between the principal tone of the piece and its overtonal implications; and intellectual montage, a conflict that arises when similar actions are seen in conjunction but have been performed for different reasons (e.g., a hammer blow by a blacksmith, a hammer blow by a murderer).

These were not academic formulations. These five kinds of montage were, for Eisenstein, organs of a vibrant, live art. With them, and combinations of them, he fashioned *Potemkin* into a kind of bomb that penetrates our customary "entertainment" apperceptions to burst below the surface and shake us from within.

The story itself he phrased into five movements: Part One, Men and Maggots; Part Two, Drama on the Quarterdeck; Part Three, An Appeal from the Dead; Part Four, The Odessa Steps; Part Five, Meeting the Squadron. Each of these parts, like an act in a good drama, is a structure in itself, with its own cantilevered stress and tensions, that contributes to the structure of the whole.

Commentators have pointed out that both the montage in *Potemkin* and its five-part structure had their origins at least partly in practical considerations. Raw film stock was in very short supply in the early Soviet days. Most of what was available was in relatively short snippets, so directors had to work in short takes. Eisenstein developed the esthetics of montage out of an exigency. Also, most Soviet film theaters at the time had only one projector; there was a pause when one reel ended and another reel had to be put on the machine. The five parts of *Potemkin* are on five reels, so the pauses come at reasonably appropriate moments. But, as is so often true in the history of art, the practical needs were not constrictive but stimulating. Another great precedent: the *David* in Florence is huge because the city had a huge block of marble on its hands, left over from an unfulfilled commission, and asked Michelangelo to make use of it.

With the very opening moments of *Potemkin,* we know we are in the presence of something new, and the miracle is that we know it every time we see the film. The waves beat at the shore, the lookouts converse, the ship steams across the sea, and all this is modeled with an energy, controlled yet urgent, that bursts at us. Then, when we cut to the crew's quarters and we move among the slung hammocks, we know we are in the hands of an artist who sees the difference between naturalism and realism. The scene of the sleeping sailors is accurate enough, yet Eisenstein sees the arabesques that the hammocks form, and he uses these graceful, intersecting curves as a contrast to the turbulence of the waves earlier and the mutiny that is to come. Shortly thereafter, he uses the swinging of the suspended tables in the mess hall in the same way—another moment of irrepressible grace in iron surroundings.

Fiercely, electrically, the film charges forward into the confrontation between officers and men, the action caught in flashes that simultaneously anatomize and unify it—in Eisenstein's double aim to show things as they are yet make us see them as never before. One of his methods, which has been likened to cubism and is a forerunner of a technique used in *Last Year at Marienbad,* is to show an action and then repeat it immediately from a slightly changed point of view. A celebrated instance of this is the moment when a young sailor smashes a plate on which is inscribed "Give us this day our daily bread." We see his action twice in rapid succession, from two angles, and the effect is intensification, italicized rage.

Eisenstein shot the quarterdeck sequence on board *The Twelve Apostles,* the surviving sister ship of the *Potemkin,* which had to be altered somewhat but which nevertheless gives the sequence a steely verisimilitude. (Remember *Gas Masks!*) When the obdurate sailors are herded together and a tarpaulin thrown over them before they are to be shot—itself a simple, dehumanizing image—the firing squad prepares, and the film cuts away: to a close-up of two cannon, to a view of the ship at anchor, as if to implicate the environment. Of course it is D. W. Griffith's old technique of intercutting to distend a moment of climax, but it is used here for thematic as well as visceral effect.

At the last moment the firing squad goes over to the sailors' side, and in the fight that follows Eisenstein uses another of his favorite devices, which he himself called synecdoche. After the corrupt ship's doctor is thrown overboard, we see a close-up of his pince-nez dangling from the rigging—the same pince-nez with which he had inspected the maggoty meat and pronounced it edible. The man's corruption and what followed it are caught in that shot. And there is another such moment. Before the fight, we have seen the ship's priest, one of the clerics whom Eisenstein was constantly caricaturing in his films, lifting his crucifix and bidding the men obey. During the fight, after the priest has been knocked down a flight of steps, we see a close-up of the crucifix, an edge of its lateral bar stuck in the deck where it has fallen, like an axe plunged into wood—an axe (Eisenstein implies) that has missed the necks for which it was intended.

The most noted sequence in the film, without question the most noted sequence in film history, is the Odessa Steps. It is oceanic. With some hundreds of people, Eisenstein creates the sense of an immense, limitless upheaval. With the quick etching of a few killings, he creates more savagery than thousands of commonplace gory films. With crosscurrents of perspective and tempo, he evokes the collision of status quo and inevitable protest.

Here are two examples of Eisenstein's montage in this sequence that is a treasury of montage esthetics. First, as he himself noted, the recurring shots of the soldiers' boots coming down the steps toward the frightened and angry citizens are always in a different rhythm from the rest of the sequence, ideationally establishing a different political impulse, esthetically creating an exciting counterbeat. Second, he establishes, by typage, a woman with glasses protesting the soldiers' butchery. Shortly afterward, we see an officer swinging a saber at the camera; then we cut to her face, one lens of her glasses shattered, her eye streaming blood, her features frozen in shock. (The bank teller in *Bonnie and Clyde* who was shot through the car window is her direct descendant.) The suggestion of the blow's force by ellipsis is masterly enough; but in the brief moment in which we see the officer swinging his saber at us, totaling less than two seconds, there are *four different shots* of him, exploding his fury into a horrifying prism.

This episode raises one more point to be made about the whole sequence, the whole film. Even when one sees *Potemkin* without musical accompaniment, which is preferable to most of the scores that have been tacked on to it, when it is seen absolutely silent, the effect is of roaring tumult. One strong impulse to the development of montage in the days of silent film was the attempt to create visually the effect of sound: shots of train whistles or church bells or door knockers so that you could see what you couldn't hear. But in this film, by the way he counterpoises rhythms and faces, marching boots and guns and moving masses, Eisenstein draws from that silent screen a mounting and immense "roar" that has rarely been surpassed in sound films.

The double vision of *Potemkin*, subjectivized and also cosmic, is paralleled in its double effect throughout the world. Subjectively, it was made as a celebration for those already fervent in communism; but it was simultaneously intended as propaganda for the unconverted world. Emotionally and esthetically, if not politically, it unquestionably has had a great effect; but those who control the film have much less faith in it than its maker had. No important picture has been more seriously tampered with. Political messages have been tacked on fore and aft on some prints; some prints have been snipped internally;

thirty-five years ago in New York the picture was given a filmed prologue and epilogue spoken by American actors. The only music that Eisenstein approved was written by an Austrian, Edmund Meisel, for the Berlin premiere, and this score has only recently been rediscovered. Most prints of *Potemkin* have some other music ladled on.

Eisenstein's career, in terms of its free growth, describes a curve that coincides with the rise and fall of world-wide radical hope for Soviet communism. But at the height of his faith, he created a film that both proclaimed his faith and transcended it, a work of political fire that lives because it is a work of art.

THE GOLD RUSH

WHEN Charles Chaplin made *The Gold Rush* in 1925, he was thirty-six. He had been a world-famous star for about ten years. Trotsky said of Céline that he "walked into great literature as other men walk into their own homes." The same figure applies to Chaplin and great film. The rising young English music-hall performer met the film medium as if it had been created for him, and he met the film public as if it had been waiting for him. Up to 1920 he made about seventy films, most of them short and most directed by himself. Only one of them, *Tillie's Punctured Romance* (1914), was feature-length, and it was directed by Mack Sennett. In 1920 Chaplin directed his first feature, *The Kid,* with himself and Jackie Coogan. His next feature, *A Woman of Paris* (1923), was not a comedy, and he appears in it only briefly as a station porter. *The Gold Rush* was only the second long film of his own about the Tramp; yet he knew he was dealing with a character who was familiar to everyone, Eskimos and Malayans included. It's rather as if an author had created a world-renowned character through short stories, had written one novel about him, very successfully, and now wanted to take that character further and deeper in a second long work.

Chaplin recounts in his autobiography how he struggled to find an idea for that second feature, insisting to himself: "This next film must be an epic! The greatest!" Nothing came.

Then one Sunday morning, while spending the weekend at the Fairbankses', I sat with Douglas after breakfast, looking at stereoscopic views.

Some were of Alaska and the Klondike; one a view of the Chilkoot Pass, with a long line of prospectors climbing up over its frozen mountain. . . . Immediately ideas and comedy business began to develop, and, although I had no story, the image of one began to grow.

The role of the unconscious in creation is still unfathomed, and we can only hypothesize from results. In Chaplin's reaction to those photos, the striking element is unpredictability. He had made very few films that took the Tramp out of contemporary city or country life. Tramps are, after all, a by-product of industry, urban or rural. Evidently (we can deduce after the event) Chaplin's unconscious saw at once, in those stereoscopic pictures, the advantages of the novelty of putting the Tramp into a context that, so to speak, had no direct relation to Tramp-dom, the possibilities for the "epic" that he was seeking. And, presumably, he saw the power in putting the image of the Tramp, whose black moustache is the center of the figure's color gradations, against predominantly white backgrounds. All in all, it was a chance to simultaneously vary and heighten what he had done up to now.

Years later Chaplin told Jean Cocteau that the plot of *The Gold Rush* had grown "like a tree." Well, it is a remarkably ramified tree, a remarkably complex plot for a film that runs less than ninety minutes. In brief: Charlie, a prospector in the Alaskan gold rush of 1898, takes refuge from a storm in a lonely snowbound cabin with another prospector, Big Jim McKay, who has literally been blown in there after making a big gold strike. They spend some days of hunger together, then go separate ways. Big Jim finds a man trying to jump his claim and, in a struggle, is knocked out. He wakes without any memory of his claim's location.

Charlie, meanwhile, has arrived in a boom town, has found a job as caretaker of a cabin, and has fallen in love with Georgia, a dance-hall girl. She treats him lightly, since she is in love with a strapping young prospector, until she accidentally discovers how truly smitten the Tramp is. Before Charlie can pursue his love, Big Jim wanders into town, still amnesiac about his claim, and seizes Charlie as the sole means of guiding him back to the lonely cabin and thus the gold. He promises Charlie half the proceeds and drags him off.

They find the cabin and spend the night there, during which the cabin is blown to the edge of a cliff near the claim. (This is a reversal of the earlier device in which Big Jim was blown from the claim to the cabin.) In the morning the two prospectors escape from the cabin just before it slips over the edge—to find themselves right on the site of the gold.

In an epilogue, Charlie and Big Jim, swathed in furs, are on board a ship returning to the United States. For newspaper photos, Charlie puts on his carefully preserved Tramp outfit, and runs into Georgia. She thinks he is still really the Tramp, hides him from the ship's officers who are searching for a stowaway, and offers to pay his fare when they find him. The truth is revealed about the new millionaire, and Charlie and Georgia are united at the close.

It *is* the "epic" that Chaplin was looking for. The opening strikes his usual serious opening note, like the adagio opening measures of a Hayden symphony before the brightness; but Chaplin returns frequently to seriousness, something that has always dismayed a few and delighted many. Those first shots are of a long serpentine line of prospectors filing up the snow-covered Chilkoot Pass (filmed in Nevada, actually) and are obviously inspired by some of the pictures that Fairbanks showed Chaplin on that Sunday morning. The sequence is grim; we even see one of the prospectors collapse while the others trudge heedlessly past him.

Then a title announces "A Lone Prospector," and we see a narrow mountain path on the edge of a steep drop. I always laugh at once, not just because I know Chaplin is coming and the path is dangerous, but because—separated from the opening only by one title—the scenery is so patently phony compared with the reality of the Pass. Thus, early in the film, Chaplin sets a pattern that weaves throughout, the real world posed against the theater of that world, unblinking reality as the ground for a comic abstract of that reality. It's dangerous to mix modes like that, of course, unless you are able, as Chaplin is, to make the return to each mode instantly credible and supportive of the other.

Then in he comes, dancing along with a pack on his back. This first sequence shows the touch that made him great. As he skips and skids along the narrow path, a gigantic bear appears behind him and follows him. A lesser comic would have turned and seen the bear, and possibly would have got a lot of laughs out of panic on the slippery path. But the bear disappears into a cave just before Charlie stops to turn around and see how far he has come. *We* know the danger he has escaped, he doesn't. This is not only funnier, it is also serious: it exemplifies two of the Tramp's most important qualities—innocence and an unwitting faith in the power of that innocence.

Later, when he and Big Jim are trapped and starving in the cabin, the other man, delirious with hunger, imagines that Charlie is a gigantic chicken. (Big Jim is played by Mack Swain, a fat and endearing figure in early Chaplin films.) The delirium is funny, but Chaplin says he got the idea from the tragic story of the Donner party, the emigrants who were lost in the Nevada mountains in the winter of 1846 and resorted to cannibalism. Grimness as a source of comedy! On this point Chaplin himself said: "In the creation of comedy, it is paradoxical that tragedy stimulates the spirit of ridicule, because ridicule, I suppose, is an attitude of defiance: we must laugh in the face of our helplessness against the forces of nature—or go insane."

From the Donner story, too, he elaborated the famous sequence of the boiled shoe. (Some members of the Donner party roasted and ate their moccasins.) The two men are so famished that they eat a shoe—the Tramp's, of course. Charlie boils and serves it, and the humor comes not only from what they are eating but the way they eat it. A lesser comic inventor might have got laughs by having the two men go through grimaces of disgust as they forced themselves to chaw. But, as with the bear incident, Chaplin raises the scene to a higher power, making it funnier by means of poetic imagination. Big Jim is jealous because the Tramp got the bigger piece, and switches plates. This is funnier than grimaces because it is *truer*. And the Tramp twirls the shoelaces on his fork like spaghetti, then sucks each nail as if it were a tasty little bone. The consolations of fantasy have rarely gone further.

All through Chaplin's body of work, hunger is a recurrent subject of comedy. (One example among many: in *The Circus* the hungry Tramp steals bites from a child's hot dog over the shoulder of the father who holds the boy in his arms.) Hunger is an inevitable subject for a Tramp, particularly one whose creator had a childhood in surroundings of wretched poverty. Three times a day, life puts the Tramp at the mercy of "the forces of nature," and three times a day Chaplin has the option of transmuting those forces into laughter so that the Tramp will not "go insane." But there is an extraordinary aspect to this theme in *The Gold Rush*. Usually in Chaplin's films the pinch of hunger comes from a social stringency: no money. Here in the cabin, money is irrelevant. Chaplin takes the theme that has always had a social-political resonance for him, isolates it into the Thing Itself, and makes it funnier than ever.

The harmonics of the picture—light tone against dark, light tone arising *out* of dark and vice versa—is enriched by his first entrance into the dance hall in the boom town. Chaplin, the director, avoids the conventional sequence: showing us the bustling saloon and then showing us the Tramp looking at it—which would mean looking at the camera. He shoots past the Tramp, from behind, to the saloon interior. Charlie is in outline; the brightness is beyond him. He watches from the edge, and we watch from an edge ever farther behind him. Yet because he is seen from slightly below eye level, there is something strong, almost heroic, in the pathos, and, simultaneously, there is something comic in his silhouette. It is the classic, quintessential Chaplin shot.

Both pathos and comedy are heightened in the next moments. A man comes to stand behind Charlie, unseen by him. At the bar the barkeep says to Georgia (if we watch his mouth closely), "There's Charlie." She turns and says, "Charlie," smiles, and comes toward the Tramp. He's mystified but happy—and she goes right past him to greet the man behind him. Chaplin had used this idea of mistaken greetings before, notably in a two-reeler called *The Cure,* but only to be funny. Here it is funny, but it also crystallizes another matter: the moment of his falling in love despite his forlorn condition.

Georgia is played by Georgia Hale, whom Chaplin had seen in Josef von Sternberg's first film *The Salvation Hunters.* Her career did not go on long after *The Gold Rush,* which is odd because her performance is perfect: she supplies exactly the right qualities of sauciness, sex, and tenderness. Hale clearly plays the part with a knowledge of what would now be called the subtext, the meaning below the surface. This dance-hall girl is a prostitute; what else could she possibly be? (One of her friends at the dance hall is a beefy, older woman, with the look of the traditional madam.) Nothing is done or said to explicate this; it is simply there for those who can see it, and it deepens the film for them. Children, as I can remember from my own experience, see the characters "innocent." It seems another version of the *Petrouchka* story, a haughty soubrette who prefers a handsome extrovert and rebuffs the shy man unable to demonstrate the worth that we perceive. Adults, however, can see that the other man has some of the aspects of a prostitute's "bully." More: when

Georgia and the other girls are playing in the snow one day near Charlie's cabin, an outing that accidentally leads to her discovery of his devotion, the sequence recalls the feeling of Maupassant's "Madame Tellier's Establishment"—the staff of a bordello frisking on holiday.

The point of this subtext is not merely to slip innuendo past the censor. It provides, for those able to see it, a further stratum of reality for the *comedy* and, since the Tramp never recognizes what Georgia is, further proof of his armor of innocence. Other commentators have noted that Chaplin pointedly chose to make a picture about a gold rush in the middle of the madly moneymaking twenties. He also chose to have the world-beloved Tramp fall in love with, and finally win, a prostitute, in an American comedy—seemingly as a tacit certification of the postwar era's changing sexual standards.

During their encounter on her outing, Charlie invites Georgia and the other girls to New Year's Eve dinner in his cabin. They accept, knowing they won't come. On that evening, Charlie prepares an elaborate table setting and a big meal, then sits down to wait—and wait and wait. At last he nods off at the table and dreams that they have come, that all is joyous. In one of the most celebrated moments in all Chaplin films, Charlie entertains the adoring girls (in his dream) by doing the Oceana Roll. Sitting at the table, he sticks two forks in two sabot-shaped rolls, then kicks and jigs them as if they were his legs and he were doing a chorus-girl dance. Every time I see this sequence coming, I think, "I know every move he's going to make. He can't possibly make me laugh again." And every time he does. One reason, deduced from the very last viewing, is that he doesn't merely kick his fork "legs," he uses his whole body behind the forks, his utter concentration, in pinpoint reproduction of a chorus girl's performance.

And, typical of the picture's complex harmonics, this hilarious pantomime occurs in a dream into which the Tramp has fallen because he has been tricked and disappointed.

This dream dinner, we should also note, exemplifies another theme that runs through Chaplin's work, the mirror image of the hunger theme discussed earlier. Instead of hunger, we get here the other extreme, the feast, the laden table, which has an effect in Chaplin films like the effect of feasts in Dickens (another man who knew poverty in London). Plentiful food means not gluttony, but love: an atmosphere of community, conviviality, and affection. One of the most touching moments in *The Kid* is the huge breakfast that the Kid prepares for himself and his "father," the Tramp. In *The Gold Rush* the golden brown turkey is the Tramp's contribution to an atmosphere in which human beings can be human. Chaplin's idea of a low and dehumanized state is not hunger, but the insult to the full table. In *Modern Times,* the Tramp is strapped to an automatic feeding machine, with food enough but without feeling. It debases a daily joy.

I describe one more scene in *The Gold Rush,* although it is hard to limit oneself, as an example of Chaplin's comic invention. When Charlie and Big Jim wake up in the lonely cabin to which they have returned in their search for Jim's lost claim, they don't realize, of course, that during the night the cabin was blown to a new location: the very edge of a cliff. They can't see out the frost-covered windows. As the cabin begins to shift on the precipice, Charlie decides to have a look at the trouble. He opens the back door—and swings out into immense space, hanging onto the doorknob. (If I had to vote for the single funniest sight gag in films, I'd probably choose this moment.) Big Jim pulls Charlie back inside. Then comes a sequence in which the two men, one slight and the other burly, try to inch their way up the increasingly slanting floor toward the safe side and the front door. It is a pearl of invisible dynamics, in which they cautiously *wish* their bodies upward, a monument to spirit-flesh dichotomy.

Like so much in Chaplin's films, and in farce generally, this cabin sequence is built on danger, scary but seen from safety. It is the quantum of the banana peel greatly multiplied: we know what it would feel like if it were happening to us, but we also know that it isn't. Comedy, of all kinds, depends on perception and superiority. In high comedy, which usually deals with social criticism, we can recognize the hypocrisy or vanity or whatever it may be, acknowledge secretly that we share it, and laugh with relief that it is being pilloried in someone else. In farce, the materials are often physical, often the dangers of daily life that surround us all the time, even when crossing the street. The *farceur* makes injury and possible death simultaneously real and unreal. We know that the Tramp and Big Jim will not be killed in the cabin—it simply could not happen in this kind of picture; yet we feel the danger in our viscera. We are frightened at the same time that we enjoy the skill of the artists who have nullified death. Farce characters—important ones—never get killed. They contrive for us a superiority over mortality, even as they make us laugh at their struggles to escape it.

To this comic heritage of danger combined with subconscious assurance of safety, Chaplin adds a unique touch: grace. All through his career, it is manifest: as in the dangerous skating sequences of *The Rink* and *Modern Times.* One of the most famous remarks about Chaplin was made by W. C. Fields. With salty verbal ornament, Fields said that Chaplin was "the best ballet dancer that ever lived." What Fields omitted is that the ballet is often performed in the face of death.

The finish of *The Gold Rush* strengthens and resolves the light-dark harmonics of the whole. Some have objected to the ending because it is contrived to be happy, because the Tramp doesn't walk down the road alone at the end. But, as a matter of fact, that lonely walk is not a typical ending of his feature films: *The Kid, City Lights,* and *Modern Times* also end happily. For *The Gold Rush,* if the end was to be happy, it meant, because of the subject matter, that Charlie had to end up rich. Even this is not much different from *The Kid,* which finishes with the Tramp going into the rich woman's house to join her and the Kid, presumably to stay.

The Gold Rush differs only in that we *see* Charlie rich. Essential though the wealth is thematically, this was not the image that Chaplin wanted to leave before our eyes, so he devised a way for the rich Charlie to put on his Tramp clothes once again. This persona, resumed, gives Georgia, the prostitute, a chance to prove the genuineness of her feelings, and it gives Chaplin a chance to score a last point. The Tramp had to be dragged away from Georgia by Big Jim, had to be dragged to wealth; now the wealth brings the lovers together again on the ship. Money and happiness, Chaplin seems to say, are at the whim of two powers: Fate and authors.

But an even subtler complexity runs through the film, through most of his major films. The element that persists, through the comedy and through the pathos that makes the comedy beloved, is a sense of mystery. Who *is* the Tramp? What is the secret of his unique effect on us?

Consider. Here is a prospector who appears on a mountain trail wearing a winged collar and tie. We never question this, we never even really notice it. All right, perhaps that's because the Tramp's costume is by now an internationally accepted set of symbols. After he gets a job in the boom town, the Tramp, who has been collarless for a while, again has a collar and tie. Even though this is a rough Alaskan town, again we don't even notice the impossibility. When he and Big Jim are first snowbound in the cabin, Jim's whiskers grow and Charlie's don't.

But then the Tramp's characteristics move from costume into action, and we begin to wonder. When Georgia invites him to dance, in his silly clothes and with one foot wrapped in rags to replace the eaten shoe, he dances with exquisite style. Who *is* he? When he invites the girls to dinner, he not only knows how to cook, he knows all about table settings, party favors, dainty giftwrappings, and etiquette. Who *is* he? When he performs the Oceana Roll, he knows a chorus-girl routine. Who *is* he? When Georgia's bullyboy tries to force his way into her room against her will, Charlie bars the door to the hulking man with a knightly chivalry that is contemptuous of the danger to himself. Again—who *is* he?

I propose no supernatural answer, that he is a divine messenger in ragged clothes, a fool of God. I do suggest that part of the genius of Chaplin, part of his superiority to all other film comics except Buster Keaton, is his ability to make us believe in a comic character whose standards are better than our own, just as his body in motion is more beautiful than our bodies. I suggest that one of the reasons we have loved him all these decades—and young people seem to feel that *they* have loved him for decades, too—is that he has not concentrated on merely making us laugh, he has shown us the funniness in a hero-clown, an unsententious agent of exemplary values. He is not dully angelic; he sometimes pulls off con games, though usually to a good end or to flout oppressive authority. But in the main he compensates for the shortcomings, social and physical, of our lives and beings. In his magical movement and in his code, even in his cunning, he is what we feel we ought to be.

Bertolt Brecht wrote in 1926 that he went to see *The Gold Rush,* after some delay, because it had made his theater friends despondent about the theater. He says that the picture made him share their despondency, but not because he feels there is a hierarchical difference between the arts of theater and film. The difference is Chaplin. He says that Chaplin is an artist who "already qualifies as a historical event." Yes. *The Gold Rush* is a marvel, but it is Chaplin himself who is the event in art.

LA GRANDE ILLUSION

SINCE 1938, when it was first shown in the United States, Jean Renoir's famous film has been mistitled. It is called *Grand Illusion,* but the French title is *La Grande Illusion,* and as every high school student knows, this means *The Big Illusion.* The point is important, because the proper title avoids an opening note of lofty, half-romantic regret.

In the winter of 1936–1937, when *La Grande Illusion* was made, in the world of the Spanish Civil War, of Mussolini and Hitler gulping down the West, of Japan ravaging China, the film was a warning of the futility of war in the face of growing wars, an anatomy of the upheaval of 1914–1918 to show contemporaries how grim machineries had once been set in motion. Today its pacifist intent, as such, seems somewhat less salient (though no less moving) because so many more human beings know how futile war is and know, too, that no film can abolish it. Today the film seems a hard perception of inevitabilities, not glibly cynical but, in the largest classical sense, pessimistic: a film that no longer asks for action but that *accompanies* us, noting our best, prepared for our worst. Since this state of mind, this undepressed pessimism, is today widespread, this film continues to speak, out of the change it incorporates, to changing man.

Yet—in a wonderful and important way—*La Grande Illusion* is a period piece, and Renoir was the ideal maker for it. The history of film is full of remarkable confluences. (At least that's a cursory way to describe complicated matters of cultural and psychic history.) D. W. Griffith came along just when the newborn medium needed a genius to formulate its language. Eisenstein and Pudovkin came along in the Soviet Union just when the new society needed new artists to celebrate it in this new form. Six hundred years of Renaissance humanism, predictably ripening to decline, found a film elegist in a Frenchman born and nourished in its center, the son of a painter who had given *la belle époque* some of its sensual loveliness.

Jean Renoir, son of Pierre Auguste, was born in 1894 in Paris. He has written a biography called *Renoir, My Father,* which inevitably contains a good deal about himself. In 1913 the young Renoir enlisted in the cavalry, and in 1915 he was wounded in the leg. (He still limps.) In 1916, after his recovery, he became a pilot in a reconnaissance squadron. (Maréchal, a leading character in this film, is a reconnaissance pilot, who is wounded. Jean Gabin, who plays Maréchal, wears Renoir's very uniform.) When the war ended, Renoir worked in ceramics for about five years, then in 1923 began to write and direct films. By the mid-1930s he was one of the eminent directors of France, having made such highly regarded films as *Boudu Saved from Drowning, The Crime of Monsieur Lange,* and an adaptation of Gorki's *The Lower Depths,* and was well launched on a career that, whatever one's opinion of individual works, has had a huge influence on the later film world. (The connection between Renoir and Orson Welles has often been noted, particularly by Welles. François Truffaut dedicated his *Mississippi Mermaid* to Renoir. André Bazin wrote: "The influence of Jean Renoir on the Italian cinema is paramount and definitive.")

It would have been impossible for the man who had made those early films to be unconcerned with what he saw happening in Europe and Asia and Africa in the mid-1930s. Renoir prepared to make *La Grande Illusion,* based on a story that he says "is absolutely true and was told to me by some of my comrades in the war." This combination—of authenticity and of response to a sense of historical twilight—roots the film firmly in its period, using the best of an age to bid that age farewell.

To collaborate on the script with him, Renoir engaged Charles Spaak, one of those important film figures of whom the public knows little, like Carl Mayer in the German 1920s and Cesare Zavattini in the Italian 1950s—the screen writers who contributed greatly to celebrated eras. Spaak, the brother of Paul-Henri Spaak, the former Belgian prime minister, wrote a number of memorable screenplays in a long career. By this time he had already written *La Kermesse Héroïque (Carnival in Flanders)* for Jacques Feyder and the Gorki adaptation for Renoir.

This Spaak-Renoir screenplay tells the story of three French officers who are captured by the Germans and of one German officer who is their jailer. The drama is built in three sections. The first, after a brief prologue, takes place in an internment camp where the three Frenchmen try to tunnel to freedom but are transferred before the tunnel is ready. The second is in a fortress-prison, run by the German officer whom we met in the prologue, from which two of the Frenchmen escape with the help of the third. The last section is in a German farmhouse where the two fugitives are sheltered for a time by a young widow who has a small daughter. And there is an epilogue, balancing the prologue, in which the two fugitives finally cross into Switzerland.

The movement of the film is thus toward freedom; but that freedom implies return to other "prisons," of renewed military service or other straitenings of society. The officers' characters are unashamedly selected for contrast and symbolism—beginning with the fact that they are officers, not ordinary soldiers; but they are so well written, and played, that any suspicion of artifice is swept off by reality. Boeldieu is an aristocrat, a career officer; Maréchal is a mechanic, who might never have been an officer in an earlier, unmechanized war; Rosenthal is a Vienna-born Jew, whose parents emigrated to France, were naturalized, and prospered mightily. (A distinct suggestion of the Rothschilds.) The German is Rauffenstein, himself an aristocrat, an aviator who shoots down the first two Frenchmen, entertains them to lunch before they are sent to prison camp, and who reappears eighteen months later as the fortress commandant. Maréchal and Rosenthal, both French, are parvenus of different sorts; Boeldieu and Rauffenstein, enemies, are both aristocrats and feel an affinity. War, says the film, is exclusively a matter of national loyalty only to nonprofessionals. To the international officer caste, national loyalty is a matter of honor but is only one aspect of chivalry.

For the role of the French aristocrat, Renoir got Pierre Fresnay, formerly of the Comédie Française and a member of the Compagnie des Quinze under the famous Michel Saint-Denis. Maréchal was played by the rapidly rising Jean Gabin, who had already played for Renoir in *The Lower Depths* and was becoming a premier representative on the screen of the French working class. Marcel Dalio, an alumnus of the Paris Conservatory and of revues, already a film veteran, played Rosenthal. The German widow was played by the diminutive Dita Parlo, best known until then as the bride in *L'Atalante,* the only feature film made by the greatly gifted and prematurely deceased Jean Vigo. And, in one of the master strokes of casting in film history, Rauffenstein was played by Erich von Stroheim.

This fascinating man came from cloudy beginnings. One biography maintains that he was born in Vienna, in 1885, resigned a commission in the Austrian army in 1909 to emigrate to America, served a hitch in the U.S. cavalry, and then held a wide variety of jobs. The story becomes solider when he broke into films, under D. W. Griffith, as a stunt man in *The Birth of a Nation.* He acted monocled German officers in Hollywood during the war and became publicized as "the man you love to hate." He went on to write and direct and play in such films as *Blind Husbands* and *Foolish Wives* which, though they were rococo melodramas, were made with visual splendor and sardonic "continental" realism. In 1924 he made *Greed,* from the Frank Norris novel *McTeague,* which is generally held to be one of the best films ever made in the U.S. but which helped to seal Stroheim's fate as a prodigal and "difficult" director. After a rocky Hollywood career, he went to France as an actor in 1936 to find himself the object of a cult. (Renoir himself has said that he had seen *Foolish Wives* twelve times and that it had opened his eyes about film making.) To *La Grande Illusion* Stroheim brought the right temperament and age and experience, but he also brought an immense and exactly apposite mystique. His presence in the picture is so forceful that when Richard Griffith reviewed it (*The Nation,* October 22, 1938), he didn't begin with Renoir; his opening line was: "It is unkind of Erich von Stroheim to debunk war's illusions in this graceless year."

According to Stroheim, as reported in Thomas Quinn Curtiss's biography, he himself had an influence on the script. He was told that there were two German roles, the aviator at the beginning and the fortress commandant, was asked which he wanted, and said, "Both." Spaak was uneasy at the need for explanatory material to make clear why the same man turned up later. Stroheim suggested wearing a neck brace as the commandant which would in itself explain that Rauffenstein had been wounded and invalided out of action, and which also underscored—almost parodied—the Prussian stiff neck. (Rauffenstein does speak of his wounds in a later scene with Boeldieu, but by then it's more than mere explanatory material.) We can assume, too, that the fur muff which Rauffenstein wears as he conducts his new prisoners around the wintry fortress is a Stroheim touch.

The film immediately sets its tone, with rhetorical devices that are used throughout: irony and ellipsis. Maréchal, seen first in a French army officers' mess, has a date with a girl but is suddenly ordered to take Boeldieu on a reconnaissance flight; the date, instead of being postponed a few hours, is ironically postponed a few years, if not forever, because they are shot down. The sequence in the French officers' mess cuts immediately to a German officers' mess. Ellipsis:

we don't see the air fight. (We never see any battle in this war film.) Irony: the German place, save for a few details, is just like the French one.

In the internment camp—let's call it Act One—we live with Boeldieu, the gentleman officer who (as we come to learn) keeps his white gloves fresh in prison, who says he has always called his wife and mother *vous,* yet who insists on doing his part in the dirty tunnel-digging. Maréchal is the *homme moyen,* but his self-knowledge of this—without self-dramatization—keeps the character from being stock. Among the other officers in the barracks are a teacher and an actor, but the most interesting is Rosenthal, the wealthy Jew.

Remember that this role was written in 1936, when the Nazis were already tormenting Jews in Germany, when anti-Semitic feeling was simmering in France and even in Britain; remember, too, that Renoir is unquestionably among the most humane of men; and your admiration grows for his insistence on drawing Rosenthal with honesty, instead of making him a saintly martyr, as counterpropaganda against the times. Rosenthal is a decent enough fellow, who wants to "belong" and who knows he doesn't "belong" completely, who is rich and will not hide it, in fact who boasts as proof of his "Frenchness" that his family owns a nice chunk of France. His family sends him big parcels of good food, which the Germans pass because they then have to give less food to that barracks. (The guards usually eat worse than Rosenthal and his friends!) And Rosenthal uses these parcels as a means to be accepted.

In short, Rosenthal is a good image of the risen bourgeois European Jew, rather proud of all these facts, yet seeking to blend into a national landscape, morally no better or worse than most others, aware that he is tolerated, anxious to *be* tolerated, willing to pay for it, on the implied ground that it is better to have purchased acceptance than none at all.

Thus we have in this barracks a model of European society, with all major strands represented except the peasant/worker—who was excluded arbitrarily because this is an officers' camp. We know, as we watch, that we are being shown a model, but it is made with such fine observation and dexterity that it acquires size.

Two scenes, particularly, from Act One are notable. Rosenthal gets a basket of costumes from home for a camp show. A boyish officer goes inside to try on a dress and female wig. When he comes out—uneffeminately—silence gradually spreads around the big crowded room. Memory and loneliness float over the men's heads, and make them still.

After the camp show, Maréchal is put in solitary for insulting the German command. He sits torpidly in his cell, picking idly at the stone wall with a spoon. When his guard comes in to talk with him and offer him cigarettes, he goes berserk and rushes out through the open door. The camera does *not* go with him; it waits patiently with the understanding guard until, very shortly, the subdued Maréchal is carried back into the cell by other German soldiers. (Another ellipsis.)

A second German guard exemplifies another system of Renoir's—the epitomizing vignette. This guard is a middle-aged, round-shouldered man. His very appearance tells us of the manpower drain in Germany, his manner tells us that he too is imprisoned. Whenever I see *La Grande Illusion,* I wait for this man's brief appearance, as I wait for the haughty English officer who grinds his watch under his boot to keep the Germans from getting it and for the owl-eyed frightened orderly who attends the maimed Rauffenstein in his castle.

When we get to the castle—Act Two—more elements are joined. The reappearance of Rauffenstein, now in a neck brace and wearing gloves to cover his burned hands, is a trenchant signal of the passage of time: it not only marks how the war is wearing on and on, it seems to give the film itself a lengthening perspective, a reach of experience and journey. The quick affinity between the German and Boeldieu broadens the social fabric, by internationalizing the officer set; and, dramaturgically, it gives each of them someone to whom he can talk easily, allowing them to comment on the passing of the class paradigms, centuries old, that made their very existence. However, as a gentleman, Boeldieu never derogates his fellow officers to Rauffenstein. Clearly it is Rauffenstein, the jailer, who needs these conversations more than Boeldieu, the prisoner. (Another irony.)

The culminating irony of Act Two is the escape of Maréchal and Rosenthal, made possible by the decoy act of Boeldieu—the past recognizes that its last function is to make the future possible. Boeldieu climbs a parapet and plays a tune on a flute to distract the guards, and the irony is heightened when it is Rauffenstein himself, the other aristocrat, who shoots him when he refuses to come down. After the shot, before he falls, Boeldieu glances at his watch, to see whether he has given his friends time enough to make it over the walls.

The act ends with Boeldieu's death, surely one of the most masterly scenes ever filmed. He lies in Rauffenstein's room in great pain; the maimed German, the man who shot him, sits beside him, apologizing for his poor aim yet envying the other aristocrat his death in war. The nurse ends the conversation. Rauffenstein goes to a cabinet and pours a drink. The nurse calls him softly. He knows what has happened. Without turning, he takes the drink. Then he cuts off a geranium in a flowerpot, which we know is the only flower in the fortress.

If the film ended here, with Boeldieu dead and Rauffenstein envious of him, with Maréchal and Rosenthal making their way through the snowy countryside to the border, it would in fact be a complete work, but of smaller dimension than it ultimately achieves. Renoir is dealing not only with the past but with the future, not only with symbols of war but with war itself as a symbol of the world in which war happens.

The two fugitives trudge through the snow in mufti, which was part of their escape equipment. Rosenthal limps. He has sprained his ankle, and it keeps getting worse. His condition irritates Maréchal, and in a few days they quarrel. He says he never liked Jews anyway, and Rosenthal says he ought to have thought of that earlier. Maréchal stomps off alone, and Rosenthal sits on a rock, singing defiantly. His song breaks off as (another ellipsis) Maréchal suddenly reappears quietly. We haven't seen him change his mind, we don't hear him apologize. We know he really does have anti-Semitism in him and that Rosenthal knows it and is prepared to live with it because he knows that Maréchal regrets having it—all this in Maréchal's silent reappearance at the edge of the frame.

The two men take refuge in a barn where they are discovered by the owner, Elsa, a young widow. Her losses in the war—her husband and her brothers—have purged her of fear, even of hate. They stay with her until Rosenthal recovers, and they make a pet of Elsa's small daughter. Maréchal helps around the farm, and this leads to the film's one really weak scene. As he feeds the cow one day, he says to it: "You don't mind being fed by a Frenchman . . . You're just a poor cow and I'm just a poor soldier." How I wish that this scene had been omitted.

Maréchal and Elsa become lovers, but when Rosenthal's ankle is better, the two men must leave for the border. Maréchal tells Elsa that after the war, if he is not killed, he will come back for her and the child, and take them to France. Both he and Elsa believe it equally: that is, they both know he really means it—at the moment. This is one more belief that (we feel) will be turned into illusion by the passage of time, like the larger beliefs of class and of war-with-a-purpose.

In the last scene, the epilogue, the two Frenchmen are standing in the snow, bidding farewell to one another before they try to cross a long valley to the border. Embracing, they call each other the names affectionately that they have used angrily before. Then they start. A German border patrol spots them and fires a few times, but they have made it into Switzerland. In the last long shot, we see two small figures struggling through the snow toward a village. Toward repatriation. Toward return to the war. Toward some sort of life and some sort of death.

Enriching, supporting, fulfilling all the above is Renoir's direction—his sheerly cinematic imagination. His skill with actors shines from every scene (he has been an actor himself), but two qualities of his filmic style are especially important: his use of a moving camera and his deep-focus composition.

Two examples of the way he moves his camera. When Maréchal arrives in his first prison barracks, we see him in a close two-shot with a fellow prisoner, a former actor, talking about the theater. As they continue to converse, the camera gently pulls back disclosing Boeldieu and others also conversing in the large room, Maréchal and the actor still talking as they disappear; and the camera itself tells us that Maréchal is being integrated into a new community.

In the farmhouse sequence, Maréchal and Rosenthal say good-night to Elsa on Christmas Eve. She remains at the living-room table, pensive, as the camera goes with the two men into Rosenthal's room. Maréchal says good-night to his friend, then goes through the connecting door into his room and closes it, then goes to his own "front" door to close it, and sees Elsa still standing at the living-room table. He walks out to her and embraces her, for the first time. (Now the camera remains discreetly behind, as if to allow the new lovers a little privacy.) Maréchal's circular movement has done two things: it has allowed a minute to elapse, while *filling* it, so that by the time Maréchal sees Elsa again, still at the table, he realizes that she is tacitly waiting; and the large slow circle underlines the circle of human elements that are coming together in front of the camera.

Deep-focus is somewhat more complex. Put much too simply, one can say there are two general approaches to film making. First, the montage approach, developed by Eisenstein and Pudovkin and others out of Griffith, which relies on joining bits of film together in rhythmic and pictorial relationships so that an effect is created out of the very way the pieces are joined, an effect additional to the effects of the separate bits, just as an arpeggio is an entity in itself made up of separate musical entities.

But in the deep-focus approach, the reliance is on the content of any one shot, rather than on a succession of shots. The shot is held and people may come in or leave, the camera itself may move: it's the absence of cutting that makes the difference, the exploitation of different planes of depth within one shot to make the film progress, rather than the addition of new views. André Bazin praised Renoir because he "uncovered the secret of a film form that would permit everything to be said without chopping the world up into little frag-·ments, that would reveal the hidden meaning in people and things without disturbing the unity natural to them."

Bazin was being generous to Renoir in crediting him with uncovering a secret: you can find the conscious, deliberate use of deep-focus in Edwin S. Porter's *The Great Train Robbery* (1903), in the scene where the posse captures the bandits. More important, the point that Bazin and other deep-focus theorists have tended to disregard is that the deep-focus principle is about 2500 years old and is usually called "the theater." Renoir, who has written and directed plays, simply combined the flow of cinema with the relationships within a frame that are standard practice in the theater.

One example. Maréchal and Rosenthal are in the farmyard, and the former says he hasn't the courage to tell Elsa that they must leave. Rosenthal agrees to do it, goes into the house, and delivers the message. Elsa nods and disappears. Then Rosenthal opens the curtained window, and we see Maréchal, still where he was, out there in the yard leaning on a wagon. The opening of that window, suddenly deepening the screen, the addition of that plane to the composition, creates a tension between Maréchal outside and what has just happened in the room—a device often used in the theater by lifting a drop or lighting up a dark area.

Today the Big Illusion of the title includes at least three aspects: the illusion that war accomplishes anything of permanence; the illusion that, even without war, men will be brothers; and the illusion that truth can ever be anything more than a very necessary illusion. Yet the presentation of all these illusions is here in the hands of a man committed to love.

Inevitably, then, *La Grande Illusion* deals with transition, from a society committed to the idea of progress and perfectibility to an era in which men think less of perfection and more of achieving some proportion of good. The old world changes before our eyes. The aristocrats see that their ethos—the best of it along with the middling and worst—is dying. The bourgeoisie discover that the reliance by which their fathers lived—reliance on a society that, generation after generation, would respond predictably to ambition and application— is being changed in this cataclysmic war.

In his book about his father, Renoir says that when he and his brother were children his parents often went to the theater, leaving them in the care of a neighbor. Nevertheless his parents would jump in a cab at intermission and rush home for a few minutes to make sure the children were all right. A child who has known a home like that must grow up to inevitable disappointments, but has some security against them. For the characters in *La Grande Illusion,* their figurative parents—the traditions and ideals of the past—will not be back at intermission; they will never be back. The film is a farewell to their memory and the acceptance of a world without them.

RASHOMON

LITTLE is emptier in art criticism than the global pronouncement. Whenever we see the assertion that "X is the best in the world," we have a right to suspect enthusiastic ignorance. From time to time, we get a sharp reminder about our limited knowledge of an art, in world terms, and few such reminders have been sharper than the showing of *Rashomon* at the Venice Film Festival in 1951.

Up to then, although the Japanese film industry had been enormously active, with high annual production figures, it might as well have been situated on the moon as far as the West was concerned. World War II was not a prime reason for the gap; relatively few Japanese films had been seen in Europe and America before 1939.

When *Rashomon* opened in New York in 1951, it was the first Japanese film to be shown there in fourteen years. The barrier to import was financial, not political—the same barrier that obstructs the import of foreign literature.

The cultural shock that followed from the Venice Festival showing was a smaller mirror image of the shock felt in Japan a century earlier when Commodore Perry dropped in. Then the Japanese had learned of a technological civilization about which they knew very little; now the West learned of a highly developed film art about which they knew even less. It would, alas, be untrue to say that the import situation is greatly improved. It is not: the money barriers still intervene because Japanese films have not been very profitable in the United States. But at least we now have a much clearer idea of what we are missing, and maybe in that knowledge lies some hope.

The first Japanese director to be known in the West was Akira Kurosawa, who made *Rashomon*. This was lucky, because Kurosawa is not merely a good director, he is one of film's great masters. Moreover, his career tells us something, prototypically, about the Japanese film world. He was born in Tokyo in 1910, the son of an ex-army officer who was teaching physical education. Kurosawa, unattracted to either of his father's professions, studied painting at the Doshusha School of Western Painting. (Note its name.) In 1936 he saw an advertisement by a film studio looking for assistant directors; applicants were asked to send in an essay on the basic defects of Japanese films and how to remedy them. He replied, and—along with five hundred others—he was invited to try out further, with a screen treatment and an oral examination. He was hired, and became an assistant to a director named Kajiro Yamamoto.

This assignment was momentous in Kurosawa's career. In that invaluable book *The Japanese Film* by Joseph L. Anderson and Donald Richie, there is a chart that shows the apostolic succession of Japanese directors—who trained whom after being trained by someone else. The system of Japanese film training very early took on some of the tradition-conscious quality of Japanese culture generally. From Yamamoto, Kurosawa learned, among other things, a high regard for the script. (He has often quoted Yamamoto's remark: "To understand motion pictures fully, one must be able to write a script.") Besides his work as assistant, he also worked on screenplays. In 1941 Yamamoto made a film called *Horses,* of which he said later, "When we were making *Horses,* [Kurosawa] was still called my assistant, but he was much more than that, he was more like my other self." In 1943 Kurosawa was given his first solo directing assignment, and by 1950 he had made eleven films. Some of them, shown in the U.S. after *Rashomon,* are very much more than apprentice works, but it is this twelfth picture of his that proclaims his mastery.

The script, by Kurosawa and Shinobu Hashimoto, is based on two short stories about medieval Japan by a twentieth-century author, Ryunosuke Akutagawa, who died at thirty-five in 1927 and is so well esteemed that a literary prize has been established in his name. He is best known for his short stories, and those stories, says C. J. Dunn, have a modernity and universality of approach that "make them readily appreciated by Western readers." (Remember Kurosawa's painting school.)

From the first Akutagawa story, "Rashomon," the film takes little more than a setting—the place where the film begins, to which it returns, and where it closes—along with a mood of desolation caused by the waste of civil war. Rashomon was the name of the largest gate in Kyoto, the ancient capital of Japan; it was built in the eighth century, and by the twelfth century, the time of the film, it was already in disrepair. In this great but dilapidated gate three men—a woodcutter, a priest, and a man called simply a commoner—huddle together out of a pouring rain and recount various versions of a murder that took place recently in the vicinity.

The second story, "In a Grove," is the source of the murder narrative. There are some central facts: a samurai and his wife were traveling through a forest and were waylaid by a notorious bandit who tied up the husband and ravished the wife; the husband was killed, and his body was found by the woodcutter.

But there are four versions of the events surrounding these central facts, and we see each version as it is recounted. The first is that of the bandit who was captured soon after and told his story to a police magistrate. The bandit says that he tricked the samurai, bound him, and assaulted the wife who quickly became compliant. Afterward, at the wife's insistence, he released the husband so that they could fight, and killed the samurai in a long hazardous duel.

Then the priest gives the version he heard the wife give the magistrate. She says that, after the rape, the bandit left. She saw the hate in her husband's eyes, because she had not resisted sufficiently, and in a frenzy of grief and shame, she (apparently) killed him, then ran away.

The third version, also recounted by the priest, is that of the dead husband, who spoke through a medium. The husband says that, after the seduction, the wife urged the bandit to murder him and take her along. The bandit declined, released the husband, and left. Alone, the husband killed himself with a dagger. Later, after his death, he felt someone take the dagger away.

The woodcutter then says this can't be true—no dagger was there, he was killed by a sword. Under the commoner's pressure, the wood-cutter then revises his story of discovering the samurai's body—and gives us a fourth version. He says that he came along just after the ravishing and watched from behind a bush. The wife was crying, the bandit was pleading with her to go away with him. She said that the men would have to decide whom she was to go with. She cut her husband free with the dagger, but he was at first unwilling to fight for this woman he now despised. She taunted them into fighting—a brawl that was a parody of the noble duel recounted earlier by the bandit. The husband was killed. The woman fled. Somewhat dazed, the bandit limped off with his sword and the samurai's.

The "true" version is never established. At the end of the film the three men in the Rashomon gate are in various states: depression about human beings (the woodcutter), cynical glee (the commoner), desperate hope (the priest). Suddenly they hear a baby crying in a corner of the huge gate, an abandoned infant. The commoner tries to steal the baby's garments, and when the woodcutter stops him, the commoner turns on him fiercely, calls him a hypocrite, and accuses him of stealing the samurai's expensive dagger, which was not found at the scene of the crime. The woodcutter does not explicitly admit it, but he offers to take the infant home, into his already large family, perhaps as a penance for his lie and his (presumable) theft, perhaps as a token of his hope for human hope. This final sequence with the infant has been much criticized for its patness and sudden surge of uplift, but one can argue that Kurosawa felt that the very arbitrari-ness of this incident would make the central story's necessary ambi-guity resonate more strongly.

Why should this film have had such a strong impact? Surely not because of the script alone. It is a good enough Pirandellian teaser with somber overtones, but—on paper—it is little more than one more statement of a familiar idea, the contradictory nature of truth, the impossibility of absolutes. On film, because of its cinematic qualities that grow out of the script but surpass it, *Rashomon* becomes a work of greater size.

One general reason for the film's impact is its cultural accessibility. Many Japanese directors, including at least one who is on Kurosawa's creative plane, Yasujiro Ozu, are more difficult to approach, more "Japanese." Kurosawa has always resisted being labeled a Westerner in any sense that makes him seem unsympathetic to his own culture, but he has always asserted that "the Western and the Japanese live side by side in my mind naturally, without the least sense of conflict." His fine-arts training and his response to Akutagawa, of all Japanese authors, support this thesis. Also, as he has said many times, he greatly admires American directors, especially John Ford, William Wyler, and Frank Capra. So, at Venice in 1951, those who might have expected this film to be couched in the esthetics of Noh or kabuki—which Kurosawa has indeed used elsewhere—found instead a work that was intrinsically Japanese yet certainly not remote in style or dynamics.

But of course there are other values in *Rashomon* that give it stature, much larger and deeper than Kurosawa's cosmopolitanism. Chief among these, I think, are three particular beauties.

First, the acting. As the woodcutter, Takashi Shimura runs through the film like a quiet stream of human concern—human enough to be himself found out in wrongdoing. Shimura, who was trained in the theater, had already played in eight pictures for Kurosawa and later gave (very different) wonderful performances for this director in *The Seven Samurai* and *Ikiru*. The samurai's wife, Machiko Kyo, who began her career as a dancer, is a famous star of Japanese film. The four versions of the murder story provide, in effect, four women to play, each of whom she draws precisely. But the outstanding performance, partly because it is in the most colorful role, is that of Toshiro Mifune as the bandit.

Mifune, now the best-known Japanese actor in the world, began in films in 1946 after five years in the Japanese army. He made four Kurosawa films before *Rashomon* and made many subsequent ones, including versions of Dostoevsky's *The Idiot,* Shakespeare's *Macbeth,* and Gorki's *The Lower Depths.* He has said of Kurosawa, "I have never as an actor done anything that I am proud of other than with him." Kurosawa has told the story that, while the company was waiting to start on *Rashomon,* they ran off some travelogue films to pass the time, including one about Africa. In it there was a lion roaming around. "I noticed it and told Mifune that that was just what I wanted him to be." Mifune succeeded. He gives one of the most purely feral performances on film—animalistic in both the bestial and the elemental senses, a man concentrated wholly on physical satisfactions and with a fierce power to satisfy them.

The second important aspect of this film is the use of blocks, or plaques, of visual texture. Each of the three main locations of the story has a distinct visual "feel": the gate, the courtyard of the police station where the witnesses testify, and the forest where the stories take place. The gate scenes are drenched in rain. Until the very last moments, each of these gate scenes is seen—and heard—through torrents, frequently emphasized by being shot from ground level so that we see the rain pounding the earth. The fall of the rain is often matched by a vertical view of the scene from above.

In the testimony scenes the witnesses kneel before us, motionless. (We never see the magistrate, who "is" the camera.) In contrast to the gate scenes, these courtyard scenes are sunlit, and the compositon is horizontal. Three great parallel bands stretch across the screen: one of shadow, close to us, in which the testifying witness kneels; one of sunlight behind it, in which the preceding witnesses kneel; and the top of the low courtyard wall behind them. The camera rarely moves in these scenes. Kurosawa creates a tension between the violent stories being recounted and the serenity of the picture.

The third plaque of texture, the forest, is dappled with sunlight and filled with movement—horizontal as the characters move forward, vertical as the camera frequently looks up at the sun.

These three distinctive textures are, first, aids to our understanding of a complex narrative: we know immediately where we are at every moment. They also provide a contrapuntal texture: the somber setting for the conversation of the troubled woodcutter and the priest and the cynical commoner; the quiet place of recollection; the kinetically lighted and composed setting for the rape and murder.

The last major esthetic component of *Rashomon* is the quality of the motion in those forest scenes. Kurosawa has said:

I make use of two or three cameras almost all the time. I cut the film freely and splice together the pieces which have caught the action most forcefully, as if flying from one piece to another.

He has made this use of *motion* in motion pictures uniquely his own, and never more "forcefully" than in the forest scenes of *Rashomon*. In the forest, where there is danger to people and, more important, danger to truth, the camera hovers, darts, glides, and swoops, like a skimming bird.

The very opening of the first forest sequence sets the style. Near the end of the gate scene with which the film begins, we are looking down from high above at the men crouched below out of the rain. We cut to a close-up of Shimura's face as he begins to tell his story. Then there is a sharp cut to the bright sun, seen through tree branches as the camera travels forward—a cut accompanied by the sudden entrance of strong rhythmic music. The sequence that follows is dazzling—dazzling both in the virtuosity of the shooting and editing and in the way that these skills are used for mood and point. The next shot is of the woodcutter's axe, on his shoulder, gleaming in the sun as he strides along. Then the camera precedes him as he walks toward us, follows him, and in one especially beautiful moment, arcs across toward him as he strides toward us, crosses in front of him as he approaches, then follows him from the other side. More than underscoring the burst of sunlight and movement into the film, this camera motion sets a tone of comment, of near-teasing, implying, "Stride on, stride on. An ordinary day's work, you think, woodcutter? Stride on. And see." He does see. He and the camera's ballet around him halt suddenly when he spies a woman's hat hanging on a bush. He and the camera resume—and stop again when he spies a man's hat and some other objects. Again he and his observer resume—and this time he halts in horror. We see his face through the upright, death-rigid arms of the slain samurai. The *camera,* fulfilling its implied promise, looks through those arms at the woodcutter's face.

This marvelously intricate and graceful dance of the camera continues through all the versions of the forest story. In a sense we are always aware of it; it would be overly reticent if we were not. The language of a good poem is enjoyable at the same time that the poem moves to something for which the language is only the visible sign. Kurosawa is always sure to make his camera movement, wonderful in itself, inseparable from what it treats. For instance, the bandit and the samurai fight twice, once in the bandit's story, once in the wood-cutter's. In the first, both men fence brilliantly. The second fight is a frantic brawl in which both men look foolish. In both encounters the camera leaps around them like an imp, heightening the fever, but the camera rhythms and perspectives match the quality of the fight in each case.

Now since all this camera movement is silken smooth, at the furthest remove from sickening hand-held improvisation, every smallest action of the players and of Kurosawa's camera had to be planned in detail. Tracks had to be built on which the cameras could dolly. These sequences were obviously shot outdoors, in a real forest, so every inch of the camera's traverse had to be prepared, sometimes in a way that allowed a camera to come around and look back—without a break—at the place it had just left, without revealing the tracks on which it had traveled. These technical details of preparation would not be our concern except for what underlies them: a realization of how thoroughly Kurosawa had to know in advance what he was doing and why. A film director does not have the freedom of inspiration, in sequences of this kind, that a theater director or choreographer has. Long-range design is of the essence here; and the quicksilver insight of these designs—their feeling of spontaneous flight—is extraordinary.

That Venice festival audience must have had a bit of a shock when the music began in that first forest scene. Many have noted its strong resemblance to Ravel's *Bolero*. Not by accident. Kurosawa told his composer, Fumio Hayasaka, to "write something like Ravel's *Bolero*." Apparently the Ravel piece was not then well-known in Japan and had not become something of the self-parody that it now is to Western ears. Western music can be heard in many Kurosawa films. In the films set in the present, it is often used to show the alteration of Japanese culture. Here Kurosawa apparently thought he was appropriating a helpful Western vitality for *Rashomon*. But whatever the effect of that music was or is on Japanese ears, it is still bothersome to ours. Kurosawa is big enough to bear a blemish. If we can forgive Dickens for naming one of his female characters Rosa Bud, we can forgive Kurosawa for his Ravel imitation.

Earlier I noted that *Rashomon,* the film, is a far larger work than its good-enough script. This is a commonplace about any satisfying film, of course, even about some unsatisfying ones, but it has a special pertinence in this case. Kurosawa's vision, his steely yet sympathetic sense of drama, his power to make the screen teem with riches yet without any heavy-breathing lushness, his overwhelming faculties of rhythmic control that translate emotion into motion, all these produce a question in us. We ask: Can such a subtle and complex artist really have bothered to make a film about—as has been said—"the unknowability of truth"? Would that trite theme have been enough for such a man? Finally, the very quality of Kurosawa's art opens up this banal version of relativism to reveal the element that *generates* the relativism: the element of ego, of self. Finally, *Rashomon* deals with the preservation of self, an idea that—in this film—outlasts earthly life. That idea is not the sanctity of each individual as a political concept, not the value of each soul as a religious concept, but stark, fundamental *amour-propre*. The bandit wants to preserve and defend his ego, the wife hers, and the husband, dead and out of his body, wants the same. Even the woodcutter, who has little *amour-propre* to protect, is forced to tell a more complete version of his story in self-defense.

Ego underlies all, the film says at last. What is good and what is horrible in our lives, in the way we affect other lives, grows from ego: not merely the biological impulse to stay alive but to have that life with some degree of pride.

In the Christian lexicon, pride is the first deadly sin; but in our daily lives, Christian or not, Westerner or Easterner, we know that this sin is at least reliable. We can depend on it for motive power. All of us acknowledge that we ought to be moved primarily by love; all of us know that we are moved primarily by self. *Rashomon* is, essentially, a ruthlessly honest film. Exquisitely made, electrically exciting, it reaches down—by means of these qualities—to a quiet, giant truth nestled in everyone of us. Ultimately what the film leaves with us is candor and consolation: if we can't be saints, at least we can be understandingly human.

SOME LIKE IT HOT

"NOBODY's perfect." Possibly that is the most famous last line of any American film. Well, nobody, nothing, *is* perfect—perhaps; but the picture that closes with that line is almost the exception to the rule. It may be somewhat ungrateful to call a very funny film a masterpiece; it sounds like an attempt to take it out of human circulation. Still Billy Wilder has brought it on himself. What is worse, I have to insist that this unfailingly delightful farce is a triple milestone.

It is significant three ways in American film history. It is the best film (so far) by the last European director to flourish in this country. It is the best film of the last great sex star created by Hollywood. It is the last of the carefree American comedies that sprang up when sound came in, bloomed through the thirties, and had a revival after World War II.

Hollywood has seen two principal "waves" of European directors. The first group, including such men as Ernst Lubitsch and F. W. Murnau, were imported in the twenties by an American industry that was jealous of European artistic advances and worried about commercial competition. The second group were the political refugees of the thirties. No European director has made a career in America since the war. Wilder is one of the last fruits of a certain kind of cultural cross-pollination.

He was born Samuel Wilder in Vienna in 1906 and was called Billy by his mother, who was mad for everything American. He worked as a journalist and in the late 1920s went to Berlin, at that time probably the most sophisticated city in the world. He broke into films as a writer, moved to France when Hitler moved to Berlin, wrote and co-directed there for about a year, then went to Hollywood in 1934, where for four years he did very little. In 1938 he joined with the American writer Charles Brackett and collaborated on a number of screenplays, including Garbo's *Ninotchka*. In 1942 he directed his first American film, *The Major and the Minor,* from a Wilder-Brackett script, and launched a career that included *The Lost Weekend, A Foreign Affair,* and *Sunset Boulevard.*

Through these years Wilder was acquiring a reputation for a mordantly amusing tone, a view of human behavior derived from the old-Berlin wittiness of Ernst Lubitsch and the scathing naturalism of Erich von Stroheim. Wilder had worked for Lubitsch on *Ninotchka;* Stroheim worked for *him* in *Five Graves to Cairo* (in which he played Rommel) and in *Sunset Boulevard.* Aided by American collaborators, Wilder was making his own mixture of European and domestic influences, growing more and more skillful as he proceeded.

Another fusion lay ahead of him. Marilyn Monroe, hush-voiced, moist-lipped, all made of whipped cream, burst on the world in 1950.

Retrospectively at least, it seems inevitable that her wide-eyed sexiness would some day encounter Wilder's winking appreciation of it. In 1955 they worked together on *The Seven Year Itch,* made from a Broadway comedy. Then Wilder found a new collaborator, I. A. L. Diamond; and in 1959 the United States, in the persons of Diamond, Monroe, Jack Lemmon, and Tony Curtis, combined with Europe, in the persons of Wilder and a man named Thoeren, to create a farcical gem.

Who was Thoeren? Most reference books merely attribute the original idea of *Some Like It Hot* to a story by R. Thoeren and M. Logan. In response to an inquiry, Wilder wrote me that he had no idea who M. Logan was but that Robert Thoeren was an old chum from the Berlin days who had been a handsome actor, had co-authored a German film called *Fanfaren der Liebe* (*Fanfares of Love*), had come to Hollywood as a scriptwriter, where he had prospered, and had urged Wilder to remake his German film. Wilder was otherwise involved, but after Thoeren died in the mid-fifties, an agent raised the matter again.

We got a print of the German original and ran it. It was quite poor, a rather heavy-handed Bavarian *Charlie's Aunt,* replete with dirndls and lederhosen. And yet there was that platinum nugget: two male musicians latching onto an all-girl band. So the property was purchased . . . and my collaborator I. A. L. Diamond and I started from scratch.

The time they chose was perfect for the piece: the height of the Prohibition era—remote enough to be slightly romantic, near enough for easy identification. The plot concerns Joe, a saxophone player, and Jerry, a bass fiddler, both young and broke, who accidentally witness the Saint Valentine's Day massacre of one gang by another in Chicago, 1929. (Wilder uses a notorious real event like the cushion of a billiard table for a wild carom.) The victorious gang chief, Spats Colombo, wants the two witnesses killed, but they manage to escape. Penniless, frantic to flee Chicago, they dress as girls and grab two jobs they know about, with an all-girl band headed for three weeks in a Florida hotel.

On the southbound train they meet the luscious band vocalist, Sugar Kane, who hopes to catch a millionaire at the resort hotel. When they arrive, an aging playboy millionaire appears, named Osgood Fielding, but he falls for the disguised Jerry, now called

Daphne. Meanwhile, Joe, disguised as Josephine, re-disguises himself after working hours as a millionaire in order to woo Sugar. Things are progressing steadily toward just normal madness when suddenly Spats appears at the Florida hotel for a gangland convention.

A rival gang chief has Spats killed at a banquet, a murder that Joe and Jerry also accidentally witness. Now, doubly dangerous to the gangsters, they flee again. Sugar pursues Joe because she realizes, through a good-bye kiss, that her bandstand girl friend is really the "millionaire" whom she loves. Both of them, with Jerry, speed with Osgood out to his yacht. Osgood talks about wedding plans with Jerry, who is still in female dress, and dismisses Jerry's frenzied objections. At last, even at the risk of spoiling their means of escape from the hoods, Jerry is forced to rip off his wig and say he can't marry Osgood because he's a man. To which the smiling, unswervable Osgood replies with the famous last line.

Like many good directors, Wilder began as a scriptwriter. Such a director knows that poor films can be made from good scripts but good films cannot be made from poor scripts. This Wilder-Diamond script is a model of what farce should be.

The dialogue is not a collection of gags but a temperamental use of language: that is, vernacular is filtered through a chuckling temperament, diction is selected and arranged so that, while the characters speak always as themselves, the lines support and further the tone and action of the whole. Often a line gets a laugh, as when Jerry, after dancing till dawn with Osgood, says he has news for Joe, then tells him flatly: "I'm engaged." The laughs are pleasant when they come, but the real triumph of the writing is that, even when we don't laugh, the dialogue is funny.

In addition, there is a deft, knitted use of ideas. Themes are stated that are played back at odd angles. When the "girls" report for their jobs, the suspicious leader asks them their musical backgrounds, and they say they studied at the Sheboygan Conservatory, which awes the others. Later, when Sugar is trying to impress Joe-as-millionaire, she tells *him* that she studied at Sheboygan. Early, when Joe cajoles a booking agent's secretary into lending him her car, it's a Hupmobile. Much later, as the millionaire, when he invents a traumatic love affair to impress Sugar, it is with the daughter of the vice-president of Hupmobile. These interwoven strands are a comic-dramatic bonus: the authors' humor employed as the characters' ingenuity.

Structurally, the script obeys and profits by two traditional formal injunctions. First, it conforms to Hebbel's all-inclusive dictum on the secret of dramatic style: "To present the necessary in the form of the accidental." Second, more specific to farce, it begins with a ridiculous but engaging premise (Wilder's "nugget"), then builds on this improbable premise with rigid logic.

The one arguable moment in the logic of *Some Like It Hot* is the appearance of Spats at the very hotel where the band happens to be playing. It looks more necessary than accidental. Still, anyone who has heard an audience's response to the first sight of those spatted shoes in the hotel doorway knows that, as soon as Spats appears, the audience realizes that they *wanted* him to appear, they wanted the increased complication. If Wilder and Diamond were stretching here, they were stretching in a direction that the audience has, to put it paradoxically, foreseen ex post facto.

Credibility in farce depends very much on this matter of what the audience wants to happen, without knowing they want it. The credibility is established with the fairly likely, based on references to life, then slides into the unlikely, based on references to the piece itself. For instance, early in the film when we see Joe wheedle the car out of the booking agent's secretary, we just about believe it could happen. Later, when Joe and Jerry decide to masquerade, the picture cuts to them wigged and in female dress. Where did this penniless pair get the costumes—so quickly? By now, we ourselves supply the implicit wheedling that Joe did of some girl, and we do it both because of our experience of him and because we want them to be on that train with the band.

Farce, like melodrama, needs monochrome characters who will react predictably in given situations. *Some Like It Hot* has a well-blended spectrum of characters: the classic pair of youths, one aggressive and scheming, the other meek and wistful; the tough lady bandleader with the chromium smile; the near-sighted manager; the urbane, murdering Spats. With the exception of Joe, whose change we will come to, none of them alters through the film, and almost none of them has, or is meant to have, depth. The exception is Sugar Kane, born Sugar Kowalczyk, from Sandusky, Ohio. Marilyn Monroe.

The story of the making of this film is thickly laced with troubles, Wilder's troubles with the temperamental, unreliable, slow-learning Monroe. The reasons for her personality problems are not our business here; the result of the friction is our concern. And that result is all the more astonishing because of the stormy offscreen story. The character as written and the performance that Wilder got from her take the role beyond the jiggly-breasted sex doll of farce to a pathetic-comic portrait. The script was finished with Monroe in mind: "We didn't think of Marilyn Monroe when we started plotting *Some Like It Hot*," says Wilder, "about half-way through we signed her and went back to fit her unique requirements. . . ." As written, Sugar is not just a cardboard blonde, she is a girl who has sexual power but no instinct for using it, whose attractiveness has been converted by men to vulnerability. She is the one, not the man, who gets "the fuzzy end of the lollipop" in amorous encounters. She is the one who gets left, by the saxophone players who are her special weakness. At one point Sugar tells how a sax player sent her down at two in the morning for potato salad, how she couldn't find potato salad so she brought back cole slaw, and how he threw it in her face. This gorgeous creature tells the story as if that is how life is and was meant to be. It was diabolically insightful of Wilder and Diamond to build this role of a warm-hearted loser for Monroe. It was good when the film first appeared; seen in the light of what happened to her finally, it becomes more touching, and her last-moment happiness, at least in this picture, is all the more exhilarating.

She couldn't really act. The sharp observer can see that she just about gets through some of her scenes without forgetting what she has been told to do. But she was a great screen personality. Wilder understood that, and how to "place" her personality on the screen. We often hear that there is no such thing as film acting because directors and editors control everything and can manufacture performances. We have only to see such a film as *La Grande Illusion* to know that, as fiat, this is false. But it *can* happen that way on occasion. A gifted director can use the medium to extract and construct a performance out of a personality. Wilder does it here, superlatively.

Two other comic elements are used with dexterity. The first is a series of intra-cinematic references. When Joe poses as a millionaire, he employs a Cary Grant accent. When Spats arrives for the gangster convention, a young hood is idly flipping a coin in a doorway, and Spats says, "Where'd you pick up that stupid trick?" That coin trick was used in *Scarface,* twenty-seven years earlier, by George Raft, who plays Spats; and the young hood is played by Edward G. Robinson, Jr. At the gangster banquet, Spats picks up a grapefruit angrily as if to shove it in a henchman's face, something that James Cagney did to Mae Clarke in *The Public Enemy* in 1931. The subtlest reference, contained within the precincts of this film, is a scene, reminiscent of Restoration comedy, in which Joe, as the fake millionaire, pretends to be frigid and Sugar, anxious to hook him, kisses him and crawls all over him, trying to awaken his responses. The extra dimension of amusement comes from the fact that Sugar is not just a voluptuous girl, she is in fact the girl who at that moment was probably the most-desired female on earth, and for a long time she cannot light a fire, apparently, in Joe.

The particular grace of these references is that they are inessential but enriching. If you don't understand them, you are not left out. If you do understand them, you sense how the history of film is being used in irreverent affection.

Second, there is Wilder's use of music. This is, quite literally, a musical comedy. When Sugar makes her first appearance, walking down the train platform like "Jello on springs," a muted trumpet comments just as it used to do when a stripper walked down the runway in burlesque. When the bus drives up to the gorgeous old Victorian hotel with the band, a girls' chorus sings "Down Among the Whispering Palms"; when the girls splash in for their first swim, the same chorus sings "By the Beautiful Sea." Both times, the songs blend with the sun and that wonderful old hotel to keep our spirits both high and nostalgic.

But the best use of music is in Sugar's three songs. None of them is allowed to be just a static "number." On the train, when they all rehearse "Runnin' Wild," Sugar drops a flask hidden in her stocking. Drinking is forbidden by the leader, and she is about to be fired. But Jerry pretends the flask is his, so the song becomes a chance to establish rapport. On the hotel bandstand, when Sugar sings "I Wanna Be Loved by You," Joe uses the last portion as a cover to switch cards on a big basket of flowers sent by Osgood. Near the end, after Sugar's "millionaire" has phoned to say he is leaving suddenly, she sings "I'm Through with Love," again on the bandstand, and Joe, the fake millionaire, realizes—through her singing—how she feels and how *he* feels.

Joe is Tony Curtis, who has sometimes done well in other films but has never done better than here. He charges the role to the brim with comic energy; his timing is crisp; and his change of heart at the end, from exploiter to lover, is affectingly underplayed. Jack Lemmon is Jerry and, as always in his best comic performances, he combines clean vocal attack and nicely shaded readings with a feeling for silent-comedy profile. The moment on the beach when Jerry in a girl's bathing suit, runs past his pal Joe posing as a millionaire, recognizes Joe only after he has passed, then stops with one foot raised—that moment is one of the best delayed "takes" since Buster Keaton.

Occasionally the word "transvestite" is applied to *Some Like It Hot* in a clinical sense, as if the film were an unwitting glimpse into psychosexual murk. Literally, the term "transvestite" is accurate; psychically, it applies about as much as it does to *Der Rosenkavalier* because Octavian is played by a woman. Wilder shot the film in black-and-white (against Monroe's wishes) because he thought that in color the two male leads could be accused of transvestism if their make-up was light or of vulgarism if it was heavy. The masquerade comedy comes, not from swishing about, but from the very maleness of two young men in a harem situation, unable to do anything about it. The upper-berth party, with Jerry in nightdress visited by a horde of pretty girls in nightdresses, is a scene of hilarious torture. Sometimes the viewer of sex comedy needs a little less glib psychology and a little more innocence.

It would be foolish to burden *Some Like It Hot* with undue praise. I am interested in due praise. The beauty—no less a word will do—of a fine farce like this has little to do with the elements of high comedy: character dissection, moral reproof, social comment. There is no valid social comment in this picture: the gang wars, Sugar's millionaire-hunting, Osgood's profligate philandering, were chosen only as props, the way a juggler chooses ninepins instead of hats. If Wilder and Diamond could have thought of a better setting for their "nugget"—better in farcical terms—they would presumably have used it; they were not interested in indicting American mores but in utilizing them. The purpose of the picture is to make us laugh.

Watching it is like watching good trapezists. They, too, start from a ridiculous premise: what sane person would hang from bars in midair? Once there, they proceed with absolute logic. Farce gives us the thrill of danger (when Joe forgets to take off his bandstand earrings, racing to a date as the millionaire) and the thrill of split-second neatness (when he whisks them off just in time). Basically, that is the greatest joke of all: absolute order has been imposed on the chaos of life. Farce, as an artistic form, is identical with that order. We know that life, on either side of these two hours, is chaotic: there is pleasure here in seeing how neatly things fit together for people we like.

Possibly, to come at last to the third significance of *Some Like It Hot,* that is why it is the last really good farce produced in this country to date. There have been new imitations of old farces, there have been new farces, all inferior; they lack any real commitment to the sheer fun of design, to the ideal of a finely turned comic machine that has no purpose other than fun.

Also, the great *farceurs* believe very strongly in physical movement. Running, sliding, hurtling, wheeling, bicycling, jumping, climbing, and falling. (Monroe is tripped for a headlong fall.) The latter-day screwball comedies, which is Hollywood jargon for farce, lack real conviction in the moving body as a source of wonders.

I regret ending on a serious note, but many viewings of *Some Like It Hot* have convinced me that it belongs in the line of the best elegantly busy farces of the last century, the line of Labiche and Feydeau and Pinero. Those farces exist in a kind of limbo: they can be revived well or ill. The script of a film is inseparably wedded to its performance, whatever the latter's quality may be; and *Some Like It Hot* is happily married to a fine performance forever.

This film will make people laugh as long as future societies bear any perceptible relation to our own; and will make people laugh the second, third, sixth time they see it. If that isn't immortality, it's close enough. Nobody's perfect.

L'AVVENTURA

IN 1960, the year it was finished, *L'Avventura* was shown at the Cannes Film Festival and was loudly booed. In 1962 it was voted one of the ten best films of all time in an international poll conducted by a British cinema journal. In those intervening two years, audiences in Europe and, more slowly, in America had begun to perceive that Michelangelo Antonioni's film is a major work. Since then, it has not only influenced other film makers and the taste of the public, it has come to be seen as a milestone. Its stature testifies to the expected attributes of a fine artist, but in Antonioni's case, there is an added attribute: courage.

Even when advanced and advancing ideas have been accepted in, say, book-reading and theatergoing circles, it is still an act of courage to take those ideas, without compromise, into the world of film, a medium of immensely wider reach (and greater expense!). Of all the memorable works in film history, only a relative few have pioneered in this way, and shining among those few is *L'Avventura.*

By the late 1950s the dominant postwar intellectual climate had been explored in the novels and plays of Sartre and Camus, Pavese and Beckett, among others. The first fully committed, mature film in this general vein was made by Antonioni. But his work is much more than a me-too tail wagging after an accepted dog: its very existence as film makes it new. If different art forms are more than different containers into which identical concepts can be poured, then *L'Avventura* is an original chapter in the testament of an age.

Antonioni is a northern Italian, born in Ferrara in 1912. He took a degree in economics at the University of Bologna, where he did some amateur theater and film work. In 1939 he went to Rome, worked at various jobs, including some writing for a film journal, then entered the national film school. After only three months, he made a short film that won him a first-class diploma. He found odd bits of film work, writing and assisting, was drafted into the army, and was given leave to work on a film in France as assistant to Marcel Carné. When he returned, still in the army, he found time and means to make a short documentary.

After the war he wrote film criticism, made some more short films, worked at such other film jobs as he could get, and translated some French books into Italian, including novels by Gide and Chateaubriand. In 1950, at the relatively late age of thirty-eight, he got the backing for his first feature film; by 1957 he had made four more. None of them was notably successful (only one was shown in the U.S.), although some critics recognized from the start that a unique talent was becoming manifest.

Now aged forty-five, now increasingly determined to do only what he wanted to do and finding it increasingly difficult to get backing because he had no ringing success behind him, he spent two years before he raised the money even to begin *L'Avventura.* The subject, as usual, was his own and, as usual for him, was worked out with the aid of the novelist and poet Tonino Guerra, this time assisted by Elio

Bartolini. The picture was finished under extremely difficult conditions—the "location" shooting was hard and the money often faltered.

The hostile public reception at Cannes was, in a noncynical sense, one proof that Antonioni had succeeded: in his ambition to break new ground. Right after the disastrous première a group of directors and critics signed a statement supporting Antonioni, and within months the picture was launched on its troublesome, troubling, significant career.

The story seems simple. Anna, a wealthy young Roman, is a guest on a yachting cruise off Sicily. She has been accompanied by her lover, Sandro, a successful architect in his forties, and by Claudia, a girl friend of hers, apparently the only one on the cruise who is not well-to-do.

The yacht stops for a bit at a small rocky Aeolian island, and Anna disappears. A slight clue leads to Sicily where she might have gone, in secret whimsy, by small boat. The yacht goes to Sicily. After an inconsequential police inquiry, Sandro and Claudia begin a private search for Anna—with increasing laxness as, in a very few days, *they* become lovers.

Soon they rejoin their yachting friends in a luxury hotel. That night Claudia retires alone, and comes down early next morning, to find Sandro making love with a girl he has picked up. After her shock— and after his—Claudia is reconciled to Sandro's behavior, and also to her own acceptance of it.

Antonioni's first great act of daring is in this "simple" story. Look at three examples of that daring. To begin with, the story affronts conventional audience expectations by starting with one heroine and abruptly switching to another before the film is one-third along. The story of Anna and Sandro becomes the story of Claudia and Sandro, and what's more, the disappearance of Anna is never explained. This development follows the caprice of life rather than rigid plotting rules.

Second, the audience is asked to sympathize with a girl who replaces her friend as a man's mistress within a few days of the first girl's disappearance, and to sympathize with the man who is the lover of both. Claudia's actions are based on an honesty rarely found in private life, let alone in a popular art.

Third, at the end the audience is asked to accept Claudia's relatively quick acceptance of Sandro's infidelity. This acceptance is the explosion that forces the consequences of the film's adventure, the moral adventure of the title, into the characters' consciousness.

The story, then, rests basically on radical candor, the recognition of moral change, of dissolution and a new resolution. Such a director as Jean Renoir had shown, in *La Grande Illusion,* the poignancy of a certain Western ethos burning to its end in the fires of World War I, as the bases of that ethos shriveled. Now, after World War II, Antonioni is showing us a generation stripped even of poignancy. His film is about people looking for ways to live and relate in a moral landscape burned clean even of pathos. Anna in her discontent at the opening, Claudia, even Sandro, are people refusing to despair of decency because they no longer have ideals to cuddle them, ideals that, as the film implies, had been imposed on human reality and now lack even a comforting poetry.

"Existentialism" has become a cheapened word, but it is an increasingly serious idea: the belief that human beings can find a rationale, a morality, *in the living of their lives,* rather than huddling under a canopy of doctrine constructed to reassure. Man, says Sartre, "is nothing else but the sum of his actions, nothing else but what his life is. . . . Our aim is precisely to establish the human kingdom as a pattern of values. . . ." And he adds that, in this pursuit "it is not only one's self that one discovers . . . but those of others, too." Claudia and Sandro, thrown into a situation where they might once have behaved otherwise because of prettily fabricated moralities, try to act with such truth as they can find in themselves and each other.

But it would be an immense disservice to suggest that *L'Avventura* is a tract, demonstrating a thesis. This is a major film, not because of its ideas but because it is a fine artwork embodying those ideas. The way it is made is, therefore, part of what it is about.

That is Antonioni's second, and inseparable, great act of daring. Out of motives similar to Eisenstein's, though with very different means, Antonioni enlists his film making as part of the revolution in consciousness that is his film's subject. He has used methods of composition, of action, and of editing that disregard the traditions of film fiction, even of film realism, in order to internalize the work, to make its style consonant with the honesties of the story and the characters' quandaries.

The film opens with Anna walking toward the camera, as she leaves home for the cruise. At the front gate she meets her father and is speaking with him when Claudia arrives to join her. The camera remains on Anna and her father as Claudia crosses the background. Claudia enters the film peripherally, just as she enters the story. Antonioni is prefiguring the shift of the picture's center, with the seeming heroine in the foreground and the real heroine in the background, thus in his very composition making an ironic comment on the surprises that life has in store. When we first see *L'Avventura,* we cannot be conscious of the irony at the moment, but it has a retroactive effect. When we see it again—and like any good work, this film grows with acquaintance—that peripheral entrance strikes the first unconventionally truthful note.

Then Anna and Claudia go to pick up Sandro at his apartment, and at first Anna rather sullenly postpones going upstairs to see him after they get there. When she does go up, she surprises us, somewhat more than Sandro, by insisting on going to bed with him at once while Claudia waits below in the piazza. Antonioni handles this odd situation, with editing and camera angle, to show that the patient Claudia infers what is causing the delay; in an oblique way he implicates her in the world of sex with Sandro, as a subtle preparation for her direct involvement to follow.

All three go off on the cruise, and while the yacht is at sea, Anna plunges in for a swim. Soon she cries "Shark!" After considerable alarm, she is rescued. Later, below, she and Claudia are changing, and she confesses that she lied, there had been no shark. The pointless lie further deepens the sense of her instability, her inexplicable restlessness, but more delicately, Antonioni handles the scene between the two undressed girls to evoke an attar of sex—not lesbianism, almost interchangeability, as if one could serve for the other. He underscores this by having Anna give Claudia a blouse. Claudia wears it later, after Anna disappears, thus shocking Anna's distraught father and thus also furthering the suggestion of inheritance. She replaces Anna and inherits her position vis-à-vis Sandro.

Uniquely as these subtle matters have been handled by the camera, it is only on the island that we first meet the crucially different element in Antonioni's style: his use of time. The search for the lost Anna is carried out with disregard for traditional editing, the mechanical acceleration of pace within a sequence. Antonioni is not simply trying to replace condensed "screen" time with "real" lapsed time; he is destroying stock methods, replacing them with fidelity to mood and thought, making time a visible balance in his structure.

He choreographs the searchers, individually and in small groups, to produce at least two effects. First, there is a gradual infusion of seriousness, the realization that the longer Anna is missing, the more likely it is that she is dead—just as when we see someone go under-water for five seconds, it's a dive, but if for five minutes, it's a drowning. Second, the ballet of the search over the rocks becomes a transitional passage, like a suspended musical chord in which some notes are held and new ones are added to change their color. (Sounds, literally, are important in this sequence. The wind and the sea are handled almost as components of the dialogue.)

The tonal center finally shifts when Claudia slips on a rock and Sandro catches her arm. There is a quick glance between them and a quick withdrawal of her arm, but it is a moment of shock. We have just seen a flash of naked feeling that is, by conventional rule, grossly out of place here and now.

Sandro kisses Claudia aboard the yacht, less than a day after Anna has disappeared. After a moment's hesitation, she breaks away. The first time they really kiss is a few days later in Sicily, during their search for Anna, and here again Antonioni uses the element of time to enrich his material. He prolongs the encounter, pressing with different close-ups, as the pair lie on the ground, kissing. So deliberately are we made to watch that we look past the event to what it signifies. Sandro, the somewhat jaded, somewhat frightened middle-aged man, kisses Claudia as if this were the only rite he knows to assure himself that he is still living, as if he must have someone whom he thinks he loves, without even a three-day gap, just as he would have to eat in three days or collapse. Claudia embraces him with an air of admission, of release: as if she had always loved him, had been jealous of Anna, and is now so intoxicated by the disturbances in her life that she can confess these things unconventionally soon.

Scenes such as these can be called novelistic cinema so long as the term does not imply that Antonioni is literary but uncinematic. He is here transmuting into film terms, completely, some of the functions of the novel: suspension of time to luxuriate in character resonance and mood.

Another example of this novelistic approach occurs just before the kissing scene. Sandro and Claudia are driving and come to a town newly built but completely deserted. They stop and try, without success, to find some inhabitants, then with a slight shiver, they drive on. Presumably it is a new settlement built to house people who have not yet moved in, but this is never explained. Its emptiness, unexplained, is the very quality that Antonioni wants, a visual metaphor of everyday mystery. Significantly, the only times in the whole film that the camera moves independently, not following someone or something, are just before this scene, as it goes to meet the arriving pair, and just after, as it glides down the street that they have left. These independent movements underscore harmonically the abstracted feeling of the scene.

The final sequence of *L'Avventura* is one of the key moments in modern film. After Claudia's ruthless honesty with herself about her love for Sandro, after he has in fact proposed marriage, she discovers that he has immediately been unfaithful—and, one may say, idly so, just because the chance was offered. In the space of a few minutes Antonioni then encompasses a small revolution.

Look at this whole sequence in terms of its images, because it is an epitome of Hegel's definition of beauty: "the sensuous appearance of the Idea." It opens with a close-up of Claudia's hand, as she lies in her hotel bed. Restlessly she gets up in her white nightgown and wanders around the room, trying to distract herself, making faces in a mirror, scribbling on a magazine. Clearly she is disturbed by the fact that Sandro has not yet returned from downstairs, and this disturbance is itself a symptom of her unease at the situation she has found herself in, so quickly yet so willingly. Again Antonioni insists on our watching. Nothing of importance happens; much of importance is conveyed.

We cut to gray daybreak, seen through her window, and Claudia walks into the shot in a black dress. The different light and color change the time and intensify the mood. Sandro has not yet returned.

A cut, then, to a floor-level shot, something rarely used in this picture—a long shot of Claudia running toward us down a long empty hotel corridor. It is like a nightmare beginning to be realized. She stops in the suite of a married couple she knows, to ask them whether they have seen Sandro. They have not. For a moment here, Claudia and her friend Patrizia are seen, heads close, in a shot that distills the idea of female communion.

Claudia continues her search, which is worked out in a kind of large geometry, seen in long shots, as she moves through the great empty lounges of the early-morning hotel. There is a kinetic "echo" here, a reminder of the search for Anna on the island, only this search is for the lover of both girls and this search is successful.

The only sound is Claudia's footsteps. Indeed, from this point to the end, neither Claudia nor Sandro speaks a word. She is running away from us toward the far end of a large room when she turns and, on a sofa, discovers something that we cannot see. Instantly we cut to a shot over her shoulder, looking down on Sandro and a girl on that sofa. The swift change of view is like a sharp catastrophic shout. To see Claudia from a distance, a small figure in the universe, and then to be plunged instantly into the shock at the center of her universe—that is film art.

Dazedly she walks out into an open square, railed, which overlooks a view. It is not yet morning; the light seems suspended. Soon Sandro comes out, slowly, but does not go to her. He walks to a bench nearby and sinks on to it, facing away from her. He has come out to accept whatever she has for him, to make himself present, his presence the only apology he can offer. We see his face, tears coming down the cheeks, and the truth—the terrible truth—is that the tears are real. He *is* sorry; and we also know that he is helpless, he can make no promises about different futures.

We feel this because she feels it. Her sobbing stops. She walks to him, and stands behind him. In close-up her face looks down on him. Her tears have stopped; the future has begun, whatever it is to be. There is a close-up of her hand—the hand with which the whole final sequence began!—trembling toward the back of his head. Then, after a moment, the hand goes up and touches his head. The last view is a long shot of them from behind, against the graying light. Together, her hand on him.

Thus Antonioni tells us through images that, in a cosmos devoid of absolutes, all that human beings have is themselves, faults and all; that the possibility of love depends on our not making impossible demands on each other. This is the revolution in relations. Claudia takes Sandro for what he is, not for what he ought to be by some synthetic standard, knowing that he sees himself clearly, knowing that she herself is the woman who so quickly replaced Anna. This is a moment of figurative marriage between two people who can ache for perfection without insisting on it and who have the courage to embrace life *im*perfect.

The three principal actors utterly fulfill their roles. In a sense Lea Massari, as Anna, has the most difficult job because her part is shortest and she must be unforgettable. So she is—sexually implosive, racked with ambivalences. Gabriele Ferzetti, the Sandro, who resembles Laurence Olivier, has exactly the right, nearly overripe appeal and the right air of uncomfortable self-knowledge. But the film hangs on Monica Vitti, the Claudia, mature yet relatively innocent compared with the society she is now moving in. The main transition in the film is hers, the greatest change, and it is beautifully realized.

The society Antonioni has chosen is upper middle-class and aristocratic, leisured and discontent. He contrasts these people with others: an old shepherd who clings to that small rocky island, a pair of Sicilian servants on a train, a sourly married druggist and his new wife, but that upper-class society is his medium. He knows, as Chekhov did, that a leisured class lives closer to the border of moral changes that eventually affect a whole culture.

We can see now that, by examining love in this society, Antonioni has examined everything. He has understood that all the secrets in us—our desires, our dreads, our gods—are entailed in the words "I love you." Essentially the film asks how we can still say those words, how they can still be true for a world so profoundly changed since the world that invented love.

To ask those questions was to face the austerity of the answers. For this toweringly important task, Antonioni had the requisite gifts and the requisite courage. Yet, though this is far from a film of easy uplift, the very asking of those questions is, fundamentally, an act of affirmation. Gravely yet reliantly, Claudia and Sandro affirm a truth today: the truth that life, without illusions, can be lived.

PERSONA

THE word "persona" has several meanings: among them, mask (in the original Latin); person; and a character in a play. *Persona* is the consummate title for Ingmar Bergman's film.

Made in 1965, it is the twenty-seventh film he directed, the twenty-ninth screenplay he wrote or collaborated on. Bergman was born in 1918 near Stockholm, the son of a Lutheran minister, and began his directing career in the theater; in fact, despite his immense film activity, he has spent more than half of his directing career in the theater. But film, of course, is what made his international reputation. By the time he came to *Persona* he was known as one of the cinema's prime explorers of psyche and spirit—strongly influenced by Strindberg—

through such works as *The Virgin Spring* and his trilogy, *Through a Glass Darkly, Winter Light,* and *The Silence.* All of these were made with Sven Nykvist, his only cinematographer since 1959, and with a "company" of actors, most of whom he had worked with in the theater for many years. His specific impulse toward *Persona,* Bergman has said, came out of an addition to that company: he saw a film with a new Norwegian actress, Liv Ullmann, and was struck by her resemblance to a long-time colleague, Bibi Andersson.

Persona has often been called difficult and abstruse, yet in a poll conducted in 1972 by a British film journal to determine the ten favorite films of eighty-nine critics around the world, *Persona* tied for fifth place. (With Antonioni's *L'Avventura.* Another Bergman film, *Wild Strawberries,* tied for eighth place.) This statistical tally is relevant only in that it substantiates the position of this "difficult" work in the treasury of film art. I am not going to try to show that the picture is not difficult, that its materials are not dark. I want to analyze, if I can, why its difficulty is fruitful.

I propose three separate looks at *Persona.* But I emphasize that these looks are arbitrarily separated: in our experience of the film, all three of these views—and doubtless others as well—occur simultaneously.

First, a map of the story. The picture begins, before the titles and even through the titles, with a series of images, some of which are previsions of matters treated later, some of which only set tonalities for matters treated later. Then we are in a hospital. A nurse, Sister Alma (Bibi Andersson), is assigned by a doctor (Margaretha Krook) to the case of Elisabet Vogler (Liv Ullmann). Elisabet is an actress of about Alma's age, successful, well-known, who has become mute. She is physically well, she is alert and extremely intelligent; but from some psychic imperative, she has simply decided not to speak— not even to her husband and young son.

Although Alma has seen the actress on stage and film and idolizes her, she has inexplicable misgivings about taking the case after she meets Elisabet. But the doctor persuades her to continue. Then the doctor has a talk with Elisabet, the actress keeping absolutely silent as usual, in which the physician shows sharp perception of her patient's condition. She says that Elisabet is in a state of revulsion with the world and herself, and is convinced that every word she might speak would only add to the sum of lies in the world. What can she do? "Suicide?" reflects the doctor. "No, too vulgar." But at least Elisabet can decide to keep silent.

Elisabet's quality of attention indicates that the doctor has diagnosed matters accurately.

The doctor has a cottage by the sea. She says there is no point in keeping Elisabet in the hospital, she is sending the patient and the nurse to her cottage until, as she puts it, the actress is ready to move on to other roles.

Most of the film takes place in this isolated small house on the rocky Swedish coast; and all the rest of the film, except for one episode with one other person, is between these two women, only one of whom speaks. By this very fact that the other woman only and always listens, Alma soon progresses into details of her life at its most intimate and recessed. The cottage becomes a kind of confessional. Alma feels drawn almost entreatingly to Elisabet, her patient; she is stimulated by being here alone with this famous artist, who listens to her; and she tells Elisabet about a long wretched love affair she had with a married man, about the pleasant fiancé she has now, and more.

Then one day Alma drives to town to mail some letters, including one of Elisabet's to the doctor. Elisabet has accidentally left her letter unsealed, and Alma can't resist reading it. In it Elisabet has written patronizingly of Alma, saying that she likes the nurse who has taken to telling her secrets, and that she finds it amusing to study Alma.

The shock is severe for Alma who, though not naive, is straightforward. Her attitude toward Elisabet changes drastically. No longer a nurse and an aspiring friend, she becomes a competitor, an avenger, desperate to avenge the affront to herself in a particular way—by being recognized as a person. Eventually this leads to a physical fight between the two women, during which Alma, in a fury, almost throws a pot of boiling water at Elisabet—her patient—and provokes the one unequivocal, spontaneous utterance the actress makes in the film, a cry of "Don't!"

Later, in a long pleading scene, the tearful Alma follows the outraged Elisabet down the beach, explaining how fond she had become of the actress and how badly the letter had hurt her, saying she knows they must leave this place soon but hopes they can part as friends. But Elisabet keeps walking, as stony as the stony beach.

Now Alma, failed as a nurse, offended as a person, scorned as a suppliant, begins to crack. She begins to have fantasies on the edge of hallucination, including one about Elisabet's husband whom she has never seen. In an effort to reclaim herself, Alma puts off informal country wear and puts on her nurse's uniform; this doesn't help. She is not only no longer her earlier self, she has slipped even closer toward Elisabet, as she imagines her.

She confronts the actress and tells her—twice, once with the camera on the other woman, once with it on herself—why she thinks Elisabet had a child and why she later rejected the boy: that the actress had thought of motherhood as a role but had been frightened by the reality. The account ends with Alma frantically stuttering into gibberish.

These are the last words she speaks in the film, except for some dream utterances. We see the two women packing in silence, closing the house. We see a very quiet Alma leaving. A voice on the sound track tells us that Elisabet returned to the theater "in December" and continued her career (and we get a glimpse of her acting again). Then again we see the quiet Alma getting the bus to take her away from the coast. There is a quick reprise of two images from the very beginning, and the film ends.

Now, a second look at *Persona,* to see how and, principally, why Bergman told this story.

First, the performances by Andersson and Ullmann. They are perfect. Any lesser word would be footling. Andersson, carrying almost all the dialogue, never fluctuates from a complete grip on the truth of the moment and the means of conveying it truly. Ullmann, silent almost throughout, nevertheless creates a complex human being in herself and by the *use* of things that are said to her. To see the film again now is to "hear" Ullmann by virtue of her subsequent appearances in other films: to see *Persona* when it was released was to witness an extraordinary debut, silent but eloquent.

As for the film itself, it begins with a black screen and a thrum of electronic sound. The carbon arcs of a film projector glow into presence, and in a series of disjointed flashes, we see—among other glimpses—a strip of film beginning to roll through a projector, bits of old slapstick comedy, a sheep being dissected, a spike being driven through a hand. Then we are in a morgue, with bodies under sheets. A telephone rings. A dead old woman's eyes blink open. A dead boy sits up, puts on glasses, starts to read. Then he reaches toward the camera and, in a reverse shot, we see that he is reaching toward the immense face of a woman behind glass. It becomes another woman's face. (Later we learn that these are Elisabet and Alma.) The faces blur together. Then the title and credits of the film appear.

The very start emphasizes that what we are going to see is a film: reality is not going to be re-created, it is going to be abstracted. The "meaning" of the various disjointed images is never patly explicated. My feeling when I first saw *Persona*, enforced by subsequent viewings and unchanged by others' views, was that we are being given a quick, jagged tour of Elisabet's mind. This is one of the relatively few sequences in which the film is subjectively hers; usually it is either Alma's or it is objective. It can even be argued that the film-projector and film-strip opening are Elisabet's, since (as the doctor notes) she sees life as a show, a succession of roles.

Through the credits, too, there are flashes of what we have already seen and what we shall see, after which the screen goes absolutely white for a moment. Then, via Nykvist's magic camera, the outlines of a door are sketched in photographically. Alma comes through it and faces us. The "prologue" began with black, into which white penetrated; the body of the film begins with a reversal of this process, as if blackness and whiteness are being established as the visual poles of the work.

The camera holds on the nurse, first from the front, then from behind. The doctor who addresses her is seen only vaguely in the background. Thus Bergman insinuates that Alma is abstracted from the world, a distilled presence, that what we are seeing is only seeming realism. When the doctor says that Elisabet stopped dead in the middle of a stage performance, of *Electra,* we see a flash of this, but we also see a camera filming that performance. Again Bergman seems to be reminding us that everything we see here as reality is itself being observed by at least one other reality. Thus his very method keeps asking the question: Where is truth?

The lighting of that first scene with the doctor and the feeling of a real room floating in space are continued in Elisabet's room, as the nurse and the patient become acquainted. Two moments here are especially important to what follows. First, Alma switches on a bedside radio, for Elisabet's amusement, and a soap-opera actress begins to talk moonily of love. Elisabet giggles, then angrily switches it off. Alma then puts on some music for her—Bach, as it happens— and leaves her. Then comes a minute that is powerful in its simplicity, exquisite in its power. The camera holds on Elisabet's face turned to the radio; listening; her eyes unblinking. (Bergman has said that, to him, film means faces.) The light dims; it is twilight, yet this is a theatrical fading. (Again Bergman leads us subtly over the edge of realism.) In the dusk Elisabet stares intently, held by the music, *feeding* on it. After a long, absolutely motionless moment, she turns her head as if in pain.

This brief scene is crucial to the film. It is no facile exploitation of great music, like the Mozart in *Elvira Madigan*. Bach is not mere sound track accompaniment; he is in this scene, his music is part of the drama. It provides the best statement that Bergman could find of all that is out of Elisabet's reach, so unattainable that she has decided to be silent rather than settle for less. This music, we may infer, is particularly pertinent because of what we know about her. One of the master strokes in the script is that Bergman has made Elisabet an actress, not because she must "lie" every night, pretending to be someone else, but because the truth in that pretense—the truth of art—is greater than any truth she can achieve in her own life. So she is constantly abraded by the difference between the truth of concept and the circumscriptions of self as woman and wife and mother. (Remember, too, that she stopped cold for the first time while playing Electra, the Argive princess whose mission is to cleanse away impurity at whatever cost to herself.) This crystalline moment of Bach is a statement in art to an artist, of a perfection that never existed except in imagination; it is also a reminder of a time in which such imagination was possible but which is now gone.

This is underscored in the second of the two moments. Later Elisabet watches television at night—a filmed report of the Vietnam war. In her nightgown she shrinks into a corner of the hospital room, now lit only by ghostly television light, and watches a Buddhist monk burn himself to death, a man whose protest against imperfection is so strong that it takes the form of permanent silence. Elisabet watches in horror, perhaps with a touch of shame put possibly with some touch of reinforcement for her present "role."

These two moments, one of purity from the past, one of agony in the present, come to her through electronic media of the twentieth century.

The first scene on the island—the two women walking alongside a stone wall, then peeling mushrooms together—is one of the few sequences in sunlight. Most of these island scenes are at night or in rain or in the soft-clear gray light that Bergman and Nykvist have long since established as the climate of the human "interior."

And in this isolated place, with these two physically similar women dressed in similar country clothes, we see a drama of virtually isolated forces, opposed yet melding. One woman of strength and intellect has had a vision of nullity. The other woman, of strength and intelligence, is there to bring Elisabet back (in effect) to her (Alma's) point of view, to a plane of function. Yet the reverse happens: without philosophic process, Alma is drawn more and more to the cavern in which Elisabet is now hiding. What attracts Alma consciously is Elisabet-as-artist; the nurse is happy to be with this gifted and renowned woman. What attracts Alma unconsciously is the sense that Elisabet has found some sort of explanation for the bewilderments of existence, that the actress's so-called abnormality may be a *reasonable* reaction to the confusions and pollutions of life.

This hunger for clarity in Alma is seen most sharply in the sequence where the two women draw closest, a sequence where Alma recounts the story of a sex orgy—a quite spontaneous occasion in which she had found herself participating. As Alma tells the story she feels again the surprise and the dismay that she was able to do these things, to enjoy them, then return to her fiancé and make love with him later that night. She bursts into tears at the end of the story, shocked again at this enlarged knowledge of herself with which she cannot deal. In this sequence Bergman has Elisabet listening as she lies on her bed next to a lamp, with Alma sitting in an armchair in some shadow. The lamp and Elisabet's luminous face seem in themselves to be drawing this secret story out of Alma, almost to be promising her relief and answer.

And that night, apparently because of this closeness and this promise, the film moves for the first time into dream—deliberately difficult to distinguish from reality, perhaps because the reality in this film is itself treated as an abstraction. But it is Alma's dream; in it the breeze moves the gauzy curtains on the doorway to her bedroom and through them Elisabet floats in her nightgown. In one of the most miraculously photographed intimate scenes in all of film, the two women embrace—a communion that is physical without being overtly sexual, a gesture of affinity. This is apparently a symbol of what Alma wishes could happen, a wish that she could join Elisabet wherever, in her inner secretness, she is hiding. (Of course next morning when Alma asks Elisabet whether she came into her bedroom the night before, the actress shakes her head.)

As with this dream scene, the texture of what we see at every moment fulfills what the film is about. Take, for instance, the first scene after Alma has read the unsealed letter. The sun shines, as on the first island day. Alma, on the terrace in a bathing suit and barefoot, breaks a glass and sweeps up the pieces. She discovers one more glass splinter. She picks it up, then she hears Elisabet coming and puts the splinter back. Then she goes inside while Elisabet, also in bathing clothes and barefoot, walks up and down. We wait with Alma. The cry of pain comes, and we see Elisabet glance sharply and suspiciously at the watching Alma inside. Alma stares back stolidly—and then the film itself disintegrates. A hole burns through it and it tears apart. It is as if the tissue of this abstraction—the very film we are watching—has been torn by this sudden savage reversal of feeling.

Then the film fights its way back into being. The next sequence (after a swift reprise of a few flashes from the "prologue") begins quite out of focus, as Elisabet moves around the house, doing some little chores. Slowly, almost painfully, the picture focuses again.

Later, when Alma tells her how hurt she has been by the letter, Elisabet seems only to be startled by the fact that Alma read the letter, and does not yield an inch in apology. Alma gets more and more desperate as she realizes that soon they must leave this place, as she sees that she is getting further and further away from acknowledgment by this woman in whom she has confided so much, as she hates herself for still wanting that ackowledgment, as she feels snared and infuriated by Elisabet's unshakable silence, which now is colored by pride and resentment. That silence seems to have become a kind of victory over everything in Alma: her competence as a nurse, her attempt to draw close as a friend, even her unconscious attempts to hover on the edge of Elisabet's philosophic view.

And interwoven with these scenes of their waking hours, their conflict, Alma's defeat, are her fantasies and dreams: one in which Elisabet's husband makes love to her, thinking her Elisabet, while the actress looks on. In another, the earlier beautiful night embrace is repeated as a kind of glimpse of lost happiness. Another goes back even earlier to Elisabet's hospital room, where Alma finally gets the actress to speak just one word—the word "Nothing."

The climactic scene, in which Alma imagines and tells twice the selfish "role-playing" reasons why the actress had a child, ends with her face and Elisabet's split vertically and joined on the screen. Our first thought is of the two blurred faces that the boy saw in the morgue (especially since the talk here is of a child); but here the joining looks harsh, ugly, schizoid. It is like a danger signal, like the gibberish to which Alma is reduced. Then, in a frenzy of seeming frustration and self-hate, Alma pounds the table, scratches her forearm fiercely, draws blood. Suddenly Elisabet leans forward and sucks that blood. Perhaps she is saying: "You wanted union? I give you a blood bond." Or perhaps it is an act of expiation, the only moment when Elisabet literally and figuratively bows to Alma, as if she had implanted a poison that now she wants to draw.

If it is the latter, we never learn positively that it works. Elisabet returns to her career, we know. The shaken Alma returns to her profession and her fiancé—presumably.

The last images are of film running out of the projector and the carbon arcs burning down into darkness; and so the film, to the very end proclaiming itself a film, finishes.

A last look at *Persona*—beneath the action and also beneath the forces of the action. In the year the film was released I saw it two or three times and thought that it was an agon between, to put it crudely, intellectual and biological impulses. The mind of modern man sees the futility of life, the entropy of ideal and hope. But the biological destiny of man is to survive, possibly so that he is able to have such bleak perceptions. The entirely rational disaffection of Elisabet sucks in and almost swamps the extra-rational, vitalist Alma, who pulls herself free to go on living on the other side of this experience, profoundly altered but not by untruth.

Now, after some half dozen further viewings in the intervening years, I think the above is valid enough but incomplete. I think that what Bergman has done here is to try the possibilities for modern tragedy. It is modern because it depends neither on Aristotelian flaw nor on fate nor on vengeance nor on any of the great tragic instruments of the past but on diurnal life. The tragedy lies in the realization of the insuperable distance between truth and possibility. Not death or blindness or suicide is the outcome but *existence,* with increased perception—for both women.

Bernard Shaw once congratulated Chekhov because, as against Ibsen, the Russian understood that the tragedy of the Hedda Gablers in real life is that they do not shoot themselves, they go on living. Elisabet knows (as the doctor indicated) that she will go on living her various roles in the tragedy of *life,* rather than completing an architecturally modeled tragedy in one sequence of her life. Alma's tragedy is that, though primed by experience to be vulnerable to Elisabet's vision, she might not have reached it by herself and must now discover whether she can bear it. Her early misgivings about taking this case may have been a premonition of her vulnerability. Now her premonition is realized: she is not an intellectual "role-player," she now has a new persona she must live with. In an essay on *Persona* Robert Boyers wrote: "The tragic hero is one who loses confidence in reality as he has always known it, and articulated it." The life that Alma will make for herself, he says, "will be tragic, because to be conscious, and to go on living, is to suffer as only our heroes can."

As I understand Bergman, he feels that traditional tragedy is impossible today because, in this god-hungry, probably godless universe, tragedy consists of this very consciousness, this comprehension of the dimensions of imagination and concept as against the dimensions of act and fact. Structurally, however, Bergman has drawn on the ancient sources of the tragic mode. (Surely *Electra* is cited to suggest this.) Some critics have said that *Persona* is related to Strindberg's *The Stronger,* a short two-character play in which a wife confronts her husband's mistress, in which the mistress is silent throughout while the wife speaks, and which leaves us undecided as to which of the two is the stronger. Of course Bergman knows the play, but its domestic gnaw is a long way from the current and thrust of his own much larger work. Particularly in the light of his theater background, I think he may have been strongly influenced by the distilled quality of Greek tragedy—in its earliest form, with only two actors (which essentially are all that *Persona* has) and in one place (which essentially is also true here).

Yet, native of the modern sensibility that Bergman is, he could not rest with archaism. To the above impulse toward classic distillation, he added his understanding of contemporary self-awareness—the literal awareness of self as an entity to be watched, the compulsion or injunction to observe one's own life as a performance, plus the corollary hunger for authenticity in a world where one is now sentenced to observe himself. So, in using the twentieth century's own medium to make a twentieth-century tragedy, Bergman incorporated this modern truth by making the film itself know, so to speak, that it is a film. The work that is watched knows that it is a work made to be watched, not an all-inclusive "real" world; thus in its very being it reflects the self-awareness of its characters and its era.

Ultimately, this difficult, dark, unremitting film is exalting. First, because it shows that a superb artist can still deal with our most terrible knowledges, that high art is still possible in an age that has doubted this possibility. Second, because in the interior action of that art, we see contemporary human beings, in all their feeble self-reliance, still able to experience and survive the very worst, which is one other definition of the heroic. Like Antonioni, like other paramount artists of our time, Bergman has found art to be both a source of moral insight and a means of taking its consequences.

COMMENT

comment

NOTES ON THEATER-AND-FILM

(Performance, September/October 1972)

FOR a number of years I have spent a lot of time going to plays and films, sometimes one of each on the same day, so the two forms are constantly juxtaposed for me. The experience convinces me that there are some received ideas on the subject of theater-and-film—or theater versus film—that can use a quizzical look. My intent is not hierarchical ranking, which seems to me boneheaded, simply investigation. Here are some notes.

Attention

The art of film lives by controlling attention, we are told, and are told truly except when there is an implication that the theater lives otherwise. The film director controls attention irrevocably; you cannot look at anything in the scene except what he permits you to look at. But the theater director wants to have exactly the same power over you. His job is harder because he has to *earn* your attention. If you look elsewhere than where he wants you to be looking at any given moment, the production is wobbling as badly as when the film in a projector flutters.

The difference between the two arts here is certainly not in intent but in means. Temperament sometimes enables a director to use both sets of means—Bergman and Visconti, for just two instances—sometimes not. Antonioni once told me that he had directed a few plays, and I asked him whether he wanted to do more theater work. "No," he said. "Always the same shot."

The film's ability to vary the shots, to command our shifts of attention with no chance of our demurral, is a happy slavery when the right person is giving the orders. But the notion advanced by some film writers that the very idea of holding attention on specific points for specific lengths of time *began* with film is esthetic and pragmatic nonsense.

Time

The synoptic powers of film in regard to time are much greater than in the theater. The actor crossing the room on stage has to cross it, step by step; the film actor can come in the door and immediately be on the other side of the room. Film can juggle the present, past, and future effortlessly, and can repeat the moment, à la Resnais. The theater can try all these things to some degree (I have even seen the Resnais effect on stage), but it has to breathe hard in the attempt.

Much has been made, quite rightly, of these temporal powers in film. Much has been scanted, almost as if by contrasting obligaton, of the temporal powers in the theater. The strength, not the limitation, of the stage is that, in any given scene, time does elapse there, moment by moment. Obviously, figurative time has been used in the theater—mostly between scenes—ever since the *Agamemnon*; still, a strength of the theater is that you feel and see time passing. This is a component of theatrical structure, enrichment, companionship.

It's interesting that in the film form, which can play with time, few works dare to run over two hours. In the theater, which mostly must

NOTES ON THEATER-AND-FILM 355

accept time as it comes, chunk by chunk, many works run over two hours. To see a picture like the Russian film of *Uncle Vanya,* which, among other barbarisms, chopped the play to bits, is to miss the theater's power of letting lives flow before us in simulated passage, the theater's function as the place where such things can happen effectively.

Also, theatrical time works to the actor's advantage in many cases. A scintillating example was Rosalind Russell's performance in *Auntie Mame.* On stage it was not only a dazzling entertainment but a marathon event. Almost the same performance on screen was less effective because we knew it had been done in bits and pieces over a period of months, and the silent hum of wonder as the evening progressed was missing. Almost the only thing wrong for me with Peter Brook's film of *Marat/Sade* was the fact that I knew it had been made in seventeen days—a whirlwind in film-making time but a far distance from the span of one theater performance.

"Opening Up"

To continue with a comparison of plays and filmed plays, a relation that is not only commonplace but revealing: the surest sign of the cliché mind in film making is a feeling of obligation to "open up" plays when they become films and a conviction that this process proves superiority, that a play really comes into its own when it is filmed. We can really go to Italy in Zeffirelli's film of *Romeo and Juliet,* so it supersedes place-bound theater productions. We can dissolve and cross-fade more easily in the film of *Death of a Salesman,* so the theater is once again just a tryout place for later perfect consummation. We can go outside the house in the film of *Who's Afraid of Virginia Woolf?,* and once again the theater is shown up as cribbed and confined.

The trouble here is a confusion in esthetic logic, an assumption that we are comparing apples and apples when we are really comparing apples and pears. Fundamentally, the film takes the audience to the event, shifting the audience continually; the theater takes the event to the audience, shifting it never. Just as the beauty of poetry often lies in tensions between free flight and form-as-preserver, so the beauty of drama often lies in tensions between imagination and theatrical exigency, theater form as a means of preservation, of *avail-*

ability. To assume that the film's extension of a play's action is automatically an improvement is to change the subject: from the way the theater builds upward, folding one event on another in almost perceptible vertical form, to the film's horizontal progression. The theater works predominantly by building higher and higher in one place. The film, despite the literally vertical progress of the frames, works predominantly in lateral series of places.

The very necessity for the dramatist to arrange to get the right people together at the right time in his one place becomes, for the appropriate talent, a means to beauty rather than a burden. (See any Chekhov or Shaw play.) It is muddled to think that, by "unfolding" these careful arrangements, the film inevitably enlarges the original work. This "unfolding" can be successful when the film maker knows clearly what he is doing and treats his film as a new work from a common source, as in the admirable Lester-Wood film of *The Knack.* But most adapters seem to think that any banal set of film gimmicks constitutes a liberation for which the poor cramped play ought to be grateful.

Framing

We often read some version of the following: a difference between stage and screen is that the stage contains all of the place where the event occurs, but the screen frames only part of the film's reality, which continues away from its borders on all sides.

One can see why this idea would grow out of film scenes shot on location. The cowhand who steps before the camera steps out of all Colorado into a tiny portion of it. It is harder to credit this idea when a film actor steps onto a set, even though the camera may eventually go into the next room or outside the house.

The theater audience knows that, literally, what is out of sight is the backstage area. The film audience knows that, literally, what is out of sight—even in Colorado—is a different set of mechanical means: grips, gaffers, reflectors, sound men, and a mechanical omnipresence that the theater never has, the camera.

Seemingly desperate for distinctive esthetics, desperate, too, to formulate a mystique, the film lays claim here to an imaginative exclusivity that is invalid except to the dull-minded. When Barbara Loden in her film *Wanda* roamed through coal fields and coal towns,

she did not suggest any realer places out of sight than Ruby Dee in
Fugard's *Boesman and Lena* telling us of the towns she had tramped
through in her lifetime. In both cases there was a literal frame of
mechanics and techniques; in both cases there was an imaginative
world that stretched endlessly outside the frame.

Things as Actors

The difference here is one of degree, not—as is frequently implied—
of kind. Vachel Lindsay, with an enthusiasm that was admirable and
probably necessary at the time, said of *The Cabinet of Dr. Caligari* in
1922: "It proves in a hundred new ways the resources of the film in
making all the inanimate things which, on the spoken stage, cannot act
at all, the leading actors in the films." The discovery was important,
though overstated. One can forgive "cannot act at all" and "leading
actors" in a prophet of 1922; the idea is less forgivable when repeated without modulation fifty years later.

How beautifully Kurosawa, Welles, Ford use *things* in their films—
a breeze, a sled, a gun. This is quite outside the competence, or
business, of the theater. Although objects acquire metaphoric significance on the stage simply by virtue of having been selected to be
there, no one could maintain that they become "actors"—as the
splinter in the rain barrel seems to become an actor in *Eclipse*.

But Lindsay's pronunciamento, parroted without qualification,
tries to sweep away the affective power of such "things" in the theater
as costume and setting. Rex Harrison's cardigan in *My Fair Lady* was
a "thing" that functioned for me as well on stage as on screen. Places,
which of course are things, can be more easily enlisted in the aid of
the whole work on stage. (Excepting the exceptions, like *Caligari*
itself.) Of course, set design is important in film, and all sets are not
equally good. But John Bury's setting for *The Homecoming,* which
was a collection of "things," contributed to the drama in a way that
was theatrically valid but would have been cinematically obtrusive.*

Words

Many have noted, myself among them, that words often fight films,
which is why classic plays are hard to film. Let's define "classic" in

* For the film of *The Homecoming,* which arrived subsequently, Bury greatly
modified his designs. See p. 243.

old theatrical terms: the classic style is one in which you must play on the line, not between the lines. In films the action usually stops for the words, the words for the action. In addition, the camera brings classic language too close, as the camera brings the singing too close in films of opera. But the facile implication behind this, in much film criticism, is that prolixity doesn't matter in the theater. In fact, as all theater people know, a superfluous line in the theater is, in its own scale, as impedimental as it would be on film.

Further, when language is designed for film and is understood as contributory dynamics, it is as cinematic as any other film element. Bibi Andersson's account of the sex orgy in *Persona,* many of the dialogues in *My Night at Maud's* and *Claire's Knee,* John Gielgud's speeches in *The Charge of the Light Brigade,* Ray Collins's farewell at the railroad station in *The Magnificent Ambersons,* these are only a few of the instances where words, understood and controlled, become *film* components.

Of course there are still some who think that the film art died the moment Jolson sang. A quite valid case can be made to show that the silent and the sound film are esthetically separate; but it is a different case from the one that words are intrinsically and inevitably the enemy of the film.

The Need for an Audience

We may be coming to the end of the age in which film acting is judged by theater standards. So-and-so is not an actor, we are told, even though successful in films, because on stage he could not project beyond the third row; or because cameraman and editor patched together a performance out of his efforts; or because he has to work out of sequence; or because he has the chance to try things a dozen times and to preserve only the best effort. (This last reason would prove that Rubinstein is not a good pianist on records.) Now we are beginning to judge acting by standards appropriate to the particular medium.

Still all performing media have certain standards in common. This can be shown empirically, and it destroys a sentimentality to which the theater clings: that an actor cannot really act unless he has an audience. Think of Mastroianni in *The Organizer,* Huston in *Treasure of the Sierra Madre,* Oscarsson in *Hunger,* Baranovskaia in

Mother, Garbo in *Camille* . . . and on and on and on. No matter the sequence in which each of those films was shot, can one say that those are not sustained performances? And can one imagine how they could possibly have been improved by being done in front of an audience?

Conversely, there are theater performances that seem to proceed wonderfully without any real cognizance of or relation to an audience. The three plays of the Grotowski company that I saw were among the few really momentous theater experiences of my life, but it is hard to believe that those actors play to and with an audience. They reveal certain matters; the audience takes them up or not. I cannot think that *Akropolis* would be played differently if there were no audience present, or that different audiences affect the performances.

The one element that "live" acting inevitably contains is the possibility of mistake. We are never really aware of the confidence that an actor earns until he fluffs a line; and it usually takes a considerable time before he gets us back in his grip. The fissure is in a way pleasurable because it underscores the fact of the making of the art right before us and gives us a kind of added pride in the actors who have not fluffed.

Theater comedy must, of course, take account of laughs, and directors of film comedy have to develop some sense of how to anticipate what the laughs will be so that they don't smother or rush them. But laughter is an overt response. Other tensions, sensations, "feels" are more often than not theater sentimentalities, as far as the actor's need for them is concerned.

To settle the matter subjectively, which is at last the only way, my response to film actors is never less than to theater actors just because the former are on film. The medium is never the reason for response or lack of it. And the fact that film actors *can* move me, and often do, is sufficient proof to me that they don't need my presence at the time they are acting in order to create.

Most talk by actors about the nourishment they get from the audience affects me much like Don Marquis's Mehitabel reminiscing about the old theater days, putting her hand on her heart, and saying, "They haven't got it here." The theater has unalterable powers: it doesn't need to cling to claptrap.

Actor and Role

Any play that we see, we can see again with a different cast; most films never. This is wonderful and terrible, for both the theater and the film.

The London production of *Old Times* did little for me; the New York production did a good deal. Individual actors improve in the same role: Christopher Walken's Caligula which was good to begin with, was even better when I sampled it again some weeks later. On the other hand, there are numberless plays that have seemed lesser later on because of cast or whole company changes; and the same actor can deteriorate in a part. (Not a rarity.)

In films the performance is fixed, for good or ill. When I urge people, as I do, to see Peter O'Toole in *Brotherly Love* if ever it is revived, I know they will see precisely the same performance I saw. When I urge people to see a play, I hope they will go on a good night.

When I saw *Sugar* on Broadway, I thanked providence that the performances of Jack Lemmon and Tony Curtis and Marilyn Monroe in *Some Like It Hot* were fixed immutably. When I sat through Welles's *Macbeth* and *Othello* films, I thanked providence that the scripts weren't fixed immutably to those performances.

As has often been noted, most film roles, if they are memorable at all, are inseparable from their performances. The role has no separate conceptual existence, even if the performance is more than a personality display. Who can conceive of an actor other than George C. Scott playing in *The Hospital*, if a remake were ever conceivable? A film role has no separate existence; most theater roles are apprehensible as entities, even during original productions, because the theater is a place where actor and role meet and, eventually, part. Concepts of actor and role in film may be in as much need of change, vis-à-vis the theater, as standards of acting.

Glamour

No contest. Film actors now have it, some of them, theater actors do not. This is a serious loss to the theater, not frivolous baggage. The mythopoeic quality of actors was an instrument in the mythopoeic functioning of the theater. The theater now gets no such assistance from its casts, no matter whose name is above the title—unless of course it's a film or TV star!

Possibly one of the reasons, among many, for the latter-day theater interest in ensemble work and matrix performance, is the realization that the actor's persona, as armatured by the playwright, is no longer a prime power.

Death

No contest. The effects of death belong entirely to the film. Anyone who saw *Wild Strawberries* before Victor Sjöstrom died and saw it again afterward knows that his performance, the whole film, took on added poignancy and truth. In January of 1972 I read about Dita Parlo's death shortly before I saw *La Grande Illusion* again; when I saw the film and she came into the barn, I felt suddenly as if more was being given me than I knew how to cope with. It was more than moving, it seemed to confirm the death of the actress herself in a very cruel appropriative way and to confirm, by the very fact that what was on the screen was invulnerable, the certainty of my and my fellow viewers' death.

In the theater, play scripts and photographs are souvenirs of productions, no more, if one happens to have seen the now-dead performers. In film, as TV movies demonstrate every night, inevitabilities laugh at us all.

Criticism

The crucial historical difference between theater and film is this: the theater began as a sacred event and eventually included the profane. The film began as a profane event and eventually included the sacred.

No serious person objects to the theater's being judged by sacred standards (as the term is relevant here) because of its origins. But many serious people object to the film's being judged by sacred standards because of its origins.

It is tyrannical and priggish and self-cheating to militate against the profane. But it is a curious critical gift that militates against the sacred, or, more curious, equivocates by insisting that the sacred is *in* the profane. This difference in origin is, at worst, hard luck for the film, not esthetic or spiritual hierarchy. No Dionysus happened to be available when the film was beginning, but, fundamentally, it was born out of the same needs and to comparable ends. Its extra burden is that it has had to fashion its Dionysus as it goes, fitfully, patchily. But what a proof of its power and its potentiality that it has been able to do it. Why should film be reproved or patronized for this? Why should the one art born in this century be scolded for treating *everything* that anguishes and exalts human beings in this century? Or, more strangely, why should some of its devotees apply critical standards that implicitly urge it to aim low? What a price to pay for being apt!

The theater's struggle is not to forget its past. The film's struggle is not to be afraid of its future.

FOREIGN AND DOMESTIC: *Exchanges*
Through Film History

I

MORE and more, as I look at the history of film, one factor becomes especially significant for me: the tension, the interchange, the argument between American and foreign films. This relation has existed from the very beginnings of the art. The influence of American film abroad has long been past question; and American judgments on American film very frequently state or imply a comparison with foreign films. In 1908 a critic began an analysis of film style by saying: "First, let us classify the film product of the world as American and foreign."* In 1909 another critic wrote an article called "An American School of Moving Picture Drama" and censured "American film manufacturers who too frequently, in our opinion, go abroad for their themes."†

Obviously cultural tensions and interchanges with other countries did not begin with film. Emerson and Thoreau and Whitman are only three of the strongest voices that, before 1850, called for American

* "Earmarks of Makers" in *The New York Dramatic Mirror,* November 14, 1908.
† "An American School of Moving Picture Drama" in *The Moving Picture World,* November 29, 1909.

In slightly different form, this essay was given as a lecture at the University of Illinois, Urbana, in April 1974.

literary independence from Europe, long delayed after political independence. The first native theater star, Edwin Forrest, did not appear until some fifty years after political independence; until the 1830s, the American stage was dominated by British or British-born stars. American painters and sculptors of the nineteenth century worked in the midst of tugs and countertugs from abroad. This condition of inheritance and derivation was inevitable in this newest of powerful Western nations; our cultural sources were almost entirely European. The new country had to live awhile, had to develop its own language and moral landscape, before the unmistakable American voice could be heard—around the middle of the nineteenth century.

While this was happening in the traditional arts, a new art began to stir. Photography—still photography—appeared in France in the 1830s and, during the century, flowered technically and esthetically on both sides of the Atlantic. As the United States grew to selfhood, the moving picture camera was developed; and the film form reached utility just as the United States reached political might.

A great difference between American-foreign tensions in film and comparable tensions in other arts is that, almost from the start, the American product had tremendous influence abroad. Unlike the other arts, international relations in film were at once a matter of influence and counterinfluence. Of course if the novel and the poem and painting had been invented around 1890, American and foreign counterinfluences would have been reciprocal in those forms, too. But even then the interplay would not have been identical with the film situation because, as we shall see, of some social qualities peculiar to the new art.

Now if we arbitrarily extract this one element, international relationships, from the complex of film history, we may get some perspective from an overview of it.

In the first decade of film, before 1910, foreign films in the United States meant mostly French and Italian films, and their photography was held to be superior to American work, their pantomime more subtle, their cultural ambitions more elevated. Toward the end of that decade the French were making potted versions of famous plays, called Films d'Art, usually with famous actors of the Comédie Française, and were sending them here, where they were taken as evidence of film's potentialities at a time when most of our films were still about banal melodramatic or comic subjects. In fact the whole field was still so suspect here that most American actors, unlike those

Frenchmen, did not even want to be identified when they appeared on screen.

Around 1910 the Italians began to make five- to ten-reel films while Americans still rarely ventuerd beyond two reels. Such Italian spectacles as *The Fall of Troy, Cabiria,* the first *Quo Vadis?,* the first *Ben Hur,* were all great successes in America before World War I, and their success caused an epochal split in American production and exhibition. There were those here who felt that American one- and two-reel production was paying quite nicely, and the goose should be allowed to go on laying those small but numerous golden eggs. There were those who felt that more complex stories, longer films, higher admission prices, and more elegant places for exhibition were indicated. The second group, persuaded by foreign example, made their moves, were quickly proved right, and soon dominated the U.S. film industry.

By this time, however, a reverse flow, the popularity of American films abroad, had become very strong. In 1912 one critic offered an odd explanation:

> The European school is based more upon bodily movements than upon the mobility of the face. . . . Facial expression is the keynote of American pantomime. It has made American pictures popular all over the world.*

If this peculiar thesis needed amplification, it soon got it. In early 1914 Charles Chaplin appeared—his body *and* his face—and, with a speed that has never been surpassed, soared to world-wide fame. A point that is often overlooked: he made this global reputation while World War I was going on. Military convoys must have carried as many Chaplin films as war supplies and soldiers.

Less well remembered now is the then-famous French comedian who surely influenced Chaplin, Max Linder, who made a reverse reputation in the United States during the war and was invited here to make films. He stayed two years, 1917 and 1918, and returned later in 1921–22. Linder's American films were not box-office hits, still it was his French films that had got him his American contracts.

At about the same time such American directors as D. W. Griffith and Thomas Ince were heavily influencing French directors like Louis Delluc and his friends. Griffith was one of the only two directors who

---

* H. F. Hoffman, "Cutting Off the Feet" in *The Moving Picture World,* April 6, 1912.

ever influenced the Danish director Carl Dreyer (as Dreyer said later in his career). American films were even pouring into Japan, to fill the gap left by the stifling of European production during the war.

Long before 1920 American films had cornered the world market. By that time, more than 90 percent of the films shown in foreign countries were American. By about 1920 a rough, debatable, but persistent generalization had come into being: America made entertainment films, Europe made art films.

Even then some observers knew that there were great exceptions on both sides of that generalization, particularly the second part. That generalization has become increasingly suspect as it has become increasingly plain that good entertainment films cannot be made by the ungifted; further, that some men of alpine talent have spent their whole careers in entertainment films. But for compact purposes here, the terms "entertainment" and "art" can serve to distinguish between those films, however well made and esthetically rewarding, whose original purpose was to pass the time; and those films, however poorly made and esthetically pretentious, whose original purpose was the illumination of experience and the extension of consciousness. In this view, the generalization about American and European films has some validity—less than was assumed for decades, still some validity.

Every film-making country makes entertainment films; they are the major portion of every nation's industry. But no country's entertainment films have had the international success of American films. Some historians have speculated that the swift success of American entertainment films around the world came from the fact that the United States is a heterogeneous country without old class stratifications; that the United States thus had a quick affinity with popular works in a new theatrical medium, an affinity more immediate than in countries where the theater was historically associated with the upper classes of society, an affinity closer to the international common man. This theory, hardly watertight, is just sound enough to be stimulating. Particularly when one looks at the contrast with older countries with relatively homogeneous cultures. Their entertainment films had a parochialism, resulting from that homogeneity, that often made them unexportable. For instance, take Sweden. Very few Swedish entertainment films were seen outside Scandinavia.

But I choose Sweden because that's the country where the art film, the serious film, is said to have begun; and that, too, was the result of homogeneity, of class tradition. Unlike the United States, Sweden had a substantial homogeneous cultural heritage, and the cultivated people of Sweden wanted at least a small portion of their national film output to respond to that heritage. That serious minority of Swedish films—that serious minority of all foreign films—were what usually reached the United States; so we got the impression that other countries made nothing but serious films. This misconception, together with a blindness to the intrinsic merits of the best entertainment films made in this country, led to the generalization quoted above.

Two extrinsic factors helped the less "national" and more "popular" American film on the road of global conquest: World War I, which (as mentioned) hampered European production, and the international organization of American distribution facilities. Again, this is not to say that other countries had no international organizations: several did, very efficient ones. But that 90 percent domination by 1920 reflected, in some degree at least, American business agility.

Naturally, however, this success came ultimately from the films themselves. We can distinguish at least two principal esthetic components in this success. One, at the lowest-common-denominator level, is the simplicity of Victorian melodrama in plot, in values, in character: Mary Pickford, Lillian Gish, Richard Barthelmess were essentially figures from a local stock company, archetypally magnificent and magnified. The second component, at the highest esthetic level, was the superb quality of American comedy. Along with Chaplin, the Englishman who made his career in America, there were the equal genius Buster Keaton and the near peer of both, Harold Lloyd, together with such lesser but appealing figures as Harry Langdon, the Keystone Kops, and many others.

A third, almost mythical factor figured in this global success, I believe: the factor of America itself. American films were exporting within themselves the very size of America: the reach of the horizon, the bustle and immensity of the cities, the spirit—true or not—of infinite possibility. Federico Fellini once told me that he often dreamed about New York when he was a boy in Rimini. Many Europeans have told me that I, a New Yorker, cannot appreciate the effect that American films had on them in their, as they thought, constricted provincial early years. The very geography of America, Rocky Mountains and metropolitan skyline; the very distances that one could ride a horse or drive a car or ascend in the social scale; the chance for air and the prospect of fortune—all these things, quite apart from individual talents and individual pictures, helped American films to the world eminence that they gained quickly and have never lost.

But, as with all history, closer examination brings contradiction and complexity. In the midst of the American deluge of the world, German films began to be imported into the United States—seemingly on the day after the armistice—and began to have considerable success and even more considerable influence. The quality of such films as Lubitsch's *Passion*, Wiene's *The Cabinet of Dr. Caligari*, and Murnau's *The Last Laugh* made some American critics domestically discontent and made some American studios jealous. In November 1921, a mere three years after the end of the war, Alfred B. Kuttner wrote an article called "The Foreign Invasion," which began:

It is probably as much beyond dispute as anything can be that the outstanding event of the past year in the American motion picture world has been the exhibition of a series of German pictures beginning with *Passion* and ending with *All for a Woman*.

Kuttner deplored the popular idea that this was a harmful phenomenon to be resisted. He urged that these German films be allowed to affect American thinking, and concluded:

Already men like Chaplin, Herbert Brenon, Joseph Urban, and others have made generous admission of a debt of inspiration to foreign film achievement, and many studios are full of whispers about promising schemes of emulating the work from abroad. May something come of it.*

Something certainly did. The substantial success of German and other films in the United States, along with their critical acclaim, led American producers to a simple counteraction: not so much to fulfill "a debt of inspiration" as to buy the competition. The studio chiefs made shopping trips to Europe in the early 1920s and returned with prizes like the directors Ernst Lubitsch, Paul Leni, Dmitri Buchowetzki, F. W. Murnau, from Germany, and Victor Seastrom and Mauritz Stiller from Sweden: along with actors from both countries—Emil Jannings, Pola Negri, Lars Hanson, and Greta Garbo.

* Alfred B. Kuttner, "The Foreign Invasion" in *Exceptional Photoplays*, November 1921.

These people increased very sharply in American film a "continental" flavor that had already been implanted by, for example, Maurice Tourneur, the French director who worked in Hollywood from 1914 to 1926, by Erich von Stroheim, the Austrian-born director-actor whose film career began here but whose hallmarks of style were middle-European, and by Rudolph Valentino, whose sex appeal was exotic.

It is easy to mark the work that these imported artists did in Hollywood. What is less easy but almost equally significant is to mark the effect that directors such as Lubitsch and Murnau had on native directors. Very few sophisticated comedies made after Lubitsch's arrival would have been done exactly as they were done if he had not become American-based; and the influence of the German expressionists, particularly in lighting, can still be seen—even on our television screens. So the economic threat of European competition was solved in the most direct way possible, by acquisition. European films, it need hardly be noted, continued to thrive, but they never again posed a real money threat to America.

At the same time, however—to continue this outline of interplay—American influence was considerable in the most important political event of the 1920s: the building of the Soviet revolution. Surely no single item of influence in film history is more vivid than the effect of D. W. Griffith and other Americans on the preeminent Soviet directors, Sergei Eisenstein and V. I. Pudovkin, whose work helped to consolidate the USSR at home and to win it acclaim abroad. Why did these Soviet directors turn to American directors instead of more sophisticated Europeans? Eisenstein tells us:

On the one side there was the cinema of our neighbor, postwar Germany. Mysticism, decadence, dismal fantasy followed in the wake of the unsuccessful revolution of 1923, and the screen was quick to reflect this mood. . . . Expressionism left barely a trace on our cinema. This painted, hypnotic "St. Sebastian of Cinema" was too alien to the young, robust spirit and body of the rising class. . . . There was the role of another film-factor that appeared . . . captivating and attractive, in its own way engaging the attention of young and future film-makers, exactly as the young and future engineers of the time were attracted by the specimens of engineering techniques unknown to us, sent from that unknown, distant land across the sea. What enthralled us was not only these films, it was their possibilities . . . it was the boundless temperament and tempo of these amazing (and amazingly useless!) works from an unknown country that led us to muse on the possibilities of a profound, intelligent, class-directed use of this wonderful tool.*

So the USSR drew on American films, while American films drew on the more subtle and involuted Germans and Swedes and others. Another way of putting it is that the Russians wanted only grammar, in which to express their concepts; the United States, which had the grammar, wanted concepts, although not Russian ones.

That statement, within its context, is modestly accurate; but when we look at European countries other than Russia, the matter gets more complex. One side of the statement remains fixed: in the 1920s many Americans wanted Hollywood to be more like Europe. Carl Sandburg, in 1921 the film critic of the *Chicago Daily News,* said of *The Cabinet of Dr. Caligari:* "It is a healthy thing for Hollywood . . . that this photoplay has come along at this time. It is sure to have healthy hunches and show new possibilities in style and method to our American Producers."† On the other hand, through the 1920s, European countries other than Russia wanted more than American grammar, they wanted American approaches. Henri Langlois, founder of the *Cinémathèque Française,* recalls the effect of Howard Hawks's *A Girl in Every Port* on the Paris of 1928: "It was the Paris of the Montparnassians and Picasso . . . of the 'Six,' of Gertrude Stein, of Brancusi's masterpieces. . . . To the Paris of 1928, which was rejecting expressionism, *A Girl in Every Port* was a film conceived in the present, achieving an identity of its own by repudiating the past."‡

This is only one ripple from a torrent. That flooding of Europe by the United States—a movement that went east across the Atlantic at the same time that European artists were being bought up and shipped west—grew so great that by December 1927 the American critic Harry Alan Potamkin wrote a worried article called "The Plight of the European Movie," whose opening sentence was "Europe has America on the brain." Potamkin called the roll of European countries and checked them vis-à-vis American influence. England (contradictorily) was too resentful of that influence, he said, particularly

* Sergei Eisenstein, *Film Form* (New York: Harcourt, Brace, 1949), pp. 202–204.
† Harry M. Geduld, ed., *Authors on Film* (Bloomington: Indiana University Press, 1972), p. 48.
‡ Joseph McBride, ed., *Focus on Howard Hawks* (Englewood Cliffs, N.J.: Prentice-Hall, Inc., 1972), p. 65.

in view of the low state of English films. But Germany, whose films he admired, was being debased by close business ties between German studios and Hollywood power and by the talent raids mentioned above. Likewise Sweden. Italy, whose industry after World War I was even flabbier than England's, "almost invariably" showed American films in its theaters. "The fight for dictatorship of Italy will some day be between Mussolini and Tom Mix." There was one European exception.

One country has met the onslaught of America and met it with grace and self-preservation. France, which recognized the merit of the American film long before America did, promises, despite little progress, to develop a distinguished film art. . . . Although most French films are bad imitations of bad American films, and French audiences are Wild West mad, there are independent producers who, if faulty, have integrity; and there is an intelligent critical interest in the movie.*

Potamkin's prediction was extraordinarily sound. As Clair and Carné and Duvivier and Renoir developed, the French film became the dominant foreign influence in the United States during the 1930s.

The anomaly in this French influence is that it came after the advent of sound, when language might have been supposed to be a barrier. But French sound films were quite successful here, notably René Clair's. *Sous les Toits de Paris* ran for six months in New York, and, said Herman G. Weinberg in early 1933, "Clair's influence on Hollywood has been probably greater than that of any other European director" since Murnau and Dupont.† German films, particularly operettas, continued to have success and influence in America in the sound age until the rise of Hitler; but French work, through the decade until the start of World War II, because of its talent and honesty and touching sense of approaching doom, was the leader among imports.

Other countries, too, kept sending films, and the figures are rather surprising. For instance, in 1936, *The New York Times* reviewed 548 films, 314 of which were American, thirty-three British, and 201 in foreign languages. (Of course only a few of the last group got really widespread release in America.)

* Harry Alan Potamkin, "The Plight of the European Movie" in the *National Board of Review Magazine,* December 1927.

† Herman G. Weinberg, "The Foreign Language Film in the United States" in *Close-Up,* June 1933.

The second large wave of immigration to this country, after the 1920s shopping trip, was caused by Hitler. At first came such figures as the directors Fritz Lang, Billy Wilder, Max Ophüls, Otto Preminger, and Douglas Sirk, the cinematographer Rudolph Maté, the composer Friedrich Holländer, the producers Erich Pommer and Sam Spiegel. As the German occupation spread, we got, among others, the directors René Clair, Jean Renoir, and Julien Duvivier, the cinematographer Boris Kaufman, the actors Jean Gabin and Michèle Morgan. But during the 1930s European production kept rolling and, in France, reached new heights. Welford Beaton, writing of *Carnival in Flanders* in 1937, said: "If the insane people who rule the destinies of European countries do not plunge the continent into another general war, the development of picture making over there will become a real threat to the world dominance of the American film industry." This worry, which, as we have seen, was not new, might have been expected from a Hollywood commentator; less predictably for a trade journalist, Beaton went on to join a by-then familiar chorus: "Another advantage Europe has—the one which eventually will count most—is that across the Atlantic they recognize there is such a thing as an art of the screen and allow consideration of it to influence production."*

This (recurrent) statement is, as noted, much too glib because it ignores the large amount of poor foreign work—almost as high a proportion as in America—and because of the generally high level of execution—with occasional high level in entirety—of Hollywood films. But the more subtle point that the statement overlooks is that the influence of foreign styles and talents on American film had never been stronger. This could be seen in the work of such a seemingly homespun director as Frank Capra and later was seen in the work of Orson Welles, Samuel Fuller, Nicholas Ray, and Joseph Losey. It could also be seen in the originating point of view of some American films: for example, *Casablanca* (1942) can be called a Jean Gabin picture transplanted, Hollywood's osmosis of the French temper of the 1930s.

At the end of World War II, in 1946, Kenneth Macgowan, himself the producer of fifty Hollywood films, took up again the recurrent refrain. Discussing a group of new films, he wrote that the screen had

---

* Welford Beaton, "A Lesson from Overseas" in *Hollywood Spectator,* January 30, 1937.

lately "brought pleasure enough to those who care to generalize on the familiar but perhaps boring subject of the faults of Hollywood and the virtues of the Old World cinema. . . . Certainly our best is not so good as the best of Europe; this cannot be said too often."*
Well, it was said often enough, though not always so carefully.

At this point, immediately after the war, the imports were coming chiefly from Britain, but before 1950, Italy, whose films had been insignificant here since 1914, found its cinematic feet again, more solidly than ever; and in reaction to twenty-five years of fascist film fabrication, produced the school of neo-realism—more properly, neo-naturalism—headed by Visconti, Rossellini, and De Sica. Soon Italy was very visible on American screens; soon after, France was too, particularly in the work of Jean Cocteau. By 1951 Richard Griffith felt impelled to write an article in which he deplored the poor distribution of foreign films and urged efforts to get them a larger American public.†

The exchange pattern that emerged in the late 1940s remained fairly constant for about ten years. American films reclaimed their universal power to grip, to inhabit dreams, to win affection, to inspire near-worship. (A Yugoslav director told me in 1964 that he felt less grieved when his faraway brother died than when Gary Cooper died.) As for imports, the only completely new element—a very considerable one artistically though sadly negligible at the box office—was the appearance here of Japanese films, led by the success of Akira Kurosawa's *Rashomon* at the Venice Festival in 1951. Very few Japanese films had been shown widely in the United States even prior to World War II; now they had at least a great effect on critics and film makers. Aside from evidences of Kurosawa's style in American film, the overt effect can be seen in such American remakes of Kurosawa films as *The Outrage* from *Rashomon* and *The Magnificent Seven* from *The Seven Samurai*. What makes the influence of Kurosawa especially pertinent to this discussion is that he himself has acknowledged the early influence on him of such Americans as Howard Hawks and George Stevens, and has said that his three favorite directors are John Ford, William Wyler, and Frank Capra.

I must note, in passing, that the remaking of foreign films in

* Kenneth Macgowan, "Summer Films, Imported and Domestic" in *Hollywood Quarterly*, No. 2, 1946–47.
† Richard Griffith, "European Films and American Audiences" in *The Saturday Review*, January 13, 1951.

American settings is not a recent phenomenon. Only a few past examples: the Soviet film *Road to Life* by Nikolai Ekk (1931) was remade by William Wellman as *Wild Boys of the Road* (1933); Fritz Lang's *M* (1931) was remade by Joseph Losey (1951); Marcel Carné's *Le Jour Se Lève* (1939) was remade by Anatole Litvak as *The Long Night* (1947).

Then, at the end of the 1950s and through the first half of the 1960s there arrived the strongest foreign influences in our film history, because of the conjunctive emergence of extraordinary talents in Europe: in Sweden Ingmar Bergman, in Italy the two post-neo-realists Michelangelo Antonioni and Federico Fellini, in France the group of directors labeled the New Wave. All of these directors have testified to American influences on them, but those French directors particularly are clear examples of the international syncretism we are examining. Most of them were young, most of them had grown up through the Second World War and the German occupation and had been deprived of films, certainly of American ones. Soon after the liberation they fell upon a feast of films in general and of American ones in particular—not only the new issues but the backlog of seven or eight years that they had missed, indeed the whole history of American film which had been inaccessible to them. Films became in an operative sense their university and their cosmos, and most especially American films. Through the stimulation and prisms of American film they turned to and treated their own lives and times. Out of a host of possible examples, just one: Jean-Luc Godard dedicated his first feature *Breathless* (1959) to Monogram Pictures, the most B of American B studios.

These foreign directors, French and otherwise, nurtured by America, had a tremendous effect on America in the 1960s. I have speculated elsewhere about the reasons for the rise of this Film Generation.* Here I cite only some of the specific stimuli. Take the first year of that decade, 1960. If you stretch that year a few months either way, these are some of the films that arrived in that brief period: Godard's *Breathless,* Truffaut's *The 400 Blows,* Resnais's *Hiroshima, Mon Amour,* De Broca's *The Love Game,* Antonioni's *L'Avventura,* Fellini's *La Dolce Vita,* De Sica's *Two Women,* Wicki's *The Bridge,* Satyajit Ray's *The World of Apu,* Kurosawa's *Ikiru,* and Bergman's *The Virgin Spring.* Within two years we had seen further

* "The Film Generation" in *A World on Film* (New York: Harper & Row, 1966; Delta Books, 1967).

films from almost all these men, plus Bresson's *Pickpocket,* Olmi's *Il Posto* (*The Sound of Trumpets*), Germi's *Divorce Italian Style,* Reisz's *Saturday Night and Sunday Morning,* Anderson's *This Sporting Life,* and Chabrol's *Landru.* The paradox is that most of these directors have acknowledged their debt to the traditions and styles of Americans—Bergman and Ray and Germi and Anderson and Fellini and Truffaut have specified John Ford—but their effect on the United States was to shake traditions and styles. The changes here occurred in virtually every aspect: from a fundamental concept of the function of film to cinematic syntax to ideas of narrative to views of character to the frontiers of subject and theme. For instance, to take possibly the most obvious aspect, the new sexual breadth of American films, now in some legal danger but nevertheless present, would have been inconceivable without the effect of the foreign films of the 1960s.

The immense eruption of film enthusiasm in that decade, the rhapsodies of news magazines, the torrent of film books that swelled through the decade, the fantastic increase in the number of film courses in colleges and universities, including film majors and doctoral programs—all these were stimulated by, if not derived from, the force of these numerous extraordinary foreign films, arriving at a particularly apt cultural moment for American youth. Concurrently the interest in foreign pictures was accompanied, intensified, by a crescent interest here in American films of the past. While young people were responding to Godard and Bergman, they were also discovering the seminal pictures from which those men had learned so much. These two factors, the foreign influx and the domestic interest heightened by it, made the 1960s the most significant decade in our film history: not in terms of production or box-office receipts, which had declined because of the impact of television, but in terms of changes in American film-making methods and manners, and changes in audience knowledge, discrimination, and hope. Films were being seen by fewer people than in the 1930s and 1940s but those who now saw them cared more and felt different about them.

II

IN the few years since the end of the 1960s the situation has changed in several respects. Situations are always changing in the film world in a few years, but these changes are strongly marked and historically important.

The single most striking change is that the flood of good and occasionally fine films from abroad has dwindled to a trickle. The sense of things marvelous continually arriving has faded. The foreign directors of the 1960s have not continued to grow. Some have withered painfully, like Godard and Kurosawa. Antonioni has been in creative trouble (the single biggest worry to me). Truffaut breathes by never sticking his nose outside a film studio. And there have been no truly significant replacements for these men. The new directors of Germany are, to put it calmly, a rather specialized taste. Bernardo Bertolucci is ludicrously overrated. (The best of the younger Italians, Marco Bellocchio, is still scarcely known here.) The gifted Hungarian, Miklós Jancsó, is becoming esthetically eremitic. The gifted Swede, Jan Troell, is, so to speak, a swallow, not a summer. I don't pretend to offer a complete survey or full report, but I think most interested persons would agree that the continual tingle of excitement from abroad during the 1960s is gone.

Why did the flood falter? Several reasons can be suggested, one of them—appropriately enough in a chronicle of interchange—involving the United States.

The influence of World War II, as jet-propellant or hatchery, wore out. Connected with that was the problem of material, a pressing problem for many kinds of contemporary artists. It's no longer easy for the artist who deals with characters and with life-simulation in some form—the novelist, the dramatist, the film maker—to have an extensive career. The convictions of relevance, of grip on the world, that sustained Ibsen and Strindberg and Zola and Shaw are harder to come by. The ability to fabricate—synthesis in the best sense—that sustained Dickens and Lope de Vega and Griffith and Chaplin is harder to rely on, for serious artists, in an age of increasingly subjective art, where the degree of "confessional" pertinence has almost become a touchstone of truth. If the artist limits himself to personal experience, or the personal transfigured, he can find years of his life used up in one film—in one sequence!

Bresson is an exception to this problem of material: he is one of the few deeply religious men in film making, and his cosmos is ordered, or is anyway invitingly mysterious. Buñuel is an exception chiefly because he has embraced again the faith that started his career—surrealism. Bergman is an exception; as I've said elsewhere, I think that his concurrent theater career has played a psychic role in fertilizing his film career. Crudely put, this is to say that nine months' work each year on other men's work builds impulses in him to do three months' work entirely on his own. Visconti, though active, is not an exception; apart from *The Stranger,* his work in the past decade has been of surpassing unimportance. (He, too, works in the theater, but I don't suggest that Bergman's situation constitutes a pattern that applies to every director with two careers.)

Another reason for the faltering of the import flood was money. Generally speaking, as these men were acclaimed, more was invested in their films (Godard the great exception here), more was expected of them in "production values" and at the box office. But the work of many of them, by its nature, couldn't attract bigger audiences, so they found themselves making box-office flops. By no means had all their previous films been hits, but now the flops were emphasized, and it became more difficult for these directors to get financing even on their previous modest level.

To complicate this aspect, American producers and distributors, attracted by the dazzle of these foreign films, began to invest in foreign production, and thus changed cultural balances. A Portuguese film (to be hypothetical) used to be made for Portugal, and if it was really good, it might appeal to the rest of the world as a Portuguese film. But with American money involved, an explicit appeal to the American market, to the world market, became a consideration; and the result was usually a film that was not purely Portuguese, not very good, and not very marketable. Over and over again in recent years I have heard foreign directors say that American investment was forcing them to make quasi-American pictures. Even allowing for the copout aspects of this complaint, there must be some truth in it.

But there have also been drastic changes at home in recent years. This account of international relations culminates in a domestic situation unlike any that preceded it, one in which foreign films have played a decisive part.

Ever since the end of World War II it has been patent that the traditional method of American film production—seven or eight giant plants, each one producing between fifty and eighty pictures a year—was doomed. The increase in television production and viewing, the divorce between studio ownership and theater ownership decreed by law, the soaring expense of film making, the vagaries of public taste as against the public's almost sheeplike obedience in much of the past, have finally killed the assembly line. Film production, still numerically substantial, has become independent. This is one of the funniest words in the film lexicon: it means independent only of the old assembly line. In some ways it is more harried, less self-confident, than the old studio procedure where picture people knew precisely what they were doing, or thought they did, and for whom they were doing it. Now independent production means that, for each project, a producer not only needs to acquire script and director and actors and studio facilities and distribution, he also has to acquire an audience—possibly a different audience for each film, or at least not a relatively dependable general audience as in the past. No longer is there any resemblance to a keeper throwing fish to trained seals. Making pictures is now much more like publishing books: each venture is a separate business enterprise, a separate risk and search.

One important result of this fragmented production, which is at least partly occasioned by a fragmented audience, is that it has allowed more young people, more new people of differing ages, to work in films than ever before in this country. Producers and financiers, in their eagerness to scatter shots and hit less precisely defined audiences, have taken chances that they might not otherwise have taken. For a while, a short while, this resulted mainly in so-called youth pictures, like *Easy Rider* and its imitations; in the large, it has simply meant that fresh talents have had a chance to work. So in the past few years we have seen the talent of such directors as Barbara Loden in *Wanda,* Peter Fonda in *The Hired Hand,* John G. Avildsen in *Save the Tiger,* Daryl Duke in *Payday,* Frank D. Gilroy in *Desperate Characters,* Bob Rafelson in *Five Easy Pieces,* Francis Ford Coppola in *The Conversation,* Terrence Malick in *Badlands,* and Sam Peckinpah in *The Wild Bunch.* There are others. Some of these directors have not yet made one wholly satisfactory picture, but all of them have shown distinctive gifts and all of them clearly share one characteristic: all of them reflect the influence of foreign films made during the 1960s.

Some of this foreign influence on some Americans, even on pictures by some of the people named, has been regrettable: because it was based on a belief that mere imitation, without any of the cultural genesis of a mode, will produce work in that mode. Still, much of that foreign influence has been legitimately ingested, in a way that is different from the ingestion of influences described earlier because the American film situation is now different.

When Lubitsch and Clair and Murnau were influencing Hollywood, it was a question of adapting what was learned from those men to the relatively precise and constricting demands of the studio:

because the studio knew quite well, over the long run, what the audience wanted. But neither the studio nor the audience exists as before; so the influence of those foreign directors of the 1960s can now be used here for the making of "personal" pictures, films much closer to art as roughly defined earlier, in a distinction from entertainment that is itself rough. Now, in such a complex medium as film, no picture can be made with the solitary creation of a poem; and I emphasize that some good, highly personal films were made under the old studio system; still the best pictures from abroad represent the originating vision of one man and a large measure of his control. Both of these conditions are very unlike the overwhelming preponderance of American production in the past. The American present makes the future look possibly different.

So we stand, or anyway may be standing, at an important point in cultural history. In this long and tensile relation between foreign and American films, the influence of America's films on foreign production has been principally through the force of individual talents expressed through genres and schools. The force of foreign films on American productions has of course also been through individual talents but as expressed in individual, realized works—not the evidence discernible in a body of consciously compromised entertainment films, but the evidence of completely realized, uncompromised works of art. The search in America for new audiences—which, not to be unduly mystical, is in some ways a search to discover whether America still exists in any prognosticable sense—that search apparently permits the production of at least a small proportion of personal films. And many of the stylistic qualities in those personal films come from abroad. As noted, some foreign countries have had, along with their entertainments, a tradition of the personal film; this country, despite its personal films, has had no such tradition. Now there seems to be a chance that, along with the majority of our other films, such a personal tradition may come into being. And foreign films will have played an important part in this evolution.

All one would want is the possibility of such a tradition in this country. In the theater I would not want all American works to be musicals and thrillers, even if they were all excellent, with the good new serious plays all imported. The American theater, with its ludicrous lamenesses, has never felt arbitrarily debarred from the highest aspiration, from the best personal productions it could try to make. Whatever its failings, our theater has never automatically assumed that America's job is to excel in entertainment, exhibiting high talent in commercial genres, resigning noncommercial work to the theaters of other countries. But the American film, allowing for exceptions, has seemed to make such an arbitrary assignment in the past.

Out of generational changes, out of self-respect and respect for film, even out of shame from the comparison with what has happened in foreign films in the past two decades, American film makers and film audiences have opened up possibilities for themselves. And the new, foreign-influenced American film may in time stimulate and influence production abroad!—as American films have so often done in the past.

The doom-crying we hear about film from time to time, along with the very safe nostalgia for the old Hollywood days, may just be fear of maturity. At any rate, change seems more possible than ever because conditions are insecure and production is much less susceptible to formula, because promising talent, some of it coming from film schools, has never been more evident. After the talent is trained, what it needs are courage, recklessness, self. The current uncertainties in the American film scene guarantee nothing, but they do offer possibilities. I hope that the next decade of American film will be as adventurous and aspiring and unordained as it certainly could be.

FILMS PREVIOUSLY REVIEWED

films previously reviewed

The following, of possible use to the readers of this book, is a combined alphabetical listing of all films reviewed in my two previous collections. Titles set in roman are in *A World on Film* (Harper & Row, 1966; Delta Books, 1967). Titles set in *italics* are in *Figures of Light* (Harper & Row, 1971; Harper Colophon, 1971).

The index to the present book follows this list.

S.K.

Abysses, Les	Amiche, Le
Accattone	Angry Silence, The
Adalen 31	Aparajito
Alice's Restaurant	Apartment, The
All Fall Down	Ashes and Diamonds
All These Women	Avventura, L'

Back to the Wall
Bad Sleep Well, The
Ballad of Cable Hogue, The
Ballad of a Soldier
Bandits of Orgosolo
Barbarian and the Geisha, The
Becket
Bed Sitting Room, The
Belle de Jour
Ben-Hur
Beyond the Law
Bezhin Meadow
Billy Budd
Billy Liar
Birds, The
Birthday Party, The
Blow-Up
Bonnie and Clyde
Breathless
Bridge, The
Brotherly Love
Bullitt
Carabiniers, Les
Caretaker, The (The Guest)
Cat on a Hot Tin Roof
Catch-22
Chapman Report, The
Charge of the Light Brigade, The
Cheyenne Autumn
China Is Near
Chinoise, La
Chronicle of a Summer
Circus, The
Cleo from 5 to 7
Closely Watched Trains
Collector, The
Condemned of Altona, The
Connection, The
Contempt
Cool Hand Luke

Cool World, The
Criminal Life of Archibaldo de
  la Cruz, The
Darling
Desire Under the Elms
Devil and the Ten Command-
  ments, The
Devil's Eye, The
Diary of a Chambermaid
Doctor's Dilemma, The
Dr. Strangelove
Dolce Vita, La
Duet for Cannibals
Easy Rider
Eclipse
Elvira Madigan
Elusive Corporal, The
Enemy Below, The
Entertainer, The
Everybody Go Home
Expresso Bongo
Face of War, A
Faces
Falstaff
Fate of a Man
Fellini Satyricon
Fiancés, The
Fist in His Pocket
Five-Day Lover, The
For Love of Ivy
400 Blows, The
From Russia with Love
Fugitive Kind, The
Funny Girl
Getting Straight
God's Little Acre
Gone Are the Days
Goodbye, Columbus
Graduate, The
Grand Illusion

index

389